The Fourth Turning

Previous Books by William Strauss and Neil Howe

13TH GEN: ABORT, RETRY, IGNORE, FAIL?

GENERATIONS: THE HISTORY OF AMERICA'S FUTURE

Also by Neil Howe (coauthored with Peter G. Peterson)

ON BORROWED TIME: HOW THE GROWTH IN
ENTITLEMENT SPENDING THREATENS AMERICA'S FUTURE (1988)

Also by William Strauss (coauthored with Lawrence Baskir)

CHANCE AND CIRCUMSTANCE: THE DRAFT, THE WAR,
AND THE VIETNAM GENERATION (1978)

The Fourth Turning

An American Prophecy

William Strauss
and Neil Howe

BROADWAY BOOKS

New York

First trade paperback edition published 1998.

Designed by Marysarah Quinn

The Library of Congress has catalogued the hardcover edition as:
Strauss, William.
The fourth turning : an American prophecy : what the cycles of history tell
us about America's next rendezvous with destiny /
William Strauss and Neil Howe. — 1st ed.
p.   cm.
Includes index.
ISBN 0–553–06682-X (hc)
1. United States—History—1945– 2. Cycles. 3. Twenty-first
century—Forecasts. I. Howe, Neil. II. Title.
E839.S84   1997
303.4973—dc20   96–31309
CIP

ISBN 0-7679-0046-4

15 30 29 28 27 26 25 24 23 22

To Janie and Simona, who share our time

And to Eric, Giorgia, Melanie, Nathaniel, Rebecca, and Victoria, who, God willing, will share a time beyond

That which hath been is now;
and that which is to be hath already been;
and God requireth that which is past.

—Ecclesiastes 3.15

Contents

The Fourth Turning

CHAPTER 1

Winter Comes Again

AMERICA FEELS LIKE IT'S UNRAVELING.

Though we live in an era of relative peace and comfort, we have settled into a mood of pessimism about the long-term future, fearful that our superpower nation is somehow rotting from within.

Neither an epic victory over Communism nor an extended upswing of the business cycle can buoy our public spirit. The Cold War and New Deal struggles are plainly over, but we are of no mind to bask in their successes. The America of today feels worse, in its fundamentals, than the one many of us remember from youth, a society presided over by those of supposedly lesser consciousness. Wherever we look, from L.A. to D.C., from Oklahoma City to Sun City, we see paths to a foreboding future. We yearn for civic character but satisfy ourselves with symbolic gestures and celebrity circuses. We perceive no greatness in our leaders, a new meanness in ourselves. Small wonder that each new election brings a new jolt, its aftermath a new disappointment.

Not long ago, America was more than the sum of its parts. Now, it is less. Around World War II, we were proud as a people but modest as individuals. Fewer than two people in ten said yes when asked, Are you a very important person? Today, more than six in ten say yes. Where we once thought ourselves collectively strong, we now regard ourselves as individually entitled.

Yet even while we exalt our own personal growth, we realize that millions of self-actualized persons don't add up to an actualized society. Popular trust in virtually every American institution—from businesses and governments to churches and newspapers—keeps falling to new lows. Public debts soar, the middle class shrinks, welfare dependencies deepen, and cultural arguments worsen by the year. We now have the highest incarceration rate and the lowest eligible-voter participation rate of any major democracy. Statistics inform us that many adverse trends (crime, divorce, abortion, scholastic aptitudes) may have bottomed out, but we're not reassured.

Optimism still attaches to self, but no longer to family or community. Most Americans express more hope for their own prospects than for their children's—or the nation's. Parents widely fear that the American Dream, which was there (solidly) for their parents and still there (barely) for them, will not be there for their kids. Young householders are reaching their midthirties never having known a time when America seemed to be on the right track. Middle-aged people look at their thin savings accounts and slim-to-none pensions, scoff at an illusory Social Security trust fund, and try not to dwell on what a burden their old age could become. Seniors separate into their own Leisure World, recoiling at the lost virtue of youth while trying not to think about the future.

We perceive our civic challenge as some vast, insoluble Rubik's Cube. Behind each problem lies another problem that must be solved first, and behind that lies yet another, and another, ad infinitum. To fix crime we have to fix the family, but before we do that we have to fix welfare, and that means fixing our budget, and that means fixing our civic spirit, but we can't do that without fixing moral standards, and that means fixing schools and churches, and that means fixing the inner cities, and that's impossible unless we fix crime. There's no fulcrum on which to rest a policy lever. People of all ages sense that something huge will have to sweep across America before the gloom can be lifted—but that's an awareness we suppress. As a nation, we're in deep denial.

While we grope for answers, we wonder if analysis may be crowding out our intuition. Like the anxious patient who takes seventeen kinds of medicine while poring over his own CAT scan, we find it hard to stop and ask, What is the underlying malady really about? How can we best bring the primal forces of nature to our assistance? Isn't there a choice lying somewhere between total control and total despair? Deep down, beneath the tangle of trend lines, we suspect that our history or biology or very humanity must have something simple and important to say to us. But we don't know what it is. If we once did know, we have since forgotten.

Wherever we're headed, America is evolving in ways most of us don't like or understand. Individually focused yet collectively adrift, we wonder if we're heading toward a waterfall.

Are we?

IT'S ALL HAPPENED BEFORE

The reward of the historian is to locate patterns that recur over time and to discover the natural rhythms of social experience.

In fact, at the core of modern history lies this remarkable pattern: Over the past five centuries, Anglo-American society has entered a new era—a new *turning*—every two decades or so. At the start of each turning, people change how they feel about themselves, the culture, the nation, and the future. Turnings come in cycles of four. Each cycle spans the length of a long human life, roughly eighty to one hundred years, a unit of time the ancients called the *saeculum*. Together, the four turnings of the saeculum comprise history's seasonal rhythm of growth, maturation, entropy, and destruction:

- The *First Turning* is a *High*, an upbeat era of strengthening institutions and weakening individualism, when a new civic order implants and the old values regime decays.
- The *Second Turning* is an *Awakening*, a passionate era of spiritual upheaval, when the civic order comes under attack from a new values regime.
- The *Third Turning* is an *Unraveling*, a downcast era of strengthening individualism and weakening institutions, when the old civic order decays and the new values regime implants.
- The *Fourth Turning* is a *Crisis*, a decisive era of secular upheaval, when the values regime propels the replacement of the old civic order with a new one.

Each turning comes with its own identifiable mood. Always, these mood shifts catch people by surprise.

In the current saeculum, the First Turning was the *American High* of the Truman, Eisenhower, and Kennedy presidencies. As World War II wound down, no one predicted that America would soon become so confident and institutionally muscular, yet so conformist and spiritually complacent. But that's what happened.

The Second Turning was the *Consciousness Revolution,* stretching from the campus revolts of the mid-1960s to the tax revolts of the early 1980s. Before John Kennedy was assassinated, no one predicted that America was about to enter an era of personal liberation and cross a cultural divide that would separate anything thought or said after from anything thought or said before. But that's what happened.

The Third Turning has been the *Culture Wars,* an era that began with Reagan's mid-1980s Morning in America and is due to expire around the middle of the Oh-Oh decade, eight or ten years from now. Amid the glitz of the early Reagan years, no one predicted that the nation was entering an era of national drift and institutional decay. But that's where we are.

Have major national mood shifts like this ever before happened? Yes—many times. Have Americans ever before experienced anything like the current attitude of Unraveling? Yes—many times, over the centuries.

People in their eighties can remember an earlier mood that was much like today's. They can recall the years between Armistice Day (1918) and the

Great Crash of 1929. Euphoria over a global military triumph was painfully short-lived. Earlier optimism about a progressive future gave way to a jazz-age nihilism and a pervasive cynicism about high ideals. Bosses swaggered in immigrant ghettos, the KKK in the South, the mafia in the industrial heartland, and defenders of Americanism in myriad Middletowns. Unions atrophied, government weakened, third-parties were the rage, and a dynamic marketplace ushered in new consumer technologies (autos, radios, phones, jukeboxes, vending machines) that made life feel newly complicated and frenetic. The risky pleasures of a "lost" young generation shocked middle-aged decency crusaders—many of them "tired radicals" who were then moralizing against the detritus of the "mauve decade" of their youth (the 1890s). Opinions polarized around no-compromise cultural issues like drugs, family, and "decency." Meanwhile, parents strove to protect a scoutlike new generation of children (who aged into today's senior citizens).

Back then, the details were different, but the underlying mood resembled what Americans feel today. Listen to Walter Lippmann, writing during World War I:

> We are unsettled to the very roots of our being. There isn't a human relation, whether of parent or child, husband and wife, worker and employer, that doesn't move in a strange situation. We are not used to a complicated civilization, we don't know how to behave when personal contact and eternal authority have disappeared. There are no precedents to guide us, no wisdom that was not meant for a simpler age.

Move backward again to an era recalled by the oldest Americans still alive when today's seniors were little children. In the late 1840s and early 1850s, America drifted into a foul new mood. The hugely popular Mexican War had just ended in a stirring triumph, but the huzzahs over territorial gain didn't last long. Cities grew mean and politics hateful. Immigration surged, financial speculation boomed, and railroads and cotton exports released powerful new market forces that destabilized communities. Having run out of answers, the two major parties (Whigs and Democrats) were slowly disintegrating. A righteous debate over slavery's westward expansion erupted between so-called Southrons and abolitionists—many of them middle-aged spiritualists who in the more euphoric 1830s and 1840s had dabbled in Transcendentalism, utopian communes, and other assorted youth-fired crusades. Colleges went begging for students as a brazen young generation hustled west to pan for gold in towns fabled for their violence. Meanwhile, a child generation grew up with a new regimentation that startled European visitors who, a decade earlier, had bemoaned the wildness of American kids. Sound familiar?

Run the clock back the length of yet another long life, to the 1760s. The recent favorable conclusion to the French and Indian War had brought eighty years of conflict to a close and secured the colonial frontier. Yet when England tried to recoup the expense of the war through taxation, the colonies seethed with a directionless discontent. Immigration from the Old World, emigration across the Appalachians, and colonial trade arguments all rose sharply. As debtors' prisons bulged, middle-aged people complained of what Benjamin Franklin called the "white savagery" of youth. Middle-aged orators (peers of the fiery young preachers of the circa-1740 Great Awakening) summoned civic consciousness and organized popular crusades of economic austerity. The youth elite became the first to attend disciplined church schools in the colonies rather than academies in corrupt Albion. Gradually, colonists began separating into mutually loathing camps, one defending and the other attacking the Crown. Sound familiar again?

During each of these periods, Americans celebrated an ethos of frenetic and laissez-faire individualism (a word first popularized in the 1840s) yet also fretted over social fragmentation, epidemic violence, and economic and technological change that seemed to be accelerating beyond society's ability to absorb it.

During each of these periods, Americans had recently achieved a stunning victory over a long-standing foreign threat—Imperial Germany, Imperial New Spain (alias Mexico), or Imperial New France. Yet that victory came to be associated with a worn-out definition of collective purpose—and, perversely, unleashed a torrent of pessimism.

During each of these periods, an aggressive moralism darkened the debate about the country's future. Culture wars raged, the language of political discourse coarsened, nativist (and sectional) feelings hardened, immigration and substance abuse came under attack, and attitudes toward children grew more protective.

During each of these periods, Americans felt well-rooted in their personal values but newly hostile toward the corruption of civic life. Unifying institutions, which had seemed secure for decades, now felt ephemeral. Those who had once trusted the nation with their lives were growing old and dying. To the new crop of young adults, the nation hardly mattered. The whole *res publica* seemed on the verge of disintegrating.

During each of these previous Third Turnings, Americans felt as if they were drifting toward a cataclysm.

And, as it turned out, they were.

The 1760s were followed by the American Revolution, the 1850s by Civil War, the 1920s by the Great Depression and World War II. All these Unraveling eras were followed by bone-jarring Crises so monumental that, by their end, American society emerged in a wholly new form.

Each time, the change came with scant warning. As late as December 1773, November 1859, and October 1929, the American people had no idea how close it was. Then sudden sparks (the Boston Tea Party, John Brown's raid and execution, Black Tuesday) transformed the public mood, swiftly and permanently. Over the next two decades or so, society convulsed. Emergencies required massive sacrifices from a citizenry that responded by putting community ahead of self. Leaders led, and people trusted them. As a new social contract was created, people overcame challenges once thought insurmountable—and used the Crisis to elevate themselves and their nation to a higher plane of civilization: In the 1790s, they triumphantly created the modern world's first democratic republic. In the late 1860s, wounded but reunited, they forged a genuine nation extending new guarantees of liberty and equality. In the late 1940s, they constructed the most Promethean superpower ever seen.

The Fourth Turning is history's great discontinuity. It ends one epoch and begins another.

History is seasonal, and winter is coming. Like nature's winter, the saecular winter can come early or late. A Fourth Turning can be long and difficult, brief but severe, or (perhaps) mild. But, like winter, it cannot be averted. It must come in its turn.

Here, in summary, is what the rhythms of modern history warn about America's future.

The next Fourth Turning is due to begin shortly after the new millennium, midway through the Oh-Oh decade. Around the year 2005, a sudden spark will catalyze a Crisis mood. Remnants of the old social order will disintegrate. Political and economic trust will implode. Real hardship will beset the land, with severe distress that could involve questions of class, race, nation, and empire. Yet this time of trouble will bring seeds of social rebirth. Americans will share a regret about recent mistakes—and a resolute new consensus about what to do. The very survival of the nation will feel at stake. Sometime before the year 2025, America will pass through a great gate in history, commensurate with the American Revolution, Civil War, and twin emergencies of the Great Depression and World War II.

The risk of catastrophe will be very high. The nation could erupt into insurrection or civil violence, crack up geographically, or succumb to authoritarian rule. If there is a war, it is likely to be one of maximum risk and effort—in other words, a *total war*. Every Fourth Turning has registered an upward ratchet in the technology of destruction, and in mankind's willingness to use it. In the Civil War, the two capital cities would surely have incinerated each other had the means been at hand. In World War II, America invented a new technology of annihilation, which the nation swiftly put to use. This time, America will enter a Fourth Turning with the means to inflict unimaginable horrors and, perhaps, will confront adversaries who possess the same.

Yet Americans will also enter the Fourth Turning with a unique opportunity to achieve a new greatness as a people. Many despair that values that were new in the 1960s are today so entwined with social dysfunction and cultural decay that they can no longer lead anywhere positive. Through the current Unraveling era, that is probably true. But in the crucible of Crisis, that will change. As the old civic order gives way, Americans will have to craft a new one. This will require a values consensus and, to administer it, the empowerment of a strong new political regime. If all goes well, there could be a renaissance of civic trust, and more: Today's Third Turning problems—that Rubik's Cube of crime, race, money, family, culture, and ethics —will snap into a Fourth Turning solution. America's post-Crisis answers will be as organically interconnected as today's pre-Crisis questions seem hopelessly tangled. By the 2020s, America could become a society that is *good*, by today's standards, and also one that *works*.

Thus might the next Fourth Turning end in apocalypse—or glory. The nation could be ruined, its democracy destroyed, and millions of people scattered or killed. Or America could enter a new golden age, triumphantly applying shared values to improve the human condition. The rhythms of history do not reveal the outcome of the coming Crisis; all they suggest is the timing and dimension.

We cannot stop the seasons of history, but we *can* prepare for them. Right now, in 1997, we have eight, ten, perhaps a dozen more years to get ready. Then events will begin to take choices out of our hands. Yes, winter is coming, but our path through that winter is up to us.

History's howling storms can bring out the worst and best in a society. The next Fourth Turning could literally destroy us as a nation and people, leaving us cursed in the histories of those who endure and remember. Alternatively, it could ennoble our lives, elevate us as a community, and inspire acts of consummate heroism—deeds that will grow into mythlike legends recited by our heirs far into the future.

"There is a mysterious cycle in human events," President Franklin Roosevelt observed in the depths of the Great Depression. "To some generations much is given. Of other generations much is expected. This generation has a rendezvous with destiny." The cycle remains mysterious, but need not come as a total surprise. Though the scenario and outcome are uncertain, the schedule is set: The next Fourth Turning—America's next rendezvous with destiny—will begin in roughly ten years and end in roughly thirty.

How can we offer this prophecy with such confidence? Because it's all happened before. Many times.

THEORIES OF TIME

From the Grim Reaper of the Christians to the blood-drenched Kali of the Hindus, mankind has traditionally viewed time darkly. Time, we realize, must issue in our dissolution and death. Its passage is destined to annihilate everything familiar about our present—from such trivial pleasures as a morning cup of coffee to the grandest constructions of art, religion, or politics. "Time and his aging," observed Aeschylus, "overtakes all things alike."

Over the millennia, man has developed three ways of thinking about time: chaotic, cyclical, and linear. The first was the dominant view of primitive man, the second of ancient and traditional civilizations, and the third of the modern West, especially America.

In *chaotic time,* history has no path. Events follow one another randomly, and any effort to impute meaning to their whirligig succession is hopeless. This was the first intuition of aboriginal man, for whom change in the natural world was utterly beyond human control or comprehension. It is also how life and time appear to a small child. Yet pathless time has also become a supreme spiritual goal, the "knowing beyond knowing" of many Eastern religions. Buddhism teaches that a person reaches nirvana by ritually detaching himself from any connection to the meaning of space or time or selfhood. Over the last century, various strains of chaoticism have gained influence in our own society—from the Just Do It popular culture to the deconstructive nihilisms of academe.

The practical shortcoming of chaotic time is that it dissolves society's connective tissue. If cause and effect have no linkage in time, people cannot be held morally accountable for their choices. Nothing would legitimize the obligations of parents to children or neighbors to community. This is why no society or religion has ever given more than a very limited endorsement to chaotic time—not even Buddhism, in which all who fail to reach nirvana remain subject to the orderly reign of karma.

Cyclical time originated when the ancients first linked natural cycles of planetary events (diurnal rotations, lunar months, solar years, zodiacal precessions) with related cycles of human activity (sleeping, waking; gestating, birthing; planting, harvesting; hunting, feasting). Cyclical time conquered chaos by repetition, by the parent or hunter or farmer performing the right deed at the right moment in the perpetual circle, much as an original god or goddess performed a similar deed during time's mythical first circle. Eventually, great cycles came to mark the duration of kingdoms and prophecies, the coming of heroes and shamans, and the aging of lives, generations, and civilizations. Cyclical time is endless, yet also endlessly completed and renewed, propelled by elaborate rituals resembling the modern seasonal holidays.

Unlike chaotic time, cyclical time endowed classical societies with a prescribed moral dimension, a measure by which each generation could compare its behavior with that of its ancestors. Those who believed in cycles could engage in what anthropologist Lévy-Bruhl calls a "participation mystique" in the divine recreation of nature's eternal round. The power that this concept has exercised on mankind is conveyed by the colossal monuments to recurring time (the obelisks, pyramids, ziggurats, and megaliths) so many archaic societies left behind. Yet even as belief in cyclical time overcomes the chaotic primitive view, it leaves less room for what modern people think of as originality and creativity. "For the traditional societies, all the important acts of life were revealed *ab origine* by gods or heroes. Men only repeat these exemplary and paradigmatic gestures *ad infinitum,*" observes religious scholar Mircea Eliade. "This tendency may well appear paradoxical, in the sense that the man of a traditional culture sees himself as real only to the extent that he ceases to be himself (for a modern observer) and is satisfied with imitating and repeating gestures of another."

So what's the alternative? Enter the third option: *linear time*—time as a unique (and usually progressing) story with an absolute beginning and an absolute end. Thus did mankind first aspire to progress. In Greco-Roman civilization, the cyclical view of time was punctuated by inklings of human improvement. The Greeks sometimes hoped that Promethean reason might deliver mankind from perpetual destitution, while the Romans believed that a powerful polity could endow its citizens with a glorious destiny. Most important, the rise and spread of the great Western monotheisms inspired the hope that mankind was fated for more than just fortune's wheel. The Persian, Judaic, Christian, and Islamic cosmologies all embraced the radically new concept of personal and historical time as a unidirectional drama. Time begins with a fall from grace; struggles forward in an intermediate sequence of trials, failures, revelations, and divine interventions; and ends with redemption and reentry into the Kingdom of God.

Linearism required hundreds of years to catch on, but when it did, it changed the world. In medieval Europe, unidirectional time as outlined by the early Christians remained a relatively arcane idea, fully understood by only a small clerical elite. But in the sixteenth century, the Reformation and the spread of the printed Gospel ushered in a new urgency (and popular application) to linear history. Ordinary people began speculating about the historical signs of Christ's Second (and final) Coming and inventing new sects according to their expectations about this. Two centuries later, the Enlightenment transmuted Christian linearism into a complementary secular faith, what historian Carl Becker called "the heavenly city of the eighteenth-century philosophers"—the belief in indefinite scientific, economic, and political improvement.

By the late nineteenth century, with the Industrial Revolution roaring at maximum speed, the Western dogma of history-as-progress reached its apogee. Either as a religious credo, a positivist dogma, or an evolutionary science, it was not to be questioned. The 1902 edition of *The Cambridge Modern History* explained: "We are bound to assume as a scientific hypothesis on which history is to be written, a progress in human affairs. This progress must inevitably be towards some end." "Progress was Providence," was how Lord Acton later described the prevailing Victorian view. "Unless there was progress there could be no God in history."

England's first New World settlements began as an outpost of radical Calvinism and the radical Enlightenment. Not surprisingly, America has come to embody the most extreme expression of progressive linearism. The first European explorers often saw in this fresh land mass—this New Atlantis, El Dorado, or Utopia—an authentic opportunity to remake man and therein put an end to history. Successive waves of immigrants likewise saw themselves as builders of a millennial New Jerusalem, inaugurators of a revolutionary Age of Reason, defenders of "God's chosen country," and pioneers in service of a Manifest Destiny. Early in the current century, Herbert Croly wrote of a "progressive nationalism" and James Truslow Adams of an "American Dream" to refer to this civic faith in linear advancement. Time, they suggested, was the natural ally of each successive generation. Thus arose the dogma of American exceptionalism, the belief that this nation and its people had somehow broken loose from any risk of cyclical regress.

Along the way, linear time has succeeded in suppressing cyclical time. Ages ago, cyclical time conquered chaotic time. But in recent centuries, the conqueror has in turn been chained and shackled. The victory of linearism was neither immediate nor absolute. For example, the core Christian ritual— the yearly celebration of a dying and reborn savior—still resembles the regenerative midwinter rituals of the archaic religions it superseded. But by degrees, cyclical time as a living faith has been pushed ever deeper into obscurity.

The suppression dates back to the early Christians who tried to root out calendrical paganism, denounced classical cycles, and pushed underground entire branches of nonlinear learning, such as the hermetic fields of alchemy and astrology. "Only the wicked walk in circles," warned St. Augustine. At the dawn of the modern era, the assault grew more fierce. The Reformation not only triggered a renewed attack on pagan holidays (chopping down maypoles) but also popularized the calibrating clocks, calendars, and diaries that enabled people to employ time as an efficient means to a linear end—be it holiness, wealth, or conquest. More recently, the West began using technology to flatten the very physical evidence of natural cycles. With artificial light, we believe we defeat the sleep-wake cycle; with climate control, the seasonal cycle; with refrigeration, the agricultural cycle; and with high-tech medicine, the rest-recovery cycle.

Triumphal linearism has shaped the very style of Western and (especially) American civilization. Before, when cyclical time reigned, people valued patience, ritual, the relatedness of parts to the whole, and the healing power of time-within-nature. Today, we value haste, iconoclasm, the disintegration of the whole into parts, and the power of time-outside-nature.

Before, the dominant numerical paradigm for change was four, originally a feminine symbol in most cultures. In the great quaternities of seasons, directions, and elements, the fourth element always circles back to the others. Today, the dominant paradigm is three, originally a masculine symbol. In the great triads of Christianity and modern philosophy, the third element always transcends the others.

Before, people prized the ability to divine nature's energy and use it. Today, we prize the ability to defy nature's energy and overcome it.

OVERCOMING LINEARISM

The great achievement of linear time has been to endow mankind with a purposeful confidence in its own self-improvement. A linear society defines explicit moral goals (justice, equality) or material goals (comfort, abundance) and then sets out deliberately to attain them. When those goals are reached, people feel triumphant; when they aren't, new tactics are applied. Either way, the journey never repeats. Each act is original, granting a sense of authentic creativity unknown to those who reenact the past. In America, as Mark Twain observed, nothing is older than our habit of calling everything new.

Yet the great weakness of linear time is that it obliterates time's recurrence and thus cuts people off from the eternal—whether in nature, in each other, or in ourselves. When we deem our social destiny entirely self-directed and our personal lives self-made, we lose any sense of participating in a collective myth larger than ourselves. We cannot ritually join with those who come before or after us. Situating us at some intermediate moment eons away from both the beginning and the end of history, linear time leaves us alone, restless, afraid to stand still lest we discover something horrible about ourselves. Most Americans would agree with Mary McCarthy that "The happy ending is our national belief"—but few of us have any idea what we would do if we ever got there.

When things go well, this weakness is no problem. But when things go badly, the linear view can crack—exposing the horror of time as an unfamiliar void. The experience of World War I affected the entire Western world in precisely this fashion, casting a shadow of despair and relativism that loomed until the uplifting finale to World War II reenergized faith in the future. But today that faith is again in steep decline. *Progress* has acquired mostly pejorative connotations—of robotic technology, bureaucratic statism, and jaundiced culture. It no longer describes where we wish history to go. The more we persist in believing time to be linear, the more we fear that the path to the future might now be linear *downwards*.

Many Americans have responded to this dimming faith in progress with aggressive denial. In every recent decade, the public has rallied around yet another manifesto of three-stage triumphalism. In 1960, it was Walt Rostow's *The Stages of Economic Growth* (culminating in a "takeoff" into a fabulous mass-consumption society); in 1967, Herman Kahn's *The Year 2000* (traditional, industrial, and then postindustrial societies); in 1970, Charles Reich's *The Greening of America* (Con I, II, and III); in 1980, Alvin Toffler's *The Third Wave* (First, Second, and Third Waves); and in 1992, Francis Fukuyama's *The End of History and the Last Man* (a new take on G.W.F. Hegel, who carved all of history into threes). The linear school views all human history as akin to a ski jump: After crouching dumbly for millennia, mankind is just now taking off on its glorious final flight.

To linearists, the future can often be reduced to a straight-line extrapolation of the recent past. Because they don't see any bends or reversals in what has already happened, they can't see any in what will happen. "Trends, like horses, are easier to ride in the direction they are already going," writes *Megatrends'* John Naisbitt. It is likewise typical of linearism, new and old, to herald the imminent arrival of history's last act. Today's avid believers, just like the crowds who gathered around Reformation preachers, are apparently flattered into believing that they just happen be alive at the moment of mankind's ultimate transformation.

Yet despite the undaunted linearism, even more Americans are reverting to the belief in chaotic time—the belief that life is a billion fragments, that events come at random, and that history is directionless. In pop culture, the past is mainly grist for Planet Hollywood artifacts, *Forrest Gump* morphs, and Oliver Stone infotainments. In politics and business, the past is little more than a tool chest of tactical images. In academe, many historians grimace at the suggestion that the past offers any lessons whatsoever. They see no intrinsic and unifying story, merely a grab bag of bygone details or footnotes to some passing social theory. Indeed, some historians now say there is no single history at all—just a multitude of histories, one for each region, language, family, industry, class, and race. Many academics see the past as subservient to politics, yet another weapon on the Culture Wars battlefield.

This scholarly rejection of time's inner logic has led to the devaluation of history throughout our society. At Ivy League universities, undergraduates are no longer required to study history as a separate field. In public school textbooks, tidbits about past events are mixed together with lessons about geography, politics, and the arts into a sort of social studies stew. Polls reveal that history is now the subject high school students find of least interest or worth. In pop parlance, *that's history* has come to mean "that's irrelevant." Taught a lessonless past, today's students have trouble reciting even the core names and dates. Yet, if their teachers are correct, why should students care when the Civil War was fought? Does it really make any difference whether it started in 1861, 1851, or 1751? If time is chaos, an event like the Civil War could never happen again or could recur tomorrow. If time is linear, then the entire nineteenth century is of no more consequence than some discarded ballistic booster, its relevance fading with each passing year.

Americans today fear that linearism (alias the American Dream) has run its course. Many would welcome some enlightenment about history's patterns and rhythms, but today's intellectual elites offer little that's useful. Caught between the entropy of the chaoticists and the hubris of the linearists, the American people have lost their moorings.

There *is* an alternative. But to grasp it, Americans need to return to the insights of the ancient circle.

Nothing would be lost. We can retain our hopeful intuition of progress and our skeptical awareness of randomness. Yet at the same time we can restore the one perspective that we have too long suppressed and the insights that no other perspective can offer.

We need to realize that without some notion of historical recurrence, no one can meaningfully discuss the past at all. Why even talk about the founding (or decline) of a city, a victory (or defeat) in battle, the rise (or passing away) of a generation, unless we accept that similar things have happened before and could happen again? Only through recurrence can time reveal the enduring myths that define who we are. When Aristotle said that poetry is superior to history because history only tells us "what Alcibiades did or had done to him," he had in mind history as the mere compilation of facts. To matter, history has to do more. It has to reconnect people, in time, to what Aristotle called the "timeless forms" of nature.

We need to recall that time, in its physical essence, is nothing but the measurement of cyclicality itself. Whether the swing of a pendulum, the orbit of a planet, or the frequency of a laser beam, the assumed regularity of a cyclical event is literally all we have to define what time is. Etymologically, the word *time* comes from *tide*—an ancient reference to the lunar cycle still retained in such expressions as "yuletide" and "good tidings." Similarly, the word *period* originally meant "orbit," as in "planetary period." The word *annual* comes from *annus,* whose ancient root meant "circle." The words *year* and *hour* come from the same root as the Greek *horos,* meaning "solar period." The word *month* is a derivative of *moon.* Without cycles, time would literally defy any kind of description.

Most important, we need to understand that our modern efforts to flatten natural and social cycles often meet with only superficial success. Sometimes, all we do is substitute one cycle for another. When we dam a river or industrialize a society, for example, we might eliminate the cycle of floods or wars; then again, we might just ensure that the cycle is both less frequent and more devastating. Often, "progress" ends up generating entirely new cycles. Just ponder them all: business cycles, financial cycles, electoral cycles, fashion cycles, opinion cycles, crime cycles, traffic cycles, and so on. Ironically, linear time creates or deepens social cycles by disabling our natural capacity to achieve homeostasis by continual minor readjustment. Instead, readjustments occur in jumps—that is, in more powerful cyclical movements. The saecular cycle is a profound case in point: Relatively weak in traditional settings, it assumes its most potent form in modern societies that subscribe to linear time.

The society that believes in cycles the least, America, has fallen in the grip of the most portentous cycle in the history of mankind. Many Americans might prefer to think of their country as immune from nature or to think of their history as riding on such serendipities as a slim electoral margin, a barely won battle, an improbable invention, or an assassin's fateful marksmanship. Yet many such supposedly external factors are linked to cyclical change. And even when truly random events occur, our response is governed by circular rhythms that are beyond our power to eradicate. In an eloquent defense of the cyclical perspective on American history, Arthur M. Schlesinger Jr. writes:

> A true cycle . . . is self-generating. It cannot be determined, short of catastrophe, by external events. War, depressions, inflations, may heighten or complicate moods, but the cycle itself rolls on, self-contained, self-sufficient and autonomous. . . . The roots of this cyclical self-sufficiency lie deep in the natural life of humanity. There is a cyclical pattern in organic nature—in the tides, in the seasons, in night and day, in the systole and diastole of the human heart.

Among today's historians, Schlesinger leads the courageous few who challenge the linear orthodoxy. He thereby joins a long and rich tradition of historians, philosophers, writers, and poets who have seen, in affairs of state and war, rhythms similar to what Schlesinger has seen in "the natural life of humanity."

What are these rhythms? In traditional societies, they can assume any number of forms and periodicities. In modern societies, two special and related rhythms come to dominate all the rest. One beats to the length of a long human life. The Etruscans ritualized it and the Romans first gave it a name: the *saeculum.* Today, it loosely goes by the name of *siècle,* or "century." In modern times, those who have glimpsed what Arnold Toynbee called history's "long cycle" have seldom strayed from the core logic of the saeculum: that cycles of human affairs are approximately the length of a long human life (or in the case of half-stroke cycles like the Kondratieff wave, half a human life).

The other rhythm beats to the four phases of a human life, each about twenty years or so in length. What the ancient Greeks called *genos,* and what we call the *generation,* has been known, named, and respected as a force in history by practically every civilization since the dawn of time. From the Sumerians to the Mycenaeans to the Mayans, archaic societies knew of few other ways to describe the passage of social time. In the Hebrew Bible, it was the "new generation . . . who knew not the ways of the Lord" that periodically reenacted the enduring human drama of apostasy, punishment, repentance, and renewal. Over the ages, most of those who have pondered the underlying cause and motive force behind cyclical change—from Plato and Polybius to Toynbee and Schlesinger—have pointed to the generation.

The saeculum lends history its underlying temporal beat. Generations, and their four recurring archetypes, create and perpetuate history's seasonal quality. Together, they explain how and why cycles occur.

CYCLES AND ARCHETYPES

During the Middle Ages, travelers reported an unusual custom among illiterate villagers in central France. Whenever an event of local importance occurred, like the marriage of a seigneur or the renegotiation of feudal dues, the elders boxed the ears of a young child to make sure he remembered that day—and event—all his life.

In today's world, the making of childhood memories remains a visceral practice. Grand state ceremonies box the ears with the thunder of cannons, roar of jets, and blast of fireworks. Teenagers' boom boxes similarly etch young aural canals with future memories of a shared adolescent community. Like medieval French villagers, modern Americans carry deeply felt associations with what has happened at various points in their lives. We memorialize public events (Pearl Harbor, the Kennedy and King assassinations, the *Challenger* explosion) by remembering exactly what we were doing at the time. As we grow older, we realize that the sum total of such events has in many ways shaped who we are.

Exactly *how* these major events shaped us had much to do with how old we were when they happened. When you recall your personal markers of life and time, the events you remember most are suffused with the emotional complexion of your phase of life at the time. Your early markers, colored by the dreams and innocence of childhood, reveal how events (and older people) shaped you. Your later markers, colored by the cares of maturity, tell how you shaped events (and younger people). When you reach old age, you will remember all the markers that truly mattered to you. Perhaps your generation will build monuments to them (as today's seniors are now doing with the new FDR and World War II monuments in Washington, D.C.), in the hope that posterity will remember your lives and times in the preliterate way: as legends. It is through this linkage of biological aging and shared experience, reproduced across turnings and generations, that history acquires personal relevance.

Human history is made of lives, coursing from birth to death. All persons who are born must die, and all who die must first be born. The full sweep of human civilization is but the sum of this. Of all the cycles known to man, the one we all know best is the *human life cycle.* No other societal force—not class, not nationality, not culture, not technology—has as predictable a chronology. The limiting length of an active life cycle is one of civilization's great constants: In the time of Moses, it was eighty to a hundred years, and it still is, even if more people reach that limit. Biologically and socially, a full human life is divided into four phases: *childhood, young adulthood, midlife,* and *elderhood.* Each phase of life is the same length as the others, capable of holding one generation at a time. And each phase is associated with a specific social role that conditions how its occupants perceive the world and act on those perceptions.

A *generation,* in turn, is the aggregate of all people born over roughly the span of a phase of life who share a common location in history and, hence, a common collective persona. Like a person (and unlike a race, religion, or sex), a generation is mortal: Its members understand that in time they all must perish. Hence, a generation feels the same historical urgency that individuals feel in their own lives. This dynamic of generational aging and dying enables a society to replenish its memory and evolve over time. Each time younger generations replace older ones in each phase of life, the composite life cycle becomes something altogether new, fundamentally changing the entire society's mood and behavior.

History creates generations, and generations create history. This symbiosis between life and time explains why, if one is seasonal, the other must be.

Americans' chronic failure to grasp the seasonality of history explains why the consensus forecasts about the national direction usually turn out so wrong.

Back in the late 1950s, forecasters widely predicted that America's future would be like Disney's Tomorrowland. The experts foresaw well-mannered youth, a wholesome culture, an end of ideology, an orderly conquest of racism and poverty, steady economic progress, plenty of social discipline, and uncontroversial Korea-like police actions abroad. All these predictions, of course, were wildly mistaken. It's not just that the experts missed the particular events that lay just ahead—the Tet Offensive and *Apollo 11,* Watts and Kent State, the Summer of Love and Watergate, Earth Day and Chappaquiddick. It's that they missed the entire mood of the coming era.

Why were their predictions so wrong? When the forecasters assumed the future would extrapolate the recent past, they expected that the next set of people in each phase of life would behave just like the current occupants. Had they known where and how to look, the experts could have seen history-bending changes about to occur in America's generational lineup: Each generation would age through time as surely as water runs to the sea. Over the ensuing two decades, the current elder leaders were due to disappear, a new batch of kids to arrive, and the generations in between to transform the new phases of life they were entering.

This dynamic has recurred throughout American history. Roughly every two decades (the span of one phase of life), there has arisen a new *constellation* of generations—a new layering of generational personas up and down the age ladder. As this constellation has shifted, so has the national mood. Consider what happened, from the late 1950s to the late 1970s, as one generation replaced another at each phase of life:

- In elderhood, the cautionary individualists of the *Lost Generation* (born 1883–1900) were replaced by the hubristic *G.I. Generation* (born 1901–1924), who launched America into an expansive era of material affluence, global power, and civic planning.
- In midlife, the upbeat G.I.s were replaced by the helpmate *Silent Generation* (born 1925–1942), who applied their expertise and sensitivity to fine-tune the institutional order while mentoring the passions of youth.
- In young adulthood, the conformist Silent were replaced by the narcissistic *Boom Generation* (born 1943–1960), who asserted the primacy of self and challenged the alleged moral vacuity of the institutional order.
- In childhood, the indulged Boomers were replaced by the neglected *13th Generation* (born 1961–1981), who were left unprotected at a time of cultural convulsion and adult self-discovery. Known in pop culture as Generation X, its name here reflects the fact that it is literally the thirteenth generation to call itself American.

Viewed through the prism of generational aging, the mood change between the late 1950s and the late 1970s becomes not just comprehensible, but (in hindsight) predictable: America was moving from a First Turning constellation and into a Second. Replace the aging Truman and Ike with LBJ and Nixon. Replace the middle-aged Ed Sullivan and Ann Landers with Norman Lear and Gloria Steinem. Replace the young *Organization Man* with the Woodstock hippie. Replace Jerry Mathers with Tatum O'Neal. This top-to-bottom alteration of the American life cycle tells much about why and how America shifted from a mood of consensus, complacency, and optimism to one of turbulence, argument, and passion.

What about the most recent twenty years? The most prevalent late-1970s forecasts of late 1990s America assumed that the trends of the 1960s would continue along a straight line. This led to predictions of an acceleration of government planning, ongoing protests against social conformity, more God-is-dead secularism, delegitimized family life, less emphasis on money and weapons in a "postmaterialist" age, and spectacular economic growth that would either allow unprecedented leisure—or plunge the planet into a huge ecological catastrophe.

None of that came to pass, of course. But in their triumphal enthusiasm, virtually all the late-seventies forecasters made a more fundamental error: Whether their visions were utopian or apocalyptic, veering toward *Epcot Center* or *Soylent Green,* they all assumed that America was heading *somewhere* in a hurry. No one imagined what actually happened: that through the 1980s and 1990s, while different societal pieces have drifted in different directions, America as a whole has gone nowhere in particular.

As before, these forecasters missed the target because they failed to look at life-cycle trajectories. They failed to realize that all the generations were poised to enter new phases of life—and that, as they did, people up and down the life cycle would think and behave differently. In elderhood, the confident G.I.s were due to be replaced by the more hesitant Silent, who would prefer a more complex, diverse, and individuated social order. In midlife, the conciliatory Silent were ready to give way to the more judgmental Boomers, who would enforce a confrontational ethic of moral conviction. In young adulthood, the passionate Boomers were set to vacate for the more pragmatic 13ers, whose survivalism would be born of necessity. In childhood, the neglected 13ers were about to be replaced by the more treasured Millennials amid a resurgent commitment to protect and provide for small children. As a result of all these life-cycle shifts, the national mood would change into something new. Back in the 1970s, the experts could have envisioned what this mood would be. How? By looking at an earlier Awakening era with a similar generational constellation and by inquiring into what happened next.

And what about today? Forecasters are still making the same mistakes. Best-selling books envision a postmillennial America of unrelenting individualism, social fragmentation, and weakening government—a nation becoming ever more diverse and decentralized, its citizens inhabiting a high-tech world of tightening global ties and loosening personal ones, its Web sites multiplying and its culture splintering. We hear much talk about how elder life will improve and child life deteriorate, how the rich will get richer and the poor poorer, and how today's kids will come of age with a huge youth crime wave.

Don't bet on it. The rhythms of history suggest that none of those trends will last more than a few years into the new century. What will come afterward can be glimpsed by studying earlier Unraveling eras with similar generational constellations—and by inquiring into what happened next.

To do this correctly, we must link each of today's generations with a recurring sequence of four generational archetypes that have appeared throughout all the saecula of our history. These four archetypes are best identified by the turnings of their births:

- A *Prophet* generation is born during a High.
- A *Nomad* generation is born during an Awakening.
- A *Hero* generation is born during an Unraveling.
- An *Artist* generation is born during a Crisis.

Each archetype is an expression of one of the enduring temperaments—and life-cycle myths—of mankind. When history overlays these archetypes atop the four turnings, the result is four very different generational constellations. This explains why a new turning occurs every twenty years or so and why history rolls to so many related pendular rhythms. One turning will underprotect children, for example, while another will overprotect them. The same is true with attitudes toward politics, affluence, war, religion, family, gender roles, pluralism, and a host of other trends.

Dating back to the first stirrings of the Renaissance, Anglo-American history has traversed six saecular cycles, each of which displayed a similar rhythm. Every cycle had four turnings, and (except for the anomalous U.S. Civil War) every cycle produced four generational archetypes. We are presently in the Third Turning of the Millennial Saeculum, the seventh cycle of the modern era.

By looking at history through this saecular prism, you can see why the American mood has evolved as it has during your own lifetime. Reflect back as far as you can and recall how the persona of people in any phase of life has changed completely every two decades or so. Every time, these changes have followed the archetypal pattern. Consider the generational transitions of the past decade, which are once again proving the linear forecasters wrong.

As the Silent have begun reaching retirement age, national leaders have shown less interest in making public institutions do big things and more interest in making them flexible, fair, expert, nuanced, and participatory. Why? The elder *Artist* is replacing the elder *Hero*.

As Boomers have begun turning fifty, the public discourse has become less refined and conciliatory and more impassioned and moralistic. Why? The midlife *Prophet* is replacing the midlife *Artist*.

As 13ers have filled the "twentysomething" bracket, the pop culture has become less about soul, free love, and feeling at one with the world and a lot more about cash, sexual disease, and going it alone in an unforgiving world. Why? The young-adult *Nomad* is replacing the young-adult *Prophet*.

. As Millennials have surged into America's elementary and junior high schools, family behavior has reverted toward greater protection. Why? We are now raising the child *Hero,* no longer the child *Nomad*.

When you compile these four archetypal shifts through the entire life cycle, you see how America's circa-1970s constellation has transformed into something new, from top to bottom, in the 1990s. *That* is why the nation has shifted from a mood of Awakening to one of Unraveling. When you apply this secular logic forward into the Oh-Oh decade and beyond, you can begin to understand why a Fourth Turning is coming and how America's mood will change when the Crisis hits.

REDISCOVERING THE SEASONS

"The farther backward you look, the farther forward you are likely to see," Winston Churchill once said. The challenge is to look at the future not along a straight line, but around the inevitable corners. To know how to do that, you have to practice looking at how the past has turned corners.

In American schools, where most of us first learn history, our teachers and books seldom if ever discuss events from a seasonal perspective. Recall those pictures of U.S. presidents that line so many classroom walls: Were you ever taught to link the mood and events of those presidents' youth eras with the mood and events of their terms of leadership? Recall the usual litany about the rise of the modern West over the five centuries from Columbus to *Apollo 11:* Were you ever taught about the ebbs and flows *within* each of those centuries of supposedly monotonous progress? Recall all the lessons you heard about the American Revolution, Civil War, and the Great Depression and World War II: Were you ever taught anything more than bits and pieces about the decades that *preceded* those Crises, that is, about the 1760s, 1850s, and 1920s? Did you ever study the public mood in those other Third Turnings? Or what premonition (if any) people had about the Crisis about to hit? Probably not.

If you learned history in the usual linear style, you probably felt a void. Perhaps you yearned for a more personal connection with the past and future, a path through which you could attach a larger drama to your own life experience. Perhaps you yearned for a closer connection to the ancestral wisdom gained by real people who struggled to build the civilization you inherited. Perhaps you yearned for a feeling Americans haven't known in decades: to be active participants in a destiny that is both positive and plausible.

You are about to embark on a new journey through modern history. There is much to learn—but before embarking, there are some things to unlearn.

You should try to *unlearn* the linear belief that America (or the entire modern world) is exempt from the seasonal cycles of nature. As you become acquainted with the saeculum, you will meet a very different view, one arising with the ancients—the view that the rhythms of social change are reflected in the rhythms of biological and seasonal nature. In their search for deeper meanings, the ancients translated events into myths and heroes into archetypes, players in a recurring drama in which new civic orders (or values regimes) are perpetually created, nurtured, exhausted, destroyed—and, in the end, regenerated. In the ancient view, this cycle repeats, pursuant to the same beat, in a history without end. Time can bring an upward spiral of progress or a downward spiral of decline, much like the processes of natural evolution.

Try to *unlearn* the linear need to judge change by one-dimensional standards of progress. Because nature was more central to their cosmology than to ours, the ancients understood some things better than we moderns do. They knew that natural change is neither steady nor random. They knew that nature neither guarantees progress nor precludes it. They knew that the oscillations within a cycle are greater than the differences across a full cycle. They knew that one year's (or one saeculum's) winter is more like the prior winter than like the autumn that came right before it. They knew that a Fourth Turning is a natural season of life.

Try to *unlearn* the obsessive fear of death (and the anxious quest for death avoidance) that pervades linear thinking in nearly every modern society. The ancients knew that, without periodic decay and death, nature cannot complete its full round of biological and social change. Without plant death, weeds would strangle the forest. Without human death, memories would never die, and unbroken habits and customs would strangle civilization. Social institutions require no less. Just as floods replenish soils and fires rejuvenate forests, a Fourth Turning clears out society's exhausted elements and creates an opportunity for fresh growth.

Finally, *unlearn* the linear view that positive change always comes willingly, incrementally, and by human design. Many Americans instinctively sense that many elements of today's Unraveling-era America—from Wall Street to Congress, from rock lyrics to pro sports—must undergo a wrenching upheaval before they can fundamentally improve. That instinct is correct. A Fourth Turning lends people of all ages what is literally a once-in-a-lifetime opportunity to heal (or destroy) the very heart of the republic.

With all that unlearned, you can *relearn* history from the perspective of seasonality.

This is a book that turns history into prophecy. It takes you on a journey through the confluence of social time and human life. In Part One ("Seasons"), you will acquire new tools for understanding self, family, society, and civilization. You will learn about the cycles of life, generational archetypes, turnings, and history. In Part Two ("Turnings"), you will revisit post–World War II American history from the perspective of turnings and archetypes. You will gain a new insight about why the first three turnings of the current Millennial Saeculum have evolved as they have. You will read why this saecular journey must culminate in a Fourth Turning and what is likely to happen when it does. In Part Three ("Preparations"), you will explore what you and your nation can do to brace for the coming Crisis. Given the current Unraveling-era mood of personal indulgence and public despair, now may seem like a hopeless time to redirect the course of history. But you will learn how, by applying the principles of seasonality, we *can* steer our destiny. There is much that we can accomplish in a saecular autumn, many steps we can take to help ensure that the coming spring will herald glorious times ahead.

An appreciation for history is never more important than at times when a saecular winter is forecast. In the Fourth Turning, we can expect to encounter personal and public choices akin to the harshest ever faced by ancestral generations. We would do well to learn from their experience, viewed through the prism of cyclical time. This will not come easily. It will require us to lend a new seasonal interpretation to our revered American Dream. And it will require us to admit that our faith in linear progress has often amounted to a Faustian bargain with our children. Faust always ups the ante, and every bet is double or nothing. Through much of the Third Turning, we have managed to postpone the reckoning. But history warns that we can't defer it beyond the next bend in time.

As Arthur Wing Pinero has written, "The future is only the past again, entered through another gate." Increasingly, Americans are sensing that the next great gate in history is approaching. It's time to trust our instincts, think seasonally, and *prepare*. Forewarned is forearmed.

PART ONE

■

Seasons

CHAPTER 2

∎

Seasons of Time

IN THE PRE-ROMAN CENTURIES, ITALY WAS HOME TO Etruria, among the most mysterious and exotic of ancient civilizations. The Etruscans were unrelated to other Italic peoples and may have come from Lydia, in present-day Turkey. Their alphabet resembles ancient Greek but defies translation. To understand their rituals, modern historians have little more than rumors handed down by raconteurs, plus artifacts dug from tombs. From these clues, historians have concluded that the Etruscans were an unusually fatalistic people who looked upon time as the playing out of an unalterable destiny. According to legend, an old sibyl issued a prophecy that their civilization would last for ten lifetimes, at which time *finem fore nominis Etrusci:* Etruria was doomed.

Around the time this prophecy was issued, perhaps in the ninth century B.C., the Etruscans invented the ritual with which they came to measure the portents of their prophecy. No one knows its Etruscan name, but by the time the Romans adopted the ritual, it was known as the *saeculum.* The word carried two meanings: "a long human life," and "a natural century," approximating one hundred years. The word's etymology may be related to the Latin *senectus* (old age), *sero* (to plant), *sequor* (to follow), or some lost Etruscan root. Much of what we know about the saeculum comes from Varro (Augustus's librarian) via Censorinus, a Roman historian of the third century A.D. By then, Etruria had become a distant memory to a Rome that was itself weakening.

In *De die natale,* an essay on time and history dedicated to a friend on his birthday, Censorinus described "natural saeculae" as "very long spaces of a human life defined by birth and death" and explained how the Etruscans measured them:

Although the truth is concealed in the darkness, in any civilization which has natural saeculae the books there are seen to teach the rituals of the Etruscans, in which it is written that the beginnings of saeculae are brought forth in this way: Among those who are born on the day on which a city or civilization is founded, the one who lives the longest completes, with the day of his death, the standard measure of the first saeculum, and among those alive in the city on that day, the one who lives the longest completes the second saeculum.

Although he furnished the traditional numbers for the first six Etruscan saeculae (which averaged 107 years), Censorinus admitted that these calculations must have encountered many practical difficulties. Who kept track of "the one who lives the longest"? How did the various Etruscan towns, founded in different years, agree on a common system of reckoning? Censorinus reported that the Etruscan priests confirmed the dates by noting comets and "strange lightning" in the heavens. We know little for certain except that the Etruscans considered the natural human life span to be the central unit of their history and destiny.

Like all ancients, the Etruscans were well aware of the annual cycle of the sun and seasons—of spring, summer, autumn, and winter. Gripped by prophecy and superstition, they also believed that Etruria's history was progressing through a similarly seasonal cycle of history—of growth, maturation, entropy, and death. Of these two cycles, one lasted a year, the other too long for a mortal to imagine. Perhaps the Etruscans felt they needed an intermediate measure of time, a natural cycle between the other two. If so, they made the obvious choice: the human life, with its natural progression from springlike growth to summerlike maturation to autumnlike entropy to winterlike death.

The saeculum served a mnemonic purpose as well. The Etruscans are believed to have been an affective people, attuned more to the personal than the abstract, alert to the energies of youth and the wisdom of age, and (as D. H. Lawrence observed) fascinated with the biology of human procreation. For them, history meant more if somebody were still alive who could personally remember it. Upon the death of the last person who recalled a given event, Etruscans were inclined to move on to fresh memories of newer events. The saeculum became their way of recording history from the inside out—as people actually lived it and remembered it—not from the outside in, as the scribblings of priests in a king's court.

In the end, Etruria's ten-saeculum prophecy proved alarmingly correct: The last vestiges of their culture were buried under the advance of Rome during the reign of Augustus, nearly one full millennium after the Etruscan year zero.

The Romans had their own mythical prophecy. When Romulus founded Rome, he supposedly saw a flock of twelve vultures, which he took to be a signal that Rome would last twelve units of time. Eventually, the early Romans (who turned to Etruscan learning on such matters) came to assume that the vulture omen must refer to twelve saecula. This assumption was confirmed by a set of prophetic books presented by an old sibyl to Tarquin, the last king of Rome who was himself Etruscan. Thereafter, these Sibylline Prophecies were kept under close guard in the Temple of Jupiter, to be consulted only at moments of crisis and doubt.

As their city prospered and conquered, the Romans became obsessed with the saeculum as a rhythmic measure of their destiny. Not long after their republic was founded in 509 B.C., Rome instituted the tradition of saecular games. These three-day, three-night *ludi saeculares* combined the athletic spectacle of a modern Olympics with the civic ritual of an American July Fourth centennial. Held about once per century, these extravaganzas were timed to give most Romans a decent chance of witnessing them at some point in their lives. By the second century B.C., the first Roman historians routinely employed the saeculum (or saecular games) to periodize their chronicles, especially when describing great wars and new laws.

When Augustus established the empire, popular optimism about putting an end to chronic political disorder expressed itself in Virgil's poetic hopes that an aging Rome could "reestablish its youth" and give birth to a new *saeculum aureum,* another "age of gold." After Augustus, emperors typically claimed that their ascendancy to power heralded a new saeculum, a dawning age that would rejuvenate a vast empire gradually shuddering into decadence and ruin. During the late Republic, writers explicitly referred to their own era as Rome's eighth saeculum. A century later, after a round of civil wars, Lucan and Juvenal assumed they were living in the ninth.

Why were the Romans so fascinated by the saeculum? It wasn't just an odd way of groping toward 100 years as a convenient round number. Censorinus himself raised and dismissed this possibility, noting that the Romans always distinguished between a civil saeculum (a strict 100-year unit of time) and a natural saeculum (the stuff of life, history, and imperial destiny). A more probable explanation is that the Romans were impressed by a strong 80 to 110 year rhythm that seemed to pulse through their history. During the Republic, this rhythm appeared in the timing of great perils and Rome's subsequent eras of renewal and innovation (the struggle to found the Republic, the do-or-die wars against the Veii and the Gauls, the catastrophic Great Samnite War, the disastrous invasion of Hannibal, and the Gracchi reforms and slave revolts). During the Empire, the saecular pattern arose after fearful episodes of civil strife or barbarian invasion (the founding of the principate under Augustus, the early-second-century recovery under Trajan and the Antonines, the early-third-century recovery under the Severii, and yet a later recovery under Diocletian and Constantine).

Ultimately, even the Eternal City was fated to meet a crisis from which it could not recover. In one of history's more bizarre coincidences, the vulture augury proved to be even more accurate than the original Etruscan prophecy. Rome fell to the Visigothic chieftain Alaric in A.D. 410, exactly thirty-seven years before the twelve hundredth anniversary of its legendary founding, ninety-seven years for each of the twelve vultures seen by Romulus. As Europe plunged into the Dark Ages, St. Augustine launched his City of God attack on the cyclical futility of the imperial City of Man. Yet even if the Etruscans and Romans vanished from history, the saeculum did not. A millennium later, it appeared again, boosted by Renaissance philosophers who rediscovered the classical insight of cyclical time. In due course, modern man redefined the practice of saecular games—in the form of major wars and new balances of power that have recurred roughly once every hundred years.

Although the Etruscans were unique among archaic peoples for using the length of a long human life as the central unit of time, many other ancient cultures reached similar conclusions about the seasonality of their world. They saw the same natural elements as the Etruscans did, and they too noticed great circles in the seas, skies, and animal life. They reached these conclusions by instinct, not by science. Even so, these beliefs became the stuff of powerful myths and enduring religions. Along the way, ancient cyclical visions pointed toward the saeculum, even if they did not always identify it. Whatever its influence over the ancient world, the saeculum was destined to become even more potent in the modern world, where it would underlie a recurring cycle of history.

THE WHEELS OF TIME

Late each December, many Americans place large circles of sculpted evergreens over their front doors. Most of us think of this year-end wreath as a Christmas decoration, but the ritual is originally pagan. It dates back to the Roman Saturnalia and totems used by other ancients to protect themselves from winter. Consider the natural symbolism: The wreath's circle symbolizes an eternity of unbrokenness; its evergreens, the persistence of light and life through the death and darkness of winter; its location on the home portal, the conviction that the family will survive; its postsolstice timing, an acknowledgment that the days of greatest cold must now yield to warmth and promise of spring. Another year-end practice—the New Year's Eve party—resembles not just the Saturnalia, but also the Babylonian Zagmuk, Persian Sacaea, and other annual festivals of wildness and social inversion.

As the year turns, many of our later holidays also have roots in the ancient ritual year, whose spring festivals celebrated newness, fertility, and creation; whose midsummer bonfires honored kings and staved off witches; whose autumnal rites extolled the bounty and thanked the earth; and whose winter festivities marked great moments of discontinuity, from death to re-birth. The ancients did not fear the seasons of nature (or history) changing as much as they feared them *stopping,* leaving the world in a perpetual state of cold or hot (or anarchy or despotism).

The ritual year endures in modern America, especially around the time of the "winter break" between the old year and the new. The baby Jesus symbolizes hope for the soul, while the New Year's baby symbolizes hope for the world. In the week between the two holidays, many modern Americans feel unfocused, much like the ancients did after the solstice. Now as then, the break passes. Spurred along by seasonal rites, the year resumes its circular voyage. The original purpose of these solstitial rituals was less to congratulate the seasons than to propel them on, to help nature complete what ancient cultures deemed a wheel of time.

The quaternal round of annual seasons was one of many wheels of time ritualized by the ancients. The shortest were governed by the sun and moon, each traversing its own circular pattern of waxing, fullness, waning, and disappearance. Of intermediate length were the cycles of life—animals and humans, priests and kings, dynasties and civilizations—each possessing an orderly morphology of growth and decline. The longest cycles were abstract periods of universal creation and destruction, ranging from the Hebrew *yom* (1,000 years) to the Mayan *pictun* (8,000 years), to the inconceivable Buddhist *kalpa* (4,320,000,000 years). The 12,000-year "great year" or *yuga* was especially popular in the Babylonian, Hindu, and Hellenistic world, since it roughly coincided with an astronomical cycle today known as the precession of the ecliptic.

Whether Eastern or Western, whether as short as an hour or as long as a *kalpa,* whether measures of real or of eternal or of sacred time, the ancient ritual cycles nearly always manifested the same attributes:

■ Each cycle is represented by a circle, symbolizing perfect and unbreakable recurrence.

Nearly every primitive or archaic society came to see sacred time as rounded. In ancient India, Hindus and Jainists described it as a *yantra* (circle) or *chakra* (disk), the Buddhists as a *mandala* (wheel of law or life). To the ancient Chinese, the principle of stability underlying all change, *tai chi,* was drawn as a circle. Likewise, the ancient Greek word *kyklos* meant both "cycle" and "circle." On the temple to Athena at Athens was inscribed the epigram "All human things are a circle"—a sentiment echoed by Greco-Roman philosophers from Aristotle to Marcus Aurelius. Ancient Babylon and Egypt gave birth to the zodiacal great year, which inspired the wheels of time and fortune so popular among later Christian and Islamic writers. In Europe, the Celtic god Mag Ruith (wizard of the wheels) set time in motion, while Germanic tribes symbolized time as a ring, emphasizing its power to bind and constrain. Mayan calendars were circular, while natives in the North American plains referred to the year as a sacred hoop.

Two particular symbols of circular time are nearly universal. One is the looping serpent, a sign of evil in the Judeo-Christian tradition but believed by many ancient societies to be a benign chthonic force of nature. Supposedly immortal, the snake periodically renews itself by shedding its skin, just as time sheds years. Another is the traditional circle dance—the European *carole,* the Punjabi *bhangra,* the South American *cueca,* the Balkan *kolo*— with which communities greet a new season of nature or life. The human ring, like the wedding ring, symbolizes the unbreakable continuity of time.

■ Each circle is divided into phases—sometimes two, nearly always four.

When the ancients contemplated time's circular voyage, they were impressed by how every extreme is defined, balanced, and necessitated by its opposite. As the day turned, light alternated with dark. As the year turned, hot and dry alternated with cold and wet. As the saeculum (or its equivalent) turned, peace alternated with war. The ancient Chinese called this the reciprocal interaction of *yin* (passivity) and *yang* (aggression). The ancient Greeks called it the dynamic pulsation of *philia* (love and harmony) and *neikos* (strife and separation). The Jainists believed that time's wheel oscillates between *utsarpini* (ascending motion) and *avasarpini* (declining motion), literally, "up serpent" and "down serpent." The ancients believed that each cyclical extreme, mirroring the hopes and fears of the other, helps generate the other. The night longs for the day, the day for night. In war, people yearn for relief from strife, leading to peace. In peace, people yearn to champion what they love, leading to war.

Overlapping with two-phase time, and surpassing it in popularity among the ancients, was fourfold time. Some ancient religions deified the number four: The holy *mandala* of the Hindus was typically drawn into four quadrants; the Pythagoreans held the *tetrad* sacred. Whenever the ancients described the physical universe in its totality, they regularly turned to a fourfold division of directions, colors, elements, humors, winds, and planets, even a supposed fourfoldedness of rivers, trees, cities, and mountains of aboriginal space. Quaternities of time were likewise common. Usually, the ruling prototype was the fourfold seasonality of annual time: spring to summer to fall to winter. Similar quaternities were also applied to days or nights (the Romans' four *vigilia),* to months (the four phases of the moon), and to people (the four phases of life).

When the ancients speculated on universal time, quaternities turned up constantly. The Hindus and Buddhists divided their *yugas* into four phases of declining virtue. The Persians believed that the twelve thousand years of earthly time were divided into four eras of three thousand years each. The Babylonian and Hellenistic "great year" was subdivided into four "seasons." Ancient Greek myth told of four ages, each corresponding to a metal (gold, silver, bronze, and iron), a concept echoed in the Hebrew prophet Daniel's "four ages of man" and in the Christian Book of Revelations. Among American native peoples, from the Maya to the Dakota, fourfold time is nearly universal.

Like the *yin* and *yang* of two-phase time, four-phase time alternates between opposite extremes (spring versus autumn, summer versus winter). Yet along with the solstices, the four-part wheel includes transitional equinoxes, eras of developmental change that allow for a richer metaphor of organic growth and decline. Time's circle moves not only from cold to hot to cold but also from growth to maturity to decay to death.

Each season thus assumes a unique identity, which attaches meaning to the spring or autumn of a life or empire. China was said to have four types of ruling houses, each associated with its own season, element, emotion, geographic direction, and color. According to Han Dynasty historian Tung Chung-shu, rulers are supposed to administer punishments and rewards with regard to the suitability of the season. "The ruler's likes and dislikes, joy and anger, are equivalent to Heaven's spring, summer, autumn, and winter . . . When Heaven brings forth these four qualities seasonably, the year is fine; when unseasonably, it is bad." "In general," summarizes Tung's translator, "pardon, benevolence, and generosity should be manifested in spring and summer to foster the expansive processes of growth; punishments, severity, and strict justice in autumn and winter to aid the tightening up processes of nature."

■ Each circle of time has a great moment of discontinuity.

In the ancient view, a new round of time does not emerge gradually from the last but only after the circle experiences a sharp break. In the lunar cycle, this break occurs during the three nights of darkness; in the annual cycle, during the natural death of winter; in the social cycle, after the death of a father or ruin of a village or, by extension, after the death of a king or ruin of a dynasty. In their great year cycle, the Hellenics called this discontinuity the *ekpyrosis,* when all things, even human souls, are destroyed in fire. Thus cleansed, nature and history can begin again.

Classical cultures developed elaborate rituals to usher in each new circle, just as their mythical gods and heroes and prophets had presumably done at the beginning of time. All over the world, time's rite of passage required three steps. First, rituals of *kenosis* (emptying)—fasting, sacrificing, or scapegoating—purified the community of sins committed in the last circle and thereby allowed a new circle to begin. In the typical new year celebration, the ancients assumed that an aboriginal god or king had once died for precisely this purpose and that a sacrifice (literally, a "making sacred") had to be reenacted before each new circle could start. The second step was a liminal, chaotic phase in which the old circle was dead but a new circle not yet born. In this phase, all rules were breakable: The dead could awaken, insults go unpunished, and the social order be inverted, as in the traditional twelfth-night Feast of Fools. The third step required rituals of *plurosis* (filling)—feasting, celebrating, and marrying—to propel the new circle to a happy and creative beginning. In the modern Christian world, this discontinuity is ritualized each year in the atavistic gestures of emptying and filling that extend haphazardly from Christmas and New Year's through Mardi Gras and Lent.

■ Each circle requires that time be restarted, at the moment of each creation.

When a month is over, we push the day back to the first. When a year is over, we push the month back to the first. But is there ever a time when we should push the *year* back to the first? The ancients thought so. Whenever heroic or prophetic deeds occurred, they often moved all measures of time back to the number one. Their calendrical dates typically denoted numbered years of a particular reign or generation or dynasty. Most modern religions (Christianity, Judaism, Islam) are so firmly wed to the concept of linear time that they do not welcome the concept of periodic new beginnings. But modern revolutions, on occasion, have attempted to restart (and purify) time. On September 22, 1792, the new French Assembly proclaimed "Year One of the Republic" and introduced an entirely new calendar, which lasted only thirteen years. In 1871, the revolutionary leaders of the Paris Commune shot the hands off church clocks to express their release from ancestral time. In our own century, Benito Mussolini ordered 1922 to be hailed as "Year I" (in Roman numerals) of his self-proclaimed Fascist Era.

In popular parlance, Americans often set fixed boundaries between eras of active historical remembrance and eras of diminished relevance. We describe the last half-century as a "postwar" era, part of a circle of time that began with the civic heroism of countrymen still alive. Prior events feel substantially more distant in the national memory.

■ Each circle is presumed to repeat itself, in the same sequence, over a period of similar length.

Periods repeat—celestial ones exactly, social ones approximately. In ancient Greek, the word *periodos* meant "a going around, a cycle." Nearly all non-Western cultures accept the periodic regularity of time. In the West— from the Stoics to the Epicureans, Polybius to Ibn Khaldun, Machiavelli to Vico, Yeats to Eliot, Spengler to Toynbee—circular time has been a peren-

nial theme. As the philosopher R. G. Collingwood remarked, "The historical cycle is a permanent feature of all historical thought."

There are many cycles of time, each with a different periodicity. Each cycle measures hours or days or years or great years of human activity according to its own particulars. This prompts the question: Through the
millennia, which wheel has dominated the others as a marker in people's
personal and social lives?

Among traditional societies, where behavior is prescribed by ritual time,
any circle may be as useful as any other. Some activities are governed by
rules for the day, others by rules for the month, season, year, reign, dynasty,
and so on. When an unnatural intervention occurs (say, a solar eclipse or an
untimely royal death), people engage in purification rites to push the dis-
tended circle back to its natural groove, after which time is presumed to keep
turning as before. As a society modernizes, however, one circle gradually
emerges as paramount over all the others: This is the circle of the natural human life span—what the Etruscans defined and the Romans knew as the
saeculum.

Why should the saeculum be so special? One reason is that the natural
life span is probably the only circle that mankind can neither avoid nor alter. The planetary rhythms of light, heat, and precipitation can be mutated
or circumvented by modern technology and global markets. The political
rhythms of dynastic change can be twisted or frozen by ideologies and nation states. The natural human life cycle and its seasons, by contrast, remain
relatively invariant.

Yet a more important reason is that as modern people exercise their freedom to reshape their natural and social environment, often in efforts to escape circular time, their innovative energy typically reflects their own
life-cycle experiences. Thus, for example, a modern generation impressed
young by the need for peace (or war or justice or art or wealth or holiness)
is empowered to change society's direction accordingly as it assumes leadership. Later on, another generation may choose to reverse this direction,
giving rise to a history that beats to the rhythm of a life span. In a traditional
society, no group possesses such freedom or power. The liberation of the life
cycle thus points to a central irony in the development of saecular rhythms:
The life span plays a dominant role in the rhythm of history precisely when
modern society has largely abandoned cyclical time in favor of linear time.

The Saeculum Rediscovered

After Rome fell, the idea of the saeculum lay dormant in the Western world
for roughly a thousand years. Although linear time was always implicit in
medieval Christian dogma, it lent little direction to the daily affairs of the
nobles, burghers, and peasants. In the Augustinian lexicon, the word *saecu-*

lum lost its meaning as a specific length of time and came to refer to un-
bounded biblical time, as in *saecula saeculorum,* or "endless ages." Dates
referring to the linear Christian drama (the years *Anno Domini)* became the
exclusive province of monastic chroniclers. For everyone else, the ancient
circles persisted—in the quaternity of the cross, the circularity of halos, and
the annualized rituals of Christ's birth, death, and resurrection.

This changed with the Renaissance, when the elites of Western societies
began to perceive themselves as rational and self-determining actors capable of altering the destiny of civilization. With the advent of the Reformation, laypeople felt the rush of events as a preliminary to Christ's return.
Before that millennial event, they had reforms to fight for, fortunes to work
for, ideals to be martyred for, and signs of grace to pray for. As time became
more linear, history became more urgent. Right at this threshold of modernity—when Columbus was voyaging, da Vinci painting, and princes nation
building—the saeculum reentered Western culture. In the romance languages, the word became vulgarized into the derivatives still used today: the
Italian *secolo,* Spanish *siglo,* and French *siècle.* All these new words retained the old Latin term's dual meaning: an era measured by one hundred
years and a long human life. From *centurio* (the rank of a Roman officer
who commanded one hundred soldiers), Renaissance humanists invented an
additional word: *centuria.* Initially, it meant one hundred years, but soon it
acquired a life-cycle connotation as well.

The 1500s became the first hundred-year period to be proclaimed a century and the first to be affixed a century number. In 1517, Erasmus ex-
claimed "Immortal God, what a century I see opening up before us!" As
scholars searched for an event that would mark the beginning of a new century, the philosopher Campanella found it in the discoveries of Galileo. Following the Gregorian calendar reform of the 1580s, Protestant historians
busily categorized Western history into centuries. The epochs that interested
them were *antiquitas* and *modernitas.* What lay between they called the
medii aevi, a medieval period in which time seemed directionless and of less
consequence.

During the seventeenth century, while calendars and almanacs began referring routinely to hundred-year civil centuries, contemporary writers invented references to such natural centuries as the prior "century of Spanish
gold" or the current "grand century of Louis XIV." At the century's end, poetic celebrations of time's rebirth were observed in courtly circles—as with
John Dryden's "Secular Masque" of 1700 ("'Tis well an old age is out, / And
time to begin a new."). On the eve of the French Revolution, the thought of
another century's end engendered fanatical optimism and grim pessimism.
Others sensed an end-of-century awareness of completion, finitude, exhaustion, escapism, and resignation—what scholars came to define as a *fin-
de-siècle* mood that has periodically reappeared in Europe since the
Renaissance. When Madame de Pompadour's *"après nous, le déluge"* au-

gury did indeed come to pass, people realized that yet another century (an *ancien régime* that had also been an *age des lumières)* had indeed passed into history.

After Napoleon, ruminations on the meaning of the historical century assumed romantic overtones. Gustav Rümelin wrote that the word itself had come to mean "a mystical, sublime, almost natural measure of formidable distances of years." Ralph Waldo Emerson described each century as "loaded, fragrant." Sentimental interest in the manners and mores of "lost centuries" clashed with the new belief in progress to produce a true *fin-de-siècle* distemper between 1880 and 1914. The actual phrase was popularized in 1888 when a play with that title opened in Paris. References to "decadence" and "degeneration" became commonplace—as did yearnings for an *élan vital,* a release from time's prison. Never before had the Western world talked so much about a saecular calendar that seemed to be running down. The French essayist and critic Rémy de Gourmont attributed this to modernity itself: "We think by centuries when we cease to think by reigns."

During and after the ensuing world war, historians regarded the quiet months of 1914 as the *fin* of one *siècle* and the assassination of the Austrian archduke as the *commencement* of the next. Before long, the word started marching forward again, now dressed in the uniform of collective action—whether as Mussolini's "century of fascism," Henry Luce's "American Century," or Henry Wallace's "century of the common man." More recently, as people have watched the modern mass man of that century's dawn transform into the postmodern demassified man of that century's twilight, many have wondered if yet another epoch of civilization might be growing old.

Meanwhile, Western scholars began to see *siècle*-length rhythms in many corners of their past. The markers weren't exactly a hundred years long and didn't necessarily correspond to hundred-year breakpoints in the Christian calendar, but they were increasingly regarded as building blocks of the modern European experience. As Antoine-Augustin Cournot observed during the 1870s, "The ancient Romans did not fix the return to their secular games with such a degree of precision; and when we talk of the *siècle* of Pericles, of the *siècle* of Augustus, of the *siècle* of Louis XIV, we mean that it has to do with *siècles* in the Roman sense, not with centuries." Cournot's *siècle,* of course, was the saeculum.

After the mass violence of the twentieth century's second quarter, Arnold Toynbee perceptively noted that "mankind's built-in measure of time is the average duration of an individual human being's conscious life." But there was more to it than just that. He made this observation while writing an opus in which he reached a chilling conclusion: Over much of human history, *siècles* have shown a recurring alternation between peace and war.

THE SAECULUM OF WAR AND PEACE

In the late 1960s, when young anti-Vietnam protesters were chanting "ain't gonna study war no more," one of their elderly supporters, a retired University of Chicago history professor named Quincy Wright, was systematically doing just that. Having watched his own Lost Generation get thanklessly chewed up by World War I, Wright had crusaded in vain for the U.S. Senate to ratify the League of Nations. In the 1920s, as Europe festered with new enmities, he began his epic *Study of War,* a consortium of over fifty separate research projects that he completed in 1942, at the depth of America's fears about a second world war that was proving to be much costlier than the first.

In his *Study,* Wright observed that war waging occurred "in approximately fifty-year oscillations, each alternate period of concentration being more severe." Wright uncovered this pattern not only in modern American and European history but also in Hellenistic and Roman times, and noted that others had glimpsed it before him. He attributed this pattern mainly to generational experience. "The warrior does not wish to fight against himself and prejudices his son against war," he observed, "but the grandsons are taught to think of war as romantic." While Wright also pondered over more epochal "long-wave" cycles of warfare, his saecular rhythm has drawn the most interest from later historians.

Despite its apparent periodicity, Wright remained convinced that war could be avoided through rational peacekeeping. By the time he died in 1970, however, his hopes were crumbling under the powerful insights of his scholarship. The United Nations (whose creation he had encouraged) had become a helpless bystander. The most rational planners any war scholar could want had somehow plunged America into a demoralizing conflict in Southeast Asia, right on the cusp of the "minor war" quadrant of his cycle.

Only a few years after his book appeared, Wright's timetable was corroborated by a famous British contemporary, Arnold Toynbee. In *A Study of History,* best known for its theory of the rise and fall of civilizations, Toynbee identified an "alternating rhythm" of a "Cycle of War and Peace." Punctuating this cycle were quarter-century "general wars" that had occurred in Europe at roughly one-century intervals since the Renaissance. Toynbee identified and dated five repetitions of this cycle, each initiated by the most decisive war of its century:

■ The *overture* began with the Italian Wars (1494–1525).
■ The *first cycle* began with Philip II's Imperial Wars (1568–1609).

- The *second cycle* began with the War of Spanish Succession (1672–1713).
- The *third cycle* began with the French Revolutionary and Napoleonic Wars (1792–1815).
- The *fourth cycle* began with World Wars I and II (1914–1945).

In addition to these five modern centuries, Toynbee identified similar cycles spanning six centuries of ancient Chinese and Hellenistic history, all situated in what he called "break-up" eras of great civilizations. Everywhere, he found the span of time between the start of one general war to the start of the next to have averaged ninety-five years with a "surprising degree of coincidence" across the millennia.

Underlying this periodicity, noted Toynbee, were "the workings of a Generation Cycle, a rhythm in the flow of Physical Life," which had "imposed its dominion on the Spirit of Man." Like Wright, he linked this to the gradual decay of the "living memory of a previous war." Eventually, he observed, the veterans' heirs who "know War only by hearsay" come into power and resume the original war-prone pattern of behavior. Also like Wright, Toynbee diagnosed "supplementary wars" at the midway point of each cycle. Early in his career, Toynbee believed that "human control . . . can diminish the discord and increase the harmony in human life." In old age, he grew more fatalistic—and came to feel transcendence through religion might be a worthier goal than control over worldly affairs.

Toynbee added an important new dimension when he subdivided the war cycle into four periods and distinguished between the "breathing space" after a big war and the "general peace" after a small war. Yet he was wrong to imply that no wars occur during these intervening quarter-century eras. Plainly, *some* wars, at least minor wars, have occurred during practically every quarter century of European (and American) history. To account for these, L. L. Ferrar Jr. reconstructed Toynbee's four-phase war theory and replaced the breathing space and general peace eras with what he calls "probing wars." Richard Rosecrance similarly posited a four-part war cycle, which alternates between bipolar eras of war and multipolar eras of "power vacuum." Although he doesn't specify the periodicity of this cycle, he notes that "one of the tragedies of western international history has been that this cycle has been repeated time and time again."

Some historians cite casualty data to argue with Wright, Toynbee, and Ferrar about their list of which wars qualify as major, general, or hegemonic—yet anyone who ranks wars solely according to their severity misses the point. Whatever the nomenclature, a cycle-ending war is one with decisive social and political consequences. It must *end an era.* Here is where the war cycle needs the assistance of Ludwig Dehio's classic study demonstrating how the European balance of power has shifted profoundly once a century. From this perspective, some of history's bloodiest wars (like the Thirty Years' War or World War I) do not classify as cycle ending because they did not replace the old order with something fundamentally new.

Several recent scholars have broadened the Toynbean cycle beyond war into a more general thesis about long waves of social behavior. In the field of economics, Terence Hopkins and Immanuel Wallerstein have explained the Toynbean cycle as a consequence of capitalist development. In the field of international relations, William Thompson and George Modelski have also advanced theories of political cycles that match Toynbee's rhythm. "Over a period of time (roughly 100 years) a world power emerges from a global war only to experience a gradual decay in its position of preponderance," writes Thompson. "Global order decays at a parallel rate until a new global war occurs and facilitates the emergence of a new world power."

Modelski divides this global political cycle into four quarter-century phases, each succeeding the last in a natural entropic progression. In the first *world power* phase, both the (social) demand for order and the (political) supply of order is high. In the *delegitimizing* phase, the demand for order declines. In the *deconcentration* phase, the supply of order declines. The cycle culminates when the demand for order rises, leading to an order-producing era of *global war.* The last phase is distinguished not by the mere scale of human destruction, though this will likely be high, but rather by a universal perception that an old global structure of politics has perished and a new one is born. He describes this global passage as myth generating in its scope: "The major event clusters of the cycle, the global war campaigns and the celebrated settlements, the ceremonial observances of the great nations, and the passing into obscurity of others, these make up the rituals of world politics. They are the key markers of world time."

In the chart on page 39, notice the similarity between these modern cycles of war and the ancient wheels of time. The alternations between war and peace, or between growing and decaying order, resemble the Asiatic *yin* and *yang* or Hellenic love and strife. These theories reflect the seasons of nature and the ritual year that celebrated them: a springlike era of growth followed by a summerlike era of jubilation, and an autumnlike era of fragmentation followed by a winterlike death—and regeneration. The final phase brings to mind the Stoics' *ekpyrosis,* the purifying and transmuting fire that ends one circle and starts the next.

What is at work here? What did Quincy Wright proclaim in his youth and resist in his old age? What rhythm did Arnold Toynbee see rippling through the modern age of every civilization he studied? It's the unit of history the Etruscans discovered: the natural saeculum, history turning to the beat of a long human life.

The culminating phase of the saeculum is a quarter-century era of war, upheaval, and turmoil. Early humanist scholars called this the *revolutio,* a word derived from the Copernican *revolutiones orbium cælestium* (a pre-

The Modern Saeculum of War and Politics

Author	First Quarter	Second Quarter	Third Quarter	Fourth Quarter
WRIGHT (1942)	peace	minor wars	peace	major wars
TOYNBEE (1954)	breathing space	supplementary wars	general peace	general wars
ROSECRANCE (1973)	decreased involvement	power vacuums	increased involvement	war
FERRAR JR. (1977)	probing wars	adjusting wars	probing wars	hegemonic wars
HOPKINS-WALLERSTEIN (1982)	hegemonic maturity	declining hegemony	ascending hegemony	hegemonic victory
MODELSKI-THOMPSON (1987)	world power	delegitimization	deconcentration	global war
NATURE	*Spring*	*Summer*	*Autumn*	*Winter*

dictable moment of astronomical return). With the Reformation, the word *revolution* connoted a path to a golden age, to paradise, to justice. A century later, Thomas Hobbes linked it to politics, a meaning that matured with the epic revolutions of the eighteenth century. In recent years, Americans have devalued the word through repeated reference to episodes (such as the "post-Watergate," "Reagan," and "Gingrich" revolutions) that borrow from the prestige of earlier events without producing anything close to the same outcome.

A better word is *crisis*. Its Greek root *krisis* refers to a decisive or separating moment. In disease, the *krisis* is when physicians know whether a patient will recover or die; in war, it is the moment in battle that determines whether an army (or nation) will triumph or fall. Thomas Paine attached the word to political revolution in 1776, when he began publishing his renowned *American Crisis* pamphlets. From Metternich to Burckhardt to Nietzsche, a host of nineteenth-century thinkers applied it to the periodic total wars that Marx called "express trains of history." By World War I, historian Gerhard Masur explains, the word was widely understood to mean "a sudden acceleration of the historical process in a terrifying manner," sufficient to "release economic, social, and moral forces of unforeseen power and dimensions, which often make return to the status quo impossible."

The Crisis ends one saeculum and launches the next. Yet if it denotes the cycle's maximum moment of *yang,* or strife, a curious asymmetry seems to arise: What denotes the cycle's opposite extreme, the maximum moment of *yin,* or love? If we can locate and describe history's winter solstice, we should be able to do likewise with its summer solstice.

An important clue lies in Modelski's description of his second-quarter delegitimizing phase, which he describes as the season of "internal renovation" and "revitalization of the system's normative foundations." Just as a fourth-quadrant era is necessary to replace the outer-world structure of political and social institutions, a second-quadrant era is necessary to replace the inner-world structure of culture and values.

What defines these eras? Forty years ago, the religious anthropologist Anthony Wallace drew on worldwide research to offer the definitive answer to this question. A "revitalization movement," he wrote, is a "deliberate, organized, conscious effort by members of a society to construct a more satisfying culture." In origin, these movements are a collective response to "chronic, psychologically measurable stress." When successful, they generate an entirely new "cultural mazeway," a transformed understanding of "nature, society, culture, personality, and body image." After categorizing such movements (as nativistic, revivalist, millennarian, messianic, and so forth), Wallace hypothesized that all of today's established religions are the ossified remains of the "prophetic and ecstatic visions" of past movements. Wallace did not say how often these revitalization movements arise, but he did note that "they are recurrent features in human history" and—hinting at the saeculum—that "probably few men have lived who have not been involved in an instance of the revitalization process."

Until recently, scholars seldom inquired into the periodicity of these prophetic and ecstatic eras of modern history. But that is changing. In a provocative essay announcing that "against all the predictions of nineteenth-century sociologists, religious movements have survived and flourished in the modern world," Princeton sociologist Robert Wurthnow reports that revitalization movements "have been distributed neither evenly nor at random in space and time." In fact, their timing since the Renaissance is quite regular. His list of movements is presented here, along with their two-decade spans of peak enthusiasm. The dry phrase *revitalization movement* is dropped in favor of a gnostic image long popular among Westerners—the image of an awakening of the spirit, or simply *Awakening:*

- The Protestant Reformation (1530s–1540s)
- The Puritan Awakening (1630s–1640s)
- The Pietist Awakening (1740s–1750s)
- The Evangelical-Utopian Awakening (1830s–1840s)
- The New Age Awakening (1960s–1970s)

These movements had much in common. All were loaded with passionate attacks against the morality of cultural and religious norms that felt old at the time. All were spearheaded by young people. All set forth new normative priorities (what today we call "values"). And all except the last followed a predictable timing: Each was separated from the prior Awakening by the approximate length of a saeculum, and each occurred roughly halfway between two neighboring Crises.

An Awakening is the other solstice of the saeculum: It is to Crisis as summer is to winter, love to strife. Within each lies the causal germ of its opposite. In the second quarter of the saeculum, the confidence born of growing security triggers an outburst of love that leads to disorder; in the fourth quarter, the anxiety born of growing insecurity triggers an outburst of strife that reestablishes order. An Awakening thus serves as a cycle marker, reminding a society that it is halfway along a journey traversed many times by its ancestors. Wurthnow observes that "periods of religious unrest . . . have, of course, been regarded as portents of change—as historical water-sheds—at least since Herodotus."

If Awakenings are the summers and Crises the winters of human experience, transitional eras are required. A springlike era must traverse the path from Crisis to Awakening, an autumnal era the path from Awakening to Crisis. Where the two saecular solstices are solutions to needs eventually created by one another, the saecular equinoxes must be directional opposites of one another. Where the post-Crisis era warms and lightens, the post-Awakening era chills and darkens. Where the cyclical spring brings consensus, order, and stability, the autumn brings argument, fragmentation, and uncertainty.

As the wheel turns from Crisis to Awakening and back again to Crisis, modern history shows a remarkable regularity. In Europe, every cycle but one ranges from 80 to 105 years. The conspicuous anomaly is the interval between Waterloo and V-J Day, a Toynbean cycle that lasts a full 130 years.

The exceptional length of this interval in Europe may be just that—an anomaly. Or it may raise the possibility that the Toynbean template has wrongly conflated two cycles into one. What historians call the "long nineteenth century" was a period of extraordinary peace among the great powers, except for a flurry of nation-building wars fought between the mid-1850s and mid-1870s (involving Germany, France, Italy, England, Russia, and the Balkans—as well as the U.S. Civil War). If this were deemed another Crisis era, and if the turn of century were regarded as another Awakening era, the result would be one anomalously short cycle (1815 to about 1870) followed by another of nearly the usual length (1870 to the circa-1950 origins of the Cold War). Replacing one unusually long cycle, therefore, would be a foreshortened cycle followed by another of the typical recent length. At the end of this chapter, it will become clear why this interpretation may be preferable to Toynbee's.

Either way, this sort of irregularity is hardly surprising. Looking at global history, after all, means looking at many different societies. Like the various Etruscan towns, each could be running on its own somewhat different saecular cycle, and each could be interfering (by means of war and ideology) in the affairs of its neighbors. Societies that are less modern than others may be more resistant to the rhythm of the saeculum. Amid all this noise of history, perfect regularity can hardly be expected.

If you wonder how history can become more precisely seasonal, you might want to test the following hypothesis. Imagine a scenario in which most of history's "noise" is suppressed. Imagine a single large society that has never had a powerful neighbor and that, for centuries, has remained relatively isolated from foreign interference. Imagine that this society was born modern on a near-empty continent, with no time-honored traditions to restrain its open-ended development. Imagine, finally, that this thoroughly modern society has acquired a reputation for pursuing linear progress, and for suppressing the cycles of nature, unequaled by any other people on earth. From what you know about the saeculum, wouldn't you suppose that its history is governed by a cycle of astonishing regularity? Indeed you would.

But, of course, this society is no hypothesis. This society is America.

THE SAECULUM IN AMERICA

Inspect the left-hand seal on the back of a U.S. one-dollar bill. It's a circle with a four-sided pyramid, above which hovers an eye—an Egyptian or Masonic symbol of the divinity who sees all of history at one glance. Read the inscription above the pyramid: *annuit coeptis* (God smiled on the creation), words borrowed directly from Virgil's praise of the Augustan *saeculum aureum*. Read also the inscription underneath: *novus ordo seclorum* (the new order of the centuries). When the founders designed the Great Seal, they put the saeculum right on the money.

The circle of time was not something that the Europeans had to bring to America. In the mysteries of unrecorded history, over a hundred American saecula had been witnessed by the ancestors of the native people who first glimpsed white sails on their horizon. These New World ancients were intimately familiar with the same astral and seasonal circles that preoccupied their Old World counterparts—as evidenced by the abundance of crosses, swastikas, tetramorphs, and squared mandalas used in their ritual art. The rhythm of human life, often expressed in terms of generations, was regarded as a sacred link between ancestors and posterity and as a normative standard for wise stewardship.

Indeed the circle of time was the one thing Europeans expressly did *not* bring to America, the one piece of baggage missing among all the nails, plows, Bibles, and contracts they hauled out of their longboats. Columbus' "discovery" of America, coinciding with the very birth of modernity in the West, inevitably gave rise to a European image of America as the ultimate destination of time's circle: the fabled Cathay, El Dorado, New Atlantis, or

New Jerusalem. When the newcomers first met the natives, what they chose to see were golden-age "Indians" or infernal devils—static images of the end of history. When they began carving towns out of the Atlantic forests, what they sought were final answers to mankind's perennial wheel of deprivation: the richest gold mine, the fattest harvest, the holiest commonweal, the most rational polity. What these migrants did not seek—indeed, what they were fleeing—was a pagan resignation to the seasonality of nature.

For native Americans, this invasion of linear time had tragic consequences. It created an insuperable barrier between the newcomers' culture and their own—a barrier that sealed the fate of many native nations and decimated or scattered the rest. For the world, this invasion set in motion the most remarkable experiment in modern history: a society born new, liberated from every constraint of tradition or nature that human creativity could overcome. Both Europeans and Americans sensed that something epochal was under way. Hegel described America as "the land of the future where, in the ages that lie before us, the burden of the world's history will reveal itself." As the founders intuited, a new order of the saecula had been created.

Until the eighteenth century, the saeculum in America and Europe beat to a similar rhythm. Ever since, the American saeculum has shown a timing that is more regular and even better defined than the European cycles chronicled by Toynbee.

Anglo-American Crises

To see the pattern best, start with the present and move backward. Eighty-five years passed between the attack on Pearl Harbor and the attack on Fort Sumter. That is exactly the same span as between Fort Sumter and the Declaration of Independence. Add two years (to Gettysburg), and you reach President Lincoln's famous "fourscore and seven years" calculation. Back up again, and note that eighty-seven years is also the period between the Declaration of Independence and the climax of the colonial Glorious Revolution.

Add another decade or so to the length of these saecula, and you'll find this pattern continuing through the history of the colonists' English predecessors: Ninety-nine years before the Glorious Revolution was England's empire-founding triumph over the Spanish Armada, and 103 years before *that* was Henry Tudor's dynasty-securing victory in the Wars of the Roses.

Not just in retrospect, but even when these events occurred, people realized they were participating in historical recurrences of legendary proportions. In 1688, supporters of England's Glorious Revolution rallied crowds by reminding them that the year was, providentially, the centennial of Queen Elizabeth's "Great '88" Armada victory. In 1776, Thomas Paine fired up the colonists by reminding them of the fate of the last Stuart king. At Gettysburg, Lincoln moved the nation by evoking what "our forefathers brought forth upon this continent." FDR's funeral near the end of World War II brought to mind, for millions of Americans, Walt Whitman's valedictory to Lincoln ("Oh Captain! My Captain! our fearful trip is done.").

Over time, American historians have built a nomenclature around these successive dates. In the 1930s, Charles and Mary Beard declared the Civil War to be the "Second American Revolution"—a name since reused countless times. In the 1970s, Carl Degler called the New Deal the "Third American Revolution." In his recent and magisterial history of the American Constitution, Bruce Ackerman identifies "not one, but three 'founding' moments in our history: the late 1780s, the late 1860s, and the mid-1930s."

Today, although we still think of ourselves as inhabitants of the post–World War II era, we suspect that we may be closer to the next "founding moment" than to the last. The journalist Michael Lind has subtitled his book on America's future "The New Nationalism and the Fourth American Revolution." The renowned political scientist Walter Dean Burnham, after summing up three prior "revolutions," predicts "that the present politics of upheaval may lead to a fourth American republic." Since these authors say nothing about timing, their forecasts are not as audacious as they might seem. Given time, any postwar era is destined to become prewar.

The list of Anglo-American Crises is a familiar one, and there can be little argument about the dates.

The *Wars of the Roses Crisis* (1459–1487; climax, 1485) began with an irrevocable break between the ruling House of Lancaster (red rose) and the powerful House of York (white rose). After mutual recriminations, declarations of treason, and opening skirmishes, the rival houses plunged England into an unparalleled quarter century of political anarchy, in which the crown changed heads six times, dozens of the highest nobility were slaughtered, kings and princes were murdered, and vast landed estates were expropriated. The Battle of Towton (1461), at which the Yorkists triumphed, was the bloodiest ever fought on English soil. At the Battle of Bosworth Field (1485), dynasty-founding Henry Tudor defeated and killed Richard III, the last English king ever to die in combat. England entered the Crisis a tradition-bound medieval kingdom; it emerged a modern monarchical nation-state.

The *Armada Crisis* (1569–1594; climax, 1588) began when newly Protestant England felt the encircling global threat of the mighty Catholic Hapsburgs. A spectacular crescendo soon followed: repeated efforts to assassinate Queen Elizabeth; Francis Drake's voyage around the world in a ship loaded with pirated Spanish treasure; and Philip Sidney's heroic battle death in the Lowlands. Then came England's Great Fear, the summer of the

Spanish Armada invasion, which ended in a victory so miraculous that church bells pealed annually for decades in its remembrance. England entered the Crisis a strife-ridden heretical nation; it emerged a first-rank European power and the heart of an expanding global empire.

The *Glorious Revolution Crisis* (1675–1704; climax, 1689) began in England's Atlantic colonies with two simultaneous catastrophes: Bacon's Rebellion, a violent insurrection in Virginia; and King Philip's War, New England's genocidal struggle with the Algonquin Indians, whose per-capita casualties exceed those of any other conflict fought by Americans. Afterward, the colonists slid into further political upheavals, starting with the absolutist visions of the Stuart-heir duke of York, the pancolonial Glorious Revolution in favor of King William, and then a further decade of war against Canadian New France. The ordeal ended with the exhaustion of New France and news of the duke of Marlborough's victory over King Louis XIV at Blenheim—a victory that Winston Churchill (the duke's direct descendant) described as having "changed the political axis of the world." As for the New World, observes historian Richard Maxwell Brown, "it would be no great exaggeration to call the years 1670 to 1700 the first American revolutionary period." English-speaking America entered the Crisis a fanatical colonial backwater; it emerged a stable provincial society whose learning and affluence rivaled the splendor of its European home.

The *American Revolution Crisis* (1773–1794; climax, 1781), began when Parliament's response to the Boston Tea Party ignited a colonial tinderbox that Samuel Adams's "committees of correspondence" had carefully prepared. The line of no return—from the arming of militias and the first battle deaths to the signing of the Declaration of Independence—was quickly crossed. During the dark 1778 winter of General George Washington's retreat from New York, people feared that the rebellion might fail and all its leaders be hanged as traitors. The struggle climaxed with the American triumphs at Saratoga and Yorktown. The mood of emergency did not calm until after the ratification of the Constitution and the Thermidorean end of the Jacobin temptation—as fledgling U.S. citizens watched a revolution in France end much less happily than their own. British America entered the Crisis as loyal if violence-prone colonies; it emerged the most ambitious experiment in republican democracy the world had ever seen.

The *Civil War Crisis* (1860–1865; climax, 1863) began with John Brown's raid and Abraham Lincoln's election, which several southern states immediately interpreted as an invitation to secede. So they did, triggering the most violent conflict ever fought on New World soil, with greater casualties than all other U.S. wars combined. The war reached its climax with the Emancipation Proclamation and the Battle of Gettysburg. Within two years, Robert E. Lee surrendered on Palm Sunday, and Lincoln was assassinated five days later, on Good Friday—prompting aging preachers to glory in the religious symbolism. Whether the outcome was worth the suffering became a question that historian James McPherson says "will probably never cease to be debated—but in 1865 few black people and not many northerners doubted the answer." Unlike other Crises, the denouement of the Civil War produced less optimism than a sense of tragedy having run its course. The United States entered the Crisis a racially divided agrarian republic; it emerged an industrializing dynamo, battle scarred yet newly dedicated to the principle of equal citizenship.

The *Great Depression and World War II Crisis* (1929–1946; climax, 1944) reached from the Black Tuesday stock market crash through the darkest hours of World War II, an era roughly spanning the rise and rule of Franklin D. Roosevelt. Having begun as a time of despair, the Crisis dragged on through the Hoovervilles and dust bowls of the Great Depression, during which the national spirit nonetheless coalesced around a renewed dream of community. The Japanese attack on Pearl Harbor ignited a swift and united public response. Within months, America was planning, mobilizing, and producing on an unprecedented scale. Peaking with heroic naval assaults on two distant continents, the mood of emergency wound down with the Axis capitulation, demobilization, and unexpected peacetime prosperity. The United States entered the Crisis an isolationist, industrializing also-ran; it emerged a global superpower whose industrial prowess, democratic institutions, and Marshall Plan generosity became the wonder of the free world—and the envy of its new Soviet rival.

Anglo-American Awakenings

While a Crisis rearranges the outer world of power and politics, an Awakening rearranges the inner world of spirit and culture. While a Crisis elevates the group and reinvents public space, an Awakening elevates the individual and reinvents private space. While a Crisis restarts our calendar in the realm of politics, an Awakening does something similar with the culture. When today's Americans speak of elections or alliances, we tend to begin by saying, "Since the 1930s [or 1940s] . . ." When we speak of music or religion, we are more likely to say, "Since the 1960s [or 1970s] . . ." In a Crisis, older people give orders while the young do great deeds; in an Awakening, the old are the deed doers and the young are the order givers.

Just as World War II prompted historians to study war cycles, the Consciousness Revolution sparked new interest in the periodic recurrence of cultural upheaval. The youth fury, communes, and spiritualism of the late 1960s and 1970s brought to mind similar episodes in America's past. Some recalled the muckrakers, missionaries, and militant feminists of the 1890 to 1910 decades. Others, coining the term "New Transcendentalist," harked back to the youth ferment of the 1830s. In 1970, when historian Richard Bushman summed up the Great Awakening of the 1740s, he likened this "psychological earthquake" to "the civil rights demonstrations, the campus disturbances, and the urban riots of the 1960s combined."

All the turmoil on campus inspired several prominent scholars to reflect on Awakenings in American history. Berkeley sociologist Robert Bellah points out that they have periodically renewed "a common set of moral understandings about good and bad, right and wrong." Brown historian William McLoughlin, who borrows directly from Wallace's theory, describes them as eras of "culture revitalization" that extend "over the period of a generation or so" and end with "a profound reorientation in beliefs and values." American Awakenings, he notes, have a symbiotic relationship with national Crises: Each Awakening was nourished by the security and affluence of the old order it attacked, and each gave birth to the normative foundation on which the next new order was founded. McLoughlin identifies five American Awakenings: the "Puritan Awakening" in the seventeenth century; the "Great Awakening" in the eighteenth; and the "Second," "Third," and "Fourth" Great Awakenings starting in the 1820s, 1890s, and 1960s, respectively.

For many years, political conservatives resisted the notion that the tumult of the 1960s was a form of spiritual expression. Lately, many have changed their minds and have claimed the 1960s as the spawning ground of the born-again religion and moralism of the 1990s. Approving references to the "Fourth Great Awakening" have multiplied in the conservative media—from columns by George Will to essays in the *Wall Street Journal*. Scholars in fields far removed from religion are now calling attention to this recurring Awakening paradigm. In 1995, the Nobel laureate economist Robert Fogel declared that "to understand political trends and future economic developments, one must understand the cycles of religiosity in American history and the reform movements they spawn." He observed that, from one awakening to the next, "the typical cycle lasts about 100 years," and he says that the "fourth Great Awakening" (which "began around 1960") has passed its revival phase yet is still reshaping public attitudes.

Just as Americans may be starting to sense that we are closer to our next Crisis than to the last, so do scholars intuit we are closer to our last awakening than to the next. The exact dates of the Anglo-American Awakenings may vary, but most historians would broadly agree on the following eras.

The *Protestant Reformation* (1517–1542; climax, 1536) began when Martin Luther posted his famous protest against papal doctrine. Thus began a quarter century of religious and social upheaval. On the Continent, it touched off peasant uprisings, fanatical heresies, the sack of Rome, and the disintegration of Catholicism throughout much of Germany and Scandinavia. In England, the enthusiasm seethed until King Henry VIII's formal break with the papacy, unleashing popular reform movements that split towns and churches across the kingdom. The Awakening peaked with the publication of William Tyndale's Bible, the suppression of Catholic rebellions, and Parliament's confiscation of vast Church estates. It subsided when reformers tired, leaders grew defensive, and foreign wars fired the popular imagination. The Awakening transformed England from a loyal supporter of the Roman Church to a nation possessing its own religion and newly individualized principles of spiritual authenticity.

The *Puritan Awakening* (1621–1649; climax, 1640) began as a dramatic resurgence of radical Protestant fervor throughout Europe. On the Continent, it ignited in Bohemia and led to the Thirty Years' War. In England, it boiled over in 1621 when the House of Commons issued its Great Protestation denouncing the arbitrary and unholy rule of King James I. After the accession of James's son, the reform fervor gained popular momentum but no official headway. Undaunted, John Winthrop led a "saving remnant" of true believers to America, touching off the Great Migration to New England. At home, the Puritan enthusiasm led inexorably to Cromwell's Revolution and the beheading of King Charles I; in the colonies, the excitement subsided when the new Puritan communities stiffened their moral orthodoxy. England entered the Awakening still dreaming of empire and gold, a dream that had not enabled any European nation to establish a self-sufficient colony in the New World; England emerged with a new dream of Heaven that enabled these colonial transplants to survive.

The *Great Awakening* (1727–1746; climax, 1741) began as a series of isolated spiritual revivals in the Connecticut Valley, many of them led by the charismatic young Jonathan Edwards. It spread quickly, especially in the northern and middle colonies, and reached a peak in 1741 during the rousing American tour of the English-born evangelist George Whitefield. As "new light" challenged "old light," the revival split colonial assemblies and pitted emotional young believers in faith against stolid old defenders of works. After mass gatherings and "concerts of prayer" in the early 1740s, the fervor receded. Before the Awakening, colonial America adhered to what young people called their elders' "Glacial Age of Religion"; it emerged having permanently eradicated Old World notions of class distinction and social solidarity from American soil.

The *Transcendental Awakening* (1822–1844; climax, 1831) was triggered by the evangelical preaching of Charles Finney, Denmark Vesey's slave revolt, and a widespread excitement over religious conversion and radical idealism. At times merging with Jacksonian populism, it peaked with Nat Turner's violent rebellion, the founding of abolitionist youth societies, and the rise of radical political parties. After spawning a transcendentalist school of philosophy and literature, what one historian calls a "heyday of sectarianism" produced America's first feminist movement along with a new profusion of prophetic religions, spiritualist clubs, utopian communes, and dietary fads. The excitement faded after the Millerites' predicted apocalypse failed to appear and a revived economy refocused popular interests. America entered the Awakening a staid temple of natural-law rationalism; it emerged riding a tidal swell of romantic idealism and evangelical piety.

The *Third Great Awakening* (1886–1908; climax, 1896) began with the Haymarket Riot and the launching of the global student missionary movement. Agrarian protests and urban labor violence sparked the tumultuous 1890s, a decade that Henry Steele Commager calls a "cultural watershed" and that Richard Hofstadter describes as a "searing experience" to those who came of age with it. Following Bryan's revivalist run for president, a cadre of inspired youth challenged elder values, as settlement workers uplifted the poor, muckrakers blasted the immoral establishment, and feminists hailed the "new woman." With the economy's quick recovery from the Panic of 1907, the national mood stabilized. But before it was over, this spiritual upheaval launched the Bible Belt and Greenwich Village, the NAACP and the Wobblies. America entered the Awakening gripped with the steam-and-corset mentality of the Victorian twilight; it emerged with the athleticism, vitalism, and utopianism of a dawning century.

The *Consciousness Revolution* (1964–1984; climax, 1974) began with urban riots, the campus Free Speech movement, the first anti-Vietnam protests, and fiery new arguments over the morality of America's institutional order. As the 1960s progressed, the fervor grew with the Summer of Love and the rise of a drug and hippie counterculture. After violence at Kent State and Jackson State, the mood of free-floating dissent peaked with Watergate and the first presidential resignation in U.S. history. Through the rest of the 1970s, the enthusiasm turned inward—toward the Human Potential Movement, the divorce revolution, a New Age transformation of lifestyles and values, a new narcissism, and a grindingly pessimistic Zeitgeist that came to be known as malaise. It ended in the early 1980s, when one-time hippies reached their yuppie chrysalis. Entering the Awakening, America's global reputation was a nation whose institutions could build anything but whose culture could imagine nothing; it emerged with that reputation reversed.

The Saeculum in America

The chart on page 50 shows the rhythm of the natural saeculum coursing through Anglo-American history. America's ancestors completed five saecula. The present-day American nation is beyond the Awakening of the sixth saeculum.

Notice the powerful two-stroke pendularity. At 103, 101, and 92 years, the spans of the first three cycles roughly match the civil saeculum (century) of the Romans. The fourth and fifth, though a bit shorter at 82 and 81 years, still approximate Censorinus's definition of a natural saeculum—a long hu-

The Anglo-American Saeculum

Saeculum	Time from climax of Crisis to climax of Awakening	(climax year) Awakening *(full era)*	Time from climax of Awakening to climax of Crisis	(climax year) Crisis *(full era)*	Time from one Crisis climax to next Crisis climax
LATE MEDIEVAL				(1485) Wars of the Roses *(1459–1487)*	
REFORMATION	51 years	(1536) Protestant Reformation *(1517–1542)*	52 years	(1588) Armada Crisis *(1569–1594)*	103 years
NEW WORLD	52 years	(1640) Puritan Awakening *(1621–1649)*	49 years	(1689) Glorious Revolution *(1675–1704)*	101 years
REVOLUTIONARY	52 years	(1741) Great Awakening *(1727–1746)*	40 years	(1781) American Revolution *(1773-1794)*	92 years
CIVIL WAR	50 years	(1831) Transcendental Awakening *(1822–1844)*	32 years	(1863) Civil War *(1860–1865)*	82 years
GREAT POWER	33 years	(1896) Third Great Awakening *(1886–1908)*	48 years	(1944) Great Depression and World War II *(1929–1946)*	81 years
MILLENNIAL	30 years	(1974) Consciousness Revolution *(1964–1984)*	51 years?	(2025?) Millennial Crisis? *(2005?–2026?)*	81 years?

man life. (The next chapter will suggest why the saeculum has shortened slightly since the early nineteenth century.) Reflect back on the question raised earlier about the Toynbean global cycle: Do the years between the French Revolution and NATO comprise *one* or *two* global saecula? The American experience suggests that cycle scholars might consider the latter possibility for other societies as well.

The saecular rhythm foretells another American Crisis in the first quarter of the twenty-first century, deep into the old age of those (like Newt Gingrich or Bob Kerrey) who were toddlers on V-J Day. The next Crisis era will most likely extend roughly from the middle Oh-Ohs to the middle 2020s. Its climax is not likely to occur before 2005 or later than 2025, given that thirty-two and fifty-two years are the shortest and longest time spans between any two climax moments in Anglo-American history.

War cycle theorists have drawn similar conclusions. Thompson calculates that "the average interwar interval period" is about eighty years. From this, he concludes: "If we look 80 years beyond the end of the last global war in 1945, the year 2025 appears to represent a reasonable projection of the history evidence." Modelski and Ferrar have each targeted the year 2030 as the next likely epicenter for a "general" or "global" war. Another scholar of long cycles, Joshua Goldstein at the University of Southern California, agrees that he would "put the highest danger of great power war sometime around the decade of the 2020s." The dates are suggestive, even if the Crisis need not be as terrible as these images of Armageddon imply. The saeculum's last quadrant does not specifically require total war, but it does require a major discontinuity or *ekpyrosis*—the death of an old order and a rebirth of something new. A saecular winter is indeed an era of trial and suffering, though not necessarily of tragedy. Though it can produce destruction, it can also produce uncommon vision, heroism, and a sudden elevation of the human condition.

We should take solace that the saecular rhythm is only approximate. If it were precise, it would show human events to occupy the simple, inorganic domain of physical time, rendering our society hardly more interesting than an orbiting comet or a ticking metronome. Instead, the imprecise saeculum shows that society occupies the complex, organic domain of natural time. Nature offers numerous examples of this domain: the beating of a heart, the budding of a flower, the molting of a sparrow. The mere act of breathing involves hundreds of physiological feedbacks involving blood chemistry, neuronal signals, hormonal balance, and body temperature. No one can calibrate or predict its timing with exact precision. But every phase of breathing must follow another in the proper order and at roughly the right moment, or a person would quickly die.

Likewise with the saeculum. History moves in a progression of ebbs and flows whose schedule is regular yet not precisely fixed. Modelski has likened the study of war cycles (what he calls *chronomacropolitics)* to the study of natural cycles (*chronobiology*). Even when winter arrives a bit early or late, it is still possible to foretell in what order the leaves will fall, the birds will migrate, and the streams will freeze. By correctly foretelling these things, people can prepare for the coming of a harsh season.

But foretelling requires understanding. With physical time, there is no need to know *why* a cycle exists—only that it does. With natural time, you need a feel for a cycle's rhythm and component parts. You need assurance that the saeculum is not some wild coincidence. You also need assurance that the saeculum has not been rendered obsolete by such recent innovations as multilateral peacekeepers, New Age awareness, digital technology, or global markets.

To gain this understanding, you have to move beyond the saeculum's external timing and learn about its internal dynamics. You have to see history from the inside out. The key lies in finding the link between the seasons of history and the seasons of a human life. Paradoxically, modern history does not beat to a rhythm invented by great nations, with all their vast economies, armies, and institutions—but to a natural rhythm, the rhythm of life itself, that nature accords to each person.

CHAPTER 3

Seasons of Life

"LIFE'S RACECOURSE IS FIXED," WROTE CICERO NEAR THE end of his life. "Nature has only a single path and that path is run but once, and to each stage of existence has been allotted its appropriate quality." Across all cultures and epochs, all classes and races, the experience of aging is a universal denominator of the human condition. "From a biological standpoint," observed Chinese philosopher Lin Yü-t'ang, "human life almost reads like a poem. It has its own rhythm and beat, its internal cycles of growth and decay."

The ancients made sense of Cicero's stages and Lin Yü-t'ang's rhythm and beat by portraying human aging as a circle that nature and society divides into four parts. To several North American native societies, life was experienced as four "hills" (childhood, youth, maturity, old age), each corresponding to a wind and a season and each possessing its own challenge, climax, and resolution. To the Hindus, it was a journey through four *ashramas,* four phases of social and spiritual growth. Pythagoras was among the first Western thinkers to interpret life as a cycle of four phases, each roughly twenty years long and each associated with a season: the spring of childhood, the summer of youth, the harvest of midlife, and the winter of old age. The Romans likewise divided the biological saeculum into four phases: *pueritia* (childhood), *iuventus* (young adulthood), *virilitas* (maturity), and *senectus* (old age).

In the modern era, the quaternal seasonality of the human life cycle has remained a constant in literature, philosophy, and psychology. "Metaphorically, everyone understands the connections between the seasons of the year and the seasons of the human life," writes sociologist Daniel Levinson. "Each has its necessary place and contributes its special character to the whole. It is an organic part of the total cycle, linking past and future and containing both within itself." Carl Jung similarly describes the "arc of life" as "divisible into four parts."

We connect our life cycle with the seasons of nature not only to link our personal past to our personal future but also to locate our own life within a larger social drama. Modern history has its own seasons—its own wets, hots, drys, and colds. Now consider what happens when one group of people grows up in a wet season and comes of age in a cold, while a later group grows up in dry season and comes of age in a hot. Because the seasons of history shape the seasons of life differently, the result is different *generations*. More fundamentally, because the seasons of history arrive in a fixed pattern, generations will also arrive in a fixed pattern—a recurring cycle of four *archetypes*. Rooted in ancient temperaments and enduring myths, these archetypes connect personal time with social time. Forged in youth by the seasons of history, the four archetypes re-create those seasons, in the same order, as successive generations pass through life.

THE FOURSCORE JOURNEY

"There is no history, only biography," observed Ralph Waldo Emerson, who noted that most of us recall little from most accounts about distant times and places except how individual people confront the personal challenge of living. Nearly everyone embarks on a life journey of potentially similar duration. Nearly everyone can expect to pass through four seasons of life that have remained much the same since Pythagoras identified their quaternity nearly three millennia ago. The life cycle had four seasons in Greco-Roman times, each twenty to twenty-five years long. It still does today.

The modern extension of the average life expectancy has not lengthened these phases of life. Most of the advance has been due to a dramatic decline in the mortality of infants, children, and young adults. For men or women who do not succumb to early disease or poor nutrition, the natural life span has changed little. The Old Testament declares that "the days of our years" are either "threescore and ten" or "fourscore." According to actuarial tables, today's typical fifty-year-old American can still expect a final birthday to occur sometime between these two ages. Moreover, a phase of life does not necessarily change just because more people are around to complete it. Jung justly observes that "a human being would certainly not grow to be seventy or eighty years old if this longevity had no meaning for the species." This meaning would not differ if 50 percent rather than 5 percent of all newborns reached age eighty. Nature desires that there be at least a few elders in every tribe, but nature may not especially care how many.

What determines the length of a phase of life is not so much the typical age of dying as the social and biological dynamic of living. Over the last two centuries, as the average life span has lengthened, this dynamic has actually

changed in the other direction. It has speeded up, resulting in a slight shortening of the first three phases of life. This has occurred over the same span
of time in which the saeculum has also shortened from a full century to
eighty to eighty-five years.

By definition, each phase of life imparts an entirely new social role and
self-image to those who enter it. We appeal to this role and image every time
we say to someone, "Act your age." Seventeenth-century moralists even invented a doctrine they called *tempestivitas* to describe the ideal of acting according to one's life season. To emphasize the significance of each shift from
one life season to the next, all societies institute various rites of passage, initi-
ations into the new duties and privileges that accompany a new social identity.

The first season is childhood, the spring of life, the time for growing and
learning, acquiring competence, accepting protection, and absorbing traditions at the behest of elders. In American history, the protective barrier between childhood and adulthood has at times been strengthened (as in the
1850s, 1920s, and now) and at other times weakened (as in the 1890s and
1970s). Recent improvements in public health and pediatric medicine have
reduced the risks and traumas once faced by children but have not fundamentally altered children's social role.

Childhood ends in life's best-known rite of passage, the coming-of-age
moment, what the Romans called *adulescentia* (literally, a "ripening" or
"flaming up"). Many traditional societies ritualize this moment with a brief
trial of pain, fear, or isolation, ceremonializing one's death as a child and rebirth as an adult. In contemporary America, the passage is stretched into a series of events, each by degrees acclimating youths to adulthood (bar mitzvah,
confirmation, first driver's license, first job, first vote, high school and college graduation, moving away from home, entering military service). The
coming-of-age period is also when youths learn to substitute the approval of
their friends for that of their parents—a substitution that helps forge a generational identity. As Yale life-cycle scholar John Schowalter notes: "Going
from child to adult you go over a bridge of your peers." Although the age of
adulescentia has fluctuated over the course of American history, its overall
trend has been slightly downward. The age of biological adolescence (first female menses and male puberty) has dropped by an estimated three years over
the past two centuries. The typical age at which young people begin to vote,
sign contracts, incur debt, and enter the market economy has likewise fallen.

Beyond this bridge of adolescence comes young adulthood, the summer
of life. This is the age for converting dreams and ideas into projects and
plans, for launching careers and families, for soldiering, for providing the
muscle and energy of society. Levinson describes it as a life-cycle season
"caught up in the emotional involvements and conflicts of childhood" yet
"hard-pressed to cope with the demands of family, work, and community."
In some eras (the 1880s and 1950s), the absorption of young people into careers and marriages has been seamless and rapid; other times (the 1920s and

1990s), the process has been rockier and taken longer. The average age at marriage and leaving home is now relatively high—yet the newlyweds and starting careerists of the late 1950s were the youngest in America's history. Over the long run, the opening threshold of this phase has compressed somewhat. Through the nineteenth century, for example, the average age of college students and soldiers was in the mid-twenties. In the late 1960s, the average age of college undergraduates and (Vietnam) combat soldiers was in both cases under twenty—the youngest such ages in U.S. history.

Next comes midlife, the great harvest, what Henry Adams referred to as the "Indian Summer of Life . . . a little sunny and a little sad, like the season." Thomas Hardy termed midlife "the centre of your time, and not a point at its circumference." It is Ortega y Gasset's phase of "dominance," an age for confirming lifestyles, implementing ideas and dreams, realizing projects and plans, mentoring young adults, setting standards for children—and, notes Levinson, "taking the mantle of power." This is also when individuals realize that the rising generation is no longer their own. Feeling the first signs of physical aging, people realize that they are passing beyond their biological prime. Midlife brings Carl Jung's phase of "individuation," a time when "man's values, and even his body, do tend to change into their opposites."

When does midlife begin? According to many authorities (Browne, Ortega, Jung, Levinson), it begins sometime between the fortieth and forty-fifth year. Aristotle wrote that a person's physical zenith is reached at age thirty-five, his mental zenith at age forty-nine; the average is age forty-two. Over the last two centuries, the American age of entry into midlife roles has gradually moved downward. Before the Civil War, newly elected U.S. presidents averaged fifty-eight years of age; ever since, they have averaged fifty-four. Throughout the nineteenth century, the youngest president (Ulysses Grant) entered office at age forty-six. Thus far in the twentieth, three (Theodore Roosevelt, John Kennedy, Bill Clinton) have reached office between the ages of forty-two and forty-six. Great swings occur in the leadership roles assumed by people in their early forties: In the early 1960s, they were unusually powerful in politics, while today they are more powerful in the culture.

For most people, life ends in elderhood, the winter of life, time for engaging in leisure and reflection, for retiring from the exhausting duties of career and family, and for passing the reins to younger hands. As Ogden Nash has rhymed, "Senescence begins / And middle age ends / The day your descendants / Outnumber your friends." Yet this is also a time for setting standards, passing on wisdom, making endowments, and taking advantage of society's highest leadership posts. Liberated from the grinding burdens of work and family, many elders are able to step back and provide the strategic wisdom every society needs. This ideal remains embodied in our word *senate,* an update of the ancient Roman *senatus,* which originally meant "an assembly of the old."

A much higher proportion of Americans are nowadays surviving into their seventies and eighties, yet the key rituals marking the onset of elder-hood come earlier today than in times past. A century ago, *retirement* meant too worn out to work; now it conjures an image of active play. Fifty years ago, nearly two-thirds of all men aged sixty-five to sixty-nine were em-ployed; now only one-quarter are even seeking work. The social role of el-ders often shifts from one era to another. From the 1960s to the 1990s, elder influence on politics has risen, but elder influence on the culture has de-clined commensurately.

Like the seasons, the four phases of life blend one into the other, guided by a rhythm that allows variation. Where a season's length is determined by the time from solstice to equinox, the length of each life-cycle phase is de-termined by the span of time between birth and the coming of age into young adulthood. In American society, the ritual acknowledgment today oc-curs at twenty-one, the age of college graduation and initial career launch. Afterward, a person is deemed to be an autonomous adult. The length of life's first phase fixes the length of the other life phases as well. Once one batch of children has fully come of age, *it and it alone* comprises the soci-ety's young adults, casting its next elders into a midlife social role. This now happens when the latter reach age forty-two, which is also the minimum age U.S. history (though not the Constitution) has declared acceptable for a pres-ident. And, in turn, the group entering midlife pushes another into an elder role, now starting around age sixty-three, today's median age for receiving one's first old-age benefit check from the government.

Since the share of people able to survive deep into elderhood has grown enormously over the last fifty years, it may make sense to define a new phase of life: *late elderhood* (age eighty-four on up). The social role of late elders is mostly dependence, the receiving of comfort from others. Apart from consuming resources, few of the very oldest of today's Americans are altering the quaternal dynamics of the life cycle. If late elders keep swelling in number, and if they ever collectively assert an active social role, the im-pact on the saeculum (and on history) could be substantial.

The phases, and social roles, of the modern American life cycle can be summarized as follows:

- **Childhood** *(pueritia,* ages 0–20); social role: growth (receiving nurture, acquiring values)
- **Young Adulthood** *(iuventus,* ages 21–41); social role: vitality (serving institutions, testing values)
- **Midlife** *(virilitas,* ages 42–62); social role: power (managing in-stitutions, applying values)
- **Elderhood** *(senectus,* ages 63–83); social role: leadership (lead-ing institutions, transferring values)
- **Late Elderhood** (ages 84+); social role: dependence (receiving comfort from institutions, remembering values)

The first four (childhood through elderhood) comprise the quaternity of the human life cycle. The combined length of these four phases, roughly eighty-four years, matches the span of the American saeculum dating back to the Revolution.

Generations and History

The seasonality of the life cycle is what makes possible the creation of generations. To see how this works, imagine a traditional society in which all four phases of life are clearly defined and strictly prescribed. Each new phase-of-life group tries to perform its social role—growth, vitality, power, or leadership—exactly as the last group performed it. There are no generations to speak of. There are no unique life-cycle dramas and no creative biographical trajectories.

Now imagine that the society is suddenly hit by a Great Event (what Karl Mannheim called a "crystallizing moment"), some sort of emergency so fraught with social consequence that it transforms all of society's members, yet transforms them differently according to their phase-of-life responses.

For children, this response might mean showing an awestruck deference to elders (and staying out of their way); for young adults, taking up arms and risking death to meet the enemy; for midlifers, organizing the troops, managing the home front, and mobilizing society for maximum effort; for elders, setting strategy and clarifying the larger purpose. The stress of the Great Event leaves a different emotional imprint according to the social role each is called on to play—differences reinforced by the social interaction within each group. Children mirror each other's dread, youths each other's valor, midlifers each other's competence, and seniors each other's wisdom.

If the Great Event is successfully resolved, its enduring memory imparts to people in each phase of life a unique location in history—and a generational persona. In particular, it marks young adults as collective heroes, around whom grand myths later arise. When this hero generation reaches midlife, its leaders show greater hubris than their predecessors. As elders, they issue more demands for public reward. Meanwhile, the generation following them—the trembling children of the Great Event—bring a more deferential persona into later life-cycle phases, altering their social roles accordingly. The generation born just after the Great Event will likely be seen in hopeful colors as the golden-age children for whom the triumph was won. And, as the Great Event echoes still further through time, this generation may, in turn, judge later generations according to whether they measure up to its own standards.

To make this illustration more up to date and personal, today's Americans need only recall World War II, which deeply affected every generation it touched. Look at the chart on page 59.

American Generations and World War II

Generation	Birth years	Sample member	Generational connection to World War II
PROGRESSIVE	1843–1859	Woodrow Wilson	prewar elders (unsuccessful multilateralists)
MISSIONARY	1860–1882	Franklin Roosevelt	elder leaders: principled visionaries
LOST	1883–1900	Dwight Eisenhower	midlife generals: pragmatic managers
G.I.	1901–1924	John Kennedy	rising-adult soldiers: can-do heroes
SILENT	1925–1942	Michael Dukakis	sheltered children: deferential helpmates
BOOM	1943–1960	Bill Clinton	postwar children (victory babies)
THIRTEENTH	1961–1981	Tom Cruise	postwar children (symbol of lost civic virtue)
MILLENNIAL	1982–2002(?)	Class of 2000	postwar children (last personal contact)

World War II left a massive impression on the phase-of-life social roles of everyone alive at the time. It cast Missionary elders as champions of long-held visions, stamping the peers of Henry Stimson, George Marshall, Douglas MacArthur, and Albert Einstein as the "wise old men" of their era and separating them, in America's memory, from the prior Progressive Generation. The war enabled the middle-aged Lost to get a big job done, spotlighting the gritty exploits of a George Patton or a Harry Truman and rooting a peer group that had earlier been slow to settle down. The victory empowered young-adult G.I.s to acquire the hubris of world conquerors, enhancing their reputation for "ask not" civic virtue and Great Society teamwork and later earning them the longest presidential tenure of any U.S. generation. The war bred caution and sensitivity among Silent children, lending them a persona that produced a lifelong preoccupation with process, fairness, and artistic expression.

So powerful was the social impact of World War II that it came to define several generational boundaries. The G.I.s include nearly everyone who saw combat in this war. The Lost, by contrast, include the combat eligibles of the *prior* world war, and the Silent are those who remember the war personally and may have even enlisted but mostly missed combat action. The initial Boomer birth cohort of 1943 includes the first "victory babies," those who were nurtured from the start with enormous optimism and were too young to recall the wartime absence of fathers.

Among generations born afterward, the symbolic memory of that epic war keeps resonating, but with dampened echoes. As G.I.s passed into retirement, the 13th Generation came of age without heroes and amid adult criticism for allegedly having forgotten the war-era sense of community. Today's child Millennials will be the last generation to have much personal contact with G.I. Joe and Rosie the Riveter, whose old civic values are being freshly emphasized by families, schools, churches, and the media. By the time the next generation arrives, World War II will be pure history, as distant from their lives as the Civil War was for the child Silent.

What happens as a Great Event and its echoes fade with the passage of time? In a traditional society, nothing. Absent another Great Event, generations gradually disappear. Twenty-one years afterward, only three distinct generations shaped by the event remain alive. After forty-two years, only two remain; after sixty-three years, only those who were then children can recall it; and after eighty-four years, only a few raspy voices survive to convey personal memories of bygone glories. By then, social inertia will have nudged people of all ages back to the pregenerational life cycle. In countless ancient epics, this is where the falling curtain of time puts an end to the saga.

In a modern society, however, new Great Events keep occurring, and with great regularity. These are the solstices of the saeculum: Crises and Awakenings. Through five centuries of Anglo-American history, no span of more than fifty years (the duration of two phases of life) has ever elapsed without the occurrence of a Crisis or Awakening. Every generation has thus been shaped by either a Crisis or an Awakening during one of its first two phases of life and has encountered both a Crisis *and* an Awakening at some point through its life cycle.

The chart on page 61 shows how this has clearly been the case for twentieth-century America.

From the climax of World War II, shift your attention ahead roughly forty years to the end of the next Great Event of the saeculum, the postwar Consciousness Revolution. From the early 1940s to the early 1980s, each generation had aged by two phases of life. Two generations that were earlier active (Lost and Missionary) had by now passed from the scene, and two new generations that were earlier unborn (Boom and 13th) had now arrived.

This Awakening—this societywide obsession with breaking rules, celebrating the spirit, and shedding social discipline—again defined generations, but in ways entirely unlike the earlier Crisis. Back in World War II, sixty-five-year-olds were moralist visionaries; now, in the Consciousness Revolution, they were defenders of a rationalist establishment. Before, forty-five-year-olds were hard-scrabble midlife pragmatists; now they were sensitive navigators of midlife "passages." Before, twenty-five-year-olds were uniformed soldiers; now they were preachy narcissists. And the children? Gone were the sheltered "goody two-shoes"; in their place were latchkey kids growing up hard.

Every forty years or so, the persona of each phase of life becomes nearly the opposite of that established by the generation that had once passed through it. Dating back to the start of modernity, this rhythm has been at work. English children born in the first years of Queen Elizabeth I's reign came of age as ambitious empire builders. Children born in the last years of her reign came of age obsessed with holiness. Two generations later, the American youths of the Glorious Revolution preferred teamwork over spir-

Recent Generations and Their Locations in History

	1908–1929	1929–1946	1946–1964	1964–1984	1984–?
ERA		(Crisis)		(Awakening)	
KEY EVENTS	Four Freedoms World War I Prohibition Scopes Trial	Crash of 1929 New Deal Pearl Harbor D-Day	McCarthyism Levittown Affluent Society Little Rock	Kent State Woodstock Watergate Tax Revolt	Perestroika National Debt Culture Wars Simpson Trial
ENTERING ELDERHOOD (AGE 63–83)	**Progressive** Woodrow Wilson John Dewey	**Missionary** Franklin Roosevelt Douglas MacArthur	**Lost** Dwight Eisenhower Norman Rockwell	**G.I.** Lyndon Johnson Ronald Reagan	**Silent** Colin Powell Mario Cuomo
ENTERING MIDLIFE (AGES 42–62)	**Missionary** Herbert Hoover Andrew Volstead	**Lost** George Patton Humphrey Bogart	**G.I.** John Kennedy Walt Disney	**Silent** Gloria Steinem Woody Allen	**Boom** William Bennett Candice Bergen
ENTERING YOUNG ADULTHOOD (AGES 21–41)	**Lost** Al Capone F. Scott Fitzgerald	**G.I.** Robert Oppenheimer Jimmy Stewart	**Silent** Martin L. King Jr. Elvis Presley	**Boom** Angela Davis Jim Morrison	**Thirteenth** Mary Lou Retton Kurt Cobain
ENTERING CHILDHOOD (AGES 0–20)	**G.I.** Jackie Cooper *Pollyanna*	**Silent** Shirley Temple *Little Rascals*	**Boom** Jerry Mathers Dr. Spock babies	**Thirteenth** Tatum O'Neal *Rosemary's Baby*	**Millennial** Jessica McClure *Barney's Gang*

itual conversion; the youths of the Great Awakening preferred the reverse. In the Transcendental Awakening, young adults tried to fire the passions of the old; in the Civil War Crisis, young adults doused old men's fires. It is incorrect to suppose, as some do, that most young generations come of age with attitudes (toward life, politics, culture) similar to those of their elders when young. Going back five hundred years, this has never happened.

Generational aging is what translates the rhythm of the past into the rhythm of the future. It explains why each generation is not only *shaped by* history but also *shapes* later history. It regulates the velocity of social change. It connects life in its biographical intimacy to history in its social or political grandeur. In all these ways, the generation lies at the root of the saeculum.

If the connection between generations and history is so powerful, why haven't people always known about it? People have. Yet in the ancient world, the connection was blurred by a confusion between family lineages and peer groups. And in modern times, boosters of progress have been reluctant to acknowledge a rhythmic force that would undermine their agenda.

At the dawn of recorded history, the *generation* (not the day or month or year) was the universal standard of social time. When translating the myths of prehistoric Aegea into verse, early Greek poets used sequential generations to mark the successive appearance of Gaea, Uranus, Cronus, and Zeus. Philo, writing of the legendary founding of Phoenicia, began his story with Genos, the first ruling male god. The Old Testament begins with Genesis, the begetting of the universe, and measures time ever after with a chain of generations, each begetting and raising the next. A similar generational clockwork reveals itself in the myths and legends of the Egyptians, Babylonians, Persians, Celts, Teutons, Slavs, and Hindus.

Ancient societies were often vague about what they meant by the word. The word's Indo-European root, *gen-,* means nothing more specific than "to come or bring into being" or (as a noun) any new entity "brought into being." Applied to people, this broad concept can assume alternative definitions. One meaning is the *family generation:* everyone whom a single biological parent brings into being. Family generations are intended when lineage is at issue, as when Herodotus spoke of "345 generations" of Egyptian priests or in such terms as "fourth-generation" heir. The other meaning is the *social generation:* everyone whom nature or society brings into being around the same time. Social generations are intended when an entire peer group is at issue, as when the New Testament speaks of "a generation of vipers" or Hesiod of the "generations" of gold and silver and bronze.

Few traditional societies bothered to clarify matters because, being organized around family tribes, there was little need for a distinction: Among elites, each new marriage implied a new social generation. Besides, large generational differences did not often arise in a traditional setting. When they did, they were seldom important for more than two or three phases of life in a row. Over such a short time span, a shorthand reference to family generations (parent of hero, hero, child of hero) must have seemed adequate.

With the arrival of modernity, this changed. At about the same time that Europeans began to talk self-consciously about centuries, they also began to talk explicitly about peer groups. During the *fin-de-siècle* mood preceding the French Revolution, social generation theories exploded on the scene. Every *salon* in Paris buzzed with talk (some of it from Thomas Jefferson) about how to define the length and natural rights of each generation.

Over the next 150 years, many of the best minds in the West struggled to enlarge and refine this concept. Nearly all of them agreed with Auguste Comte that generations had become, in the modern world, the master regulator of the pace of social change. John Stuart Mill formally defined a generation as "a new set of human beings" who "have been educated, have grown up from childhood, and have taken possession of society." Wilhelm Dilthey described a generation as "a relationship of contemporaneity . . . between those who had a common childhood, a common adolescence, and whose years of greatest vigor partially overlap." Giuseppe Ferrari based his whole theory of society on movements among what he termed *"i capi della società, i re del pensiero, i signori della generazione"* (the heads of society, the kings of thought, the lords of each generation). In the direct aftermath of World War I, Karl Mannheim, José Ortega y Gasset, François Mentré (who coined the term *social generation* in a book by that name), and many others produced perhaps the most cogent body of generations writing ever.

Along with the rise of new theories of progress, Europeans were becoming acutely aware of generational differences in their cultural and political life. By the end of the nineteenth century, the European elite chattered incessantly of generations, each named after a critical year that shaped the circle of young writers or activists in question, such as the (European) generations of 1815 or 1848 or 1870 or the (Russian) generation of 1820, the (French) generation of 1830, or the (Spanish) generation of 1898. The 1920s produced the first serious talk of a transatlantic generation, as the war-ravaged European "generation of 1914" and American Lost Generation mingled at many of the same Paris cafés. After World War I, when the United States became a global symbol of progress, the interest of Americans in generations began to surpass that of Europeans. Since then, no peer group has come of age in America without encountering a determined effort to name and describe it.

This Euro-American experience confirms that the faster a society progresses, the more persistently generational issues seem to keep springing up. At the same time, however, the more modern a society thinks itself, the more resistant its people become to legitimizing generational change as an *idea*. While modernity is about rational progress toward the future, generations stand as reminders of how much people remain tied to the subconscious vestiges of their past. While modernity is about social control, generational change has a tendency to explode in the face of the social controllers. At the extreme, modernist political revolutions have sometimes sought to eradicate generations entirely by stigmatizing (or, as in Kampuchea, even exterminating) citizens whose memories were shaped by the "wrong" regime. Most modern elites simply seal off the historical importance of generations with a high wall of skepticism. Because they don't look for generational change, people always seem to be surprised when it hits.

In America, these surprises arrive about once every twenty years—roughly the interval between new youth generations coming of age (and older generations entering new phases of life). Around 1950, Americans were taken aback by youths who didn't show the solidarity, optimism, and political activism of prewar CCC workers. In the late 1960s, the most prominent social scientists (from Margaret Mead to Kenneth Keniston) were blindsided by the sudden rage expressed by youths everyone expected to be docile. Since the early 1990s, three phase-of-life transitions have been taking place, to much media fanfare. A series of World War II commemoratives has evoked nostalgic talk about whether what Robert Putnam has termed "a great civic generation" would now pass from the scene or (as Bob Dole proposed) undertake "one last mission." Boomers entering midlife have leapfrogged the Silent to national power (Clinton and Gore in 1992, followed by Gingrich and the House freshmen in 1994) amid much talk of "train wrecks" replacing compromise. And the realization that Boomers are no longer America's youth has produced a flurry of interest (mostly derogatory) in Generation X.

Today, politicians and marketers are discovering the payoff of life-cycle marketing. Generational references appear constantly in TV ads, political speeches, movies, and pop culture vernacular. Even so, the broader implications of the concept continue to be trivialized, as if Bob Dylan, Jim Morrison, or Kurt Cobain said all there was to say about it. Each generation's links with voting and car buying have become far better understood (and accepted) than their more profound connection to nature and time. Academics are only gradually beginning to find merit in the judgment of William and Mary historian Anthony Esler that "the generational approach may, in fact, provide one of the royal roads to total history."

IDENTIFYING GENERATIONS

"You belong to it, too. You came along at the same time. You can't get away from it," Thomas Wolfe wrote (in *You Can't Go Home Again*) about his own Lost Generation. "You're a part of it whether you want to be or not." To Wolfe, as to F. Scott Fitzgerald, Ernest Hemingway, Malcolm Cowley, and other writers of the 1920s, membership in that generation reflected a variety of mannerisms: weary cynicism at a young age, risk taking, bingelike behavior, disdain for a pompous older generation. Wolfe's peers stood across a wide divide from moralistic midlifers and across another divide from a new batch of straight-arrow kids. To belong to it, you had to come of age not long before World War I started. No one formally defined it that way; people just *knew.*

Wolfe's Lost Generation literati never explained exactly how they identified their generation. But the question must be raised: In a world in which people are born every minute, how can social generations be located and their birth-year boundaries defined?

To answer it, you first have to determine the *length* of a generation. As the Great Event scenario showed, history puts a different stamp on different peer groups according to their age-determined social roles. Thus the length of a generation (in birth years) should approximate the length of a phase of life (in years of age). Before the early nineteenth century, American generations should average about twenty-five years in length; since then, they should average about twenty-one years. Necessarily, these lengths can vary somewhat for each generation, depending on the vagaries of history and the precise timing of Great Events.

To apply these lengths to real birth years, you have to locate an underlying generational persona. Every generation has one. It's a distinctly human—and variable—creation, with attitudes about family life, gender roles, institutions, politics, religion, lifestyle, and the future. A generation can think, feel, or do anything a person might think, feel, or do. It can be safe or reckless, individualist or collegial, spiritual or secular. Like any social category (race, class, or nationality), a generation can allow plenty of individual exceptions and be fuzzy at the edges. But unlike most other categories, it possesses its own personal biography. You can tell a lifelong story about the shared experiences of the Silent Generation in ways you never could for all women, all Hispanics, or all Californians. The reason, to quote Ferrari, is that a generation "is born, lives, and dies." It can feel nostalgia for a unique past, express urgency about a future of limited duration, and comprehend its own mortality.

There is no fixed formula for identifying the persona of a real-life generation. But it helps to look for three attributes: first, a generation's common location in history; second, its common beliefs and behavior; and third, its perceived membership in a common generation.

Common location refers to where a generation finds itself, at any given age, against the background chronology of trends and events. Location in history gives shape to a generation.

At critical moments in history, members of each generation tend to occupy a single phase of life. At the end of World War II, the Silent, G.I., Lost, and Missionary Generations each fit snugly into the age brackets of youth, young adulthood, midlife, and elderhood age. The same close fit between generations and phases of life occurred in the late 1920s (just before the

Great Crash) and in the early 1960s and early 1980s (just before and after an era of cultural upheaval). These phase-of-life alignments are generational crucibles. A peer group therein acquires what Mannheim called "a community of time and space, . . . a common location in the historical dimension" in which members encounter "the same concrete historical problems." Ortega refers to "zones of dates" that make members of a generation "the same age vitally and historically."

At any given moment, history inevitably touches a generation's oldest and youngest cohorts in different ways. The Vietnam War put far more pressure on Boomers born in 1945 than those born in 1955, for example; and World War II put far more pressure on G.I.s born in 1920 than those born in 1910. Yet within each generation, a few special birth cohorts can pull on older or younger people and gravitate them into a sense of common location. Cheryl Merser observes in *Grown Ups* that for Americans born in the 1950s (like herself), their "sixties took place in the seventies." This "sixties" experience felt authentic enough to bind Merser and her peers to older Boomers who knew the genuine article. But no one could have their "sixties" in the "fifties" or "eighties." People born in 1944 and 1954 thus share a common age location, while those born in 1954 and 1964 do not.

Generations can be separated at exact birth dates by paying attention to what the philosopher Julián Marías defines as the "social cartography" of successive birth cohorts. "In this analogy," he suggested, "each generation would be the area between two mountain chains, and in order to determine whether a certain point belonged to one or the other, it would be necessary to know the relief." Sometimes the watershed is obvious, sometimes subtle. Occasionally, even a split-second can be decisive in binding and separating adjacent generations. In contemporary America, a one-minute delay in birth can mean the difference between kindergarten and first grade six years later. Down the road, depending on the conscription laws, that can mean the difference between gliding through college just ahead of a controversial war or belonging to a class that feels real pressure from a wartime draft. A one-minute difference did in fact separate the new-born babies of December 31, 1942, from those of January 1, 1943—a critical tick of the clock that later helped ignite the fiery college class of 1965 and create a lasting cohort boundary between the Silent and Boomers.

Common beliefs and behavior of a generation show its members to be different from people born at another time. They are the means by which a generation moves history.

No element of belief or behavior ever appears uniformly across all members of a generation, of course. But conspicuous elements often do appear in a decisive majority of members, leading Comte to conclude that each generation develops a "unanimous adherence to certain fundamental notions" and Dilthey to talk of a "generational *Weltanschauung*," a worldview that shapes a generation's direction from youth through old age. To quantify these elements for recent generations, you can turn to a wealth of age-graded data—from opinion surveys and educational tests to crime records and census reports. The changes from one generation to the next are often striking and revealing.

To see how generational traits differ, consider shifts in political affiliations, such as the huge contrast between the Republican-leaning Lost (lifelong skeptics of progress and organization) and the Democratic-leaning G.I.s (lifelong optimists about science and government). Consider the changing attitudes toward risk, such as the young Silent's well-documented quest for marital and career security in the 1950s, versus the 13ers' 1990s-era aversion to early marriage and corporate ladder climbing. Consider the variable gap between acceptable gender roles for men and women, a gap that G.I.s once widened but that Boomers have since worked hard (in careers, families, and public life) to narrow. And consider a generation's overall life goals. Back in the late 1960s, Boomer college freshman believed by a two-to-one majority that "developing a meaningful philosophy of life" was more important than "getting ahead financially." Since the mid-1980s, the 13er response to this question has registered a two-to-one majority *the other way.* Between two elections, an opinion reversal of this magnitude would be considered seismic. Between two generations, these dramatic survey results show how a new persona can entirely transform the emotional texture of people who come of age two decades apart.

For generations born more than a century ago, the data become thinner, making behavior and beliefs hard to quantify. To distinguish between generations, you have to infer from anecdote, case study, and contemporary observation. Sometimes a well-recorded event will reveal underlying personas. For example, the U.S. election of 1868 turned out to be the largest generational landslide ever recorded, as the weary voters and candidates who fought the Civil War threw out the principled leaders and generals who led it. In that single year, the elder Transcendental Generation (of Lincoln) lost a full third of its seats in Congress and state houses to the younger Gilded Generation (of Grant). During that and the next two presidential elections (1868, 1872, and 1876), a younger pragmatist challenged and defeated an elder reformer. With these elections, one of the most dramatic clashes between two adjacent yet very different generations finally drew to a close.

Common perceived membership refers to how a generation defines itself and to a popular consensus about which birth cohorts belong together. Perceived membership gives a generation a sense of destiny. Marías once remarked that "to ask ourselves to which generation we belong is, in large measure, to ask who we are." Whenever a generational boundary seems murky, the best way to clarify it is often simply to *ask* people which side of the line they would put themselves.

Perceived membership confirms what many pollsters have long suspected about Boomers—that their true boundaries (the 1943 and 1960 birth years) are located a few years earlier than the fertility bulge between 1946 and 1964 often used by demographers to define this generation. Ask some people born between 1943 and 1945 whether they've always thought of themselves as Boomers. Chances are, they'll say yes. Ask the same question of people born between 1961 and 1964. Chances are, they'll say (more emphatically) no. The term *Generation X* was a self-label first popularized by young literati born between 1961 and 1964, and its central purpose was to deny Boomer membership. Even when a generation can no longer be asked directly, it often leaves plenty of evidence about its perceived peer membership. This evidence is what links the famous circle of Lost Generation authors born in the late 1890s with writers just a bit older (Randolph Bourne, T. S. Eliot, Ezra Pound), but not with writers just a bit younger (John Steinbeck, Langston Hughes, W. H. Auden).

To say that you identify with your generation does not, of course, mean that you care for your generation. Ortega wrote that the generational experience is a "dynamic compromise between the mass and the individual." To refuse this compromise is not easy; indeed, total refusal forces a person to become painfully aware of outsider status. The German sociologist Julius Peterson observed that any generation includes what he called "directive," "directed," and "suppressed" members. The directive members set the overall tone; the directed follow cues (and thereby legitimize the tone); and the suppressed either withdraw from that tone or, more rarely, battle against it.

Perhaps the most important aspect of a generation's self-perception is its sense of direction. Ortega wrote that each generation is "a species of biological missile hurled into space at a given instant, with a certain velocity and direction," which gives it a "preestablished vital trajectory." Mannheim likewise referred to each generation's sense of "essential destiny." For some generations, this sense of destiny can be overwhelming. The cohesion of postwar G.I.s reflected a massive generational consensus about the world they wanted and were expected to build. Thomas Jefferson's peers once felt the same way after the Revolution. Yet for other generations, this sense of destiny is something quite different. The Silent see their work as smoothing out the harsh edges of life—a task reminiscent of Theodore Roosevelt's Progressive peers. Boomers see in themselves a mission of vision and values—a quest others accede to them, if begrudgingly. Lincoln's generation was much the same. And 13ers have come to expect little of themselves as a generation—a fact that itself has become part of their collective persona. A similar trait arose in the generations of George Washington and Dwight Eisenhower.

A generation can collectively choose its destiny. But you cannot personally choose your generation any more than you can choose your parents or your native land. That much is fate, conditioning everything about your life whether or not you like it or care to notice it. As Martin Heidegger observed, "the fateful act of living in and with one's generation completes the drama of human existence."

THE GENERATIONAL PANORAMA

In 1992, when news weeklies and TV ads suddenly began to focus on Generation X, the American popular culture broke a long silence on the question of whether any new youth had arrived, a silence that had lasted since the end of the Vietnam War. Through two whole decades, no one had given the question much thought because no new generation seemed to be rising—but then, in the 1990s, the topic was back in the news. So has it always been. Roughly once every twenty years, America discovers a new generation—a happenstance triggered by some striking event in which young people appear to behave in ways manifestly different than the youth who came just before.

The chart on page 70 lists some of these events. Their average periodicity is, of course, significant. At 21.5 years, it is very close to the average recent length of a phase of life—and of a generation. Altogether, they reflect the rhythm of the most memorable generational surprises that America has encountered since the early eighteenth century. Yet there's something more important going on here as well. If you reflect closely on these events, you will find that each gives expression to the youthful persona of a distinct generation—a generation with its own location in history, its own worldview, and its own sense of essential destiny.

If you belong to America, you belong to an American generation. The same probably applies to many of your ancestors and heirs. All of history is nothing more than a sequence of collective biographies like yours and theirs.

The generational roster on page 71 has been corroborated by scholars who have written about American generations over the last century. From Liberty through Missionary, Arthur Schlesinger Sr. identifies eight generations. From Liberty through Boom, Brandeis historian Morton Keller identifies eleven political generations. From Liberty through G.I., literary scholar Henri Peyre identifies nine American literary generations. And from Republican through G.I., Harvard political scientist Samuel Huntington identifies eight political and social generations. While not all these lists specify exact birth years, the close correspondence among them confirms one fact: Every scholar who has looked closely at American generational rhythms has seen a similar pattern at work.

How long are the generations shown here? Assuming the Millennials' final birth year turns out as here projected, the American generational panorama divides 570 birth years into twenty-four generations, for an average length of twenty-four years each. Among the fourteen generations born before and during the American Revolution, the average length was 25

American Generations Coming of Age

Generation Coming of Age	Year When New Youth Generation Was Widely Noticed
AWAKENING	1734: Edwards' Northampton Revival
LIBERTY	1755: Washington at Battle of the Wilderness
REPUBLICAN	1776: Jefferson's Declaration of Independence
COMPROMISE	1804: Lewis and Clark Expedition
TRANSCENDENTAL	1831: Turner's Rebellion and Garrison's *Liberator*
GILDED	1849: California Gold Rush
PROGRESSIVE	1876: Edison and Westinghouse at Centennial Exposition
MISSIONARY	1896: William Jennings Bryan's populist crusade
LOST	1918: Doughboys and literati in Paris
G.I.	1935: CCC and WPA youth teams
SILENT	1954: McCarthy-era "silent" youth
BOOM	1967: Hippies at San Francisco's Summer of Love
THIRTEENTH	1992: Media discovery of Generation X

years. Ever since, the average has shortened to 21 years, matching the recent duration of a phase of life. Dating back to the Revolution, every generation but one has had a duration ranging from 17 to 24 years.

The generational birth years also coincide with the saecular rhythm of alternating Crises and Awakenings. When you compare dates, you will find that the first birth year of each generation usually lies just a couple of years before the opening or closing year of a Crisis or Awakening. The leading edge of every generation thus emerges from infancy just as society is entering or leaving one of these eras. Likewise, a generation's leading edge comes of age just before the next mood shift. Reflect on your own generation's life cycle to date, and you can see how this applies for you and people you know. It was no less true for ancestral generations.

Finally, notice the recurring pattern within each saeculum. The first generation comes of age with an Awakening, while the second has an Awakening childhood; the third comes of age with a Crisis, while the fourth has a Crisis childhood. Each of these four locations in history is associated with a generational archetype: *Prophet, Nomad, Hero,* and *Artist.* Throughout

Twenty-Four Anglo-American Generations

Generation	Birth years	Famous Member (Man)	Famous Member (Woman)	Era in Which Members Came of Age	Arche-type
ARTHURIAN	1433–1460	King Henry VII	Elizabeth Woodville	Wars of the Roses Crisis	Hero
HUMANIST	1461–1482	Thomas More	Elizabeth of York	—	Artist
REFORMATION	1483–1511	John Knox	Anne Boleyn	Protestant Reformation	Prophet
REPRISAL	1512–1540	Francis Drake	Queen Elizabeth I	—	Nomad
ELIZABETHAN	1541–1565	William Shakespeare	Mary Herbert	Armada Crisis	Hero
PARLIAMENTARY	1566–1587	William Laud	Anne of Denmark	—	Artist
PURITAN	1588–1617	John Winthrop	Anne Hutchinson	Puritan Awakening	Prophet
CAVALIER	1618–1647	Nathaniel Bacon	Mary Dyer	—	Nomad
GLORIOUS	1648–1673	"King" Carter	Hannah Dustin	Glorious Revolution Crisis	Hero
ENLIGHTENMENT	1674–1700	Cadwallader Colden	Mary Musgrove	—	Artist
AWAKENING	1701–1723	Jonathan Edwards	Eliza Lucas Pinckney	Great Awakening	Prophet
LIBERTY	1724–1741	George Washington	Mercy Warren	—	Nomad
REPUBLICAN	1742–1766	Thomas Jefferson	"Molly Pitcher"	American Revolution Crisis	Hero
COMPROMISE	1767–1791	Andrew Jackson	Dolley Madison	—	Artist
TRANSCENDENTAL	1792–1821	Abraham Lincoln	Elizabeth Cady Stanton	Transcendental Awakening	Prophet
GILDED	1822–1842	Ulysses Grant	Louisa May Alcott	Civil War Crisis	Nomad
PROGRESSIVE	1843–1859	Woodrow Wilson	Mary Cassatt	—	Artist
MISSIONARY	1860–1882	Franklin Roosevelt	Emma Goldman	Third Great Awakening	Prophet
LOST	1883–1900	Harry Truman	Dorothy Parker	—	Nomad
G.I.	1901–1924	John Kennedy	Katharine Hepburn	Depression—WWII Crisis	Hero
SILENT	1925–1942	Martin Luther King Jr.	Sandra Day O'Connor	—	Artist
BOOM	1943–1960	Newt Gingrich	Hillary Clinton	Consciousness Revolution	Prophet
THIRTEENTH	1961–1981	Michael Jordan	Jodie Foster	—	Nomad
MILLENNIAL	1982–?	Brad Renfro	Olsen twins	Millennial Crisis?	Hero?

Anglo-American history, with only one exception (the Civil War, when the Hero was skipped), these archetypes have always followed each other in the same order.

Due to this recurring pattern, America has always had the same *generational constellation* during every Crisis or Awakening—that is, the same archetypal lineup entering the four phases of life. During a Crisis era, Prophets enter elderhood, Nomads midlife, Heroes young adulthood, and Artists childhood. During an Awakening era, Heroes enter elderhood, Artists midlife, Prophets young adulthood, and Nomads childhood. These constellations push the saeculum forward, since generations that are predictably *shaped by* history become, as they age, generations that predictably *shape* history. Thus does the scripted reappearance of archetypes govern time's great wheel.

But what *are* the archetypes that are so predictably created by their location in history? How do they function? How do they relate to each other?

Why do they lie so near the heart of mankind's interaction with history? Answering these questions means journeying back to the ancient doctrine of quaternal temperaments—and to the great myths that arose alongside them.

THE FOUR ARCHETYPES

Perhaps no ancient people were as fascinated with the four sidedness of nature as were the Greeks. By the time of Heraclitus in the sixth century B.C., Hellenic philosophers understood that all worldly phenomena are definable as two pairs of opposites. This belief gave birth to the theory of four elements: fire and air (embodying the opposites of hot and cold), and earth and water (embodying the opposites of dry and wet). In the Hellenic cosmology, all matter was reducible to these elements, and all change expressible as a dynamic equilibrium between each elemental quality and its opposite. Anaximander described winter as the way cold and wet punishes hot and dry for their incursion during the previous summer. Summer, he said, was the reverse.

In time, these quaternities evolved into a theory of human physiology—and personality. The legendary physician Hippocrates identified four bodily liquids, or "humors" (blood, yellow bile, black bile, and phlegm), which supposedly produce four "temperaments," each linked to the four elements and the four seasons of the year: *sanguineus* with the moist cheer of spring, *cholericus* with the hot temper of summer, *melancholicus* with the dry depression of autumn, and *phlegmaticus* with the cold grimness of winter. During each of these seasons, people were presumed to be afflicted with an excess of its associated humor. To Hellenics, a sanguine person was optimistic and pleasant; choleric, demonstrative and quick to react; melancholic, pessimistic and sullen; and phlegmatic, apathetic and slow to react.

As with the seasons themselves, the Greeks looked on the four temperaments as two sets of quaternal opposites: *sanguineus* versus *melancholicus,* and *cholericus* versus *phlegmaticus.* An individual's personality was defined by whatever combination of the four he exhibited. Using a political metaphor, Alcmaeon of Croton taught that health was preserved by the balance *(isonomia)* of the quaternities, whereas disease was caused by the rule of just one *(monarchia).* According to myth, each temperament was associated with one of the four deities commissioned by Zeus to make man more like the gods (Prometheus, Dionysus, Apollo, and Epimetheus).

Through the next two millennia, this Hellenic paradigm dominated Western speculation about personality differences and disorders. During the Renaissance, it spun off many words that readily entered the English and the romance languages—from *sanguine, choleric, melancholic* and *phlegmatic,* to *humorous* and *temperamental.* Then came the Enlightenment, which declared human nature to be conquerable. The ancient quaternities fell out of favor for more than a century—eclipsed by scientific medicine, experimental psychology, and Freud's theory of the malleable ego.

In the current century, the four temperaments have regained some of their former esteem. The turnabout came in the years around World War I, when a new generation of European psychologists revolted against positivism and made fourfold thinking popular again. E. Adickes wrote of four worldviews (traditional, agnostic, dogmatic, innovative); Eduard Spranger of life types (theoretical, aesthetic, religious, economic); Ernst Kretschmer of abnormal temperaments (anesthetic, hyperesthetic, melancholic, hypomanic); and in the twentieth century's best-known quaternity, Swiss psychologist Carl Jung wrote of attitude types based on psychological functions (reason, intuition, feeling, sensation).

In Jung's view, certain symbols, aspirations, and behavioral modes (archetypes) are biologically hard wired into mankind. In all eras and cultures, he said, these archetypes have become so deeply embedded in mankind's "collective unconscious" that no degree of progress, real or imagined, could weaken their grip. Identifying these archetypes by probing dreams and myths, Jung fashioned his theory after the ancient quaternities, best represented visually by the quadrisected Hindu mandala. His four archetypal functions draw energy from the dynamic antagonism between two sets of opposites: thinking versus feeling, sensing versus intuiting. When one function dominates the psyche, its opposite is necessarily suppressed as the psyche's "shadow." Past midlife, people become conscious of the limits of their dominant archetype and draw energy (constructively or destructively) from its shadow. Jung called this quest for life-cycle self-correction "individuation."

In recent decades, the Jungian quaternities have inspired a growing number of psychosocial theories and therapies, including the well-known Myers-Briggs personality type indicator. Today's bookstores display a proliferation of self-help guides that explicitly invoke Jungian archetypes, often in their titles: *King, Warrior, Magician, Lover,* and *Awakening the Hero Within.* Other writers interpret history by means of personality archetypes, as in William Irwin Thompson's suggestion that modern social personas can all be traced back to four tribal archetypes: headman, clown, shaman, hunter.

These theories reflect what Heraclitus called *enantiodromia* (a natural running contrariwise), a gradual conversion of things into their opposites. See the chart on page 74. The quaternities identify two sets of two, balancing and correcting the human condition. Jungian scholars Robert Moore and Douglas Gillette acknowledge that none of the archetypes works well alone: "We need to mix with the Magician the King's concern for generativity and generosity, the Warrior's ability to act decisively and with courage, and the Lover's deep and convinced connectedness to all things."

Though archetypes are ordinarily applied only to individual personalities, they can also be extended to generations. Like an individual, a generation is shaped by the nurture it receives in childhood and the challenges it

Temperaments and Archetypes

Classical Temperament	*Sanguineus* (outer-driven, optimistic)	*Cholericus* (emotionally expressive)	*Melancholicus* (inner-driven, pessimistic)	*Phlegmaticus* (emotionally reserved)
ASSOCIATED DEITY	Prometheus	Dionysus	Apollo	Epimetheus
ASSOCIATED SEASON	spring	summer	fall	winter
HERACLITEAN QUATERNITY	wet	hot	dry	cold
CARDINAL VIRTUE	*temperentia*	*prudentia*	*iustitia*	*fortitudo*
ADICKES WORLDVIEWS	traditional	agnostic	dogmatic	innovative
SPRANGER LIFE TYPE	theoretical	aesthetic	religious	economic
KRETSCHMER TEMPERAMENT	anesthetic	hyperesthetic	melancholic	hypomanic
JUNGIAN FUNCTION	reason	intuition	feeling	sensation
MYERS-BRIGGS PERSONALITY TYPE	intuitive thinking	sensation perception	intuitive feeling	sensation Judging
THOMPSON SOCIAL FUNCTION	headman (king)	clown (artist)	shaman (priest)	hunter (soldier)
MOORE-GILLETTE MALE TYPE	king	lover	magician	warrior
GENERATIONAL ARCHETYPE	hero	artist	prophet	nomad

faces coming of age. When it assumes a persona, a generation, like an individual, can choose from only a limited number of possible roles, each pre-scripted by a societal collective unconscious. Hippocrates believed that a functional person must balance all four temperaments. So too must a functional modern society, immersed in directional time, experience the sequential unfolding of all four archetypes.

The ancient Hellenics' sequence of four temperaments (and their associated seasons) corresponds with the historical order in which generational types enter midlife—the age at which a generation asserts maximum power over the direction of society. The Hero enters midlife in the saecular spring, the Artist in summer (an Awakening), the Prophet in autumn, and the Nomad in winter (a Crisis). Everything matches—temperaments, archetypes, seasons of the year, and seasons of the saeculum.

ARCHETYPES AND MYTHS

The miraculous humble birth. The early evidence of superhuman power and strength. The rise to fame. The triumphant struggle with forces of evil. The overweening hubris. The fall. The climax of betrayal, or heroic sacrifice, and death. Perhaps you recognize this as the saga of Hercules, Superman, Jason and the Argonauts, or the boys of Iwo Jima.

Jung saw this Hero Myth as perhaps the most potent expression of his archetypes, recurring in a wide range of eras and cultures. Some hero myths, like Superman, are pure fable; others, like our memory of World War II veterans, are rooted in historical reality. Yet as time passes, the details that distinguish fable from reality tend to fade until most of what's left is myth, the raw outline of the archetype itself.

Many academic historians decry mythmaking whenever they spot it and lament the fact that much of what students "know" about the 1960s and 1970s comes from such films as *JFK, Nixon,* and *Forrest Gump.* Yet deliberate mythmaking is as old as history itself. Margaret Mitchell constructed myths from the Civil War, Shakespeare from the Wars of the Roses, and Homer from some otherwise-forgotten skirmish near the Hellespont. In any era, mythical archetypes assist people's understanding of who they are and what they should live up to. By converting events into myths, a culture can transcend chaotic or linear history and allow the instinct for reenactment to express itself. The myths that endure are those that illuminate the virtues (or vices) that successive generations see recurring in their own time.

Of all myths, the most widely noticed is the Hero Myth. But as the contrasting stories of Hercules and Orpheus suggest, heroes can be secular or spiritual; they can possess what Jung called either extraverted or introverted behavior. "There are two types of deed," insists Joseph Campbell in *The Power of Myth.* "One is the physical deed, in which the hero performs a courageous act in battle or saves a life. The other is the spiritual deed, in which the hero learns to experience the supernatural range of human spiritual life and then comes back with the message."

The secular hero-king and spiritual hero-prophet often appear in the same myth. Yet when they do, they are never the same age—not even close. Typically, they are two phases of life apart. In legends where the young hero-king makes his perilous journey, his first encounter is often with what Campbell describes as "a protective figure (often a little old crone or old man) who provides the adventurer with amulets against the dragon forces he is about to pass." The prophet can be a ritual elder, holy man, or what Campbell calls a shaman—a person who has undergone a spiritually transforming rite of passage and, entering old age, uses the powers thereby gained to assist the young. This elder possesses little worldly power but supernatural gifts of magic and access to the gods.

Recall all the classic Western pairings of the young hero and the elder prophet: Joshua and Moses in the Old Testament, the Argonauts and the centaur Cheiron in Hellenic myth, Aeneas and the Sybil of Cumae in Roman myth, King Arthur and Merlin in Celtic myth, Siegfried and Hildebrand in Teutonic myth, and Cuchulain and Skatha the Wise in Gaelic myth. Outside the West, such pairings are nearly as common. In Hindu myth, the young Prince Rama meets the old hermit Agastya; in Egyptian myth, Horus, son of Osiris, is taught by Thoth, the all-knowing adviser; in Navajo myth, the questing young sun gods are told powerful secrets by the cronish Spider Woman. Even today, this timeless tale continues to be retold as Disney's Apprentice and the Sorcerer, Tolkien's Frodo and Gandalf, *Star Wars*' Luke Skywalker and Obi-Wan Kenobi, and *The Lion King*'s Simba and Rafiki (who, like the Egyptian Thoth, takes the form of a wise baboon).

For the young hero, the elder prophet is not necessarily an ally. He (or, often, she) can also be a lethal enemy, as Medea was for Theseus and as the crone sorcerers were in *Snow White* and *The Wizard of Oz*. Yet more often, as Campbell notes, the young hero's close bond with a wise elder is essential to his ultimate success. Like Merlin, he will be a loving teacher. Like Obi-Wan Kenobi, he will feel the unseen Force of the universe. Like Gandalf, he will rescue the young hero through mysterious mental powers. Like Mickey's Sorcerer, he will warn against the dangers of hubris. In the end, the old prophet helps the young king found (or save) his dynasty.

Myths involving young hero-kings and old prophets are universal in part because people are comforted to hear tales of the valor of youth tempered by the wisdom of age. Yet people of all eras know that such a mythlike symbiosis between young and old occurs only on occasion. In America, certainly, it has not been present for decades. The last time heroic youth and wise elders had this kind of constructive relationship was during World War II. The reason these young Hero Myths are so embedded in our civilization is because they explain events when the secular world (the domain of kings) is being redefined beyond prior recognition—in other words, in Crisis eras.

Another popular type of myth—that of the young prophet and the old king—is much the opposite. These legends tell not of the founding of kingdoms but of religions. They invoke memories not of a world threatened by dire peril but of a world suffocating under mighty dynasties that have become oversecure and soul dead. They speak to the insight (not valor) of youth and the blindness (not wisdom) of elders.

When we encounter sacred myths of young prophets (Abraham in Ur,

Moses in Egypt, Jesus before the Roman magistrate), the dominant image of persons roughly forty years older is typically one of expansive wealth and rationalism, resplendent in power but bereft of values (Hammurabi, the Pharaoh, Pontius Pilate). While the Hero Myth ends in the palatial city, the Prophet Myth *starts* there. In the Buddhist myth, young Siddhartha escapes the sumptuous pleasure dome of his royal father. In Persian myth, young Zoroaster defies the too-worldly kavis and karpans. In Islamic lore, young Muhammad challenges the immorality of the rich merchant families. In Western fables, young Merlin stands up to the mighty King Vortigen, young Bacchus puts the gold curse on old King Midas, and the Pied Piper steals the children away from the stolid burghers of Hamelin.

These Prophet Myths reveal what Jung would call the shadow of the aging hero archetype. The Hero is seen not through his own eyes, but through the fresh vision of the youth Prophet. The one who sees that the emperor has no clothes is not one of the emperor's own peers, but a child who dares to speak the truth. Occasionally, these myths present kindly older people, often women, who help youths express their visions. Yet the recurring tone of these myths is one of stress and hostility across the generations. By teaching lessons about vision (or self-centeredness) among the young and power (or corruption) among the old, these young Prophet Myths speak of Awakening eras.

Myths evoking the Nomad and Artist are less grand and more personal, mainly because they encounter history's turning points at a less critical phase of life. These archetypes encounter their first turning point not coming of age, but growing up as children (the Nomad in an Awakening, the Artist in Crisis). They encounter their second turning point not entering the peak of elder power, but entering midlife (the Nomad in Crisis, the Artist in an Awakening).

Compared to the Hero and Prophet Myths, their tales speak more to human relations than to the rise and fall of dynasties and religions. Yet they too embody shadow life cycles that mirror each other in reverse. Nomads are abandoned and alienated children who later, as adults, strive to slow down, simplify, and brace their social environment. Artists are sheltered and sensitive children who later, as adults, strive to speed up, complicate, and adorn their social environment. Nomads are raised to manage alone and are burdened with low expectations. Artists are raised to cooperate with others and are burdened with high expectations.

One common story line features a Cinderella-like hated child, immersed in a hostile or neglectful social environment, who must apply competitive instincts first to survive, then to succeed. In similar myths, hard-scrabble youths must use their wits to evade murder *(Aladdin)*, cannibalism *(Hansel and Gretel)*, slavery *(Pinocchio)*, or meltdown *(Toy Soldier)*. Parental figures are typically missing, and the enemies are less often elders than prime-of-life people possessed of a ruthless vanity. If aging people are wizards, they are friendly helpmates, more like fairies than sorcerers, their powers flowing from whimsical kindness more than stern wisdom. These myths depict the child Nomad being nurtured by an older Artist amid the darker sides of an Awakening.

When a myth shows the Nomad archetype in midlife, the story tells of an aging adventurer, savvy but going it alone. If older generations are present, they represent an older Prophet and a younger Hero—never the other way around. The Nomad is neither as dutiful (or naive) as the younger Hero nor as transcendently wise (or wicked) as the older Prophet. The best the Nomad can hope to experience is a brush with others' greatness. In the *Star Wars* trilogy, Han Solo looks down the age ladder and sees the good Luke Sky-walker and Princess Leia—and looks up and sees the wise Obi-Wan Kenobi and the evil Darth Vader. These are times of Crisis, during which the Nomad does the dirty work with little expectation of public praise or reward.

The opposing child myth is that of the sensitive, dutiful youth enveloped in protections constructed by no-nonsense adults. Recall the classic myth of the Little Dutch Boy, doing his small part to save the mighty dike, or anthropomorphic tales of sweetly vulnerable little animals *(Bambi, Peter Cottontail)* or machines *(The Little Engine That Could)*. These myths depict children who look for ways to be helpful in a closed social environment where dos and don'ts are unquestioned. Sometimes adults have built such an impenetrable perimeter of protection that the outer world is invisible *(Uncle Remus, Winnie the Pooh)*. Relations across generations are harmonious. Where the emotional timbre of the young Nomad stories is blunt and horrifying, here it is subtle and heartwarming. These myths depict the child Artist being nurtured by an older Nomad. Looking carefully through a child's prism, we can recognize the possibility (Christopher Robin), if not the fact (Little Dutch Boy), that the adult world is in Crisis.

In these four archetypal myths, you can recognize two sets of opposing temperaments as well as two sets of inverted life cycles. When multiple generations enter the myths, you typically see the Nomad sandwiched between the younger Hero and the older Prophet, and the Artist between the younger Prophet and the elder Hero.

This same archetypal ordering arises again and again in nearly every time and culture. Why? A society will not elevate an event (or story) into myth unless it illustrates enduring human tendencies. This ordering reflects a latent understanding of the shadow suppressed within each archetype. Were it possible for generations to come in some different order (say, from Hero to Prophet to Artist to Nomad), it would be much harder for the shadows to reveal themselves or for a society to have that *enantiodromia* that enables civilization to correct its worst excesses.

What Jung observed about individuals is also true for generations: Each archetype's shadow is best revealed by the one directly across the cycle, two phases-of-life distant. The too-sanguine aging Heroes are countered by the fresh insights of young Prophets; the too-melancholic aging Prophets, by the valor of young Heroes; the too-phlegmatic aging Nomads, by the sensitivity of young Artists; and the too-choleric aging Artists, by the survival skills of young Nomads.

This sequence further explains the oft-noted similarities between very old and very young generations, whose location in time lies a full cycle apart. If a generation's shadow is *two* phases of life older (or younger), then a generation's matching archetype is *four* phases of life older (or younger). "It is one of nature's ways," Igor Stravinsky once observed, "that we often feel closer to distant generations than to the generation immediately preceding us." The affinity between grandparent and grandchild is universal folk wisdom. If each *family* generation is assumed to be a rough proxy for two *phase-of-life* generations—meaning that you shadow your parents and match your grandparents—then this folk wisdom directly reflects the sequence of archetypes.

In one of America's grandest historical myths, *Gone with the Wind,* Margaret Mitchell has her characters acknowledge the similarities between archetypes born more than sixty years apart. At one point in the story, Rhett Butler tells Scarlett:

> If you are different, you are isolated, not only from people of your own age but from those of your parents' generation and from your children's generation too. They'll never understand you, and they'll be shocked no matter what you do. But your grandparents would probably be proud of you and say: "There's a chip off the old block," and your grandchildren will sigh enviously and say: "What an old rip Grandma must have been!" and they'll try to be like you.

Describing his "pirate" grandfather, Rhett admitted "I admired him and tried to copy him far more than I ever did my father, for Father is an amiable gentleman full of honorable habits and pious saws—so you see how it goes." Rhett predicted that Scarlett's children "will probably be soft, prissy creatures, as the children of hard-bitten characters usually are. . . . So you'll have to get approval from your grandchildren." In Mitchell's story, Rhett and Scarlett represented the (Nomad) Gilded Generation; their parents the (Artist) Compromise Generation; their children the (Artist) Progressive Generation; and their grandchildren most likely the (Nomad) Lost Generation.

What these modern myths illustrate is this: Your generation isn't like the generation that shaped you, but it has much in common with *the generation that shaped* the generation that shaped you. Archetypes do not create archetypes like themselves; instead, they create the shadows of archetypes like themselves.

THE CYCLE OF ARCHETYPES

These myths suggest that for any generational differences to arise at all, a quaternity of opposing archetypes becomes a logical necessity. How else could young heroes emerge, if not in response to the worldly impotence of self-absorbed elder prophets? How else could young prophets emerge, if not in response to the spiritual complacency of hubristic elder heroes? This in turn requires that each generation exert a dominant formative influence on people who are *two phases of life younger,* that is, on the *second younger* generation.

This critical cross-cycle relationship is just what we see in most societies. It arises because a new child generation gathers its first impressions about the world just as a new midlife generation gains control of the institutions that surround a child. Even though a child's biological parents will be distributed about equally over the two prior generations (because generations average about twenty-one years in length), the older parental group has the dominant role. Boomers were parented by G.I.s and Silent, but the G.I.s exerted a far greater power over 1950s-era schools, PTAs, pediatric advice, TV, and movies. In the 1990s, similarly, Boomers and 13ers are together giving birth to Millennial children, but the tone is being set by William Bennett, Hillary Clinton, Steven Spielberg, Bill Gates, and their Boomer peers. Likewise, the Lost Norman Rockwells set the tone for the Silent, and the Silent Bill Cosbys for 13ers, just as the 13er Jodie Fosters will set the tone for the generation born early next century.

Move up one phase-of-life notch, and this pattern repeats. When a child generation comes of age, it does so just as that older generation enters elderhood and gains control of the institutions surrounding the young adult's world. A younger generation reaches military age just as its cross-cycle shadow reaches its maximum power to declare war. In American history, for instance, a generation's dominance in national leadership posts typically peaks around the time its first cohorts reach age sixty-five—just as footsoldiers are on average about forty-two years (or two phases of life) younger. The G.I.s fought in (Missionary-declared) World War II, the Silent in the (Lost-declared) Korean War, Boomers in the (G.I.-declared) Vietnam War, and 13ers in (Silent-declared) Desert Storm.

This cross-cycle relationship has been true throughout American history. Franklin's (Prophet) Awakening Generation set the tone for Jefferson's (Hero) Republicans, which in turn did so for Lincoln's (Prophet) Transcendentals. In between, Washington's (Nomad) Liberty Generation set the tone for Daniel Webster's (Artist) Compromisers, which afterward did it for Grant's (Nomad) Gilded.

The reaction of each archetype to its shadow can be friendly or antago-

Seasons of Life and Time

ERA		Years 0–20	Years 21–41	Years 42–62	Years 63–83	Years 84–?
			(Crisis)		(Awakening)	
ENTERING ELDERHOOD (AGE 63–83)		Artist	Prophet	Nomad	Hero	Artist
ENTERING MIDLIFE (AGES 42–62)		Prophet	Nomad	Hero	Artist	Prophet
ENTERING YOUNG ADULTHOOD (AGES 21–41)		Nomad	Hero	Artist	Prophet	Nomad
ENTERING CHILDHOOD (AGES 0–20)		Hero	Artist	Prophet	Nomad	Hero

nistic. Like Luke Skywalker's dual relationship with his father, it is usually some of both. Intentionally or not, most parents enter midlife trying to raise a new generation whose collective persona will complement, and not mirror, their own. Later on, however, the results of that nurture often come as a surprise. The G.I. pediatrician Benjamin Spock declared just after World War II that "we need idealistic children," and his peers raised Boomers accordingly, though many later voiced anger over the narcissistic product. Silent author Judy Blume wrote at the height of the Consciousness Revolution, "I hate the idea that you should always protect children," and her peers raised 13er children accordingly, though many later voiced anguish over the hardened product.

A key consequence of these cross-cycle shadow relationships is a recurring pattern that lies at the heart of the saeculum: an oscillation between the *overprotection* and *underprotection* of children. During a Crisis, Nomad-led families overprotect Artist children; during an Awakening, Artist-led families underprotect Nomad children. Following a Crisis, Hero-led families expand the freedoms of Prophet children; following an Awakening, Prophet-led families curtail the freedoms of Hero children.

These powerful cross-cycle phenomena explain why myths always depict the archetypes in one fixed order, the only order that is possible in the seasons of time: Hero to Artist to Prophet to Nomad. Recurring in this order, the four archetypes produce four possible generational constellations.

Read the chart on page 81 along the diagonal. Notice the timeless connection between each archetype and its life cycle's location in history. Heroes, for example, always appear as children after an Awakening and come of age during a Crisis. Prophets always appear as children after a Crisis and come of age during an Awakening.

Now return to the earlier generational overview of modern American history. Give each generation an archetype label and an adjective describing how people in its age bracket were generally regarded by others at the time.

Now read the chart on page 83 along the same diagonal paths. Recognize the familiar life-cycle personas of today's generations, each appearing as a collective biography cutting diagonally across time and age. Read these diagonals as a sequence of generational archetypes. Notice that each archetype *shadows* its two-apart neighbor and *matches* its four-apart neighbor. Move four diagonals forward from the Progressives and find (in the Silent peers of Michael Dukakis and Gary Hart) the first generation since then to be dubbed "neo-progressive." Move four forward from the Missionaries and find (in youthful Boomers) the first generation since then to which the labels "student radical" and "muckraker" have been applied. Move four forward from the Lost and find (in 13ers) frequent media references to a "New Lost" Generation.

As each archetype ages, its persona undergoes profound yet characteristic changes, echoing the ancient Hellenic doctrine that all living things de-

Recent Generations and Their Archetypes

ERA	1908–1929	1929–1946 (Crisis)	1946–1964	1964–1984 (Awakening)	1984–?
KEY EVENTS	Four Freedoms, World War I, Prohibition, Scopes Trial	Crash of 1929, New Deal, Pearl Harbor, D-Day	McCarthyism, Levittown, Affluent Society, Little Rock	Kent State, Woodstock, Watergate, Tax Revolt	Perestroika, National Debt, Culture Wars, Simpson Trial
ENTERING ELDERHOOD (AGE 63–83)	Progressive (Artist) empathic	Missionary (Prophet) wise	Lost (Nomad) tough	G.I. (Hero) powerful	Silent (Artist) empathic
ENTERING MIDLIFE (AGES 42–62)	Missionary (Prophet) moralistic	Lost (Nomad) pragmatic	G.I. (Hero) hubristic	Silent (Artist) indecisive	Boom (Prophet) moralistic
ENTERING YOUNG ADULTHOOD (AGES 21–41)	Lost (Nomad) alienated	G.I. (Hero) heroic	Silent (Artist) sensitive	Boom (Prophet) narcissistic	Thirteenth (Nomad) alienated
ENTERING CHILDHOOD (AGES 0–20)	G.I. (Hero) protected	Silent (Artist) suffocated	Boom (Prophet) indulged	Thirteenth (Nomad) abandoned	Millennial (Hero) protected

velop toward a destination contrary to the form in which they first present themselves. Yet each archetype also has an underlying identity that endures unchanged. "Value orientations do not change much during a generation's life time," writes sociologist J. Zvi Namenworth. "Committed during its early stages, a generation most often carried its value commitments into the grave." Once a generation fully occupies the leadership role of midlife, it succeeds in reshaping the social environment to reflect that orientation. Meanwhile, knowingly or not, it nurtures a new child generation as its shadow, equipping it to challenge its own ruling mentality. As the parental generation enters elderhood blind to its shadow, the child generation comes of age, emerges as the shadow, and reacts against its elders' perceived excesses.

When this rhythm is filled out with the full range of historical examples, a four-type cycle of generations emerges. They are listed here beginning with the Prophet archetype—the one born in the saecular spring.

■ A *Prophet* generation grows up as increasingly indulged post-Crisis children, comes of age as the narcissistic young crusaders of an Awakening, cultivates principle as moralistic midlifers, and emerges as wise elders guiding the next Crisis.

■ A *Nomad* generation grows up as underprotected children during an Awakening, comes of age as the alienated young adults of a post-Awakening world, mellows into pragmatic midlife leaders during a Crisis, and ages into tough post-Crisis elders.

■ A *Hero* generation grows up as increasingly protected post-Awakening children, comes of age as the heroic young teamworkers of a Crisis, demonstrates hubris as energetic midlifers, and emerges as powerful elders attacked by the next Awakening.

■ An *Artist* generation grows up as overprotected children during a Crisis, comes of age as the sensitive young adults of a post-Crisis world, breaks free as indecisive midlife leaders during an Awakening, and ages into empathic post-Awakening elders.

Has anybody noticed this four-type cycle before? Yes—many times over the millennia.

ARCHETYPES AND HISTORY

During the reign of King Solomon, as the Hebrews began committing their sacred history to writing, no event loomed so large and fresh in collective memory as their deliverance from Egypt and settlement in Palestine. This event was about the same distance from them as the voyage of the

Mayflower is from us. Even today, it dominates six of the twenty-four books of the Old Testament.

Exodus is, at root, the story of four generations.

1. *The holy peers of Moses.* As young adults, they awakened their people to the spirit of God. Rejecting worldly privilege, they defied the authority of Pharaoh's Egypt. Later in life, they led the Hebrews on a miracle-filled journey across the Red Sea and through the wilderness to the threshold of Canaan, the Promised Land.

2. *The worshipers of the Golden Calf.* It was for the sins of these wanderers and "men of little faith" that God punished the Hebrews with extra trials and tribulations. They were too young to join Moses' challenge against the Pharaoh, yet old enough to remember the enticing fleshpots of Egypt.

3. *The dutiful soldier peers of Joshua.* Born after the Exodus, they came of age waging victorious battles and were thereafter anointed for leadership by the patriarch Moses. As they entered Canaan (none older was allowed to do so), their unity and martial discipline enabled them to conquer the natives and bring substance to Moses' dreams.

4. *The original generation of Judges.* Overshadowed by Joshua's battles, these "inheritor" youths were reminded by the dying Joshua that they enjoyed "land for which ye did not labor, and cities which ye built not." Their exercise of power was marked by political fragmentation, cultural sophistication, and anxiety about the future.

The Old Testament assumes twenty years as the length of a phase of life—this being the age at which males were "able to go forth to war." We can thus locate an eighty-year life cycle encompassing the length of four generations and four phases of life (if we assume that the cited ages for Moses and Joshua are exaggerations). Exactly forty years elapsed between the Moses-led Exodus and the Joshua-led invasion of Canaan. When the Hebrews won their climactic victory over Jericho, Moses was an elder, the Golden Calf wanderers were in midlife, Joshua's soldier peers were young heroes, and the Judges were emerging as inheritor children. Another forty years led to the consolidation of the Hebrew conquest, the old age of Joshua's disciplined generation, and the first Judges' belated climb to leadership. Afterward, "there arose another generation after them, which knew not the Lord, nor yet the works which he had done for Israel."

Pulsing through this story is the rhythm of the saeculum, eighty years long, beginning with an Awakening and extending through a Crisis and its optimistic aftermath. Propelling the saecular cycle are the four archetypes, each possessing its expected location in history: the generations of Moses (Prophet), the Golden Calf (Nomad), Joshua (Hero), and the Judges (Artist).

Because biblical chronology lapses into confusion soon after the conquest of Canaan, no one knows whether a new saeculum picked up where the last one ended. Scholars suggest that successor generations inhabited recurring fourfold cycles of complacency, prophecy, punishment, and deliverance. When events did occur, bad ones especially, the Old Testament often warns that the consequences (usually curses and punishments) will extend "unto the fourth generation" but never beyond. Yet the ancient Hebrews did not recollect later spiritual revelations to match Moses' or secular triumphs to match Joshua's. If a generational cycle had once existed, it dampened out. As written in Ecclesiastes, "One generation passeth away, and another generation cometh: but the earth abideth forever."

The story of Exodus is believed to have occurred in the thirteenth century B.C., around the time another generational saga is supposed to have unfolded in the ancient Aegean world. Like the authors of the Old Testament, Homer had a natural feel for the rhythm of generations. "As is the generation of leaves, so too of men," he observed in *The Iliad*. "At one time the wind shakes the leaves to the ground but then the flourishing woods / Give birth, and the season of spring comes into existence; / So it is with the generations of men, which alternately come forth and pass away."

Four key characters in *The Iliad* and *Odyssey* are mythical personifications of the four generational archetypes: Nestor (Prophet), Agamemnon (Nomad), Odysseus (Hero), and Telemachus (Artist). Their life cycles unfold chronologically. Roughly a generation before the Trojan War, the middle-aged Nestor, renowned for his piety, is ruler of Pylus; Agamemnon, having survived a childhood of family atrocities, is a young prince of immense wealth; Odysseus is a boar-hunting youth in Ithaca; and Telemachus is not yet born. During the war years, Nestor presides with "white-haired" wisdom over the Achaean alliance. Now past prime fighting age, a haunted yet shrewdly pragmatic Agamemnon leads the younger troops. The war forges Odysseus, Achilles, Ajax, and Diomedes into triumphant giants. Meanwhile, Odysseus's wife, Penelope, raises Telemachus, a sensitive child who defers to the advice of elders. Twenty years later, the war over, Nestor returns safely to his homeland—as does Agamemnon, only to be murdered for his many sins. Odysseus returns to Ithaca where he now plays the midlife hero and saves the kingdom. Telemachus comes of age, obediently and with his father's help, looking forward to inheriting the kingship in an era of peace.

The saga ends after three-fourths of a saeculum, centered around a Crisis but with no mention of an Awakening. Homer does not say what happens next. As with the Hebrews, the saecular rhythm is again worn down by the unchanging round of social tradition from which it had briefly emerged. The cycle vanishes, and the dark ages return—no longer giving rise to the stuff of epic poetry.

As in the Old Testament and the Homeric epics, classical literature abounds with provocative bits and pieces of generational cycles. The great early poets and historians—Homer, Thucydides, Virgil, and Livy—typically focused on cycles launched by Hero archetypes, while sacred myths focused on cycles launched by Prophet archetypes (such as those beginning with Abraham, Moses, Lao-tzu, Buddha, Christ, or Muhammad).

Apparently, ancient societies knew of two basic types of generational sagas: one beginning with a martial or institutions-founding event, the other with a spiritual or values-founding event. It was only a matter of time before someone intuited that there might be a historical (not merely mythical) connection between the two.

Perhaps the first to make this connection was the renowned political philosopher Polybius. In the second century B.C., Polybius studied the histories of Greco-Roman city-states and noticed a recurring progression of political regimes—from kingship to aristocracy to democracy to anarchy —from which a new kingship would emerge. This progression itself was nothing new: Plato and Aristotle had said something similar. But Polybius went further. He specifically linked it to a pattern of generational succession. In his view, the city-states' first kings are generally powerful and good, but their children so weak and corrupt that an aristocratic rebellion eventually arises among the children's peers. The founding aristocrats govern well enough, but their children sink to oligarchy, prompting a democratic rebellion among *their* peers. A generation afterwards, the initial democrats' children sink to a mob rule ochlocracy, leading to a state of anarchy. In due course, a new king seizes control, and the cycle repeats. Polybius never says how long it takes for this sequence to occur. Apparently, it could occur slowly, over a period of many centuries—or rapidly, over the course of one saeculum (four generations).

Some fifteen hundred years later, the dashing philosopher-statesman Ibn Khaldun observed a similar pattern in the politics of the medieval Islamic world. In his treatise, the *Muqaddimah,* Khaldun observes that the "prestige" of medieval Islamic dynasties endures "only four generations." The first generation establishes rule by conquest, after which it governs with unquestioned authority. The second generation witnesses and admires that achievement, which it weakly emulates. Lacking firsthand knowledge of how the dynasty was established, the third generation not only lacks the founders' qualities but ignores them, so the dynasty weakens further. Coming of age under ignorant tutelage, the fourth generation reaches adulthood despising the dynasty, which then crumbles. Out of the chaos, a later generation produces a new king and new dynasty, and the cycle repeats. The entire cycle of dynastic virtue lasts about a century, and Khaldun used abundant metaphors to liken its trajectory and longevity to the cycle of human life itself.

Polybius and Khaldun are often hailed as pioneers of modern social theory because of two discoveries: first, that history moves through stages (circular or linear) of social change; and second, that parent-child tensions provide the motive force pushing society from one stage to the next. After the French Revolution, the influence of both concepts grew rapidly. By the nineteenth century, most educated people believed that history moved according to organic and developmental stages. Likewise, they assumed that generational flux played some vital role in steering this motion. Inevitably, these two ideas began to cross-fertilize. When the French philologist Paul-Émile Littré suggested that history moves in a fourfold progression—from moral to industrial to scientific to aesthetic—he likened it to the way generations follow each other. When the Russian novelist Ivan Turgenev published *Fathers and Sons,* his contemporary readers assumed he was critiquing a theory of social change.

No one took this cross-fertilization more seriously than the scholar Giuseppe Ferrari. Born around the time of Napoleon's demise and having come of age with the young radicals of the 1840s, Ferrari observed in Western history a cycle quite similar to that of Khaldun's. Ferrari was an Italian republican when his native Piedmont was in the grip of the Austrian monarchy. Following the failure of the 1848 uprising, he joined other Italian intellectuals and fled to Paris, where he wrote *Teoria dei periodi politici,* a treatise on the generational causes of "political periods." Ferrari believed that generational change was the single motive force behind all civilized progress since the end of the Roman Empire. His *Teoria* offers an encyclopedic list of *Generazioni* over the centuries, grouped into four-type cycles that, he insisted, were "the prime element of ebb and flow" in the history of France, Germany, Russia, Italy, and elsewhere. According to Ferrari, a revolutionary generation launches a new idea, a reactionary generation battles against that idea, a harmonizing generation uses that idea to establish community and build political institutions, and a preparatory generation subtly undermines that harmony, after which the cycle repeats.

A half-century later, another overdose of history—the impact of World War I on the European generation then coming of age—inspired German historian Eduard Wechssler to write about generations as a succession of "struggles over world views." He identified "four classical bases of all perception, thought, experience, and understanding, dating from the ancient Greeks," which he said follow each other in a fixed sequence. Describing the four types as physical-mechanical, rational-mathematical, cosmic-organic, and ethical-personal, he noted how each type has its own *Denkform* for almost everything in life: its hates, its loves, its approach to art, its view of

God, and so on. To each generational type, he ascribed a genre of thinking (science, rhetoric, myth, epic) and a geometric pattern of thinking (pyramid, cone, circle, spiral).

Soon after World War II, Arnold Toynbee described the "Physical Generation Cycle" that underlay his war cycle, which is in fact a theory of generational types. The reason major wars occur at periodic intervals, Toynbee asserted, is because of the effect they have on people of different ages. The young soldiers of one great war later refrain, as elder leaders, from declaring another. Those who have no memory at all of the first later become the declarers of the next great war. When you insert transitional generations between the war fighters and the war declarers, you can construct a four-type cycle over the span of one Toynbean war cycle.

The recent Consciousness Revolution prompted two new four-type generational theories, one European and the other American. Back in the 1920s, when Ortega y Gasset described in detail the "vital trajectories" of prefascist European generations, he never organized his theories into a system. After Ortega y Gasset's death, his student did. Julián Marías applied his teacher's ideas to what was then happening with the riotous "generation of 1968" (the European peers of American Boomers). Marías identified a four-part cycle: The first generation creates and initiates, the second fabricates a conformist personality, the third reflects and theorizes, and the fourth stylistically challenges forms and customs.

Around the same time in America, Harvard government professor Samuel Huntington found himself on the receiving end of a Generation Gap that pitted his G.I. faculty peers against riotous Boomer students. He responded by defining a four-part recurring IvI (Institutions versus Ideals) cycle, an alternation between periods of institutional growth and values growth, spanning the two centuries between the 1770s and 1960s. Huntington's periodicity matches the saeculum. And though he does not explicitly identify a generational typology, he directly implies one: The first generation constructs institutions, the second perfects those institutions while becoming aware of their moral failings (an attitude he calls hypocritical), the third propounds new ideals, and the fourth tests those ideals while becoming aware of their practical failings (an attitude he calls cynical).

More recently, a four-type cycle has been observed by George Modelski, in the context of his Toynbean long cycle of war and peace. Looking at world history but especially at America, Modelski described a cyclical alternation between the setting of norms and the attainment of goals. Persuaded by the teachings of Talcott Parsons that social change takes place in four stages, Modelski insists that a society cannot go directly from norm setting to goal attaining to new norm setting without passing through intermediate phases. What Modelski calls the "generational mechanism" underlying his four-part saecular dynamic is a sequence that runs from a constructive to an adaptive to a normative to a competitive generation coming of age.

Four-Type Generational Cycles

Source	Prophet	Nomad	Hero	Artist
OLD TESTAMENT	Moses (prophetic)	Golden Calf (faithless)	Joshua (heroic)	Judges (administrative)
HOMER	Nestor (sagacious)	Agamemnon (accursed)	Odysseus (hubristic)	Telemachus (deferential)
POLYBIUS	populist	anarchic	kingly	aristocratic
KHALDUN	ignoring	despising	founding	admiring
FERRARI	revolutionary	reactionary	harmonizing	preparatory
WECHSSLER	organic (myth, circle)	personal (epic, spiral)	mechanical (science, pyramid)	mathematical (rhetoric, cone)
TOYNBEE	war declaring	too old to fight	war fighting	too young to fight
MARÍAS	reflective	anticustom	initiating	conformist
HUNTINGTON	moralizing	cynical	institutionalizing	hypocritical
MODELSKI	normative	competitive	constructive	adaptive

All these theories reflect a pattern dating back to the Old Testament—a four-type cycle that has been seen across four millennia, multiple cultures, and every imaginable political and social system. The labels vary, but the archetypal order (Prophet to Nomad to Hero to Artist) is always identifiable—and always the same.

Among ancient societies, this cycle of four archetypes emerged whenever a Crisis produced a Hero generation or whenever an Awakening produced a Prophet generation. Afterward, the inertia of tradition dampened this cycle and pushed society back to a prescribed and changeless role for each phase of life. As the modern era dawned, this generational cycle emerged yet again. This time, however, tradition gave way, and the cycle of four archetypes continued on its own power. Whatever the historical problem, Namenworth observes that it takes "four whole and consecutive generations to traverse the complete problem solving sequence." He goes on to suggest that, for us moderns, "this generational succession might therefore well delineate our wheel of time."

At no other place and time in human history has the cycle of generations propelled this wheel of time with more force than in America.

CHAPTER 4

■

Cycles of History

MOUNT RUSHMORE'S GRANITE IS A MONUMENT TO FOUR great American leaders. Born over a span of 126 years, George Washington, Thomas Jefferson, Theodore Roosevelt, and Abraham Lincoln represent four different generations (Liberty, Republican, Progressive, and Transcendental). But the mountain depicts more than that: Looking from left to right, the visitor sees permanent testimony to the best-regarded president of each archetype chiseled not in chronological order, but in *saecular* order: *Nomad, Hero, Artist,* and *Prophet.* In the vision of Rushmore sculptor Gutzon Borglum, the power of the archetypal myths asserted itself once again.

Millions of Americans have sensed in this monument a magnificently balanced rendering of their national history. Some generations are remembered for championing great principles, others for building great institutions. Some are remembered for pragmatism and boldness, others for learning and flexibility. Each archetype has produced its own greatness, its own special virtues and competencies. To grow, prosper, and survive the shocks of history, America has required not one or two of these types, but truly all four.

This fourfold collaboration is not accidental. It reflects a dynamic balance that originated when humanity began asking the question, How can we make society *better?*

THE ORIGIN OF THE AMERICAN CYCLE

The self-sustaining cycle of archetypes originated at the very moment that the world made its enduring break with cyclical time and tradition. This happened in Western Europe during the last quarter of the fifteenth century.

This Renaissance—what Jules Michelet and Jacob Burckhardt both called "the rediscovery of the world and of man"—marked the true Western threshold into modern history. It was an age of glorious art and architecture, demonstrating that "man" was now indeed "the measure of all things." It was an age of autocratic nation building, when rulers built vast central authority and forged a bloody new balance of power by means of cannons, gunships, muskets, and massed infantry. It was an age of buoyant commercial activity, sustained population growth, and stunning overseas explorations that gave rise to instant global empires.

Yet even with the sea route to Cathay and the innumerable *palazzi ducali,* the birth of modernity remained only half complete. The other half did not arrive until forty or fifty years later. That was when modernity's alter ego appeared in the spiritual white heat of the Reformation and its attendant heresies, reforms, reactions, and persecutions. The Reformation redefined the search for moral conviction, a search which no longer interested worldly clerics and rulers, in terms of principles discernible by each person alone. By clearing away the intermediaries between the individual and God, the Reformation gave birth to an entirely modern definition of faith and conscience. Where the Renaissance shattered and reassembled the medieval secular order, the Reformation did likewise with the medieval religious order. Where the Renaissance redefined historical time as worldly progress toward happiness, the Reformation redefined it as spiritual progress toward salvation. Once both had run their course, the Western view of history and future would never be the same again.

Energizing these changes were two remarkable European generations. The first, embodying the Hero archetype, was born during the middle two decades of the fifteenth century. Its best-remembered names resonate with conquest, rationalism, and practical invention: rulers like Lorenzo "the Magnificent" of Florence, Charles "the Bold" of Burgundy, Ivan "the Great" of Russia, Ferdinand and Isabella of Spain; artists like Botticelli, da Vinci, and Bramante; and explorers like Christopher Columbus, Amerigo Vespucci, and Vasco da Gama. The other generation, born about forty years later, embodied the Prophet archetype. On continental Europe, its best-remembered names—Martin Luther, John Calvin, Ulrich Zwingli, William Tyndale, Charles V of Spain, Ignatius Loyola—resonate with inner fervor, self-absorption, and judgmentalism.

Modernity was thus created out of a stunning clash of generational archetypes. While the first Hero generation celebrated the outer splendor of man's power over nature, its two-apart Prophet shadow, disgusted by the "stinking" immorality of this hubristic show (as Luther recounted of his coming of age visit to Italy), glorified the inner fire of God's power over man. Propelled by this original cycle, other cycles would follow, setting in motion the rhythm of modern history and a Western fascination with generational contrasts that has lasted to this day.

While the modern generational cycle can be said to originate in Western Europe during the late 1400s, the origin of the American generational cycle can be specified with greater precision. The place was the British Isles—home to the society that long dominated the development of English-speaking North America. The date was 1485, when the army of a courageous young noble named Henry Tudor defeated and slew King Richard III near the town of Market Bosworth. This event put an end to the Wars of the Roses and secured for England a dynamic Tudor monarchy. In so doing, it transformed England into a nation with modern principles of political legitimacy. Forty-nine years later, Henry's son enlisted his people in a raging fever of enthusiasm and reform to evict the vast spiritual (and temporal) power of the Church of Rome. In so doing, he secured for England a "protestant" national church with modern principles of religious legitimacy.

As with the rest of Europe, England's launch out of the Middle Ages was propelled by two history-bending generations, each the archetypal shadow of the other. The first, the Heroic Arthurian Generation of Henry VII and John Cabot, laid the political foundations. The second, the Prophetic Reformation Generation of Henry VIII and John Knox, laid the religious foundations.

Over the next two centuries, an alternating sequence of Heroes and Prophets gestated a new American civilization:

- William Shakespeare's Elizabethan Generation produced the Heroes who founded (circa 1600) the first permanent English settlements on the Atlantic seaboard.
- John Winthrop's Puritan Generation produced the Prophets who summoned (circa 1640) the first Great Migration to America.
- "King" Carter's Glorious Generation produced the Heroes who transformed (circa 1690) a chaotic colonial backwater into a stable provincial society.
- Jonathan Edwards's Awakening Generation produced the Prophets who declared (circa 1740) the New World's social and spiritual independence from the Old.
- Thomas Jefferson's Republican Generation produced the Heroes who created (circa 1790) the United States of America.

To observe that the American generational cycle has its roots in England is not, of course, to ascribe the personal roots of most Americans to that one small corner of the globe. You have to go back to the beginning of this century—to 1900—to find an America in which over half of the inhabitants considered themselves to be of English ancestry. Now only about one-fifth do. A large majority still consider themselves to be of Western European ancestry, but that share too is in steady decline. To trace the family lineage of tens of millions of Americans today, you would have to tell a story that largely disregards the nation-states that arose within the frontiers of the ancient Roman Empire.

For Native Americans, such a story would start thirty millennia ago, when the first Asiatic peoples trekked the land highway across the Bering Strait and founded tribal civilizations on the tracks of receding glaciers. For black Americans, such a story would start among the kingdoms of central Africa and tell tales of capture, bondage, sale, and the deadly Middle Passage to the New World. For countless later immigrants, such stories would crisscross over the earth—from potato farms along the Shannon to rice fields along the Yangtze; from the dense communes of the Ukraine to the barren landskap of Sweden; from the braceros of Mexico to the boat people of Indochina.

Notwithstanding the ethnic diversity of today's Americans, the fact remains that the *cyclicality* of New World history originated with British immigrants—those who monopolized the development of the colonial civilization that would later become the United States. For more than two centuries after the founding of Jamestown and Plymouth, Native Americans were pushed almost entirely outside the settled boundaries of that civilization. Except for scattered pioneers and trappers on the outskirts, few colonists had meaningful intercourse with native peoples. African Americans—living side by side with colonists in substantial numbers and amounting to nearly a fifth of the population by 1776—were undoubtedly a greater defining influence on American society. But the vast majority lived in four southern colonies where that influence was strictly controlled by the institution of slavery.

Natives and blacks aside, America's ethnic diversity is of relatively recent origin. Among white colonists, Anglo-Saxon immigrants were long dominant. By 1720, a full saeculum after Plymouth Plantation, an estimated 90 percent of free colonists had English, Scottish, or Ulster Scot ancestors. By 1820, two saecula later, this figure was still around 80 percent; and of the remainder, roughly half consisted of German or Dutch stock—peoples whose history had been intertwined with that of England. As late as the 1830s, the free population of the United States was almost entirely Northern European and Protestant. "American" political debates were waged largely in terms of British precedents, and the use of the English language had become more standard in America than in England itself.

This complexion began to change with the large waves of Gilded Generation immigrants in the 1840s. As they came, these and other immigrants pushed and pulled on an Anglo-American generational cycle that had already acquired great historical momentum. Like new moons caught in a planetary orbit, these new immigrant waves affected the social trajectories of all parties, arriving minorities and resident majority.

Though not directly linked to the origin of the cycle, the stories of African-Americans and non-Anglo immigrants are closely linked to the cycle's rhythm. From the Stono Uprising of 1739 to Nat Turner's Rebellion of 1831, from W. E. B. Du Bois's turn-of-the-century black consciousness movement to the long, hot summers of the 1960s, America's loudest challenges against racism have coincided with the coming of age of the Prophet archetype. The rise of new ethnicities (Catholic Germans and Irish in the 1850s; Jews, Italians, and Poles in the 1910s; Hispanics and Asians today) has usually coincided with the coming of age of the Nomad archetype. Likewise, the worst nativist reactions have reflected a recurring parental urge to protect the childhood of a fledgling Hero archetype.

America's very existence as a favored destination for migrants the world over has played a crucial role in the emergence of the generation as a unit of history. In early modern Europe, England included, meaningful membership in generations was limited to elites—that is, to those who were free to break from tradition and redefine the social roles of whatever phase of life they occupied. After Jamestown and the *Mayflower,* however, the New World offered this opportunity to any person who could buy or borrow passage. From the seventeenth century through the present, the promise of generational change is one reason why America has remained such a magnet to would-be immigrants worldwide. In a series of stages—religious toleration, national independence, suffrage for nonpropertied males, emancipation of slaves, full civil rights for women and minority races—America has gradually offered more people access to a full measure of its Dream of generational advancement.

Nowadays everyone, no matter how disadvantaged or recently arrived, can be fairly said to have a bona fide chance to share in the redefinition of social roles and hence to join in what makes the generational cycle turn. Partly because of the kind of society the earliest immigrants created here, but also because of the nature of the people drawn here, America offers the world's clearest example of the generational cycle at work.

ARCHETYPES IN AMERICAN HISTORY

From the Arthurian Generation through today's Millennial Generation children, there have been twenty-four generations in the Anglo-American lineage. The first six were purely English. The next four were colonial, yet still heavily influenced by English society and politics. The eleventh (Awakeners, born 1701–1723) became the first distinctively American generation—the first whose name, birth years, and persona diverge significantly from peers in the United Kingdom. The Awakeners were also the first generation to be made up mostly of native-born Americans and, late in life, the first to know the U.S. nation and flag. So although today's Millennial children are the twenty-fourth in our full lineage of postmedieval generations, they are fourteenth in the *American* line.

In the overview of the Anglo-American Saeculum, which begins on page 123, these twenty-four generations are grouped by the saeculum in which they were born. Four generational synopses are provided per saeculum, starting with the Prophet archetype and ending with the Artist. The first Prophet birth year and last Artist birth year line up closely with the saecular boundary dates. This repeating fourfold pattern has two exceptions: the first Late Medieval Half Saeculum (whose story begins with a Hero archetype), and the Civil War Saeculum (the only true anomaly, which produced not four but three generations). Taken as a whole, this summary provides a collective biography of modernity told from the inside out, from the perspective of the cycle of life. It is quite unlike any history you will find in the vast corpus of conventional scholarship.

Notice how the four archetypes follow each other in a recurring sequence. Each archetype encounters both an Awakening and a Crisis once at some point in its life cycle and always encounters these eras at precisely the same phase of life. Notice how location in history shapes younger generations and is shaped by older generations in a predictable manner. Here again, the only exception arose during the Civil War Saeculum, which produced no Hero archetype.

To understand the connection between these generations and history, reflect on their four archetypal personas and recall the roster of prominent people who share each archetype.

We remember *Prophets* best for their coming-of-age passion (the excited pitch of Jonathan Edwards, William Lloyd Garrison, William Jennings Bryan) and for their principled elder stewardship (the sober pitch of Samuel Langdon at Bunker Hill, President Lincoln at Gettysburg, and FDR with his Fireside Chats). Increasingly indulged as children, they become increasingly protective as parents. Their principal endowments are in the domain of *vision, values,* and *religion.* Their best-known leaders include John Winthrop and William Berkeley, Samuel Adams and Benjamin Franklin, James Polk and Abraham Lincoln, and Herbert Hoover and Franklin Roosevelt. These have been principled moralists, summoners of human sacrifice, wagers of righteous wars. Early in life, none saw combat in uniform; late in life, most came to be revered more for their inspiring words than for their grand deeds.

We remember *Nomads* best for their rising-adult years of hell raising (Paxton Boys, Missouri Raiders, rumrunners) and for their midlife years of hands-on, get-it-done leadership (Francis Marion, Stonewall Jackson, George Patton). Underprotected as children, they become overprotective parents. Their principal endowments are in the domain of *liberty, survival,* and *honor.* Their best-known leaders include Nathaniel Bacon and William Stoughton, George Washington and John Adams, Ulysses Grant and Grover Cleveland, Harry Truman and Dwight Eisenhower. These have been cunning, hard-to-fool realists—taciturn warriors who prefer to meet problems and adversaries one on one. They include the only two presidents who had earlier hanged a man (Washington and Cleveland), one governor who hanged witches (Stoughton), and several leaders who had earlier led troops into battle (Bacon, Washington, Grant, Truman, and Eisenhower).

We remember *Heroes* best for their collective coming-of-age triumphs (Glorious Revolution, Yorktown, D-Day) and for their hubristic elder achievements (the Peace of Utrecht and slave codes, the Louisiana Purchase and steamboats, the *Apollo* moon launches and interstate highways). Increasingly protected as children, they become increasingly indulgent as parents. Their principal endowment activities are in the domain of *community, affluence,* and *technology.* Their best-known leaders include Gurdon Saltonstall and "King" Carter, Thomas Jefferson and James Madison, John Kennedy and Ronald Reagan. They have been vigorous and rational institution builders. All have been aggressive advocates of economic prosperity and public optimism in midlife, and all have maintained a reputation for civic energy and competence to the very ends of their lives.

We remember *Artists* best for their quiet years of rising adulthood (the log-cabin settlers of 1800, the plains farmers of 1880, the new suburbanites of 1960) and during their midlife years of flexible, consensus-building leadership (the Compromises of the Whig era, the good government reforms of the Progressive era, the budget and peace processes of the current era). Overprotected as children, they become underprotective parents. Their principal endowment activities are in the domain of *pluralism, expertise,* and *due process.* Their best-known leaders include William Shirley and Cadwallader Colden, John Quincy Adams and Andrew Jackson, Theodore Roosevelt and Woodrow Wilson, Walter Mondale and Colin Powell. These have been sensitive and complex social technicians, advocates of fair play and the politics of inclusion. With the single exception of Andrew Jackson, they rank as the most expert and credentialed of American political leaders.

As shown in the chart on page 98, these four archetypes have lent balance and self-correction to the continuing story of America. Were our ancestral legacy to have had too much or too little of any of the four, we would today be poorer for it.

Each generation has what all of history has not: a beginning, an end, and a finite path in between. As Ortega observed, a generation is not a stationary object, but rather a "vital trajectory" between the hopes of youth and the memories of old age. It never matters as much where a generation *is* as where it is *going.*

Here we return to the wisdom of the ancients: how every organism, through its development, both stays the same and yet transforms into its opposite. In certain respects, a generation always retains its persona of youth; in other ways, it expresses that persona very differently in each successive phase of life. We see this among the G.I.s, who once prided themselves on

Archetypes in History

Archetype	Hero	Artist	Prophet	Nomad
Generations	Arthurian Elizabethan Glorious Republican — G.I. Millennial	Humanist Parliamentary Enlightenment Compromise Progressive Silent	Reformation Puritan Awakening Transcendental Missionary Boom	Reprisal Cavalier Liberty Gilded Lost Thirteenth
REPUTATION AS CHILD	good	placid	spirited	bad
COMING OF AGE	empowering	unfulfilling	sanctifying	alienating
PRIMARY FOCUS COMING OF AGE	outer-world	inter-dependency	inner-world	self-sufficiency
YOUNG ADULTHOOD	building	improving	reflecting	competing
TRANSITION IN MIDLIFE	energetic to hubristic	conformist to experimental	detached to judgmental	frenetic to exhausted
LEADERSHIP STYLE ENTERING ELDERHOOD	collegial, expansive	pluralistic, indecisive	righteous, austere	solitary, pragmatic
REPUTATION AS ELDER	powerful	sensitive	wise	tough
TREATMENT AS ELDER	rewarded	liked	respected	abandoned
HOW IT IS NURTURED	tightening	overprotective	relaxing	underprotective
HOW IT NURTURES	relaxing	underprotective	tightening	overprotective
POSITIVE REPUTATION	selfless, rational, competent	caring, open-minded, expert	principled, resolute, creative	savvy, practical, perceptive
NEGATIVE REPUTATION	unreflective, mechanistic, overbold	sentimental, complicating, indecisive	narcissistic, presumptuous, ruthless	unfeeling, uncultured, amoral
ENDOWMENTS	community, affluence, technology	pluralism, expertise, due process	vision, values, religion	liberty, survival, honor

their dedication to the future but who now comprise the largest consumption lobby in American history. We see this among the Silent, who were once chided for their "lonely crowd" conformism but who now are enjoying a lifestyle of exuberant individualism full of "choices" and options. Boomers once dreamed of a Pepperland of tolerance, pleasure, and love but now sternly police the perceived excesses of youth. The first 13ers engaged in high-risk behavior coming of age, but today's fledgling householders are beginning to turn against personal and public risk. The beat goes on.

What happens to each generation separately is only part of the picture. Of more importance to history is what happens to generations together. They age in place in a manner that François Mentré described as "tiles on a roof"—overlapping in time, corrective in purpose, complementary in effect. As generations age, they together form new archetypal *constellations* that alter every aspect of society, from government and the economy to culture and family life.

Over the course of a cycle, these constellations can produce sharply different social results. Reflect on how unalike the following two societies will be: One is run by expansive old Heroes and uncertain midlife Artists, whose combined public works are torched by fiery young Prophets and whose freedoms are inconvenienced by hurried Nomad children. The other is led by judgmental old Prophets and pragmatic midlife Nomads, whose combined public works are assisted by team-playing young Heroes and whose duties are unimpeded by quiescent child Artists. The former is an Awakening constellation like that of two decades ago, during the Consciousness Revolution. The latter is a Crisis constellation like that of World War II and the Crisis to come.

ARCHETYPES AND TURNINGS

A *turning* is an era with a characteristic social mood, a new twist on how people feel about themselves and their nation. It results from the aging of the generational constellation. A society enters a turning once every twenty years or so, when all living generations begin to enter their next phases of life. Like archetypes and constellations, turnings come four to a saeculum, and always in the same order:

- The *First Turning* is a *High.* Old Prophets disappear, Nomads enter elderhood, Heroes enter midlife, Artists enter young adulthood, and a new generation of Prophets is born.
- The *Second Turning* is an *Awakening.* Old Nomads disappear, Heroes enter elderhood, Artists enter midlife, Prophets enter young adulthood, and a new generation of child Nomads is born.
- The *Third Turning* is an *Unraveling.* Old Heroes disappear, Artists enter elderhood, Prophets enter midlife, Nomads enter young adulthood, and a new generation of child Heroes is born.
- The *Fourth Turning* is a *Crisis.* Old Artists disappear, Prophets enter elderhood, Nomads enter midlife, Heroes enter young adulthood, and a new generation of child Artists is born.

Like the four seasons of nature, the four turnings of history are equally necessary and equally important. Awakenings and Crises are the saecular solstices, summer and winter, each a solution to a challenge posed by the other. Highs and Unravelings are the saecular equinoxes, spring and autumn, each coursing a path directionally opposed to the other. When a society moves into an Awakening or Crisis, the new mood announces itself as a sudden turn in social direction. An Awakening begins when events trigger a revolution in the culture, a Crisis when events trigger an upheaval in public life. A High or Unraveling announces itself as a sudden consolidation of the new direction. A High begins when society perceives that the basic issues of the prior Crisis have been resolved, leaving a new civic regime firmly in place. An Unraveling begins with the perception that the Awakening has been resolved, leaving a new cultural mindset in place.

The gateway to a new turning can be obvious and dramatic (like the 1929 Stock Market Crash) or subtle and gradual (like 1984's Morning in America). It usually occurs two to five years after a new generation of children starts being born. The tight link between turning gateways and generational boundaries enables each archetype to fill an entire phase-of-life just as the mood of an old turning grows stale and feels ripe for replacement with something new.

The four turnings comprise a quaternal social cycle of growth, maturation, entropy, and death (and rebirth). In a springlike High, a society fortifies and builds and converges in an era of promise. In a summerlike Awakening, it dreams and plays and exults in an era of euphoria. In an autumnal Unraveling, it harvests and consumes and diverges in an era of anxiety. In a hibernal Crisis, it focuses and struggles and sacrifices in an era of survival. When the saeculum is in motion, therefore, no long human lifetime can go by without a society confronting its deepest spiritual and worldly needs.

Every twenty to twenty-five years (or, in common parlance, once a generation), people are surprised by the arrival of a new saecular season—just as people are by the end of spring announced by the first oppressively humid day or the end of autumn by the first sleet storm. We keep forgetting that history, like nature, must turn. Abraham Lincoln understood as much. Speaking to a crowd just eighteen months before the bombardment of Fort Sumter, he told a story of an Asiatic monarch who directed his wise men to compose a statement "to be ever in view, and which should be true and appropriate in all times and situations." After considerable study, the sages drafted an answer: "This, too, shall pass away."

Modernity has thus far produced six repetitions of each turning. From the record of history, the following typology can be constructed.

The First Turning

A *High* brings a renaissance to community life. With the new civic order in place, people want to put the Crisis behind them and feel content about what they have collectively achieved. Any social issues left unresolved by the Crisis must now remain so.

The need for dutiful sacrifice has ebbed, yet the society continues to demand order and consensus. The recent fear for group survival transmutes into a desire for investment, growth, and strength—which in turn produces an era of commercial prosperity, institutional solidarity, and political stability. The big public arguments are over means, not ends. Security is a paramount need. Obliging individuals serve a purposeful society—though a few loners voice disquiet over the spiritual void. Life tends toward the friendly and homogeneous, but attitudes toward personal risk taking begin to loosen. The sense of shame (which rewards duty and conformity) reaches its zenith. Gender distinctions attain their widest point, and child rearing becomes more indulgent. Wars are unlikely, except as unwanted echoes of the recent Crisis.

Eventually, civic life seems fully under control but distressingly spirit dead. People worry that, as a society, they can *do* everything but no longer *feel* anything.

The post–World War II American High may rank as the all-time apogee of the national mood. The Gilded Age surge into the industrial age was supported by a rate of capital formation unmatched in U.S. history, symbolized by the massive turbines in the Centennial Exposition's Hall of Machines. In the early nineteenth century, the geometric grids of the District of Columbia and Northwest Territory townships projected a mood of ordered community that culminated in the Era of Good Feelings, the only time a U.S. president was reelected by acclamation. In the upbeat 1710s, poetic odes to flax and shipping conjured up a society preoccupied (in Cotton Mather's words) with "usefulness" and "good works."

Recall America's circa-1963 conception of the future: We brimmed over with optimism about Camelot, a bustling future with smart people in which big projects and "impossible dreams" were freshly achievable. The moon could be reached and poverty eradicated, both within a decade. Tomorrowland was a friendly future with moving skywalks, pastel geometric shapes, soothing Muzak, and well-tended families. In the Carousel of Progress, the progress remained fixed while the carousel (what moved) was the audience. The future had specificity and certainty but lacked urgency and moral direction.

The Second Turning

An *Awakening* arrives with a dramatic challenge against the High's assumptions about benevolent reason and congenial institutions. The outer world now feels trivial compared to the inner world.

New spiritual agendas and social ideals burst forth—along with utopian experiments seeking to reconcile total fellowship with total autonomy. The prosperity and security of a High are overtly disdained though covertly taken for granted. A society searches for soul over science, meanings over things. Youth-fired attacks break out against the established institutional order. As these attacks take their toll, society has difficulty coalescing around common goals. People stop believing that social progress requires social discipline. Any public effort that requires collective discipline encounters withering controversy. Wars are awkwardly fought and badly remembered afterward. A euphoric enthusiasm over spiritual needs eclipses concern over secular problems, contributing to a high tolerance for risk-prone lifestyles. People begin feeling guilt about what they earlier did to avoid shame. Public order deteriorates, and crime and substance abuse rise. Gender distinctions narrow, and child rearing reaches the point of minimum protection and structure.

Eventually, the enthusiasm cools, having left the old cultural regime fully discredited, internal enemies identified, comity shattered, and institutions delegitimized.

Many Americans recall this mood on the campuses and urban streets of the Consciousness Revolution. Earlier generations knew a similar mood in Greenwich Village around 1900, in utopian communes around 1840, in the Connecticut Valley nearly a century earlier, and in the Puritans' New Jerusalems in the post-*Mayflower* decades.

Recall America's circa-1984 conception of the future: Tomorrowland had evolved through *2001: A Space Odyssey* to *Star Wars* and *Close Encounters of the Third Kind,* a spiritual future in which human consciousness triumphs over machines. The visions alternated between perfection and disaster, between utopias celebrating love and dystopias annihilating everything. We believed that self-expression took precedence over self-control—even if we still assumed that large institutions would continue to cohere and function without much difficulty.

The Third Turning

An *Unraveling* begins as a societywide embrace of the liberating cultural forces set loose by the Awakening. People have had their fill of spiritual rebirth, moral protest, and lifestyle experimentation. Content with what they have become individually, they vigorously assert an ethos of pragmatism, self-reliance, laissez-faire, and national (or sectional or ethnic) chauvinism.

While personal satisfaction is high, public trust ebbs amid a fragmenting culture, harsh debates over values, and weakening civic habits. Pleasure-seeking lifestyles coexist with a declining public tolerance for aberrant personal behavior. The sense of guilt (which rewards principle and individuality) reaches its zenith. Gender differences attain their narrowest point, families stabilize, and new protections are provided for children. As moral debates brew, the big public arguments are over ends, not means. Decisive public action becomes very difficult, as community problems are deferred. Wars are fought with moral fervor but without consensus or follow-through.

Eventually, cynical alienation hardens into a brooding pessimism. During a High, obliging individuals serve a purposeful society, and even bad people get harnessed to socially constructive tasks; during an Unraveling, an obliging society serves purposeful individuals, and even good people find it hard to connect with their community. The approaching specter of public disaster ultimately elicits a mix of paralysis and apathy that would have been unthinkable half a saeculum earlier. People can now *feel,* but collectively can no longer *do.*

The mood of the current Culture Wars era seems new to nearly every living American, but is not new to history. Around World War I, America was steeped in reform and fundamentalism amid a floodtide of crime, alcohol, immigration, political corruption, and circus trials. The 1850s likewise simmered with moral righteousness, shortening tempers, and multiplying "mavericks." It was a decade, says historian David Donald, in which "the authority of all government in America was at a low point." Entering the 1760s, the colonies felt rejuvenated in spirit but reeled from violence, mobs, insurrections, and paranoia over the corruption of official authority.

Look at how Americans today conceive the future: Think-tank luminaries exult over the history-bending changes of the Information Age, while the public glazes at expertise, cynically disregards the good news, and dwells on the negative. The pop culture rakes with futuristic images of *Total Recall* dysfunction, *Robocop* crimes, *Terminator* punishments, and *Independence Day* deliverance from evil.

The Fourth Turning

A *Crisis* arises in response to sudden threats that previously would have been ignored or deferred, but which are now perceived as dire. Great worldly perils boil off the clutter and complexity of life, leaving behind one simple imperative: The society must prevail. This requires a solid public consensus, aggressive institutions, and personal sacrifice.

People support new efforts to wield public authority, whose perceived successes soon justify more of the same. Government *governs,* community obstacles are removed, and laws and customs that resisted change for decades are swiftly shunted aside. A grim preoccupation with civic peril causes spiritual curiosity to decline. A sense of public urgency contributes to a clampdown on bad conduct or antisocial lifestyles. People begin feeling shameful about what they earlier did to absolve guilt. Public order tightens, private risk taking abates, and crime and substance abuse decline. Families strengthen, gender distinctions widen, and child rearing reaches a smothering degree of protection and structure. The young focus their energy on worldly achievements, leaving values in the hands of the old. Wars are fought with fury and for maximum result.

Eventually, the mood transforms into one of exhaustion, relief, and optimism. Buoyed by a newborn faith in the group and in authority, leaders plan, people hope, and a society yearns for good and simple things.

Today's older Americans recognize this as the mood of the Great Depression and World War II, but a similar mood has been present in all the other great gates of our history, from the Civil War and Revolution back into colonial and English history.

Recall America's conception of the future during the darkest years of its last Crisis: From "Somewhere over the Rainbow" to the glimmering Futurama at the 1939 New York World's Fair, people felt hope, determination, and a solid consensus about where society should go: toward spiritual simplicity (home and apple pie) and material abundance (bigger, better, and more homes and pies). All this seemed within reach, conditioned on a triumph that demanded unity from all, sacrifices from many.

The overview at the end of this chapter offers a summary of all the turnings over seven saecula of Anglo-American history. Each turning made its own contribution to history. Each offered its own solutions—which, in time, created new problems and anxieties. Thus have the four turnings kept the great wheel of time in motion, infusing civilization with periodic new doses of vitality, propelling the human adventure ever forward.

The summary chart on page 105 reveals a number of cycles that unfold over the four seasons of the saeculum. This prompts the question, What would history be like if the saeculum did not exist?

In chaotic time, history would bear no pattern. Any effort to chart it would list columns and rows that describe anything—and therefore nothing. Society would zigzag aimlessly. At any time, it could accelerate, stop, reverse course, or come to an end.

In linear time, there would be no turnings, just segments along one directional path of progress. Each twenty-year segment would produce more of everything produced by the prior segment. On a chart, every cell in any

Moods of the Four Turnings

	First Turning (High)	Second Turning (Awakening)	Third Turning (Unraveling)	Fourth Turning (Crisis)
Generation Entering:				
ELDERHOOD	*Nomad*	*Hero*	*Artist*	*Prophet*
MIDLIFE	*Hero*	*Artist*	*Prophet*	*Nomad*
YOUNG ADULTHOOD	*Artist*	*Prophet*	*Nomad*	*Hero*
CHILDHOOD	*Prophet*	*Nomad*	*Hero*	*Artist*
FAMILIES	strong	weakening	weak	strengthening
CHILD NURTURE	loosening	underprotective	tightening	overprotective
GAP BETWEEN GENDER ROLES	maximum	narrowing	minimum	widening
IDEALS	settled	discovered	debated	championed
INSTITUTIONS	reinforced	attacked	eroded	founded
CULTURE	innocent	passionate	cynical	practical
SOCIAL STRUCTURE	unified	splintering	diversified	gravitating
WORLDVIEW	simple	complicating	complex	simplifying
SOCIAL PRIORITY	maximum community	rising individualism	maximum individualism	rising community
SOCIAL MOTIVATOR	shame	conscience	guilt	stigma
SENSE OF GREATEST NEED	do what works	fix inner world	do what feels right	fix outer world
VISION OF FUTURE	brightening	euphoric	darkening	urgent
WARS	restorative	controversial	inconclusive	total

given row would read just like the one before, except with a higher multiplier. The 2020s would be a mere extrapolation of the 1990s, with more cable channels and Web pages and senior benefits and corporate free agents —plus more handgun murders, media violence, cultural splintering, political cynicism, youth alienation, partisan meanness, and distance between rich and poor. There would be no apogee, no leveling, no correction. Eventually, America would veer totally out of control along some bizarre centrifugal path.

In cyclical time, a society always evolves. Usually, the circle is a spiral of progress, sometimes a spiral of decline. Always, people strive to mend the errors of the past, to correct the excesses of the present, to seek a future that provides whatever feels most in need. Thus can civilization endure and thrive.

Rhythms in History

In 1969, amid all the howl on college campuses, a young sociologist named Peter Harris quietly published a two-hundred-page monograph in the Harvard journal *Perspectives in American History*. Therein Harris reached a striking conclusion: Over three centuries of American history, a wide variety of social indicators—birth rate, marriage age, wage growth, social mobility, political activism—have always turned an abrupt corner every twenty-two years or so. Emerging out of reams of archival evidence, this insistent pattern compelled Harris to rethink the standard-issue linearism of his academic specialty—and ultimately prompted him to switch fields. (He is now a history professor at Temple University.) Maybe, he wondered, those long-term trends toward urbanization, industrialization, and education are *not,* after all, the primary forces of history. Maybe, instead, "it is possible to see, through long periods of American history, a surprisingly regular pattern of growth and change in the social system"—in other words, "a truly cyclical system of human life."

Calling this twenty-two-year period a "growth cycle interval," Harris identified the essence of the turning. He observed that "the 'mood of the nation' also goes through swings or cycles adhering closely to the familiar interval." Placed end to end, these cycles serve as a natural metric across the topography of American history. He pointed out, for example, that "it was a span of almost exactly two growth cycles from the English Civil War to the colonial revolts of the 1680s (the Glorious Revolution at home), while the War for Independence broke out about four cycles later still." Had his theory been used in 1689 to predict the future, he noted, "the hypothetical date for a crisis in the cyclical timing during this period would have been 1777."

In recent decades, many distinguished scholars have joined Harris in identifying what Arthur Schlesinger Jr. has called "patterns of alternation, of ebb and of flow, in human history." What is the *timing* of these cycles? Very often, their duration is either a full saeculum or a half saeculum. Cycles that last a full saeculum are usually divisible into four seasonal phases. Cycles that last a half saeculum (such as the economists' Kondratieff cycle or Harris's own growth interval) are usually two-stroke cycles—meshing neatly, like a double-time beat, with the full saeculum. What *causes* these cycles? Like Schlesinger, most theorists point to generational change—even if they can't say exactly how it works. Harris suggests that "the modal personality" of each generation "fluctuates according to cyclical variations in the environment in which socialization takes place."

Perhaps the main reason these cycle theorists have failed to attract more attention is because mainstream academia evaluates each newly discovered cycle as an isolated curiosity. Most academics neither look for cycles nor ponder the causes of those they happen to stumble across. And so long as the experts aren't paying attention, it doesn't matter how insistently or eloquently the seasons of history may speak to them. The saeculum remains as unheard as if it were still lying in some Etruscan tomb, still etched in a language no one can decipher.

Some cyclical trends are handicapped by the fact that no one can quantify them precisely—a deficiency skeptics use to their advantage. Consider the attitude of the rising youth generation toward political and family authority. Over the half saeculum between 1935 and 1975, survey data confirm that this attitude shifted from one extreme to another. For earlier eras, no such numbers exist. If, for example, we wanted to look at the half saeculum between 1690 and 1740, we can only infer from primary sources and historians that the distance between the CCC Youth Corps and Wheeler Ranch hippies is *analogous* to the distance between the crisp "Family Well-Ordered" essays of young Cotton Mather and the frenzied vanity bonfires of young John Davenport. We need the same imaginative power to compare the cheery young rationalists who debated *The Federalist* papers in the 1780s (using pseudonyms like "Publius") with those whom Ralph Waldo Emerson described in the 1830s as "young men born with knives in their brain . . . madmen, madwomen, men with beards, Dunkers, Muggletonians, Come-Outers, Groaners, Agrarians, Seventh-Day Baptists, Quakers, Abolitionists, Calvinists, Unitarians, and Philosophers" who gathered not to reason or build but "to chide, or pray, or preach, or protest."

Yet even when the core trend cannot be measured directly, related indicators sometimes can be. Ask yourself what the above swings in youth attitudes imply for campus rebellions. Would you figure swings of similar timing? If so, your answer is confirmed by what the record shows ever since Thomas Hobbes (born the same year as John Winthrop) denounced universities as "the core of rebellion" against the English Crown: Once each saeculum, an Awakening ushers in a dramatic surge in the number and fury of collegiate riots against symbols of social authority, with memorable peaks in the 1740s, 1830s, 1880s, and 1960s. Another telling indicator is the founding of utopian communes in America. This pattern is so overwhelmingly clustered in Awakening years (especially around 1840, 1900, and 1970) that political scientist Michael Barkun says it "strongly suggests the existence of a utopian cycle with a moderately predictable rhythm."

Describing a historical cycle requires both interpretation and quantification, within an objective framework that allows dates and magnitudes to be compared. With these caveats in mind, let's turn to other cycles that keep time with the saeculum.

Politics

The best known cycle theory of American politics was first suggested by Arthur Schlesinger Sr. Working off a casual remark of Henry Adams's, Schlesinger discerned a somewhat irregular oscillation between liberal and conservative eras since the Revolutionary War. Later, the theory was more fully developed by his son, Arthur Schlesinger Jr., who relabeled the eras as those of public energy and private interest.

The Schlesinger cycle lines up with the saeculum as follows: The public energy eras overlap largely with Awakening and Crisis turnings, the private interest eras with Highs and Unravelings. This should not be surprising: Crises and Awakenings both require a dramatic reassertion of public energy—the former to fulfill the need for social survival, the latter to fulfill the need for social expression. No such need appears in Highs or Unravelings.

Schlesinger's match is not exact and would be closer if his cycle (about fifteen years per era) were not so rapid. He justifies this rapid periodicity by pointing to Ortega's fifteen-year "generation" span—a hypothesis that Ortega never actually tested against history. One would expect a fifteen-year cycle to deviate from the saeculum rather quickly. But by identifying anomalous periods, Schlesinger has kept his cycle fairly close to the secular rhythm. Recently, though, it has started to go awry. By his extrapolation, America was ready for a major new dose of big-government liberalism in 1988. But that didn't happen. Four years later, when Bill Clinton won the White House, Schlesinger again heralded a new dawn of such liberalism. Again, that didn't happen. Timing aside, though, Schlesinger is right about the fundamental rhythm of American politics. Authoritarian government isn't dead; it's just hibernating, poised to return in the Fourth Turning, rested and refreshed.

The second best known cycle theory of American politics is the party realignment cycle, which coincides perfectly with the saeculum. Every forty years or so—always during a Crisis or Awakening—a new "realigning election" gives birth to a "new political party system." According to Walter Dean Burnham, these elections occurred in 1788 (Federalist-Republican); 1828 (Jacksonian Democrat); 1860 (Lincoln Republican); 1896 (McKinley Republican); 1932 (New Deal Democrat); and 1968, 1972, or 1980 (Nixon-Reagan Republican). By this count, Burnham reckons we are now in our sixth party system. Though these realignments don't coincide with his own cycle, Schlesinger does concede their regularity. "Over the last century and a quarter," he notes, "each realignment cycle has run about forty years." What causes these cycles? Political scientist Paul Allen Beck suggests that children who grow up during realignments come of age shunning them, whereas children who grow up during eras of "normal" politics come of age seeking them. The result is *one* realignment every *two* phases of life.

The Schlesinger and Burnham cycles both describe a two-stroke alternation, lasting a half saeculum; as such, both can be improved by reinterpreting them within the seasonal quaternity of the full saeculum. The public energy of an Awakening cannot be equated with that of a Crisis. SDS-style 1960s radicalism was hardly a reenactment of the New Deal, nor was circa 1900 muckraking reminiscent of Lincoln's Union Party. One type of public energy undermines the authority of government; the other type builds it up. Likewise, the private interests of a High cannot be equated with those of an Unraveling. In a High, private interests want to cooperate with public institutions that appear to be working; in an Unraveling, they want to flee from public institutions that appear to be failing.

The saeculum improves the two-stroke realignment cycle in several respects: Eras of partisan solidarity, high voter turnout, and mannerly campaigning typically begin near the end of a Crisis and run through a High, while eras of partisan splintering, low voter turnout, third-party crusades, and vitriolic campaigning typically begin near the end of an Awakening and run through an Unraveling. The steep slide in voter participation from 1970 to 1990 resembles a similar decline between 1900 and 1920. Ross Perot's share of the 1992 vote was the largest for a third party since the Bull Moose ticket in 1912, which was the largest since the Republicans in 1856—all Unraveling eras. In an Awakening, voters seek to disconnect from civic authority they increasingly distrust and don't need. In a Crisis, by contrast, voters seek to rebuild civic authority they increasingly trust and need. Most Awakening-era elections can be called *de*-aligning to the extent that they reflect a loosening of party discipline; most Crisis-era elections can be called *re*-aligning to the extent that they establish or reinforce one-party rule.

Foreign Affairs

Many people might suppose that nothing could be more random than changes in America's foreign policy. What pattern, after all, can possibly account for the global accidents of war and statecraft? Most diplomatic historians supposed the same thing until 1952, when the scholar Frank L. Klingberg discovered a "historical alternation of moods" in American foreign policy. He explained the clear difference between a mere *event* and society's *response* to that event. Whatever the provocation, he showed, America's response depends on whether the prevailing mood is ticking toward "introversion" or tocking toward "extraversion."

With each two-stroke alternation lasting about forty-seven years, Klingberg's cycle closely matches the saeculum, except during and just after the Civil War. In general, his introversions overlap with Awakenings and Crises; his extraversions, with Highs and Unravelings. During an Awakening or Crisis, while people are absorbed with internal social change (the New Deal until Pearl Harbor; the Age of Aquarius after the Tet Offensive), they become an introverting society. During a High or Unraveling, while people look beyond their borders (either to engage in gunboat diplomacy, Manifest Destiny, or global coalition building), they become an extraverting society. During the Civil War and Reconstruction eras, the Klingberg cycle deviates entirely from the normal rhythm of the saeculum, probably because the Civil War issued in catastrophic suffering and no triumph over a foreign power.

Klingberg explains his cycle by pointing to "generational experience"— in particular to the desire of aging national leaders to repeal the "failures" of their midlife years and return to the policy style that prevailed during their earlier "formative years." In the early 1980s, Klingberg wrote that an era of introversion had begun in 1967 and was due to last until 1987; by his clock, a subsequent era of extraversion is supposed to last until 2014.

Economy

In 1930, Stalin arrested the economist Nikolai Kondratieff and shipped him off to Siberia. His crime: daring to defy that most linear of ideologies— Marxism—by suggesting that the long-term performance of market economies is cyclical. Soon after his death in the gulag, Kondratieff became a cult figure to historical economists around the world. Today, his name is attached to a popular family of two-stroke economic "K-Cycles," some traceable back to the fifteenth century and all having a periodicity of forty to fifty-five years.

K-Cycles vary in their details, but most of them closely fit the saeculum. Cycle peaks occur near the ends of Highs and Unravelings, and troughs occur near the ends of Awakenings and Crises. (Right now, this implies that America is in a long-wave upswing that began around 1980 and will last shortly past the year 2000.) Here again, a two-way pendulum doesn't do justice to the seasonality of the saeculum. During a High, wage and productivity growth is typically smooth and very rapid. During an Awakening, a soaring economy hits at least one spectacular bust (the mid-1970s, mid-1890s, late 1830s, or mid-1730s) that is darkly interpreted as closing a golden age of postwar growth. During an Unraveling, economic activity again accelerates, but now the growth is unbalanced and fitful. During a Crisis, the economy is rocked by some sequential combination of panic, depression, inflation, war, and public regimentation. Near the end of a Crisis, a healthy economy is reborn.

The presence of public authority in the economy shifts radically from one turning to the next. During a High, government plays an obtrusive planning and regulatory role. Witness the royal trading patents of the 1610s, the congressional land grants of the 1870s, and the "military-industrial complex" of the 1950s. The rules of the game encourage saving, favor the young, and protect organized producers (monopolies, trusts, guilds, unions). During an Awakening, the popular consensus underlying this public role begins to disintegrate. During an Unraveling, public control recedes, while entrepreneurship, risk taking, and the creative destruction of the market prevail. Meanwhile, the rules of the game encourage dissaving, favor the old, and protect individual consumers. During a Crisis, a new popular consensus emerges.

A similar rhythm governs trends in income and class equality. The two most sustained and measurable poverty-rate declines (1946–1967 and 1865–1890) have roughly coincided with the last two Highs. Yet the historical moments of greatest estimated income inequality (the late 1990s, late 1920s, late 1850s, and late 1760s) have all occurred near the ends of Unravelings. Highs promote income and class equality, and Awakenings change that. Unravelings promote *in*equality, and Crises change that.

Family and Society

When Betty Friedan wrote *The Feminine Mystique* in 1963 at a trough in the public status of women, she observed that the history of women's rights is like a series of gathering tidal waves, each sweeping over American institutional life at discrete intervals before sweeping out again amid rips and eddies. The timing of these waves follows the saeculum. Feminism, as a popular movement, bursts on the scene during an Awakening. During an Unraveling, the gap between acceptable gender roles shrinks to its narrowest point. The efficacy of masculine power (and feminine morality) is reidealized during a Crisis. During a High, the gap between acceptable gender roles grows to its widest point, after which the cycle repeats.

As with turnings, so with archetypes. Prophet generations always include impassioned women (from Anne Hutchinson to Susan B. Anthony to Hillary Clinton) who are deemed the civic equals of their male peers. Hero generations favor a rational paragon of leadership (a Thomas Jefferson or John Kennedy), which reasserts the public-private division of sexual labor. Through the centuries, young Nomad women have displayed some variant of the "garçonne" look that hides sexual differences, while young Artist women have flaunted the hoops and beehives that accentuate sexual differences. In midlife, both of these latter archetypes struggle to reverse course —Nomads to expand gender differences, Artists to shrink them. Friedan implicitly had these seasonal rhythms in mind when she observed that just after World War II younger women had been steered out of public vocations and thrown "back" onto the domestic pedestal. Others have made similar observations about earlier Highs.

Seasonal shifts in gender roles are linked to shifts in the family as an institution. During a High, the family feels secure and child rearing becomes more indulgent. During an Unraveling, the family feels endangered and child rearing becomes more protective. Prior to the American High, the previous golden age of indulgent families was the 1870s—an era that family historian Mary Cable likens to the "Dr. Spock 1950s." Prior to today's Culture Wars, the previous age of family pessimism was the 1920s, a decade whose shrill hysteria over the lost family has yet to be matched.

Paralleling these family rhythms are the changing ideals or metaphors that Americans use to express their attitude toward society at large. In a High, people want to *belong;* in an Awakening, to *defy;* in an Unraveling, to *separate;* in a Crisis, to *gather.* Among racial and ethnic minorities, these attitudes play a very conspicuous role in shaping the dominant strategy for group advancement. During the saeculum following Appomattox, the image of an effective black leader progressed from Booker T. Washington (conformity) to W. E. B. Du Bois (defiance) to Marcus Garvey (separation). During the saeculum following V-J Day, cutting-edge African-American movements have retraced many of the same steps—from the Council on Racial Equality (conformity), to the Black Panthers (defiance), to the Nation of Islam (separation).

Whatever the size of a person's group, he or she is more likely to feel fairly treated in a High, where a shame ethos fosters togetherness and gratitude—and victimized in an Unraveling, where a guilt ethos fosters separateness and blame. When individuals see themselves standing outside the system, as a minority or as individuals, their objective varies with the season. In a High, they want to show they *are able* to join; in an Unraveling, they want to show they *don't need* to join.

Population

The onset of war causes birthrates to fall, and the onset of peace causes birthrates to surge. In traditional societies, this pattern is attributed to the iron laws of biology and economics. In modern societies, it is assisted by the rhythm of the saeculum—in particular, by the resurgent popularity of family life and the widening of gender role divisions that occur during Highs.

Over five centuries, every Fourth Turning has been marked by a fall in birthrates; thus, Artist generations (most recently the Silent) are typically baby bust generations. On the other hand, every High but one has been marked by a marked rise in birthrates; thus Prophet generations (most recently Boomers) are typically baby boom generations. The only exception was the Missionary Generation, born 1860 to 1882. Yet here the exception proves the rule, since the two decades after the Civil War mark the only fertility rate plateau along an otherwise steady downslope from the 1820s to the 1930s. Awakenings (when Nomads are born) and Unravelings (when Heroes are born) show a less pronounced bust-and-boom pattern. During the recent Consciousness Revolution, fertility plunged to its lowest rate in U.S. history but rebounded sharply when that era neared its end.

Immigration to America has also followed a saecular rhythm: It tends to climb in an Awakening, peak in an Unraveling, and fall during a Crisis. The climb coincides with quickening social mobility, rising public tolerance, pluralist-minded leaders, and loosening social controls. The Unraveling-era reversal is triggered by a sudden nativist backlash (in the 1850s, 1920s, and 1990s). The subsequent fall coincides with aggressive new efforts to protect the nation—and by the time a Crisis hits, immigration is often seen as unsafe by the community and unattractive by those who might in better times wish to relocate.

Across the centuries, most immigrants to America have been children or young adults when they arrived. Thus a Nomad archetype that comes of age during an Unraveling acquires a relatively large number of immigrants. Conversely, an Artist archetype that comes of age during a High typically shows a sharp decline in its proportion of immigrants. The Silent Generation, for example, is the *least* immigrant generation in American history, whereas the 13th and (very old) Lost Generations are the two *most* immigrant generations alive today.

Social Disorder

Rates of crime and worries about social disorder rise during Awakenings, reach a cyclical peak during Unravelings, and then fall sharply during Crises.

"It seems to now become dangerous for the good people of this town to go out late at night without being sufficiently well armed," the *New York Gazette* lamented in 1749. Many have echoed this complaint during subsequent Unravelings, each of which has given birth to a mythic American image of violent crime—from roaring '49er gold towns to gangland Chicago to *New Jack City*. Each time, the crime peak has coincided with equally memorable public efforts to suppress it: The term *lynching* dates from the 1760s; *vigilante,* from the 1850s; *G-Man,* from the 1920s; and *three strikes and you're out,* from the 1990s. Ultimately, public reaction has its desired effect. By the end of the Crisis, most indicators of violence and civic disorder decline to cyclical lows, where they stay through most of the following High.

Trends in substance abuse (and related pathologies) mirror and slightly precede these crime trends. In fact, indicators of per-capita alcohol consumption follow an astoundingly regular cycle: They begin rising late in a High, peak near the end of the Awakening, and then begin a decline during the Unraveling amid growing public disapproval. The sharpest drop in alcohol consumption in American history occurred near the end of the Second

Great Awakening, when it fell from an all-time U.S. peak in 1830 (four gallons per person per year) down to less than one-third of that level by the eve of the Civil War. The second-sharpest drop occurred between 1900 and 1910, near the end of the next Awakening, followed by a further decline during Prohibition. In recent decades, per-capita alcohol consumption began rising around 1960, peaked around 1980, and has since been falling. For mind-altering drugs, from opiates to hallucinogens, the trends are similar. Remarking on this eighty-year cycle, Yale medical historian David Musto notes that "a person growing up in America in the 1890s and the 1970s would have the image of a drug-using, drug-tolerating society; a person growing up in the 1940s—and perhaps in the 2000s—would have the image of a nation that firmly rejects narcotics."

Since youth is the age in which most crime and drug experimentation occurs, these trends leave a special mark on the generation moving into adulthood. Young Prophets pioneer the dysfunctional slide while indulgent elder Heroes look on. Young Nomads, habituated to this slide as children, later suffer a reputation as *under*civilized. Young Heroes reverse the bad trends while moralizing elder Prophets applaud. Young Artists, habituated to this reversal as children, later gain a reputation as *over*civilized.

Culture

In the realm of ideas, the saeculum regularly oscillates from a focus on the spirit (in an Awakening) to a focus on the world (in a Crisis). Eminent historians have noticed this pattern—as when Edmund Morgan observed: "In the 1740s America's leading intellectuals were clergymen and thought about theology; in 1790 they were statesmen and thought about politics." Metaphorically, this is a shift from the outer to the inner. The 1930s was an outer-focused decade; its culminating public event, the 1939 World's Fair, was a celebration of science and mankind's power to shape its environment. By contrast, the 1970s was an inner-focused decade, what Marilyn Ferguson called America's "Voyage to the Interior," the first step toward a "Higher Consciousness."

As it moves along this cycle of inner and outer ideals, the saeculum reveals how a society periodically rejuvenates and replenishes its culture. A Crisis totally alters the social framework for the expression of thought and feeling. In a High, the culture optimistically if blandly reflects the public consensus about the fledgling civic order. New currents arise only on the fringe, where they subtly and unthreateningly begin to undermine the consensus. Come the Awakening, the civic order feels secure and prosperous enough to enable a new culture to erupt—conforming to Cao Yu's dictum that "art for art's sake is a philosophy of the well-fed." New norms, styles, and directions first assault and then firmly implant upon the post-Crisis order. In an Unraveling, the new culture flourishes, splinters, and diversifies. As the post-Crisis order weakens, the now regnant cultural themes begin to feel less original and more like parodies and plagiarisms. When a new Crisis hits, the culture is cleansed, censored, and harnessed to new public goals. Where art was previously allowed to disturb, now its purpose is to strengthen social resolve. Afterward, the new order creates a fresh slate upon which cultural activity can (again) serve benign and decorative yet also subversive ends —establishing the beachhead on which a fresh Awakening vision will soon land.

All forms of culture reflect these patterns. Consider musical styles over the past three saecula. With Awakenings have come spirituals and gospel songs; then ragtime and early blues; and more recently soul, rock 'n' roll, and protest folk. With Unravelings have come minstrels; then blues and jazz; and more recently country, rap, and alternative rock. With Crises have come camp songs and marches and more recently swing and big bands. With Highs have come ballads; then musicals and bandstands; and more recently crooners and vintage rock.

Consider architecture and fashion. A High produces styles that are expansive yet functional, and features romantic revivals that combine confident masculinity (and large constructions) with yielding femininity (and standardization). An Awakening returns to natural, spiritual, folk, rural, and primitive motifs, always starting with a thaw in conventional social discipline and an emergence of conscience-driven lifestyle fetishes (regarding food, dress, language, sex, and leisure). An Unraveling is the most eclectic era, with a deliberate mixing and crossing of styles, periods, and genders. A Fourth Turning brings new interest in the rational and classical, in simplicity, restraint, and decorum—while gender-related fashions begin to reformalize and return to elegance.

While every turning can lay claim to cultural innovation, some shine more in certain media than in others. In music, Awakenings have been eras of special creativity. In literature, Highs and Unravelings have usually come out ahead ever since Shakespeare and Milton. During the last three saecula, Unravelings have been eras in which American culture has exercised a profound influence over the rest of the world—perhaps because this is when it exports the fruits of its recent Awakening. Surely no decades match the 1850s and 1920s for the dazzling reputation enjoyed by American authors in Europe, and surely none matches the 1990s for the global appetite for American popular culture of every variety (books, journals, news, film, software, and electronic games).

Peter Harris closed his monograph on the "cyclical system of human life" by inquiring whether it might offer "the hope of developing a predictive social science of the future." This hope, of course, goes against the linearist grain of most Americans. We like to think that we are total masters of our destiny, exempt from all cycles, able to choose whatever we desire whenever we desire it. And, in some cases, we are. But does that freedom mean that our *desires* are unpredictable? Marketers and pollsters don't think so, which is why they spend billions learning how to anticipate when people will want to buy certain kinds of products or vote for certain kinds of candidates. The statistical reliability of these patterns doesn't nullify human freedom.

The same principle applies to the saeculum. It doesn't force anybody to do anything. It doesn't limit anybody's freedom. It merely explains when most people will want to push their own lives more in one direction than in another.

ACCIDENTS AND ANOMALIES

Even if a cycle of history does not violate free will, some troublesome questions remain: They go by the name of fortune, chaos, or accident. How can the saeculum coexist with all of history's chance events and trends? Who could have predicted the steamship and locomotive? Or the stock crash on Black Tuesday? Or the sneak attack on Pearl Harbor? Or the Watergate burglary? Or the invention of the microcomputer? How can any theory of social change predict such things?

The answer is simple: The saeculum neither predicts them nor precludes them. Yes, history always dishes out accidents. But, for the saeculum, what matters most are not the accidents themselves, but rather society's *response* to them. To understand how this works, select an accident, transport it to another decade, and try to replay its effect. Move the Watergate break-in back forty years: Would circa-1934 America have been receptive to a pair of G.I. reporters eager to bring down a Missionary president recently elected by an enormous landslide? Of course not. Or move the Great Depression forward forty years: Would circa-1974 Boomers have coped with economic bust by cheerfully donning uniforms, joining paramilitary public works programs, and building a TVA? Again, not likely.

Many experts today claim that technology has become an autonomous force, by itself determining the pace and direction of major social trends. They insist that television is turning Americans into a society of a thousand niche channels, ensconcing people in private cocoons and dissolving the glue of civic life. They say that computers are enthroning the individual and undermining social authority and that a cyberspaced information revolution is overwhelming governments, globalizing the economy, and rendering national borders irrelevant.

All these arguments have some merit. But since these trends are what we would expect in an Unraveling anyway, we should wonder: Do these new technologies really change us, or do they just give us precisely *what we want when we want it?* Forty years ago, the cathode-ray technology we call television was widely considered to be a homogenizing tool that molded national opinions around the consensus messages of Walter Cronkite and Ed Sullivan. Now TV does just the opposite. Forty years ago, the organized-transistor technology we know as the computer conjured up jackbooted images of Big Brother. The whole paradigm for this technology was a mainframe atop an information pyramid. Now computers symbolize just the opposite. Today's dominant paradigm for this technology is the decentralized personal station plugged into a participatory network.

More often than not, technology tailors itself to the national mood. When automobiles, telephones, and radios were still new on the eve of World War I, they were regarded as inventions that would individualize and fragment American life by separating rich from poor, facilitating privacy, and allowing people to travel and vacation anywhere. And so they did—for a while. Then, with the convoys and propaganda machines of World War II, these same technologies symbolized civic purpose. By the 1950s, they helped standardize a middle-class lifestyle. By the 1970s, they were attacked as symbols of dehumanizing conformity. Today these technologies have again shifted back to suit an Unraveling mood: Witness the popularity of getaway vehicles, cellular phones, and niche radio.

The linearist view of technology fails to appreciate the dangers a new turning can bring. Microsoft founder Bill Gates is now predicting that everyone will soon tune in to a world of unlimited options via high-tech portable devices. What he nowhere mentions is that by merely reversing a few circuits the same technology could empower a central authority to monitor what every individual is doing. Consider a few other technologies Americans have recently associated with individual choice—birth control and genetic testing—and imagine a similar shift for *them.* While few Americans want to revisit the forced sterilization and eugenics vogue of the 1930s, we would be imprudent to declare that a higher-tech America will never again lurch in that direction.

While technologies appear gradually, other wild cards of history appear with catastrophic suddenness—often with names and faces attached. To those who perceive time as chaos, this patternless clatter of serendipities bangs away at a pace that may seem essentially random. For the twentieth century, a chaoticist might cite the likes of Adolf Hitler, Ho Chi Minh, Lee Harvey Oswald, and Timothy McVeigh. But reflect on whether these sparks of history and the national response to them are really independent of the saeculum. What about Hitler? Americans might congratulate themselves by thinking he would have provoked our nation into war in any era—but would he do so now, during an Unraveling? Maybe not. Ho Chi Minh? Definitely not. Oswald? Though a deranged act could, of course, happen at any time, most political assassination attempts in U.S. history have in fact happened

	Wars and Turnings		
First Turnings	**Second Turnings**	**Third Turnings**	**Fourth Turnings**
Queen Anne's War War of 1812 Korean War	English Civil War King George's War Spanish-American War Vietnam War	French and Indian Wars Mexican War World War I Operation Desert Storm	Wars of the Roses Armada Triumph King Philip's War Bacon's Rebellion King William's War Glorious Revolution American Revolution American Civil War World War II

during Awakenings. McVeigh? Recall how much less consensus there was in the late 1960s about the evilness of radical bombings.

History always produces sparks. But some sparks flare and then vanish, while others touch off firestorms out of any proportion to the sparks themselves. History always produces good and bad ideas. Some quickly dissipate, while others become great inspirations or horrible scourges.

As Klingberg noticed, the history of American reactions to foreign provocations is filled with such contrasts. Compare, for example, America's involvement in World War I and World War II. Both wars were preceded by aggressive foreign acts (the sinking of the *Lusitania,* the air attack on Pearl Harbor). In one case, Congress waited two years—and patiently endured further provocations—before declaring war amid significant political opposition. In the other case, it declared war the next day, and did so with only a single dissenting vote. In one case, the war helped inflame divisive issues like Prohibition, labor violence, and sedition trials. In the other, the nation mobilized with no distractions. Both wars ended in total victory. In one case, soldiers came home to moral nagging and vice squads; in the other, to ticker-tape parades. Both wars strengthened America's influence overseas. In one case, that influence was quickly squandered; in the other, it was consolidated over the next two decades.

During a Fourth Turning, generational forces tend to funnel exogenous events toward a concerted national response. When Hitler and Tōjō launched their global aggressions, America was poised for decisive action. With Prophets in power and Heroes coming of age, the archetypal order givers were in charge and the archetypal order takers were on the battlefield. The result was maximum *cooperation* between generations. Elder Prophet leaders do not back down from confrontation. Indeed, Sam Adams, John Brown, and FDR have all been plausibly accused of helping to stage an emergency for the express purpose of galvanizing younger people.

Halfway across the saeculum, no war can escape the cross-currents of a youth-fired Awakening. During the Vietnam War, the archetypal order takers were old, the order givers young. Young Prophets challenged the moral emptiness of the institutions directing them. Meanwhile, elder Heroes did everything they could to preempt the need for sacrifice—if necessary by means of sheer affluence and technology. The result was maximum *convulsion* between generations. During the late 1960s, both generations were ill at ease in their war-waging roles, each displeasing the other with its behavior.

Every major war in Anglo-American history has been shaped by the turning during which it arose. See the chart on page 118.

High-era wars were all echoes of the prior Crisis, from the War of 1812 (reconfirming the Revolution) to the Korean War (reconfirming the global postwar order). These wars tended to be stand-offs. Patience was high, enthusiasm low.

Awakening-era wars were all enmeshed with the passions of youth— from the boozy revivalists who assaulted Louisbourg in 1745 to the "Days of Rage" student strikers in 1970. Domestic turmoil drove military decisions, making each war controversial in its time and badly remembered afterward.

Unraveling-era wars were all swiftly victorious and momentarily popular, from the capture of Quebec to the liberation of Kuwait. But they were ultimately uncathartic because they failed to alter the underlying social mood. Enthusiasm was high, patience low.

Crisis-era wars were all large, deadly, and decisive. Homefront resolve conformed to the visions of elder leaders, and the outcome totally redefined the kingdom, nation, or empire.

Does the rhythm of the saeculum make a major war unavoidable? No one knows. An Awakening does not require a war. Nor, perhaps, does a Crisis— even though every Fourth Turning since the fifteenth century has culminated in total war. History teaches only that whatever wars do happen always reflect the mood of the current turning. Wars in a Fourth Turning find the broadest possible definition and are fought to unambiguous outcomes. This suggests that, had the Japanese not attacked Pearl Harbor, the United States would have found some other provocation to declare total war against the Axis powers. Whether that would have led to a worse outcome or to a better victory (say, without the concessions at Yalta) is impossible to say. The saeculum does not guarantee good or bad outcomes.

Since the saeculum is at work to some degree throughout the modern world, however, it may well say something about *when* America is likely to encounter *what sort* of allies or adversaries abroad. Soon after the American Revolution, a fledgling U.S. republic was probably fortunate that the Old World was entirely absorbed in its own Crisis, its own age of revolution. The same could be said of the 1860s: While America fought the Civil War, Europe and Japan were busy with their own wars of nation building.

World War I, which merely grazed the United States while decimating Europe, had several key markings of an Unraveling-era conflict for all participants. It began pointlessly, ended vindictively, and—notwithstanding all the carnage—settled nothing. For America, its principal consequence was to shape (among the transatlantic Lost Generation of war-ravaged soldiers) a new cadre of totalitarian leaders that U.S. forces would have to encounter again. Adolf Hitler, Benito Mussolini, Hideki Tōjō, and Francisco Franco were all between the ages of twenty-one and thirty-one in August 1914—as were Ho Chi Minh and Mao Zedong. It was not mere happenstance that triggered World War II during an American Fourth Turning. The rise of fascism had much to do with the saeculum's grip on European history.

V-E Day, V-J Day, and the creation of the Iron Curtain were profound Fourth Turning events throughout most of the world. As such, the saeculum's timing among different societies probably became better synchronized after World War II than ever before in modern history. Today, archetypal constellations all around the world show striking similarities.

At the top are elders whom everyone still associates with civic trust and big institutions, and who have recently passed from power amid fears that their strong if bullying hand on the national tiller cannot be replaced. Peers of America's G.I. Generation, they are known as the generation of the Long March (Deng Xiaoping), of the Blitz (Margaret Thatcher), of the Resistance (François Mitterrand, Giulio Andreotti), and of the Patriotic War (Leonid Brezhnev, Yuri Andropov). Taking their place as leaders is a grown-up Air Raid generation of war children (the likes of Boris Yeltsin, Helmut Kohl, Jacques Chirac, Jean Chrétien, and Romano Prodi), postmodern experts who tout *glasnost*, diplomacy, communication, and Eurocracy while all the old alliances meander and splinter.

Behind them comes the global generation that came of age amid youth riots, the invasion of Prague, Euroterrorism, and the Chinese Cultural Revolution. In Europe, this is the fiftyish Generation of 1968 (Alexander Lebed, Lech Walesa, Gerry Adams, Prince Charles, Tony Blair, and José Maria Aznar). In Israel, this is the post-Exodus generation of Binyamin Netanyahu. Values-obsessed, resistant to Western pop culture, and drawn to angry partisans, the Boomers' foreign counterparts have been slow coming to power. The 13ers' global peers, today's youthful "90s generation" (in France, the Bof generation, as in "who cares?") are described in the media as fun-loving and rootless, environmentalist and entrepreneurial, pragmatic and market-oriented, globalist economically yet xenophobic socially, and less interested in politics than in making money.

From Reagan's special friendship with Thatcher to undergrads surfing the Web from Seattle to Minsk, the cross-national affinity within today's global generations probably ensures that Americans of leadership age will continue to encounter similar temperaments abroad for the next two or three decades, at least. This may accentuate the rhythms of the saeculum and re-inforce its quaternal timing, perhaps with stormier Crises followed by higher Highs. Then again, it may do nothing of the sort. No one knows. The saeculum is not an entirely stable social dynamic, and for a very simple reason: Total stability is beyond the reach of any human system.

After all, the saeculum cannot determine the quality, good or bad, of history's endings. These endings are all open to doubt, all subject to the good and bad acts of generations (and of the parents and leaders they produce). Because the endings are open to doubt, so too is the regularity of the saeculum's timing and its generational components. If we can imagine a catastrophe so extreme that it can put an end to all historical cycles, so too must we allow for lesser tragedies that can warp or cut short a cycle. In all probability, every modern society has experienced one or more of these anomalous cycles.

In Anglo-American history, the Civil War has been the only conspicuous anomaly. Its saeculum had normal First and Second Turnings but greatly abbreviated Third and Fourth Turnings which together spanned only twenty-two years (1844–1865), the usual length of one turning. Only thirty-two years elapsed between the climax of the Transcendental Awakening and the climax of the Civil War. Also, that saeculum produced no generation of the Hero type, making this the only time in five centuries that the cycle of four archetypes has ever been disrupted.

At first glance, the Civil War Crisis appears to have come on schedule. The climax year (1863) arrived 80 years after the prior Crisis's climax, and 81 years before the next. But before the Civil War, the saecula were longer. The three prior saecula were closer to a full century in duration (103, 101, and 94 years, respectively). It seems unlikely that generations would have compressed so suddenly to their modern length. Had the rhythms been shortening at a more gradual rate, this saeculum should have been perhaps a 90 to 95 years long. Thus the Crisis of the Civil War Saeculum probably climaxed and ended some ten or fifteen years before the rhythm of history would suggest.

Why? The three adult generations alive at the time (elder Compromisers, midlife Transcendentals, and young-adult Gilded) let their worst instincts prevail. Following the failed efforts of Henry Clay, Daniel Webster, and John Calhoun to avert war, the old Compromisers of the Buchanan era were unable to rise above empty process and moral confusion. The aging Transcendentals split into two self-contained, geographically separate societies that were unable to resist waging war (and, later, peace) with ruthless finality. The young-adult Gilded never outgrew an adventurer's lust for battle or easily bruised sense of personal honor—until the war had devastated their own lives and future prospects. Together, these three generations comprised a very dangerous constellation. They accelerated the Crisis, brought it to a swift climax, and produced the most apocalyptic result that politicians, preachers, generals, and engineers were jointly capable of achieving.

For any other Fourth Turning in American history, a historian would be hard-pressed to imagine a more uplifting finale than that which actually occurred. For the Civil War, a better outcome can easily be imagined. Yes, the

Union was preserved, the slaves emancipated, and the Industrial Revolution fully unleashed—but at enormous cost. An additional century of sectional hatred left the South impoverished and in political exile. The Reconstruction collapsed into the era of lynchings and Jim Crow, and all other social agendas (everything from labor grievances to women's rights) withered until the next Awakening, when they had to rise again virtually from scratch. The political reaction of those alive at the time indicates that many Americans did indeed attribute the unusual pain of that Fourth Turning to calamitous behavior on the part of the aging Transcendentals: The Civil War was followed in 1868 by the largest generational landslide in American electoral history, when voters tossed out the old zealots for the fortyish Gilded.

Afterward, no successor generation filled the usual Hero role of building public institutions to realize the Transcendentals' visions. The Progressives (a protected, good-child generation even before the war) were next in line and could have become this. But because the Crisis congealed so soon and so violently, this man-child generation emerged more scarred than empowered. Though many young Progressives had been combat veterans, they left postwar politics in the hands of the "bloody shirt" Gilded. Asserting little collegial confidence, Progressives developed the ameliorative persona of the Artist archetype. Filling the archetypal void, the Gilded Generation aged into a hybrid of the Nomad and Hero. After presiding over a High of unusual cultural aridity, the Gilded were later repudiated by an Awakening that vilified the old as never before or since in our history.

The Civil War anomaly demonstrates how generational constellations can become dangerous, how archetypes can play their life-cycle scripts too aggressively, and how a Crisis can end in tragedy unimaginable beforehand. It also confirms that history is *not* predetermined—that the actions people take (and political choices they make) can fundamentally alter the course of history.

The Civil War anomaly offers hope as well as warning. It was followed by turnings of the usual type. A war-torn society that suffered enormous trauma restored the equilibrating sequence of saecular turnings. Even at the height of the Crisis, civic authority laid seeds that would later blossom into vast endowments: transcontinental railroads, family-farm homesteads, and land-grant colleges. It also laid a fresh foundation for nationhood: Before Appomattox, United States had been a plural noun; afterward, it became singular. And there would be another High. Postwar generations never gave up their belief in progress, repaired the damage, and invested heavily in the future. Their hard labor, wise investment choices, and foreborne consumption were substantially responsible for the twentieth-century American economic miracle.

If learning from their example enables us to avert a catastrophe in the next Fourth Turning, our debt to the generations of Clay, Lincoln, and Grant will be very great indeed.

Overview:
Seven Cycles of
Generations and
Turnings
The Anglo-American Saeculum

The **saeculum** is a seasonal cycle of history, roughly the length of a long human life, that explains the periodic recurrence of Awakenings and Crises throughout modernity.

The **Anglo-American saeculum** dates back to the waning of the Middle Ages in the middle of the fifteenth century. There have been seven saecula:

- Late Medieval (1435–1487)
- Reformation (1487–1594)
- New World (1594–1704)
- Revolutionary (1704–1794)
- Civil War (1794–1865)
- Great Power (1865–1946)
- Millennial (1946–2026?)

America is presently in the Third Turning of the Millennial Saeculum and giving birth to the twenty-fourth generation of the post-Medieval era.

On each of the following seven page pairs, the turnings are shown on the left and the generations on the right. Each generation is shown next to the turning in which it was born. (The birth dates typically precede the turning dates by about two to four years.) For any turning, the constellation of generations includes the children shown to its right, plus the three prior generations.

The chart on page 138 displays the seasons of Anglo-American history.

Turnings

A **turning** is a social mood that changes each time the generational archetypes enter a new constellation. Each turning is roughly the length of a phase of life.

The **First Turning** is a **High**—an upbeat era of strengthening institutions and weakening individualism, when a new civic order implants and the old values regime decays. (Nomads enter elderhood; Heroes, midlife; Artists, young adulthood; and Prophets, childhood.)

The **Second Turning** is an **Awakening**—a passionate era of spiritual upheaval, when the civic order comes under attack from a new values regime. (Heroes enter elderhood; Artists, midlife; Prophets, young adulthood; and Nomads, childhood.)

The **Third Turning** is an **Unraveling**—a downcast era of strengthening individualism and weakening institutions, when the old civic order decays and the new values regime implants. (Artists enter elderhood; Prophets, midlife; Nomads, young adulthood; and Heroes, childhood.)

The **Fourth Turning** is a **Crisis**—a decisive era of secular upheaval, when the values regime propels the replacement of the old civic order with a new one. (Prophets enter elderhood; Nomads, midlife; Heroes, young adulthood; and Artists, childhood.)

Late Medieval Half Saeculum: Turnings

- The **Retreat from France** (*Third Turning, 1435–1459*) was an era of dynastic decline and civil disorder. In 1435, not long after Joan of Arc's execution, the English withdrew from Paris for the last time. In the 1440s, they were pushed out of France on all fronts. Thus ended the Hundred Years' War. Meanwhile, the weak rule of young Henry VI eroded central authority in England. By the 1450s, noble houses flouted the law, vied for power, and engaged in private wars with impunity.

  Arthurians entering childhood

- The **Wars of the Roses** (*Fourth Turning, 1459–1487*) began with an irrevocable break between the ruling houses of Lancaster and York. After a bloody civil war, Yorkist kings (Edward IV, Edward V, Richard III) mostly prevailed in reigns that were punctuated with invasions and rebellions. At Bosworth Field (in 1485), Henry Tudor defeated Richard III and crowned himself Henry VII, founder of a new royal dynasty. Two years later he defeated a pretender at the Battle of Stoke, which won him the enduring confidence of his subjects.

  Arthurians entering young adulthood
  Humanists entering childhood

Generations

A **generation** is composed of people whose common location in history lends them a collective persona. The span of one generation is roughly the length of a phase of life. Generations come in four archetypes, always in the same order, whose phase-of-life positions comprise a constellation.

The **Prophet** archetype is born in a High and enters young adulthood in an Awakening, midlife in an Unraveling, and elderhood in a Crisis.

The **Nomad** archetype is born in an Awakening and enters young adulthood in an Unraveling, midlife in a Crisis, and elderhood in a High.

The **Hero** archetype is born in an Unraveling and enters young adulthood in a Crisis, midlife in a High, and elderhood in an Awakening.

The **Artist** archetype is born in a Crisis and enters young adulthood in a High, midlife in an Awakening, and elderhood in an Unraveling.

During a Fourth Turning, the constellation contains all four archetypes born in the current saeculum. During the first three turnings, the constellation includes one or more archetypes born in the prior saeculum.

Late Medieval Half Saeculum: Generations

The **Arthurian Generation** (*Hero, born 1433–1460*) grew up during England's demoralizing Retreat from France, an era of a rising pessimism and civil disorder. Raised amid elder hopes that they might save the kingdom, the Arthurians came of age with a civil war that did not end until twenty-eight-year-old Henry Tudor established his new monarchy. Entering midlife, they closed ranks around a manly new era of prosperity (led by wool exports), social discipline (led by busy local magistrates), and strong central government (led by the new Star Chamber). Entering old age, they enclosed fields, printed books, and planned voyages to the New World, securing a reputation for chivalric teamwork immortalized in *Morte D'Arthur*, their generation's treasured epic. (*English: King Edward IV, King Henry VII, John Cabot, William Grocyn, John de Vere; European: Leonardo da Vinci, Christopher Columbus*)

The **Humanist Generation** (*Artist, born 1461–1482*) passed a sheltered childhood during a bloody civil war, many of the elite attending safer schools abroad. Coming of age, they understood their mission was to embellish the new order. As young adults, they became the new humanists—Greek tutors, international scholars, ballad-writing poets, law-trained prelates, and literate merchants and yeomen. Hit during midlife by the Reformation, they adjusted awkwardly. Some wrapped themselves in Wolseyan opulence and refused to pay attention. Others waffled. A few (like the famed Man for All Seasons) exquisitely satirized the reigning hypocrisy, stood firm for the old order, and paid the ultimate price. In old age, they were startled by a ruthless new radicalism that overwhelmed their own gracious refinements. (*English: Thomas More, Thomas Linacre, John Colet, Cardinal Wolsey, Stephen Gardiner; European: Michelangelo, Copernicus*)

Turnings

- The **Tudor Renaissance** (*First Turning, 1487–1517*) was an era of political and social consolidation. To popular acclaim, King Henry VII crushed challenges to his new dynasty and strengthened royal writs and commissions. On this foundation of central authority, births rose, commerce thrived, and construction boomed. The new sumptuous worldliness was best reflected in the palaces of Cardinal Wolsey. The era closed in a mood of cultural sterility.
  Arthurians entering midlife
  Humanists entering young adulthood
  Reformation entering childhood

- The **Protestant Reformation** (*Second Turning, 1517–1542*) began in Germany with Martin Luther's famous protest and spread swiftly to England. The enthusiasm peaked (in the mid-1530s) with King Henry VIII's break with the papacy, William Tyndale's Bible, popular reform movements, and Parliament's confiscation of vast Church estates. It ended when reformers tired or (like Thomas Cromwell) were executed and when foreign wars with Scotland and France diverted the popular imagination.
  Arthurians entering elderhood
  Humanists entering midlife
  Reformation entering young adulthood
  Reprisal entering childhood

- **Intolerance and Martyrdom** (*Third Turning, 1542–1569*) was an era of social fragmentation, civil rebellion, and deadly political intrigue. Through the reigns of Edward VI and Queen Mary, the throne tacked violently over the issue of religion. The economy careened in a boom-bust cycle, with royal debasements fueling unprecedented inflation. When the era closed, early in the reign of Queen Elizabeth, a disillusioned nation looked anxiously at the future.
  Humanists entering elderhood
  Reformation entering midlife
  Reprisal entering young adulthood
  Elizabethans entering childhood

- The **Armada Crisis** (*Fourth Turning, 1569–1594*) began when the powerful duke of Norfolk was linked to a Spanish plot against the English throne, a discovery that galvanized newly Protestant England against the global threat of the Catholic Hapsburgs. A crescendo of surrogate wars and privateering culminated in England's miraculous victory over the Spanish Armada invasion (in 1588). The mood of emergency relaxed after the successful resistance of Holland and the breaking of Spanish control over France.
  Reformation entering elderhood
  Reprisal entering midlife
  Elizabethans entering young adulthood
  Parliamentarians entering childhood

Generations

The **Reformation Generation** (*Prophet, born 1483–1511*) began life surrounded by the advantages of order and affluence. They rebelled as youth, prompting first the colleges (in the 1520s) and then an egocentric young king and his Parliament (in the 1530s) to join in a religious upheaval. By the time passions cooled, the Catholic Church was liquidated, the clergy was shattered, the masses were armed with Bibles, and the Anglican faith was unshackled from Rome. In midlife, their insolence hardened into severe principle. With women figuring prominently, they became commonwealth moralists, family of love mystics, Calvinist (or Romist) proselytizers, and unrepentant martyrs burned or hanged for their heresies. Deep in elderhood, many lived to see the nation gravitate to the Puritan Settlement they had worked so long to inspire. (*English: King Henry VIII, Thomas Cromwell, John Knox, Elizabeth Barton, William Tyndale, Nicholas Ridley; European: Martin Luther, John Calvin*)

The **Reprisal Generation** (*Nomad, born 1512–1540*) spent childhood amid religious frenzy and a widespread erosion of social authority and came of age in a cynical, post-Awakening era of cutthroat politics and roller-coaster markets. They built a gritty young-adult reputation as swaggering merchants, mercenaries, spies, and sea-dog privateers who pulled off stunning reprisals through luck and pluck. Entering midlife just as their queen (a shrewd orphan herself) squared off with Imperial Spain, these daredevil adventurers knew how to "singe King Philip's beard" while stealing his gold. Making simple appeals to national honor, they aged into worldly wise elder stewards of English solidarity whose sacrifices made possible a glorious new era. (*English: Queen Elizabeth I, Francis Drake, John Hawkins, Thomas Gresham, Lord Burghley, Francis Walsingham; European: Catherine de' Medici, Michel de Montaigne*)

The **Elizabethan Generation** (*Hero, born 1541–1565*) benefited as children from an explosive growth in academies intended to mold them into perfect paragons of civic achievement and teamwork. Coming of age with the great wars against Spain, they soldiered with dazzling valor and courtly show. During their Gloriana midlife, they regulated commerce, explored overseas empires, built stately country houses, pursued new science, and wrote poetry that celebrated an orderly universe. Historian Anthony Esler explains that "ambitious projects of breath-taking scope and grandeur" distinguished these "overreachers" from the "burned-out generation" before them. In old age, many lived to see their hearty and expansive Merrie England repudiated by prickly conscienced sons and daughters. (*English: William Shakespeare, Walter Raleigh, Philip Sidney, Francis Vere, Francis Bacon, Edward Coke; European: Miguel de Cervantes, Galileo Galilei*)

The **Parliamentary Generation** (*Artist, born 1566–1587*) passed through childhood in an era of foreign threats and war. Coming of age with the dawn of imperial peace and prosperity, they built impeccable credentials in law, scholarship, religion, and arts and crafts guilds. In country houses, they swelled the influence of the newly literate gentry. At Court, they became apologists for the byzantine policies of James I. In Parliament, they promoted politeness and insisted on precedent, due process, and full disclosure. In midlife, their incrementalist ethos was shaken by younger calls for radical reform. Their Arminians argued yet resisted; their Parliamentarians applauded yet hedged. Eloquently indecisive in speech and sermon, they watched England veer toward a spiral of hysteria and violence they felt powerless to stop. (*English: King James I, John Donne, William Laud, Inigo Jones, Lord Buckingham, John Selden; European: Claudio Monteverdi, Peter Paul Rubens*)

Turnings

- **Merrie England** (*First Turning, 1594–1621*) was an age of optimism and prosperity, full of dreams of empire yet tempered by a wariness of enemies abroad. For the arts, this was the true English Renaissance, and for literature, the glorious Age of Shakespeare. After succeeding Elizabeth in 1601, James I encouraged learning, exploration, and trade. His elaborately polite relations with the Commons began to wear thin late in the second decade of his reign.

  Reprisals entering elderhood
  Elizabethans entering midlife
  Parliamentarians entering young adulthood
  Puritans entering childhood

- The **Puritan Awakening** (*Second Turning, 1621–1649*) began with Parliament's Great Protestation. Upon the accession of James's son, the reformist urge turned radical and gained popular momentum. Seeking religious exile, John Winthrop led a saving remnant of true believers to America. In England, this Puritan enthusiasm led to the Long Parliament (in 1640), civil war, and the execution of Charles I (in 1649). In the new wilderness colonies, the experimental fervor receded, leaving isolated settlements seeking an enforceable moral orthodoxy.

  Elizabethans entering elderhood
  Parliamentarians entering midlife
  Puritans entering young adulthood
  Cavaliers entering childhood

- **Reaction and Restoration** (*Third Turning, 1649–1675*) was an era of drift and fierce controversy over the ideals of the original New World immigrants. Disoriented by fast-shifting events (Cromwell's Protectorate in the 1650s, the Stuart Restoration in 1660, a war with Holland in which what is now New York was captured in 1664), each colony fended for itself and cut its own deal with England. The era ended with the authority of colonial self-government ebbing and worries about the future rising.

  Parliamentarians entering elderhood
  Puritans entering midlife
  Cavaliers entering young adulthood
  Glorious entering childhood

- The colonial **Glorious Revolution** (*Fourth Turning, 1675–1704*) began with civil upheavals and catastrophic Indian Wars—soon followed by parliamentary efforts to reassert direct royal control over the colonies. The ensuing resistance culminated in 1689 with colonial rebellions that were triggered by news of the Glorious Revolution in England on behalf of William of Orange. A further decade of war against Canadian New France ended with Britain's global triumph, vigorous institutions of colonial self-rule, and a new era of peace with native peoples.

  Puritans entering elderhood
  Cavaliers entering midlife
  Glorious entering young adulthood
  Enlighteners entering childhood

New World Saeculum

Generations

The **Puritan Generation** (*Prophet, born 1588–1617*) basked as children in the post-Armada peace. Overcome by spiritual conversions, many came of age zealously denouncing the spiritual emptiness of their elders' Jacobean achievements. While some later led England through a civil war that culminated in the beheading of King Charles I, others were called by God to lead a Great Migration to America. These young-adult Puritans established church-centered towns from Long Island to Maine. In midlife, fearing the corrupting influence of the Old World on their own unconverted children, they turned from the law of love to the love of law. Their moral authority remained unchallenged through old age, as they provided the elder diehards of the great Indian Wars and the Glorious Revolution. (*Colonial: Anne Hutchinson, John Winthrop, Simon Bradstreet, Roger Williams, John Harvard, William Berkeley; Foreign: Oliver Cromwell, René Descartes*)

The **Cavalier Generation** (*Nomad, born 1618–1647*) grew up in an era of religious upheaval and family collapse. In New England, they were the isolated offspring of spiritual zealots; in the Chesapeake colonies, they were the indentured English youth whose parents' death or poverty consigned them to disease-ridden ships bound for the tobacco fields. Notoriously violent and uneducated, they came of age taking big risks—many dying young, others becoming the most renowned merchants, trappers, mercenaries, rebels, and pirates of their century. In midlife, they struggled bravely against threats to their communities from Old World tyrants and New World native peoples. As politically tainted elders, they seldom protested the vendettas (such as the Salem witchcraft frenzy) that mainly targeted their own peers. (*Colonial: Increase Mather, William Stoughton, Benjamin Church, Metacomet, William Kidd, Nathaniel Bacon; Foreign: King Louis XIV, John Locke*)

The **Glorious Generation** (*Hero, born 1648–1673*) entered a protected childhood of tax-supported schools and new laws discouraging the "kidnapping" of young servants. After proving their valor in the Indian Wars and triumphing in the Glorious Revolution, they were rewarded with electoral office at a young age. As young adults, they took pride in the growing political, commercial, and scientific achievements of England and viewed the passion and poverty of their parents as embarrassments to be overcome. In midlife, they designed insurance, paper money, and public works and (in the South) founded a stable slave-owning oligarchy. As worldly elders, they received the colonies' first war-service pensions and land grants—while taking offense at the spiritual zeal of youth. (*Colonial: Cotton Mather, John Wise, William Randolph, Robert "King" Carter, Hannah Dustin, Peter Schuyler; Foreign: William of Orange, Czar Peter the Great*)

The **Enlightenment Generation** (*Artist, born 1674–1700*) grew up as protected children when families were close, youth risk discouraged, and good educations and well-connected marriages highly prized. Coming of age, their rising elite eased into a genteel Williamsburg-style town-and-planter prosperity. As young adults, this inheritor generation provided the colonies' first large cadre of credentialed professionals, political managers, and plantation administrators. In midlife, their Walpolean leadership style betrayed a fascination with youth, whose spiritual zeal they both welcomed and feared. Many elders lived to witness (in the Stamp Act furor) a repudiation of the tea-drinking politeness and rococo complexity on which their provincial world rested. (*Colonial: William Shirley, John Peter Zenger, Alexander Spotswood, Samuel Johnson, William Byrd II, Elisha Cooke Jr.; Foreign: George Frideric Handel, Voltaire*)

Turnings

- The **Augustan Age of Empire** (*First Turning, 1704–1727*) witnessed the first confident flowering of provincial civilization—with booming trade, rising living standards, recognizable (northern) urban centers, and massive (southern) imports of African slaves. Lauding social discipline, Americans took pride in the growing might of Britain's empire. Socially, this was the periwigged apogee of colonial politesse; culturally, it was an age of credentials, wit, and Royal Society rationalism.
    Cavaliers entering elderhood
    Glorious entering midlife
    Enlighteners entering young adulthood
    Awakeners entering childhood

- The **Great Awakening** (*Second Turning, 1727–1746*) began as a spiritual revival in the Connecticut Valley and reached a hysterical peak in the northern colonies (in 1741) with the preachings of George Whitefield and the tracts of Jonathan Edwards. The enthusiasm split towns and colonial assemblies, shattered the old light establishment, and pitted young believers in faith against elder defenders of works. After bursting polite conventions and lingering Old World social barriers, the enthusiasm receded during King George's War.
    Glorious entering elderhood
    Enlighteners entering midlife
    Awakeners entering young adulthood
    Liberty entering childhood

- The **French and Indian Wars** (*Third Turning, 1746–1773*) was an era of unprecedented economic and geographic mobility. Swept into a final war against New France in the 1750s, the colonists hardly celebrated Britain's total victory (in 1760) before renewing thunderous debates over how to salvage civic virtue from growing debt, cynicism, and wildness. With colonial leadership at a low ebb, popular fears soon targeted the alleged corruption of the English Parliament and Empire.
    Enlighteners entering elderhood
    Awakeners entering midlife
    Liberty entering young adulthood
    Republicans entering childhood

- The **American Revolution** (*Fourth Turning, 1773–1794*) began when Parliament's response to the Boston Tea Party ignited a colonial tinderbox, leading directly to the first Continental Congress, the battle of Concord, and the Declaration of Independence. The war climaxed with the colonial triumph at Yorktown (in 1781). Seven years later, the new states ratified a nation-forging Constitution. The crisis mood eased once President Washington weathered the Jacobins, put down the Whisky Rebels, and settled on a final treaty with England.
    Awakeners entering elderhood
    Liberty entering midlife
    Republicans entering young adulthood
    Compromisers entering childhood

Generations

The **Awakening Generation** (*Prophet, born 1701–1723*) arrived as the first colonial generation to consist mostly of the offspring of native-born parents and the first to grow up taking peace and prosperity for granted. Coming of age, they attacked their elders' moral complacency in a spiritual firestorm. By the 1750s, after breaking the social order of their parents and rendering the colonies ungovernable, they pushed the colonies toward pessimism—yet also toward civic renewal. They became eighteenth-century America's most eminent generation of educators, philosophers, clergymen, and abolitionists. In old age, they provided the Revolution with its dire sense of moral urgency, dominating the colonial pulpits and governorships until independence was declared. (*American: Jonathan Edwards, Benjamin Franklin, Sam Adams, Eliza Pinckney, John Woolman, Crispus Attucks; Foreign: Jean Jacques Rousseau, Empress Maria Theresa*)

The **Liberty Generation** (*Nomad, born 1724–1741*) struggled for parental comfort in an era of Hogarthian child neglect. Coming of age with an economic bust, land pressure, and rising immigration, they cut a swath of crime and disorder. As young adults, they joined the roughhewn Green Mountain, Paxton, and Liberty Boys and became the unthanked footsoldiers and daring privateers of the French and Indian Wars. Proclaiming "Don't tread on me" and "Give me liberty or give me death," they entered midlife supplying the bravest patriots (including most signers of the Declaration of Independence) as well as the worst traitors of the Revolution. As elders, they led with caution, suspicious of grand causes, while their Anti-Federalists restrained the nationalizing energy of younger people. (*American: George Washington, John Adams, Francis Marion, Daniel Boone, Ethan Allen, Patrick Henry; Foreign: King George III, Empress Catherine the Great*)

The **Republican Generation** (*Hero, born 1742–1766*) grew up as the precious object of adult protection during an era of rising crime and social disorder. They came of age highly regarded for their secular optimism and spirit of cooperation. As young adults, they achieved glory as soldiers, brilliance as scientists, order as civic planners, and epic success as statecrafters. Trusted by elders and aware of their own historic role, they burst into politics at a young age. They dominated the campaign to ratify the Constitution and filled all the early national cabinet posts. In midlife, they built canals and acquired territories, while their orderly Federalist and rational Republican leaders made America a "workshop of liberty." As elders, they chafed at passionate youths bent on repudiating much of what they had built. (*American: Thomas Jefferson, James Madison, John Paul Jones, Abigail Adams, Kunta Kinte, Robert Fulton; Foreign: Maximilien Robespierre, Wolfgang Amadeus Mozart*)

The **Compromise Generation** (*Artist, born 1767–1791*) grew up (recalled Henry Clay) "rocked in the cradle of the Revolution" as they watched brave adults struggle and triumph. Compliantly coming of age, they offered a new erudition, expertise, and romantic sensibility to their heroic elders' Age of Improvement. As young adults, they became what historian Matthew Crenson calls "the administrative founding fathers" and soldiered a Second War for Independence whose glory could never compare with the first. In midlife, they mentored populist movements, fretted over slavery and Indian removal, and presided over Great Compromises that reflected their irresolution. As elders, they feared that their "postheroic" mission had failed and that the United States might not outlive them. (*American: Andrew Jackson, Henry Clay, Daniel Webster, Washington Irving, Dolley Madison, Tecumseh; Foreign: Napoleon Bonaparte, Ludwig van Beethoven*)

Revolutionary Saeculum

Turnings

- The **Era of Good Feelings** (*First Turning, 1794–1822*) witnessed what Joel Barlow called *The Conquest of Canaan*, an era of epical social harmony and empire building. Vast new territories were mapped and settled. Canals, steamboats, and turnpikes pushed back the wilderness. Even a blundering war (of 1812) ended up unifying the nation. Civil disorder was rare—as was spiritual curiosity in an era (wrote Emerson) "able to produce not a book . . . or a thought worth noticing."
    Liberty entering elderhood
    Republicans entering midlife
    Compromisers entering young adulthood
    Transcendentals entering childhood

- The **Transcendental Awakening** (*Second Turning, 1822–1844*) began with Charles Finney's evangelicalism and Denmark Vesey's slave revolt. Soon merging with Jacksonian populism, it peaked (in 1831) with Nat Turner's Rebellion, the founding of shrill abolitionist societies, and the rise of splinter political parties. After spawning a floodtide of romantic idealism—including feminism, new prophetic religions, food fads, and utopian communes—the mood gentrified in the early 1840s into a credo of self-help, moral uplift, and Manifest Destiny.
    Republicans entering elderhood
    Compromisers entering midlife
    Transcendentals entering young adulthood
    Gilded entering childhood

- The **Mexican War and Sectionalism** (*Third Turning, 1844–1860*) was an era of "almighty dollar" commercialism, western gold fever, Whitmanesque self-worship, and nativist slogans against Mexicans and Irish. Beneath trimming national leaders, rising tempers launched competing moral crusades. By the late 1850s—from Kansas to Harpers Ferry, Dred Scott to the Underground Railroad—visions of the nation's future were separating into two irreconcilable regional loyalties.
    Compromisers entering elderhood
    Transcendentals entering midlife
    Gilded entering young adulthood
    Progressives entering childhood

- The **Civil War** (*Fourth Turning, 1860–1865*) began with a presidential election that many southerners interpreted as an invitation to secede. The attack on Fort Sumter triggered the most violent conflict ever fought on New World soil. The war reached its climax in the Emancipation Proclamation and Battle of Gettysburg (in 1863). Two years later, the Confederacy was beaten into bloody submission and Lincoln was assassinated—a grim end to a crusade many had hoped would "trample out the vintage where the grapes of wrath are stored."
    The first Transcendentals entering elderhood
    The first Gilded entering midlife
    The first Progressives entering young adulthood
    The first Missionaries entering childhood

Generations

The **Transcendental Generation** (*Prophet, born 1792–1821*), the proud offspring of a secure new nation, were the first American children to be portraited (and named at birth) as individuals. Coming of age as evangelists, reformers, and campus rioters, they triggered a spiritual paroxysm across the nation. As crusading young adults, their divergent inner visions exacerbated sectional divisions. Entering midlife, graying abolitionists and Southrons spurned compromise and led the nation into the Civil War, their zeal fired by the moral pronouncements of an aging clergy. The victors achieved emancipation but were blocked from imposing as punishing a peace as the old radicals wished. In elderhood, their feminists and poets (many with flowing beards) became unyielding expositors of truth and justice. (*American: Abraham Lincoln, Jefferson Davis, Ralph Waldo Emerson, Susan B. Anthony, Nat Turner, William Lloyd Garrison; Foreign: Queen Victoria, Karl Marx*)

The **Gilded Generation** (*Nomad, born 1822–1842*) lived a hardscrabble childhood around parents distracted by spiritual upheavals. They came of age amid rising national tempers, torrential immigration, commercialism, Know Nothing politics, and declining college enrollments. As young adults, many pursued fortunes in frontier boomtowns or as fledgling "robber barons." Their Lincoln Shouters and Johnny Rebs rode eagerly into a Civil War that left them decimated, Confederates especially. Having learned to detest moral zealotry, their midlife presidents and industrialists put their stock in Darwinian economics, Boss Tweed politics, Victorian prudery, and Carnegie's Law of Competition. As elders, they landed on the "industrial scrap heap" of an urbanizing economy that was harsh to most old people. (*American: Ulysses Grant, Mark Twain, John D. Rockefeller, Louisa May Alcott, William James, Sitting Bull; Foreign: Lewis Carroll, Maximilian*)

The Civil War Saeculum had no *Hero* archetype.

The **Progressive Generation** (*Artist, born 1843–1859*) spent childhood shell shocked by sectionalism and war. Overawed by older "bloody-shirt" veterans, they came of age cautiously, pursuing refinement and expertise more than power. In the shadow of Reconstruction, they earned their reputation as well-behaved professors and lawyers, calibrators and specialists, civil servants and administrators. In midlife, their mild commitment to social melioration was whipsawed by the passions of youth. They matured into America's genteel yet juvenating Rough Riders in the era of Freud's "talking cure" and late-Victorian sentimentality. After busting trusts and achieving progressive procedural reforms, their elders continued to urge tolerance on less conciliatory juniors. (*American: Theodore Roosevelt, Woodrow Wilson, Henry James, Booker T. Washington, Katherine Lee Bates, Clarence Darrow; Foreign: Oscar Wilde, Sigmund Freud*)

Turnings

■ The **Reconstruction and Gilded Age** (*First Turning, 1865–1886*) saw old crusaders pushed aside while, notes Van Wyck Brooks, war veterans who "might have been writers in the days of *The Dial* were seeking their fortunes in railroads, mines, and oil wells." Savings rates climbed, mass production roared, mechanical and political machines hummed, real wages surged, and middle-class families prospered in an age of pragmatism that vaunted "truth's cash value."

> *Transcendentals entering elderhood*
> *Gilded entering midlife*
> *Progressives entering young adulthood*
> *Missionaries entering childhood*

■ The **Third Great Awakening** (*Second Turning, 1886–1908*), began with the Haymarket Riot and the student missionary movement, rose with agrarian protest and labor violence, and climaxed in Bryan's revivalist candidacy (in 1896). Gilded Age realism came under harsh attack from trust-blasting muckrakers, Billy Sunday evangelicals, "new woman" feminists, and chautauqua dreamers. After radicalizing and splitting the Progressive movement, the passion cooled when William Howard Taft succeeded Teddy Roosevelt in the White House.

> *Gilded entering elderhood*
> *Progressives entering midlife*
> *Missionaries entering young adulthood*
> *Lost entering childhood*

■ **World War I and Prohibition** (*Third Turning, 1908–1929*) was an era of rapid technological change, egocentric celebrities, widening class divisions, crumbling trusts and unions, and expert—but weak—political leadership. Following World War I, the public immersed itself in moral crusades (League of Nations, Prohibition, women's suffrage). By the 1920s, a fun-filled financial boom was framed by pessimistic debates over drugs, sex, money, cynicism, violence, immigration, and the family.

> *Progressives entering elderhood*
> *Missionaries entering midlife*
> *Lost entering young adulthood*
> *G.I.s entering childhood*

■ The **Great Depression and World War II** (*Fourth Turning, 1929–1946*) began suddenly with the Black Tuesday stock-market crash. After a three-year economic free fall, the Great Depression triggered the New Deal revolution, a vast expansion of government, and hopes for a renewal of national community. After Pearl Harbor, America planned, mobilized, and produced for war on a scale that made possible the massive D-Day invasion (in 1944). Two years later, the crisis mood eased with America's surprisingly trouble-free demobilization.

> *Missionaries entering elderhood*
> *Lost entering midlife*
> *G.I.s entering young adulthood*
> *Silent entering childhood*

Generations

The **Missionary Generation** (*Prophet, born 1860–1882*) became the indulged home-and-hearth children of the post–Civil War era. They came of age as labor anarchists, campus rioters, and ambitious first graduates of black and women's colleges. Their young adults pursued rural populism, settlement house work, missionary crusades, muckrake journalism, and women's suffrage. In midlife, their Decency brigades and fundamentalists imposed Prohibition, cracked down on immigration, and organized vice squads. In the 1930s and 1940s, their elder elite became the Wise Old Men who enacted a New Deal (and Social Security) for the benefit of youth, led the global war against fascism, and reaffirmed America's highest ideals during a transformative era in world history. (*American: Franklin Roosevelt, W .E. B Du Bois, William Jennings Bryan, Upton Sinclair, Jane Addams, Douglas MacArthur; Foreign: Winston Churchill, V. I. Lenin*)

The **Lost Generation** (*Nomad, born 1883–1900*) grew up amid urban blight, unregulated drug use, child sweat shops, and massive immigration. Their independent, streetwise attitude lent them a bad-kid reputation. After coming of age as flaming youth, doughboys, and flappers, they were alienated by a war whose homecoming turned sour. Their young-adult novelists, barnstormers, gangsters, sports stars, and film celebrities gave the roar to the 1920s. The Great Depression hit them in midlife, at the peak of their careers. The buck stopped with their pugnacious battlefield and home-front managers of a hot war and their frugal and straight-talking leaders of a new cold one. As elders, they paid high tax rates to support their world-conquering juniors, while asking little for themselves. (*American: Harry Truman, Irving Berlin, George Patton, Mae West, F. Scott Fitzgerald, Louis Armstrong: Foreign: Adolf Hitler, Mao Zedong*)

The **G.I. Generation** (*Hero, born 1901–1924*) developed a special and good-kid reputation as the beneficiaries of new playgrounds, scouting clubs, vitamins, and child-labor restrictions. They came of age with the sharpest rise in schooling ever recorded. As young adults, their uniformed corps patiently endured depression and heroically conquered foreign enemies. In a midlife subsidized by the G.I. Bill, they built gleaming suburbs, invented miracle vaccines, plugged missile gaps, and launched moon rockets. Their unprecedented grip on the presidency began with a New Frontier, a Great Society, and Model Cities, but wore down through Vietnam, Watergate, deficits, and problems with "the vision thing." As senior citizens, they safeguarded their own "entitlements" but had little influence over culture and values. (*American: John Kennedy, Ronald Reagan, Walt Disney, Judy Garland, John Wayne, Walter Cronkite; Foreign: Willy Brandt, Leonid Brezhnev*)

The **Silent Generation** (*Artist, born 1925–1942*) grew up as the suffocated children of war and depression. They came of age just too late to be war heroes and just too early to be youthful free spirits. Instead, this early marrying Lonely Crowd became the risk-averse technicians and professionals as well as the sensitive rock 'n' rollers and civil rights advocates of a post-Crisis era in which conformity seemed to be a sure ticket to success. Midlife was an anxious "passage" for a generation torn between stolid elders and passionate juniors. Their surge to power coincided with fragmenting families, cultural diversity, institutional complexity, and prolific litigation. They are entering elderhood with unprecedented affluence, a hip style, and a reputation for indecision. (*American: Colin Powell, Walter Mondale, Woody Allen, Martin Luther King Jr., Sandra Day O'Connor, Elvis Presley; Foreign: Anne Frank, Mikhail Gorbachev*)

Turnings

- The **American High** (*First Turning, 1946–1964*) witnessed America's ascendancy as a global superpower. Social movements stalled. The middle class grew and prospered. Churches buttressed government. Huge peacetime defense budgets were uncontroversial. Mass tastes thrived atop a collectivist infrastructure of suburbs, interstates, and regulated communication. Declaring an "end to ideology," respected authorities presided over a bland, modernist, and spirit-dead culture.

  Lost entering elderhood
  G.I.s entering midlife
  Silent entering young adulthood
  Boomers entering childhood

- The **Consciousness Revolution** (*Second Turning, 1964–1984*), which began with urban riots and campus fury, swelled alongside Vietnam War protests and a rebellious counter-culture. It gave rise to feminist, environmental, and black power movements and to a steep rise in violent crime and family breakup. After the fury peaked with Watergate (in 1974), passions turned inward toward New Age lifestyles and spiritual rebirth. The mood expired during Reagan's upbeat reelection campaign, as onetime hippies reached their yuppie chrysalis.

  G.I.s entering elderhood
  Silent entering midlife
  Boomers entering young adulthood
  13ers entering childhood

- The **Culture Wars** (*Third Turning, 1984–2005?*), which opened with triumphant Morning in America individualism, has thus far drifted toward pessimism. Personal confidence remains high, and few national problems demand immediate action. But the public reflects darkly on growing violence and incivility, widening inequality, pervasive distrust of institutions and leaders, and a debased popular culture. People fear that the national consensus is splitting into competing values camps.

  Silent entering elderhood
  Boomers entering midlife
  13ers entering young adulthood
  Millennials entering childhood

- The **Millennial Crisis**, the *Fourth Turning* of the Millennial Saeculum has yet to arrive. Its projected generational constellation:

  Boomers entering elderhood
  13ers entering midlife
  Millennials entering young adulthood
  New Silent entering childhood

Generations

The **Boom Generation** (*Prophet, born 1943–1960*) basked as children in Dr. Spock permissiveness, suburban conformism, *Sputnik*-era schooling, Beaver Cleaver friendliness, and *Father Knows Best* family order. From the Summer of Love to the Days of Rage, they came of age rebelling against worldly blueprints of their parents. As their flower child, Black Panther, Weathermen, and "Jesus freak" fringes proclaimed themselves arbiters of public morals, youth pathologies worsened—and SAT scores began a seventeen-year slide. In the early 1980s, many young adults became self-absorbed "yuppies" with mainstream careers but perfectionist lifestyles. Entering midlife (and national power), they are trumpeting values, touting a "politics of meaning," and waging scorched-earth Culture Wars. (*American: Bill Clinton, Newt Gingrich, Steven Spielberg, Candice Bergen, Spike Lee, Bill Gates; Foreign: Tony Blair, Binyamin Netanyahu*)

The **13th Generation** (*Nomad, born 1961–1981*) survived a hurried childhood of divorce, latchkeys, open classrooms, devil-child movies, and a shift from G to R ratings. They came of age curtailing the earlier rise in youth crime and fall in test scores—yet heard themselves denounced as so wild and stupid as to put *The Nation at Risk*. As young adults, maneuvering through a sexual battlescape of AIDS and blighted courtship rituals, they date and marry cautiously. In jobs, they embrace risk and prefer free agency over loyal corporatism. From grunge to hip-hop, their splintery culture reveals a hardened edge. Politically, they lean toward pragmatism and nonaffiliation and would rather volunteer than vote. Widely criticized as Xers or slackers, they inhabit a *Reality Bites* economy of declining young-adult living standards. (*American: Tom Cruise, Jodie Foster, Michael Dell, Deion Sanders, Winona Ryder, Quentin Tarantino; Foreign: Princess Di, Alanis Morissette*)

The **Millennial Generation** (*Hero?, born 1982–?*) first arrived when Baby on Board signs appeared. As abortion and divorce rates ebbed, the popular culture began stigmatizing hands-off parental styles and recasting babies as special. Child abuse and child safety became hot topics, while books teaching virtues and values became best-sellers. Today, politicians define adult issues (from tax cuts to deficits) in terms of their effects on children. Hollywood is replacing cinematic child devils with child angels, and cable TV and the Internet are cordoning off child-friendly havens. While educators speak of standards and cooperative learning, school uniforms are surging in popularity. With adults viewing children more positively, U.S. test scores are faring better in international comparisons. (*American: Jessica McClure, the Olsen twins, Baby Richard, Elisa Lopez, Dooney Waters, Jessica Dubroff; Foreign: Anna Paquin, Prince William*)

The Millennial Saeculum's *Artist* archetype has yet to be born.

Turnings in the Anglo-American Saeculum

	First Turning (High)	Second Turning (Awakening)	Third Turning (Unraveling)	Fourth Turning (Crisis)
Generation Entering:				
ELDERHOOD	*Nomad*	*Hero*	*Artist*	*Prophet*
MIDLIFE	*Hero*	*Artist*	*Prophet*	*Nomad*
YOUNG ADULTHOOD	*Artist*	*Prophet*	*Nomad*	*Hero*
CHILDHOOD	*Prophet*	*Nomad*	*Hero*	*Artist*
LATE MEDIEVAL SAECULUM			Retreat from France *(1435–1459)*	Wars of the Roses *(1459–1487)*
REFORMATION SAECULUM	Tudor Renaissance *(1487–1517)*	Protestant Reformation *(1517–1542)*	Intolerance and Martyrdom *(1542–1569)*	Armada Crisis *(1569–1594)*
NEW WORLD SAECULUM	Merrie England *(1594–1621)*	Puritan Awakening *(1621–1649)*	Reaction and Restoration *(1649–1675)*	Glorious Revolution *(1675–1704)*
REVOLUTIONARY SAECULUM	Augustan Age of Empire *(1704–1727)*	Great Awakening *(1727–1746)*	French and Indian Wars *(1746–1773)*	American Revolution *(1773–1794)*
CIVIL WAR SAECULUM	Era of Good Feelings *(1794–1822)*	Transcendental Awakening *(1822–1844)*	Mexican War and Sectionalism *(1844–1860)*	Civil War *(1860–1865)*
GREAT POWER SAECULUM	Reconstruction and Gilded Age *(1865–1886)*	Third Great Awakening *(1886–1908)*	World War I and Prohibition *(1908–1929)*	Great Depression and World War II *(1929–1946)*
MILLENNIAL SAECULUM	American High *(1946–1964)*	Consciousness Revolution *(1964–1984)*	Culture Wars *(1984–2005?)*	Millennial Crisis *(2005?–2026?)*

CHAPTER 5

■

Gray Champions

ONE AFTERNOON IN APRIL 1689, AS THE AMERICAN COL-
onies boiled with rumors that King James II was about to strip them of their
liberties, the king's hand-picked governor of New England, Sir Edmund Andros, marched his troops menacingly through Boston. His purpose was to
crush any thought of colonial self-rule. To everyone present, the future
looked grim.

Just at that moment, seemingly from nowhere, there appeared on the
streets "the figure of an ancient man" with "the eye, the face, the attitude of
command." His manner "combining the leader and the saint," the old man
planted himself directly in the path of the approaching British soldiers and
demanded that they stop. "The solemn, yet warlike peal of that voice, fit either to rule a host in the battlefield or be raised to God in prayer, were irre-
sistible. At the old man's word and outstretched arm, the roll of the drum
was hushed at once, and the advancing line stood still."

Inspired by this single act of defiance, the people of Boston roused their
courage and acted. Within the day, Andros was deposed and jailed, the liberty of Boston saved, and the corner turned on the colonial Glorious Revolution.

"Who was this Gray Champion?" Nathaniel Hawthorne asked near the
end of this story in his *Twice-Told Tales*. No one knew, except that he had
once been among the fire-hearted young Puritans who had first settled New
England more than a half century earlier. Later that evening, just before the
old priest-warrior disappeared, the townspeople saw him embracing the
eighty-five-year-old Simon Bradstreet, a kindred spirit and one of the few
original Puritans still alive. Would the Gray Champion ever return? "I have
heard," added Hawthorne, "that whenever the descendants of the Puritans
are to show the spirit of their sires, the old man appears again."

Posterity had to wait a while before seeing him again—the length of another long human life, in fact. "When eighty years had passed," wrote Hawthorne, the Gray Champion reappeared. The occasion was the revolutionary summer of 1775—when America's elders once again appealed to God, summoned the young to battle, and dared the hated enemy to fire. "When our fathers were toiling at the breastwork on Bunker's Hill," Hawthorne continued, "all through that night the old warrior walked his rounds." This old warrior—this graying peer of Sam Adams or Ben Franklin or Samuel Langdon (the Harvard president who preached to the Bunker Hill troops)—belonged to the Awakening Generation, whose youth had provided the spiritual taproot of the republic secured in their old age.

Hawthorne wrote this stirring legend in 1837, as a young man of thirty-three. The Bunker Hill fathers belonged to his parents' generation, by then well into old age. The nation had new arguments (over slavery) and new enemies (Mexico), but no one expected the old people of that era—the worldly likes of John Marshall and John Jacob Astor—to play the role of Gray Champion.

"Long, long may it be ere he comes again!" Hawthorne prophesied. "His hour is one of darkness, and adversity, and peril. But should domestic tyranny oppress us, or the invaders' step pollute our soil, still may the Gray Champion come." Although Hawthorne did not say when this would be, perhaps he should have been able to tell.

Had the young author counted eight or nine decades forward from Bunker Hill, or had he envisioned the old age of the young zealots (like Joseph Smith, Nat Turner, and William Lloyd Garrison) who had recently convulsed America's soul, he might have foreseen that the next Gray Champion would emerge from his own Transcendental Generation. Seared young by God, Hawthorne's peers were destined late in life to face an hour of "darkness, and adversity, and peril." The old priest-warrior would arise yet again in John Brown, damning the unrighteous from his scaffold; in Julia Ward Howe, writing "a fiery gospel writ in burnished rows of steel"; in William Tecumseh Sherman, scorching Georgia with "the fateful lightning of His terrible swift sword"; in Robert E. Lee, commanding thousands of young men to their deaths at Cemetery Ridge; and especially in Abraham Lincoln, announcing to Congress that "the fiery trial through which we pass will light us down in honor or dishonor to the last generation."

Were Hawthorne to have prophesied yet another eight decades farther ahead, he might have foretold another Gray Champion whose childhood would begin just after the "fiery trial" of Hawthorne's own old age. This generation would come of age scorching the elder-built world with its inner fire—and then, a half saeculum later, complete its self-declared rendezvous with destiny as "the wise old men of World War II." By adding FDR's Missionary Generation to the recurrence, Hawthorne's tale would have been not *twice,* but *four times* told.

When ancestral generations passed through these great gates of history, they saw in the Gray Champion a type of elder very different from the bustling senior citizens of America's recent past and from the old "Uncle Sams," the Revolutionary War survivors of the 1830s, when Hawthorne wrote his tale. Who were these old priest-warriors? They were elder expressions of the *Prophet* archetype. And their arrival into old age heralded a new constellation of generations.

Where were the other archetypes at the same moments in history? Who was entering midlife in 1689? The cunning likes of ex-pirate Benjamin Church, or the reckless Jacob Leisler, leaders among a Cavalier Generation that bore more adversity (and cruelty) than any other cohort group of New World settlers. In 1775? The Liberty Generation peers of George Washington, skilled at the harsher tasks of history. 1865? Chivalrous Gilded colonels, ruined farmers, cynical industrialists, and one lone assassin. And 1944? The ex-Doughboy Lost Generation whose gutsy generals and unpretentious politicians made the tough choices while younger war heroes won the applause. These were *Nomad* archetypes.

Who was coming of adult age? The team-playing, upbeat Glorious Generation of Cotton Mather; Thomas Jefferson, James Madison, and Alexander Hamilton of the Republican Generation, the greatest civic achievers in U.S. history; and the G.I.s who scaled the cliffs of Point du Hoc and harnessed the secret of the atom. These were *Hero* archetypes.

Who were the children? The Enlightenment Generation children who later became the first students at Yale and at William and Mary College and still later the polite professionals who waited patiently to inherit the new colonial institutions founded by their elders; the Compromise Generation's John Quincy Adams, weeping as he watched from a distance as friends of his father fought and died at Bunker Hill; the Progressive Generation's Theodore Roosevelt, hoisted on a parent's shoulders as he watched Lincoln's funeral train roll by; and Michael Dukakis, age eight on Pearl Harbor Sunday and age ten on D-Day, hearing his parents talk about forging a new political and global order that he would later try to improve. These were *Artist* archetypes.

At each of these great gates of history, eighty to a hundred years apart, a similar generational drama unfolded. Four archetypes, aligned in the same order—*elder Prophet, midlife Nomad, young adult Hero, child Artist*—together produced the most enduring legends in our history. Each time the Gray Champion appeared marked the arrival of a moment of "darkness, and adversity, and peril," the climax of the Fourth Turning of the saeculum.

In nature, the season that is about to come is always the season farthest removed from memory. So too in American history, past and present. Less than 10 percent of today's Americans were of soldier (or riveter) age on

D-Day, the climax of the last Fourth Turning. Less than 2 percent have adult memories of 1929's Black Tuesday, when America last entered a saecular winter. Among their juniors, few can conjure how an Unraveling-era mood can so swiftly transform into something that feels *and is* so fundamentally different. Americans have always been blind to the next turning until after it fully arrives.

We may prefer to see ourselves as masters of nature, controllers of all change and progress, exempt from the seasons of history. Yet the more we balk at seasonality and the more we try to eradicate it, the more menacing we render our view of time—and of the future. Most of today's adult Americans grew up in a society whose citizens dreamed of perpetually improving outcomes: better jobs, fatter wallets, stronger government, finer culture, nicer families, smarter kids, all the usual fruits of progress. Today, deep into a Third Turning, these goals often feel like they are slipping away. Many of us wish we could rewind time, but we know we can't—and we fear for our children and grandchildren.

In a sense, Americans resemble a primitive people who, feeling the dry chill of a deepening autumn, grow nostalgic for spring while wondering how (or even if) the moist warmth will ever arrive again. Many Americans wish that, somehow, they could bring back a saecular spring now. But seasons don't work that way. As in nature, a saecular autumn can be warm or cool, long or short, but the leaves will surely fall. The saecular winter can hurry or wait, but history warns that it will surely be upon us.

We may not wish the Gray Champion to come again—but come he must, and come he will.

The next leg of your journey is part history, part prophecy. It begins with the end of World War II, runs through the present, and extends into the old age of today's young adults. You will relearn recent American history from a seasonal perspective, as the confluence of familiar lives and times. You will learn about the mood shifts that followed the gateway years of the middle 1940s, 1960s, and 1980s. You will reacquaint yourself with today's generations as archetypes that shift into a new constellation with each new turning. You will learn what this could mean in the next Fourth Turning.

This time, the history lesson will be your own life story.

PART TWO

Turnings

CHAPTER 6

■

The First Turning:
American High (1946–1964)

ON V-J DAY, AUGUST 15, 1945, PEACE HAD BEEN DE-clared, but America remained mobilized for total war. The nation had been locked in crisis for as long as anyone could remember, and the landscape looked it: Harbors bristled with warships, highways with convoys, depots with war materiel, bureaucracies with war planners, factories with war workers. Still geared for production, assembly lines were expected to shut down just as millions of veterans came home needing work. A return to pre-war class conflict seemed inevitable. The eminent sociologist Gunnar Myrdal warned of a coming "radicalization of labor" and an "epidemic of violence." The first threat of this came a few months after V-J Day, when auto workers went on strike against General Motors.

The strike fizzled. In what came to be known as the Treaty of Detroit, GM and the auto workers worked out an amicable deal. "At no other time in U.S. history have labor's demands been so plausible," cheered *Fortune*'s editors. There was no going back to the 1930s. These were new times, times for teamwork and trust.

Through the heart-wrenching victories and reversals of global war, Americans had wavered between a bright ideal of social unity and a dark recollection of social conflict. They thirsted to belong to a secure order, something strong and universal and beyond argument. While statesmen laid plans for global governments, politicians talked of "collective action" for the "common man." At the height of the war, in an "Open Letter to Japan," the *Saturday Evening Post* defiantly observed how "Your people are giving their lives in useless sacrifice, while ours are fighting for a glorious future of mass employment, mass production, mass distribution, and mass ownership."

As the war neared its foreseeable triumph, Americans worried that such hopes might never be attainable. Looking forward, people did what they still do when contemplating the future: They assumed it would resemble the recent past. Their most recent frames of reference—the hard-bitten 1930s and the cynical 1920s—were not remembered favorably. *Fortune* feared a resumption of "rude pushing ways" and "ill temper." Republishing a 1932 photo of police routing World War I veterans, the editors warned that "a slice of blueberry pie" would not satisfy "the veteran's gripe." Many economists saw a new depression ahead; Sumner Slichter warned of "the greatest and swiftest disappearance of markets in all history." The Research Institute's Leo Cherne predicted "insecurity, instability, and maladjustment" for "middle-class families . . . susceptible to the infections of a postwar disillusionment." A month after V-J Day, *Life* magazine forecast a sharp decline in the U.S. birthrate. Fearing a thinning population and collapsing economy, the U.S. government began planning a massive campaign, involving some two hundred organizations, to provide work relief on the scale of the original New Deal.

It wasn't necessary. Upbeat America confounded the pessimists. Veterans mustered out without any hint of riot, cheered by hometown welcomes that didn't stop when the parades were over. As the triumphant mood lingered, *Fortune* praised Americans for having found "a positive kind of middle-of-the-road," even if "the road itself is now in a different place." Few wanted to rewage old political or cultural arguments. Instead, returning vets wanted to get married, have kids, and move into nice homes and productive jobs. They did so with such exuberance that old General George Marshall chastised them for losing "the high purposes of war" in the "confusion of peace." As *Fortune* continued to monitor the national pulse, the magazine warned that "it is time to curb the boom which, if allowed to go its way, will make another depression inevitable." But when the mood persisted after the first peacetime Christmas, even the cautionaries reconsidered. The actual number of unemployed reached barely one-tenth of what labor officials had predicted. At last joining the "many prophets of hope," *Fortune* exuded that "We would seem to have it in our power to have a standard of living far beyond anything in recorded history." World War II had marked "the supreme triumph of man in his long battle with the scarcities in nature."

By June 1946, the nation realized that the postwar mood shift was permanent and massive. "The Great American Boom is on," *Fortune* proclaimed, "and there is no measuring it! The old yardsticks won't do. . . . The spectacle is so vast and confusing it is hard to understand. . . . There is a rich queerness to the U.S. scene in this summer of 1946. . . . Parallels with 1929 or 1939 or any other period break down quickly." Quoting Walt Whitman just after the Civil War, the editors prodded America to "Open up all your valves and let her go—swing, whirl with the rest—you will soon get under such momentum you can't stop if you would." The new boom was not just in economic activity, but also in fertility. Babies conceived in the ecstasy of V-J night were born in mid-April 1946, launching a procreative birth bulge that lasted until a tragedy in late 1963 altered the national mood in a different way.

Those two markers—V-J Day and the Kennedy Assassination—bracket an era variously known as "Pax Americana," "Good Times," the "Best Years," "Happy Days," and the "American High."

Thanks to vintage TV and nostalgia movies, deeply etched memories of the American High are continually recalled decades later. People now in their forties or older widely remember this as an era when large institutions were regarded as effective, government as powerful, science as benign, schools as good, careers as reliable, families as strong, and crime as under control. Government could afford to do almost anything it wanted, while still balancing its budget. From year to year, the middle class grew, and the gap between rich and poor narrowed. Worker productivity and family incomes grew at the fastest pace ever measured, with no end in sight. John Kenneth Galbraith wrote of The Affluent Society in which poverty was no longer "a major problem" but "more nearly an afterthought." "The frontiers of our economic system are formed by our mental attitude and our unity," said Harold Stassen in 1946, "rather than by any limitation of science or of productivity." Abroad, Americans saw themselves bearing a new imperial role, believing, with J. Robert Oppenheimer, that "the world alters as we walk in it." They took pride in a nation described by British historian Robert Payne as "a Colossus" with "half the wealth of the world, more than half of the productivity, nearly two-thirds of the world's machines."

The wealthier and more community-minded America grew, the nicer (if blander) it became. Crime and divorce rates declined, ushering in an era of unlocked front doors, of nicely groomed youths, of President Eisenhower celebrating the well-being of the American family.

An affluent, orderly, familial society needed appropriate living quarters. Enter suburbia: the American High's most enduring monument. The suburb's inventor was William Levitt, whose wartime stint in the Seabees enabled him to test his peers' taste for standard-issue housing. Postwar Levittowns were soon emulated everywhere. Through the 1950s, more than four of every five new houses were built in a "New Suburbia" that Fortune lauded as "big and lush and uniform—a combination made to order for the comprehending marketer." Compared to the toiletless farmhouses and urban tenements many Americans had called home before the war, suburbia was nothing less than a middle-class miracle.

The planned orderliness of suburbia was the natural lifestyle for an America bent on entering what one contemporary writer called an "age of security." With the horrors of Hitler and Stalin fresh in the public mind, the nation's domestic calm was shielded by a vigilant Cold War realism. "When World War II ended in 1945, no one dared to predict that no others would follow," explains historian Paul Johnson. "There was a general, despondent assumption that . . . future conflicts would stretch on endlessly." To guard against this threat, many of the American High's grandest edifices (interstate highways, basic research, student loans, new math and science curricula) were built explicitly in the name of national defense. The new suburbs reflected this preoccupation with security. If consumerism could be standardized, private needs could be met efficiently, saving resources for the big projects needed to ensure the long-term survival of the nation. If the new lifestyle also provided the cultural underpinnings for thrift and teamwork, with everybody pitching in like good neighbors sharing lawn mowers, all the better for America's future.

The new ethos drew plenty of criticism for its lowbrow materialism. The 1954 book *Age of Conformity* defined an American as someone who is "satisfied with not less than the best in airplanes and plumbing but accepts the second rate in politics and culture." The 1956 film *The Invasion of the Body Snatchers* satirized citizens so robotic that nobody noticed when they were taken over by aliens. Malvina Reynolds sang of "little boxes made of ticky tacky." Lewis Mumford despaired of the "multitude of uniform, unidentifiable houses, lined up inflexibly, at uniform distances on uniform roads, in a treeless command waste, inhabited by people of the same class, the same incomes, the same age group, witnessing the same television performances, eating the same tasteless prefabricated foods, from the same freezers." Newton Minow assaulted television as a "vast wasteland" of shallow, albeit wholesome, programming. When Michael Harrington wrote *The Other America,* his implicit message was that the main (middle-class) America may have been doing better than it deserved.

The High mind-set included many elements that today's Americans loathe—from racism and sexism to a stifling group-think and a philistine culture. At the time, however, the mood of the era compared very favorably with the social and economic chaos older adults recalled from their younger years. Had that circa-1950s mood been forecast to Americans in 1928 or 1944 (near the end of the two prior turnings), they might have perceived as progress a number of social trends that today's Americans are quick to criticize. Looking back, the mood of the American High strikes many 1990s-era Americans as a creaking anachronism. But at the time, it felt extremely modern—a wedding of optimism, technology, and prosperity to a crisp (if unreflective) sense of collective purpose.

What makes the years between 1946 and 1963 seem so quaint in retrospect is that today we have lost touch with the generational mind-sets of the people who lived through that era. The reclusive Old World Lost elders in dank tenements could not be further from the hip, high-tech Silent in their move-up senior condos. The "high hopes" of midlife G.I.s seem utterly stale, even insensate, to Boomer culture warriors. To young 13er entrepreneurs, the Silent's corporate compliance might as well come from a science fiction novel. And it would be nearly impossible for today's Millennial children to imagine parents who actually prod kids to explore the outer limits of adult culture and taste.

To understand how and why the American High came to be, you need to picture the generational history of those years. Consider each life-cycle transition then occurring: the hard-knocks elder Lost cordoning off the social perimeters to enable the mood to calm, the G.I.s deriving energy from midlife conformism, the Silent becoming adaptable helpmates, and the Boomers receiving new indulgences. Seen from a life-cycle perspective, the postwar mood was in many ways inevitable. There was absolutely no way that post-Crisis America would feel the same way it had back in the 1930s or 1920s.

Whether the American High was a good or bad era is beside the point. What matters is that, in the seasonal rhythms of history, it was a *necessary* era. It cleaned up after the Crisis that came before and set the table for the Awakening to follow. It lent America an infusion of optimism and constructive energy and a staleness that later had to be rooted out.

In the years between 1946 and 1963, America succeeded in many areas (such as public cooperation) where we today feel we are failing; so too was the nation notoriously weak in many areas (such as personal fulfillment) where we today think ourselves doing well. That should come as no surprise: In the middle 1950s, at the peak of the High, America lay at the opposite end of the saeculum from where we are now.

FIRST TURNINGS AND ARCHETYPES

Including this most recent era, Anglo-American history has had six First Turning Highs, dating back to the fifteenth century:

- *Tudor Renaissance* (1487–1517), Reformation Saeculum
- *Merrie England* (1594–1621), New World Saeculum
- *Augustan Age of Empire* (1704–1727), Revolutionary Saeculum
- *Era of Good Feelings* (1794–1822), Civil War Saeculum
- *Reconstruction and Gilded Age* (1865–1886), Great Power Saeculum
- *American High* (1946–1964), Millennial Saeculum

All such eras mark the construction of a new social order. All are regarded, in their own time and after, as "postwar." With the epic Crisis settled and the promised land delivered, society accelerates with a newfound solidarity and direction. It is time to reconstruct and savor victory (or recover from defeat). People want to gather, nest, plan, procreate, and build. The mood is dynamic: Each new exercise of social cooperation builds on the success of the last, until—near the end of the High—the trend toward greater order and co-hesion has become something close to an instinctual drive.

The High is an equinox era, a transition toward shorter nights and longer days, in which both the demand and supply of social order are rising. It is the vernal quadrant of the saeculum, the season of hope and innocent joy. After a winter of war and death, spring is announced by Vachel Lindsay's nightingales, who "spoke, I think, of perils past / They spoke, I think, of peace at last." Feeling a sentiment of relief, a society naturally reverts to simple pleasures and the planting of things that will grow. This becomes the season of what Thomas Nashe calls "the year's pleasant king," when nature "blooms" and "maids dance in a ring." With new life filling the earth, it is (writes Wallace Stevens) "a time abhorrent to the nihilist / Or searcher for the fecund minimum." As the procreative spirit settles in, says Robert Browning, "All's right with the world." During the saeculum's First Turning, children are indulged, academies founded, soldiers knighted, kings crowned, empires proclaimed.

Every High has embodied this mood, within the context of its own post-Crisis sensibility and technology. The first three Highs all defined eras of political consolidation, economic prosperity, and (in the realm of culture) worldly optimism. For the new United States, the Era of Good Feelings sig-nified a similar dawn. Americans had just fought for and secured their dem-ocratic self-rule. Now they could engage in the pursuit of happiness—by surveying lands, founding communities, building canals, crafting inven-tions, and (in Joel Barlow's words) applying "science" to "raise, improve, and harmonize mankind." After the Civil War, a more damaged society co-alesced around the need for Reconstruction. In the Gilded Age, Americans strengthened families and schools, glorified technology, and invested hugely in industrial infrastructure, thereby securing the continental nation whose unity had been preserved at such cost.

Through a more distant lens, Highs provide relatively few memories of noble deeds or stirring crusades or zany celebrities. Instead, they bring to mind (as Vernon Parrington described the Gilded Age) the "great barbe-cues" of history. They encompass enduring vignettes of stable community and family life—whether the stately rectangles of Williamsburg, neat log cabins of Kentucky, well-ordered "Home Sweet Homes" of Shaker Heights, or ticky-tacky suburbs of Levittown. People remake the outer world around optimistic new notions of unity and progress. Yet the flip side of this opti-mism is the suppression of bad news: Beneath the outward contentment, people ignore what are later deemed to be flagrant injustices. Highs are good times for those who inhabit and accept the majoritarian culture. They are merely secure times, at best, for those who do not.

Highs produce this mood because of the new life-cycle phase each ar-chetype is then entering: Nomads into elderhood, Heroes into midlife,

Artists into young adulthood, and Prophets into childhood. Consider the four phases (and archetypes) in turn.

■ As exhausted *Nomads* replace Prophets in *elderhood,* they slow the pace of social change, shunning the old crusades in favor of simplicity and survivalism.

Tired of big causes and ideologies, elder Nomads calm society, accept the outcome of the Crisis, and build a functioning civic order out of its glory (or ashes). Believers in functional social rituals, they become old-fashioned elders who place a high priority on protecting children and safeguarding the society's long-term future. They are less impressed than their juniors by swift progress or national triumph, and more fearful of where institutional hubris may lead. Still stigmatized, they strike other generations as burned-out, even reactionary. In old age, the Nomads' reputation for shrewdness never wins them much public reward. They claim little for themselves at a time when the public mood is focused less on rewarding the old than investing in the young.

The twilight years of Queen Elizabeth I and George Washington, though separated by two saecula, exemplify the elder Nomad style. Still the canny and picaresque warrior, each had become risk averse, worn from care, protective of a hard-won peace, graciously old regime in manner, not too proud to show occasional vanity or cupidity, and resistant yet kind to pushier and more confident juniors. During the Augustan Age, the elder Cavalier Generation stood accused of "a sad degeneracy"; indeed, their public treatment was the worst of the colonial era. After the American Revolution, Washington's Liberty peers had what historian David Hackett Fischer describes as the "unhappy fate . . . to be young in an era when age was respected, and old in a time when youth took the palm." In their last years, they became self-effacing pessimists who (like John Adams) knew for certain that "mausoleums, statues, monuments will never be erected to me."

■ As powerful *Heroes* replace Nomads in *midlife,* they establish an upbeat, constructive ethic of social discipline.

Their ears ringing with post-Crisis accolades, midlife Heroes become builders and doers, confident of their ability to make big institutions work better than their Lost predecessors. They energize and rationalize every sphere of life, from science to religion, statecraft to the arts. At their midlife peak of power, they expect to propel civilization over an unprecedented threshold of secular progress—toward wealth, happiness, knowledge, and power. Others regard them as the most-competent, if least-reflective, generation of their time.

In history, midlife Heroes provided Highs with their central protagonists.

The Arthurians founded a new dynasty, the Elizabethans adorned a new empire, and the Glorious laid the foundation of an affluent and enlightened New World civilization. "Be up and doing. Activity. Activity," Benjamin Colman preached to his Glorious peers during the Augustan Age. "A cheerful spirit is a happy and lovely thing." His peers established a stable ruling class, chiseled slavery into law, and managed the colonies' most robust era of economic growth. In the Era of Good Feelings, Jefferson asked his midlife Republican peers to "unite in common efforts for the common good" to assist "a rising nation" that was "advancing rapidly." The Republicans managed the nation through what they called "energy in government," "order and harmony" in society, "tranquillity" of mind, "usefulness and reason" in science, and "abundance" in commerce.

■ As conformist *Artists* replace Heroes in *young adulthood,* they become sensitive helpmates, lending their expertise and cooperation to an era of growing social calm.

An Artist generation comes of age just as the post-Crisis social order is solidifying. With little room to maneuver, they embark early on prosperous and secure life paths. They learn to excel at satisfying expectations and assisting the Heroes' grand constructions. As they infuse the culture with new vitality, they probe cautiously for a more inwardly fulfilling role. This effort leads to a cult of professional expertise (refining the Heroes' outer-world achievements) and to critical gestures of conscience and feeling (exposing the Heroes' inner-world limitations).

In the first two Renaissance Highs, young adults were regarded as the most educated and least adventuresome adults of their era. Likewise, the Enlightenment youths of the colonial Augustan Age called themselves "docile and tutorable." They were masters of the rococo ornaments of colonial life, yet also America's first true professionals in science, medicine, religion, and law. During the Era of Good Feelings, Compromiser youths came of age with what John Quincy Adams confessed was "our duty to remain the peaceable and the silent." The new frontier folk felt less like adventurers and more like settlers or, as with Lewis and Clark, civil servants. In the Gilded Age, the Progressive Generation started out as notoriously mild-mannered young adults, collectively described by one admirer as "a harmonious blending, a delightful symmetry, formed of fitting proportions of every high quality."

■ As *Prophets* replace Artists in *childhood,* they are nurtured with increasing indulgence by optimistic adults in a secure environment.

A High projects its optimism onto children, giving rise to a fertility bulge, a preoccupation with family life, and long investment time horizons. In the orderly post-Crisis world, parents can safely devote more time to child raising and offer new freedoms to a new generation. Nurtured by a well-ordered but spiritually depleted society, children are urged to cultivate strong inner lives. They form stronger bonds with mothers (their links to personal values) than with fathers (their links to civic deeds). Presumed to have a bright future, children are encouraged to demand much of life.

The Puritan children of Merrie England grew up in a triumphant society, booming with trade and teeming with construction. They were parented by what historian David Leverenz describes as a "mixture of relatively good mothering" and "distant . . . repressive fathers." The Augustan Age's Awakening children became the best-fed, best-housed, and most comforted generation the colonies had yet seen. Raised on Cotton Mather's *A Family Well Ordered,* they responded by cultivating what historian Gary Nash describes as "antirational, antiscientific, . . . and moralistic" feelings. The Transcendental children of the Era of Good Feelings, according to a British visitor, showed "prominent boldness and forwardness." "The elements added after 1790" to the child's world, notes historian Joseph Kett, "were increasingly on the side of freedom." The Gilded Age's Missionary kids grew up in a "long children's picnic," says historian Mary Cable, "a controlled but pleasantly free atmosphere." Jane Addams recalled how her peers had been "sickened with advantages," and Henry Canby how families had "more give and take between parents and children" than the "previous generation" had enjoyed.

Picture these four archetypes, in these life-cycle phases, layered into a constellation of generations. The behavior of each generation contrasts sharply with its predecessor's at the same age—in each case, catching society by surprise. The sum total of these four archetypal shifts is the shift in public mood, from a Crisis to a High.

Now reflect on the generational history of the most recent First Turning: the American High between 1946 through 1964. A Turning is, at bottom, a history of what millions of like-aged people do in their daily lives. As you read these sketches, filter in your own recollections and think about how people you know may have reflected these archetypes.

LOST ENTERING ELDERHOOD: OLD FOGEYS

"To err is Truman," scoffed editorialists in 1945 when this barely known "Man from Independence" replaced FDR. A year later, when John L. Lewis dared him to stop a steelworkers' strike, the president did just that—and the grandiloquent old union crusader backed down. "John L. had to fold up," Truman afterwards recounted. "He couldn't take the gaff." Six years later, Truman showed similar guts in firing Douglas MacArthur, even while younger Congressmen were likening the general's preachings to "the words of God himself."

During the American High, the Lost Generation ushered out the older authoritarians who had led their society through what MacArthur called "the crucible of war." The passing of the last Missionaries (MacArthur, along with Margaret Sanger, Frank Lloyd Wright, Albert Einstein, Helen Keller, W. E. B. Du Bois, George Marshall, and Bernard Baruch) came with the realization that their Trumanesque inheritors lacked the spiritual essence, indeed the *wisdom,* of a generation that (as a young admirer said of Nobel-laureate John Mott) had "something of the mountains and sea" in it, "very simple and a bit sublime."

The Missionaries had come of age around the turn of the century—an era whose thunder American novelist Winston Churchill attributed to "the springing of a generation of ideals from a generation of commerce." Their social causes (populism, muckraking, women's suffrage, fundamentalism, labor anarchism, Prohibition) projected what Jane Addams called a "higher conscience." Frederic Howe wrote that "the most characteristic influence of my generation" was an "evangelistic psychology . . . that seeks a moralistic explanation of social problems and a religious solution to most of them." George Santayana described his generation as "prophets" who "apply morals to public affairs." As World War II drew to a close, Missionaries dominated the American image of old age: dressed in dark colors, dogmatic and religious, preachy and principled.

This was not an act the Lost were inclined to follow. Instead, America's High-era elders became hardscrabble pragmatists, products of a lifetime of criticism. This began with the "bad-boy" fixation of Progressive-era magazines. On the eve of World War I, the *Atlantic Monthly* accused the "rising generation" of "mental rickets and curvature of the soul." During the war, the alleged stupidity of American youth became a raging issue when IQ tests indicated that half of all draftees had a mental age of under twelve. Afterwards, their morals came under constant attack from aging Missionaries. In the dark days of the Depression, when FDR blasted "a generation of self-seekers" for wrecking "the temple of our civilization," clearly he meant the middle-aged Lost, who throughout the 1930s were attacked as "Copperheads," nay-sayers, "Irresponsibles," and (as war approached) "isolationists." In old age, they were again castigated, this time as reactionary, corrupt, and antiprogress. The Lost's aging literary elite generally accepted the lifelong verdict. "The truth is," wrote Henry Miller, "under the skin we are all cannibals, assassins, traitors, liars, hypocrites, poltroons."

With a rowdy childhood and careful old age as bookends, the Lost Generation life cycle was divided roughly in thirds by two world wars. ("In the meantime, in between time, ain't we got fun?"). "I had a rotten start," lamented Babe Ruth, whose generation grew up when children were let loose to do anything they (or others) wanted—like seven-year-old George Burns, who sang for pennies in saloons. The child afterthoughts of an era of social protest, spiritual ferment, massive immigration, and rampant drug abuse, the Lost came of age popularizing the slogan "It's up to you." World War I embittered them as, in Fitzgerald's words, "a new generation dedicated more than the last to the fear of poverty and the worship of success; grown up to find all gods dead, all wars fought, all faith in man shaken." During the 1920s, they worked hard and partied hard, sensing (like Edna St. Vincent Millay) that their "candle will not last the night."

The Great Depression brought them a midlife hangover—and a change of attitude. According to Malcolm Cowley, this was a time of "doubt and even defeat" for his peers. But as life went on, they lent the 1930s much of that decade's gritty-but-solid reputation. With FDR winning term after term, the Republican-leaning Lost did not attain a majority of Congressional seats and governorships until 1941, later in their life cycle than any other generation in U.S. history. When World War II hit, the Lost shed their isolationism and provided the war-winning generals whose daring (Patton), warmth (Bradley), and persistence (Eisenhower) energized younger troops. At home, they managed the world's most efficient war machine. With little philosophizing, their first president dropped two atom bombs and then arranged a peace that was less vengeful and more secure than the one he recalled from his own soldier days.

Unprotected by families as children, unrewarded by governments as adults, and criticized by other generations all their lives, the Lost grew old with a low collective self-image. Identical psychological tests administered over two decades showed High-era Lost elders scoring far below Awakening-era G.I. seniors in measures of self-esteem. Socially and politically reticent, the old Lost reflected a lifetime's knowledge about how to deal with whatever "hard knocks" life dealt out. Distrustful of government, they "played the sap" for richer and better-educated young people and seldom lobbied on their own behalf. Their low self-image also enabled them to do the dirty work that others could not (or would not) do. The "buck stopped" with them.

As elders, the generation that had electrified America before the Crisis calmed America afterward. Those "wild young people" who made the 1920s roar either burned out entirely or matured into old-fashioned cautionaries— the likes of Virgil Thomson or Norman Rockwell—thirty years later. By the protective cordon of their stewardship, they made possible the modernizing optimism of their juniors. But it was never an optimism they shared. According to Paul Tillich, "Our generation has seen the horrors latent in man's being rise to the surface and erupt." In their view, the postwar world remained dangerous. "Tomorrow will be wonderful," wrote Joseph Wood Krutch, "that is, unless it is indescribably terrible, or unless indeed there just isn't any."

Theirs was a toughness born of desperation. "Living is a struggle," wrote Thornton Wilder, "Every good and excellent thing in the world stands moment by moment on the razor edge of danger and must be fought for—whether it's a field, a home, or a country." If corners had to be cut to protect America in an amoral world, the Lost cut them. The same generation that had earlier produced Dashiell Hammett and Raymond Chandler and Humphrey Bogart was now led by the likes of J. Edgar Hoover and the Dulles brothers, their files thick with plots and secrets they shielded from the eyes of the young. In the Lost view, Communism was less an economic paradigm than a rival bully to be thwarted *mano a mano,* with "brinksmanship" if necessary. To their eyes, America could not afford ideological recriminations: It was the Lost Joseph Welch (and, eventually, Eisenhower) who quashed McCarthy and dampened the G.I.s' anti-Communist fervor.

Having paid many a price for other generation's crusades, the Lost led with a warm realism. Their late-in-life leaders (Stevenson, Dirksen, Ervin) were famous for flowery yet self-effacing oratory and for positive "I like Ike" campaigning. The Lost liked politics to be humdrum: The 1952 and 1956 elections marked the only time in U.S. history that the same two presidential candidates ran against each other in consecutive elections with identical results. They disliked deficit financing and built a stable economic foundation beneath a prosperity for which G.I. politicians would later claim credit. They burdened themselves with unprecedented peacetime tax rates to pay for global reconstruction and domestic infrastructure—whose benefits they knew they would not live long enough to enjoy themselves.

Unlike the Missionaries, Lost leaders had few visions grander than Eisenhower's desire to project "a respectable image of American life before the world." They viewed religion mainly as a device for ritual comfort and public order. As Eisenhower once said, "Our government makes no sense unless it is founded in a deeply felt religious faith—and I don't care what it is." Ike showed similar discomfort with new technologies. He opposed the moon rocket, warned against the G.I.-fashioned "military-industrial complex," and refused to fly in a jet airplane until 1959. Historian William O'Neill described the old general as "prudent, suspicious of change, unlike those, such as John Kennedy, who believed there were no limits to what America could achieve." Adlai Stevenson shared Ike's innate cultural conservatism; he unapologetically wore old shoes, and his close advisers pointedly denied that they ever watched TV.

Accepting without pretense that they were old, the Lost unselfishly anchored an era of sharply improving fortunes for the young. Whereas for Missionaries relief from work had been late and brief, Lost elders accepted new mandatory retirement rules that required disengagement from the workplace to free job slots for younger workers. The widescale practice of forced early retirement, combined with rapidly rising wages and weak public safety nets, made the Lost one of the poorest generations, relative to the young, in U.S. history. Elder pensions were very small by today's standards; from blue-collar workers to ex-President Harry Truman, the old Lost had to scrimp and scramble to make do. While younger people were moving into gleaming new tract houses, nearly half of the old Lost had never lived in a dwelling with at least two bedrooms and a bathroom.

Throughout the High, aid to poor old people was far down on the nation's list of priorities, but few of the Lost complained. As *Harvest Year*'s editor Louis Kuplan explained, "We must not become dependent spiritually, socially, physically or financially upon relatives, friends, or government." In 1959, just after Ethel Andrus founded the American Association of Retired Persons, she refused "to bewail the hardships of old age, . . . nor to stress the potential political strength of older folk, nor to urge governmental subsidy." The 1961 White House Conference on Aging drafted a lengthy list of "obligations of the aging," stating that "the individual will assume the primary responsibility for self-reliance in old age." Though he broadly hinted that he would slash Social Security, Barry Goldwater won a larger share of votes from Lost elders than from any younger generation.

Even before the Lost fully occupied elderhood in the Kennedy years, most of them had already heard their "last hurrahs" and had disappeared from public life. Those few who remained were often disparagingly described as "old whales" and "old fogeys." Yet beyond the rough edges, this generation always retained the integrity of a survivor. Like Earl Warren, they were responsible for xenophobic tragedies (in his case, the internment of Japanese-Americans), but also stood up for the rights of accused criminals and other unpopular individuals who, per Bruce Barton's motto, were "down but not out." Their protective shield bred a God-Bless-America conformism, but their surviving literati were among the most caustic critics of what Tillich called a "patternization" of life. The new suburban communalism struck the Lost as perhaps a good thing for younger people but not for them. Instead, their pre-melting pot elders helped preserve an Old World atmosphere in urban ethnic neighborhoods, where many of today's fifty-year-olds can remember visiting grandparents who still spoke the mother tongue.

By the mid-1960s, gerontologists came to believe that thrift, self-reliance, cynicism, conservatism, and Republican voting habits were permanent aspects of the aging process in America. How times change.

G.I.s ENTERING MIDLIFE: THE POWER ELITE

A "generation of Prometheus and Adam" is how Henry Malcolm described his postwar G.I. peers. In all world history, no generation—not Alexander the Great's, not Caesar's, not Napoleon's—had conquered so large a swath of land and sea. Yet as G.I.s convoyed home when the war ended, "nervous out of the service" like the returning vet in *The Best Years of Our Lives,* what they sought was "a good job, a mild future, and a little house big enough for me and my wife." They didn't demand praise and reward from an admiring public, but they certainly received it. The Iwo Jima inscription—"when uncommon valor was a common virtue"—reflects the unusual regard in which America held this Hero generation on its homecoming. "We were a special generation," recalls historian William Manchester, "and we *were* America. You get used to that."

During their childhood, G.I.s had been fussed over by protective parents determined to raise up kids as good as the Lost Generation had been bad. Youth clubs, vitamins, safe playgrounds, pasteurized milk, child-labor laws, even Prohibition: These all were efforts to keep kids away from the danger and decadence of the prior generation. G.I.s responded by growing up as the straight-arrow achievers that adults had been praying for—as the first Boy Scouts, the first Miss Americas, and (with Charles Lindbergh in 1927) the first All-American Heroes. "There's no such thing as a bad boy," Father Flanagan had declared when G.I.s were little, distinguishing them from their "bad" predecessors who until then had been a media obsession.

By the mid-1920s, cynicism and individualism were out on college campuses; optimism and cooperation were in. By the late 1920s, G.I.s regarded themselves (recalls Gene Shuford) as America's "best generation." They learned to police themselves through what historian Paula Fass describes as a "peer society" of strict collegial standards. In the 1930s, this meant unions, party politics, and landslide votes for FDR. When the Great Depression struck, young people did their duty and came to be known not as alienated youths, but as the "Locked-Out Generation" of America's "submerged middle class." Realizing that the Missionary-imposed New Deal restacked the deck in their favor, they came to regard federal authority as a trusted friend who would always be there to help them. Thanks to government, teams of young adults planted trees, cut trails, and built dams that brought power and water to their communities. "Your power is turning our darkness to dawn," sang Woody Guthrie, "so roll on Columbia, roll on." Their unfaltering attitude served them well after the Japanese attack on Pearl Harbor. Less than four years after marching off as the most uniformed generation in U.S. history, they returned as victors. For the 97 percent of G.I. men who were not seriously injured in the service, the war provided a generational slingshot, converting a reputation for youthful virtue into one of midlife power.

As returning war heroes, G.I.s became what Stephen Ambrose termed the "we generation." They brought a peer-enforced, no-nonsense, get-it-done attitude to campuses, workplaces, and politics. Like Jimmy Stewart in *Mr. Smith Goes to Washington,* they felt a scoutlike duty to clean up a corrupt Lost world, eliminate the chaotic vestiges of the Depression, extol the "regular guy," and transfer the strength of the platoon from wartime beaches to peacetime suburbs. Beneath their sharing ("Have a smoke?") facade lay a get-back-in-line attitude toward miscreance. Polls showed G.I.s to be harsher than their elders on such topics as the Japanese occupation, the use of poison gas, and corporal punishment.

In science, the G.I.s who in war had invented radar, encryption, and the A-bomb now turned to space rocketry, TV, and new gadgets to make life easier. White-coated G.I.s began racking up their ninety-nine Nobel Prizes, most of them in hard sciences like physics. In business, hard-charging G.I.s brought can-do confidence to American manufacturing. Many of their postwar constructions—bridges, highways, tunnels, harbors, housing projects— were proclaimed to be the biggest and best in the world. Upon this infrastructure, corporations made fortunes by marketing mass goods to mass tastes. After George Gallup defined the "average man," Bob McNamara and Lee Iacocca designed the average auto, Kemmons Wilson opened new Holiday Inns to give middle-income families standard places to sleep, and the McDonald brothers homogenized fast food. Before long, retail chains stretched across America, each link as predictable and reliable as the next.

Described by historian Joseph Goulden as "a generation content to put its trust in government and authority," rising G.I. leaders saw more chaos than opportunity in the creative destruction of the marketplace. As their economists strove to flatten the business cycle, their legislators expanded social insurance to minimize family risks and regulatory agencies to minimize business risks. The federal government showered benefits on the middle-class and middle-aged, as the postwar G.I. Bill became America's largest-ever intergenerational transfer program to people entering midlife. In the latter years of the High, two of every five dollars of outstanding housing debt were covered by taxpayers, many of them older and living in housing far worse than what young veterans could buy.

What the G.I. Bill fostered was not just the suburb, but what *The Organization Man* author William Whyte called the suburban G.I. "social ethic." Much-praised in its own time but much-criticized later, that ethic embraced cooperation, community involvement, friendliness, and a sharp delineation between the correct roles for men and women. Like Sloan Wilson's hero in *Man in the Gray Flannel Suit,* the ideal male was a hard striver, the ideal female a devoted nurturer. An era that ended with "he-man" debates over missile gaps had begun with a political vocabulary whose biggest "witch-hunt" insults ("simpering," "cringing") were challenges against virility. An era that ended with Betty Friedan analyzing *The Feminine Mystique* had begun with another popular book, *The Lost Sex,* lamenting "feminism" as "a deep illness"—and *Look* magazine praising the newly submissive housewife as a "wondrous creature" who "looks and acts far more feminine than the 'emancipated' girl of the '20s or '30s."

Suburban family life centered around television, a postwar technology that promoted the G.I. "general issue" culture. Vintage TV perfectly expressed the new midlife role: taming science, nurturing children, staying upbeat, letting everybody keep up with their neighbors. The G.I.s produced TV's most enduring middle-aged comics (Lucille Ball, Jackie Gleason), its least cynical interviewers (Jack Paar, Dave Garroway), and a wholesomely macho Hollywood honor roll (Jimmy Stewart, John Wayne, Burt Lancaster, Kirk Douglas, Henry Fonda, Charlton Heston, Gregory Peck, Robert Mitchum).

A generation that believed (with John Kennedy) that "a man does what he must" had little penchant for spiritual reflection. In the late 1950s, the French philosopher Jacques Maritain remarked that "Americans seem sometimes to believe that if you are a thinker you must be a frowning bore." G.I.s equated religion with church going, a "true believer" with fanaticism. "We do not engage in loose talk about the 'ideals' of the situation," said C. Wright Mills as he heralded the arrival of a Power Elite that wanted to "get right down to the problem." Declaring an End to Ideology, Daniel Bell described his peers as inclined to overcome real-world challenges, not to explore differences in values. The G.I.s' most fervent midlife cause—anti-Communism—assumed that even the most traitorous peers adhered to a conformist ideology of an alien (Soviet) variety. Like Richard Nixon and Alger Hiss, G.I. accusers and accused were people who dressed alike, lived in similar houses, read the same magazines, and watched the same TV shows.

Preferring to celebrate similarities, G.I.s trusted that, underneath the skin, people were essentially equal. Yet aside from the 1946 breakthrough of G.I. war veteran Jackie Robinson, U.S. race relations remained frozen in place—a circumstance that seemed irrational to the G.I. author of *Black Like Me* and director of *Guess Who's Coming to Dinner*. Middle-aged blacks were presumed to share the majoritarian culture, and the goals of the early civil rights movement reflected this presumption. As the G.I. media bleached out African-American rhythms and dressed black stars in white shirts and ties, G.I. business came to realize that integration was more economically efficient than segregation. In time, this attitude would lead G.I. Congresses to enact legislation that had nothing to do with affirmative action or cultural pluralism, but followed from the logic of equal opportunity.

As this midlife generation "Spic and Spanned" America, voters of all ages came to see this generation as no less competent in peacetime than it had been in war. By 1950, one G.I. (Thomas Dewey) had twice run for president, two others (Clark Clifford, George Kennan) had become President Truman's top advisers, and several more (John Kennedy, Richard Nixon, Lyndon Johnson, Gerald Ford) had launched promising political careers. By 1953, G.I.s comprised most of the nation's governors and Congressmen. Through the 1950s, the rising G.I. elite chafed at their minor role in the Eisenhower administration. Maxwell Taylor criticized the careful, low-energy Lost-style leadership, Eric Sevareid accused the "last generation" of a "lack of controlled plans," and John Kennedy complained that "what our young men saved, our diplomats and President have frittered away." The Democratic landslide of 1958 swept into office a huge cadre of G.I.s eager to craft a more aggressive role for government.

In 1960, with an all-G.I. presidential race, this robust generation sought to bring to national leadership the same energy it had already brought to the family, economy, and culture. The older Eisenhower and Truman had their doubts. As Truman watched the campaign, perhaps the least substantive of the twentieth century, he praised both parties' "smart memoranda" but remarked how "it is not all pulled together on either side, by or into a man." Kennedy and Nixon, he said, "bore the hell out of me." Had Kennedy not received a solid majority of his peers' votes, he would have lost. Since age-based polling began in 1932, the G.I.s have *never* collectively voted for a losing candidate—and have often provided the winner's margin of support.

In his inaugural address, President Kennedy proclaimed that "the torch has been passed to a new generation, born in this century." Having campaigned on the slogan "Let's get this country moving again," he committed his peers to "bear any burden, pay any price" to bring "vigor" and "prestige" back into civic life. The new ruling generation wanted their nation to be (in Bell's words) "a world power, a paramount power, a hegemonic power" led by what David Halberstam called "a new breed of thinker-doers"—men like Bob McNamara ("the can-do man in the can-do society in the can-do era") and McGeorge Bundy ("a great and almost relentless instinct for power"). Meanwhile, Ben Bradlee and the rest of the G.I. media fraternity refrained from exposing a presidential sexual appetite that today would be front-page news.

"He's Superman!" historian James MacGregor Burns exuded about his peer in the White House, a man he heralded as "omniscient" and "omnipotent." Richard Neustadt asserted that "Presidential Power" could solve whatever problem this generation chose to target—that, for example, a U.S. president could get steel companies to lower prices just by picking up the phone. In this new era of the "imperial Presidency," there would be no limit to how far and how fast the nation could rise. Having cut their teeth on huge input-output matrices during the war, G.I. economists like Walter Heller applauded "macroeconomic" management while deriding the Puritan Ethic of thrift and survivalism. They prodded consumers to spend instead of save, and persuaded G.I. Congresses to run peacetime budget deficits to boost the Gross National Product, a term coined by G.I. economist Simon Kuznets.

In the early 1960s, Richard Rovere coined another expression to describe the new midlife G.I. elite: *The Establishment.* At the time, those two words carried a proud, totally positive connotation. The early 1960s was a time when public power was a public good, when Texaco sang (and people believed) that "You can trust your car to the man who wears the star." As Walter Cronkite liked to say, "That's the way it is"—or, more accurately, that's the way it was then.

SILENT ENTERING YOUNG ADULTHOOD: GRAY FLANNEL SUITS

"I hated the war ending," recalled Russell Baker, who nonetheless admitted that the A-bomb may have saved his skin. "I wanted desperately to become a death-dealing hero. I wanted the war to go on and on and on." Like many of his Silent Generation peers, the young Baker was expecting to join an invasion of Japan when Hiroshima, Nagasaki, and V-J Day sent him home. His Silent peers later tested their mettle in Korea, but the "Cho-Sin Few" (and *Manchurian Candidate* POWs) were no match for their superman predecessors. Like Herbert T. Gillis lording it over young Dobie, the G.I. and Silent Generations knew who had fought "the big one" and who hadn't. Denied glory, the young adults of the American High became (in historian William Manchester's words) "content to tinker with techniques and technicalities" in the new order their next-elders were forging.

In the first years of the High, Silent collegians found themselves surrounded by returning G.I. vets who got the best grades and job offers and who tolerated no "lip" from their juniors. In 1949, *Fortune* chastised the first mostly Silent college class for "taking no chances" and displaying a "gray flannel mentality." According to surveys, most of them wanted to work for big organizations; almost none wanted to start their own businesses. As Frank Conroy admitted, the Silent "clothing, manners, and lifestyle were . . . scaled-down versions of what we saw in the adults." Like Robert Morse in *How to Succeed in Business without Really Trying,* these young grads put on "sincere" ties, looked in the mirror, and saw what a professor in *Peggy Sue Got Married* chided as "a generation with strongly middle-aged values." As Manchester quipped, "Never had American youth been so withdrawn, cautious, unimaginative, indifferent, unadventurous—and silent."

The word *silent* was a G.I. put-down, but silence had been golden during their Crisis-era childhood. Norman Rockwell's portraits depicted boys and girls as clean and obedient with hardly a hint of mischief. Popular children's books *(Paddle to the Sea, The Little Engine That Could)* stressed helping others and dutiful behavior. Children were expected to behave impeccably in school—and, mostly, they did. As child illiteracy fell to 1.5 percent, the major discipline problems were reported to be gum chewing and line cutting. As a whole, Silent high-school students received lower grades but earned higher educational achievement scores than any generation before or since. Their adolescent pathologies (suicide, accidents, illegitimacy, crime, substance abuse) reached the lowest levels ever recorded. Any misconduct might elicit a withering remark from adults about uniformed men who were dying on their behalf. "Most of us kept quiet, attempting not to call attention to ourselves," recalls Conroy at a time when "to be a teenager was nothing, the lowest of the low."

The major challenge facing Silent teens was to emulate older G.I.s. The typical date-and-mate path was *The Tender Trap:* pairing off quickly, "tying the knot" after graduation, moving to the suburbs, and then blending in among G.I. neighbors. Philip Roth admitted that a High-era young man who didn't want to "settle down" in marriage "laid himself open to the charge of immaturity, if not latent or blatant homosexuality. Or he was just plain selfish. Or was frightened of responsibility." Young Silent women virtually disappeared from professions where young G.I. women made a mark before the war. America's most admired female star (Grace Kelly) abandoned her career to live with an overseas prince. For the only time ever in U.S. history, college-educated women were more fertile than those who did not complete secondary school. In 1956, the median marriage age for men and women dipped to the youngest ever measured.

Applying a similar loyalism to the work world, Silent men hastened to seal lifetime deals with big employers. *"The Man in the Gray Flannel Suit* stalked our nightmares,"* wrote Richard Schickel, "and soon enough *The Organization Man* would join him there, though of course, even as we read about these cautionary figures, many of us were talking to corporate recruiters about entry-level emulation of them." Millions of Silent men joined the "rat race," and it paid off big: The American High's cornucopia poured over people their age. By age twenty, most had exceeded their parents' lifetime education; by twenty-five, their parents' housing; by thirty, their incomes. From age twenty to forty, no other American generation ever attained such a steep rise in real per-capita income and household wealth—nor could any other generation even half believe in the Woody Allen credo that "eighty percent of life is just showing up." The bounty spread far beyond the elite: As the income gap between high- and low-achievers shrank, unskilled young workers were able to join the middle class and buy homes in suburban tracts. Young blacks who migrated North soon had higher incomes than their parents ever had—buttressed by strong families and supportive communities in even the roughest urban neighborhoods.

In the mid-1950s, sociologist David Riesman called the Silent the "Found Generation"—as benignly absorbed as the Lost had been alienated. By the time the last of them completed college, the Silent had achieved the nation's greatest two-generation advance in average years of schooling (more than thirteen years, versus less than nine years for the Lost). TV audiences took it for granted that collegiate "whiz kids" spoke in polysyllables while their Truman-like elders lapsed into slang, and corporations ran ads bragging about their brilliant young technicians.

Yet to the Silent's frustration, the High lent them no real coming-of-age challenge, and they were not of a temperament to invent a challenge for themselves. Older generations didn't expect them to achieve anything large, just to calibrate, to be what G.I. economist James Tobin called the "plumbers" of the national wealth machine. Like Colin Powell, Silent youths learned to be manipulators of systems, skilled at "meeting goals, doing what was expected." After they watched the careers of prewar leftists get chewed up in the McCarthy hearings, they avoided the unorthodox and safeguarded their permanent records. The military draft system "channeled" them into socially useful directions, pressuring young men with larger draft calls (as a percentage of the eligible pool) than Boomers would face at the peak of the Vietnam War—yet hardly anybody protested. The Silent instead displayed what Stephen Rosenfeld remembers as "a respect for authority and a toleration for discipline that came to look outlandish." But elders still did not take them seriously. *Look* magazine warned that pliable young adults were "capable of falling for the hysterical pitch of a Hitler or Stalin." Eisenhower even encouraged young people to read the *Communist Manifesto,* something he hardly would have done had he expected them to act on it.

Their aversion to risk helped spare them from outer danger, though not from inner trauma. "What, Me Worry?" said the smiling Alfred E. Neuman on the cover of *Mad* magazine. Worry they did—becoming *The Lonely Crowd,* the other-directed beneficiaries of a conformist culture. Many young people yearned to be a *Rebel without a Cause* like James Dean. In an era when "getting in trouble" meant dropping out of high school to get married, Silent "juvenile delinquents" were less youths who did wrong than youths who did nothing, who inexplicably refused to buy into the High mood. When Pauline Kael saw Dean in *East of Eden,* she wrote of the "new image in American films, the young boy as beautiful, disturbed animal, so full of love he's defenseless." "Few young Americans," wrote Silent historian David Halberstam, "have looked so rebellious and been so polite." Civic discipline was so imposing, and the need for emotional and sexual release so insistent, that songs and films depicted young people going crazy from the pressure. The youth culture bespoke a self-pity, the search for "someone to tell my troubles to," a fear of "heartbreak." Like Elvis, Silent youths felt *All Shook Up,* wondering "what's wrong with me? / I'm itchin' like a man on a fuzzy tree."

As the High wore on, many young graduates decided to lend a badly needed measure of humanity and sensitivity and beauty to a new social order that struck them as a little too rigid and geometric. They surged into expert or "helping" careers (medicine, ministry, law, teaching, social work, government), producing this century's biggest one-generation leap in the share of all workers belonging to a credentialed profession.

The Silent excelled at arts and letters, infusing subversive life and feeling into every genre they touched. Once Elvis Presley was deemed acceptable by G.I. "minister of culture" Ed Sullivan, rock 'n' roll and other Silent crossover styles helped non-Anglo cultural currents join the mainstream.

Silent "nonconformists" began convening at coffeehouses and uttering the occasional obscenity. In 1955, about the time when Allen Ginsberg read *Howl!* at San Francisco's Six Gallery, a Beat generation of goateed-and-sandaled young bohemians began sampling foreign cuisines, listening to offbeat jazz, reading hip poetry, telling "sick" jokes, and coyly deriding the G.I. "squaresville." G.I.s (like columnist Herb Caen) found these "beatniks" more amusing than threatening. After publishing *God and Man at Yale,* an erudite challenge to G.I. secularism, William F. Buckley launched the conservative *National Review* without any expectation that he could change where America was headed.

Encased in what Ken Kesey depicted as the "cuckoo's nest" sanitarium of High-era culture, the Silent bent the rules by cultivating refined naughtiness. Hugh Hefner described the consummate playboy as one who "likes jazz, foreign films, Ivy League clothes, gin and tonic, and pretty girls," with an "approach to life" that is "fresh, sophisticated, and yet admittedly sentimental." By the decade's end, hip thinking moved out of coffeehouses and into the suburbs with a style John Updike called "half Door Store, half Design Research." As Updike and Philip Roth wrote risqué novels about self-doubters, Tom Lehrer and Stan Freberg brought sophistication to satire, and Andy Warhol found art in a G.I. soup can. Apart from Dean and Presley, the typical young-adult film stars were "goofballs" like Jerry Lewis or "sweethearts" like Debbie Reynolds, usually cast alongside confident G.I. "straight men."

In politics, the G.I.'s ascendance brought a shining opportunity for the rising Silent and their reformist goals. When John Kennedy brought a bright new cast of Silent helpmates (Pierre Salinger, Bill Moyers, Robert Kennedy) into public prominence, he challenged the rest to enlist in the Peace Corps or join the civil rights movement. Millions did, nearly all of them men. Meanwhile, millions of Silent women glanced at the rings on their fingers, mops in their hands, and children at their feet and began wondering about the whole arrangement.

Whatever their social purpose or position, the Silent acknowledged the unstoppability of G.I. institutions. When Peter, Paul, and Mary sang "If I Had a Hammer," their peers knew that the G.I.s had the all hammers and were using them to build ICBMs and interstate highways. Premonitions of guilt began seeping into the Silent mind-set, a dread that horrible social crimes were being committed and hushed up, all for the sake of social discipline. A civil rights movement led by the young Martin Luther King Jr. used nonviolence with increasing success to appeal to the G.I. conscience. As young "outside agitators" started to probe the G.I. edifice for weak points, this rising generation was singing, ever more loudly, "Deep in my heart, I do believe, we shall overcome some day."

BOOMERS ENTERING CHILDHOOD: DENNIS THE MENACE

"We need idealistic children," announced pediatrician Benjamin Spock in his *Common Sense Book of Baby Care,* first published in 1946. Dr. Spock wanted to produce a new kind of child, and in many ways he did. Later, the phrase *Spock Baby* would be applied to an entire generation of American High babies—born through an era in which his book sold more than a million copies annually.

Through the American High, raising idealistic children became an anthem for G.I. parents who feared that their recent brush with apocalypse required a new temperament in the next generation. "We wanted our children to be inner-directed," explained Eda LeShan. "It seemed logical to us that fascism and communism . . . could not really succeed except in countries where children were raised by very authoritarian homes." Recalling their own youth collectivism, wincing at the McCarthy hearings, and worried about bland young adults, LeShan's G.I. peers wanted to raise children self-focused enough to resist peer pressure and "-isms" of all kinds.

Little Boomers thus grew up warmed by a strong sun of national optimism, blessed with what their chronicler Landon Jones dubbed *Great Expectations.* Postwar G.I. parents foresaw them becoming (in Manchester's words) "adorable as babies, cute as grade school pupils and striking as they entered their teens," after which "their parents would be very, very proud of them." The parental plan was for these kids to grow up living in modern houses from which they would take speedy monorails to gleaming cities where they would shop, play, and (perhaps) work. As the first Boomers filled colleges, *Time* magazine declared them "on the fringe of a golden era," soon to "lay out blight-proof, smog-free cities, enrich the underdeveloped world, and, no doubt, write *finis* to poverty and war." The baby boom itself was due partly to this adult optimism and partly to a natalism that encompassed all the fecund age brackets. While early nesting Silent produced roughly half the Boomer babies, the late-nesting G.I.s set the nurturing tone. The vast birth numbers amplified the High-era exuberance. In contrast to the Silent, the cloistered products of a birthrate plunge, Boomers came to resemble the yapping and multiplying puppies in *101 Dalmations,* symbols of plenitude.

Boomers were perceived as the modern kids of a modern age. Parents applied what LeShan termed "democratic discipline" and dealt with children "thoughtfully, reasonably, and kindly." Spock urged moms to coax (rather than threaten) in the nursery and to apply a "permissive" or "demand" feeding schedule that let infants eat when they wanted, not according to fixed rules. Throughout childhood, Boomers were nudged along by what one psychologist termed the "He'll-clean-up-his-room-when-he's-ready-to-have-a-clean-room" school of nurture. While mom's task was to tend to every complaint, dad's was to pay the bills without the kids' knowing where the money came from. At home, dads who upheld the strict male role model often felt out of place. A best-selling book advised parents to "eternally give to your children: Otherwise you are not a loving parent." Visiting Europeans joked about how strictly adult Americans obeyed their offspring.

Thanks to greater affluence, declines in adult mortality, and so many stay-at-home mothers, Boomer children enjoyed the most secure family life in American history. As G.I. dads commuted to work, G.I. moms invested endless time and energy in Boomer children. Susan Littwin recalled how "being a parent was a career, and like any career, the harder you worked, the more you gained." Few Boomer preschoolers had working mothers—and among those who did, four in five were cared for in their own homes, nearly always by relatives. Only 2 percent attended institutional day care. Spock emphasized the "mother-child bond," arguing that "creative" individuals owed their success to "the inspiration they received from a particularly strong relationship with a mother who had especially high aspirations for her children." Later in life, Boomer radicals would admit to having felt during their childhood what sociologist Kenneth Keniston termed "an unusually strong tie" to their mothers. In a Vietnam-era poll, 32 percent of white Boomers (44 percent of blacks) mentioned their mothers alone as the "person who cares about me"; only 8 percent of whites (2 percent of blacks) said the same about their fathers.

Midlife G.I. men placed a huge emphasis on fixing the physical environment to improve the child's world. Untended nature was the enemy. Bottles were preferred to breast milk, making Boomers the least breast-fed generation in U.S. history. G.I. scientists conquered such once-terrible childhood diseases as diphtheria and polio, and fluoridated the water to protect kids' teeth. Pediatrics reached its height of physical aggressiveness: No generation of kids got more shots or operations, including millions of circumcisions and tonsillectomies that would not now be performed.

Meanwhile, the high standards of G.I. science bolstered public education. American schools enjoyed their all-time peak of institutional confidence, thanks in part to a powerful mutual support network between mothers and teachers. Boomers were taught by the brightest of G.I. women, to whom most other professions were closed. Spurred by the Soviet *Sputnik* launch, taxpayers seldom refused pleas to build and equip new schools. G.I. motives weren't just geopolitical: Many Boomers recall parents telling them how hard adults were working to build a prosperous and secure country in which kids could grow up asking the big questions about the meaning of life—and maybe even coming up with some answers. Where the Missionaries taught G.I.s the basics, G.I.s taught Boomers critical thinking, instilling in them what Keniston later described as an "orientation to principle."

The most important (and scientific) new nurturing device was television.

From the mid-1940s to mid-1950s, the average daily hours a household spent watching TV rose from 0 to 4.5. Boomer kids digested a black-and-white parade of simple plots full of competent parents, smart scientists, honest leaders, and happy endings. In comics and on TV and movie screens, children were depicted as rambunctious *Dennis the Menaces,* as kids whose *Shaggy Dog* curiosity got the better of them, or as mystery-solving masters of loyal *Lassie* animals. Like Ward Cleaver, TV grownups would usually *Leave It to Beaver,* letting kids learn from their own mistakes in a world that smiled on childlike error.

Kids couldn't help but notice how attentive adults were to whatever happened to be on their minds. As the buoyant Art Linkletter put it, "Kids say the darnedest things." Anything of interest to children keenly absorbed older people. Earlier in the twentieth century, says Jones, "it would have been impossible to imagine the under-ten group starting anything. . . . But the fads of the fifties, almost without exception, were the creations of children." From Mickey Mouse ears and Davy Crockett caps to hula hoops, Silly Putty, Slinky, and Barbie, Boomers became the first child generation to be target marketed by advertising agencies. Toward the end of the High, pleasing teenagers became a very important goal for a nation that, in the recent Crisis, had shown scant interest in Silent adolescence.

Many a child's life did indeed match the *Happy Days* image preserved in vintage TV sit-coms. To Boomer kids, any problem seemed fixable by competent and rational adults. Cheryl Merser remembers how "somebody" ("God or a saint or a guardian angel or the stars") was always watching over them. The future appeared to be "the way life was on *The Jetsons*—happy, easy, uncomplicated, prosperous." To most middle-class youths, poverty, disease, and crime were invisible or, at worst, temporary nuisances that would soon succumb to the inexorable advance of affluence. At no other time in the twentieth century did the mainstream culture impart such a benign worldview to children, seldom requiring them to prepare for painful challenges or tragic outcomes. Watching the TV game *Truth or Consequences,* kids realized that the truth brought payoffs and the consequences were jokes. With life so free of danger, kids felt free to cultivate strong inner lives.

Boomer kids were made to feel welcome not just by their own parents, but also by their communities. They became the targets of libraries, recreation centers, and other civic entities that had in the Crisis been the domain of working adults (or, today, of recreating seniors). Surrounded by such open-handed generosity, child Boomers developed what Daniel Yankelovich termed the "psychology of entitlement." Landon Jones recalls how "what other generations have thought privileges, Boomers thought were rights."

Throughout the American High, the feed-on-demand Boomer spirit remained sunny. A 1960 study found kids aged nine to thirteen possessed of very positive sentiments toward the adult world. Robert Samuelson remembers reaching adolescence in "a period of high optimism when people believed that technology and society's best minds could guarantee social improvement." As the 1960s dawned, Cal-Berkeley's G.I. president Clark Kerr visited local high schools and concluded that the coming crop of students "are going to be easy to handle." "There aren't going to be any riots," he predicted.

TOWARD THE SECOND TURNING

In 1963, Stephen Spender characterized the postwar years as *The Struggle of the Modern,* proof positive that civilization carries on after a disaster. Only eighteen years of prosperity separated America from its memory of World War II, yet already people considered anything postwar as distinctly modern and anything prewar as distinctly not. In *Remembering the Thirties,* the English writer Donald Davie observed that the transatlantic verities of the prewar years now felt "more remote than Ithaca or Rome."

When the old poet Robert Frost heralded a new Augustan Age at Kennedy's inaugural, the occasion marked a triumph for his own Missionary Generation. The "good kids" Frost's generation had parented were poised to give life to his peers' parting visions. Yet the passing of the last Missionaries meant that, throughout the High, America lacked any adult generation focused on inner spiritualism. Frost's poem reached the ears of many small children born a decade after V-J Day—the same distance that separated his own birth from Appomattox. Had Frost reflected on this and on the attacks his own generation had launched against his own Gilded Age elders, he would have realized that the Augustan Age he heralded in 1960 was due to end soon. Frost died in 1963; like all but a tiny remnant of his very old Missionary Generation, he never personally witnessed what lay ahead.

In the American High, the generational archetypes shifted the mood away from the dark urgency of depression and war and toward the energy and optimism that enabled this new (if impermanent) Augustan Age. Taken together, the Lost, G.I., Silent, and Boomer life-cycle roles pushed the entire society toward public order, family stability, conformity, institution building, and a belief in secular progress. America became functional and future oriented, the national sum greater than its parts.

This mood could not last indefinitely. True to its archetype, each generation could sustain its current role through one phase of life only. Approaching the next phase, no generation showed signs of accepting the role its predecessor had assumed at like age. Would G.I.s be cautious anchors, or the Silent optimistic builders, or Boomers acquiescent helpmates? Would the next child generation enjoy an even warmer nurture? Nothing like that had ever happened before, nor would it happen this time.

Toward the end of a High, strains begin to show:

■ The *elder Nomads,* now appearing less cautious than reactionary, begin impeding the Heroes' expanding ambitions.

■ The *midlife Heroes,* now filled with the hubris of power, grow impatient to lead society toward ever-grander worldly constructions.

■ The *young-adult Artists,* now chafing at an unfulfilling helpmate's role, yearn to break away and take down social barriers.

■ The *child Prophets,* indulged by adults who are confident in their future, begin sensing a dire spiritual void at the heart of the Heroes' secular order.

By the early 1960s, as the four archetypes fully occupied these life-cycle phases, tensions deepened. As each archetype began entering its next phase of life—the Hero into elderhood, the Artist into midlife, the Prophet into young adulthood—their prior social roles were becoming unsustainable.

The postwar High was spent; it could not last. A new mood was necessary—and coming. The spark came on November 22, 1963. From the standpoint of history, the events of that day were critical but not essential. Had Oswald missed, the specifics would have been different, but the saeculum would still have carved its path. The Second Turning would have come, one way or another. It was time.

CHAPTER 7

∎

The Second Turning:
Consciousness Revolution (1964–1984)

"WHERE WERE YOU IN '62?" ASKED THE AD FOR *AMERICAN Graffiti,* one of many films, plays, and songs about what America was like just before the mood shift—*before* November 22, 1963. John Kennedy's assassination became a personal milestone for nearly everyone alive at the time. Immediately after that tragedy, people wanted to believe that nothing had been touched. Theodore White surveyed a grieving Washington and declared it "all as it had been before . . . unchanged." Yet even if America had not changed on the outside, an irreversible inner change had begun. A new wedge was penetrating the national psyche.

The next year—1964—brought the opening skirmishes of several new movements whose full meaning would reveal itself over the next two decades. That spring, Ed Sullivan invited the Beatles onto his show, implying elder approval for young people who banged drums and let their hair grow. That summer, the GOP convention that nominated Barry Goldwater set an angry new tone for politics, and inner cities unleashed the first of many "long, hot summers." That fall, Berkeley's Free Speech movement raged against the academic Establishment, and Democrats ran ads warning that Goldwater would incinerate flower-picking children. Meanwhile, LBJ had arranged a Tonkin Gulf incident that would soon enrage flower children of a different sort. A rupture appeared between the mood of the people and the mood of their leaders. "On Capitol Hill the nation's business went forward in an atmosphere of mutual understanding and respect," reported *Advise and Consent* novelist Allen Drury, "while riots and violence flared in many places over the country."

America had entered the Awakening today remembered as the Consciousness Revolution.

. . .

Following Kennedy's death, the U.S. economy roared along at a pace that Sylvia Porter exuded "has no precedent in peacetime anywhere." With the business cycle harnessed, leaders bragged about "growthmanship" and gradually pushed down on the fiscal and monetary accelerator. Extrapolating from the last twenty years, top economists declared that Americans would soon have to spend their lives consuming rather than producing. Experts began wondering if people could handle such prosperity. Robert Theobald wrote of *The Challenge of Abundance,* Roy Harrod of "the possibility of economic satiety," John Kenneth Galbraith of a "technostructure" that was programming the public into buying more goods than anyone really needed or wanted. A hot issue was whether Americans were capable of making up their own minds and simply enjoying themselves.

With the future promising such material abundance, the public began fixating on issues of conscience and dissent, prompting Alistair Cooke to warn that a "healthy rage against the pretensions and abuses of authority" could lead to "an amused distrust for any system or authority at all." Beneath it all lay a huge assumption: No matter how hard anyone raged, the physical infrastructure (power plants, highways, capital stock) and social habits (families, civic order, work habits) would remain rock solid. People came to believe that the more they got in touch with their inner desires, the more creatively they could consume what they produced—which would not only lend the cornucopia a higher purpose but also keep it going.

Although the Awakening was made possible by this durable confidence in the American way of life, the era eroded first the confidence, then the way of life. The erosion of confidence began in 1964, signaled by three apocalyptic films *(Seven Days in May, Fail-Safe,* and *Dr. Strangelove)* that indicted the High's trust in authority, government, and technology. To the new mind-set, social authority came at an unacceptable cost: Corporations crushed the individual, police oppressed the poor, academe smothered creativity, and parents deformed the child's psyche. Like long hair, this attitude began in the mid-1960s among the children of the affluent; by the late 1970s, it had filtered its way down through the middle and working classes to the poor. In *The Dream and the Nightmare,* Myron Magnet observed that an Awakening that began as an experimental euphoria among secure elites ended with pandemic family and community dysfunction whose most debilitating symptoms were observed among the poor.

With each passing year, the Awakening spirit penetrated the mainstream more deeply. Those who trusted the old verities became ever more anxious about what could come next. As he annually took America's pulse, James Reston chronicled how 1966 brought "a curious mood . . . of questioning, doubt, and frustration"; 1967 a sense of "internal crisis, . . . extremist politics" and "escapism among young persons"; 1968 "violence and defiance,

. . . protest and reaction," and "a widespread feeling . . . that things were getting out of hand"; and 1969 "frustration, destruction, counterviolence, racial tension, and fear."

Through that half decade, as Americans began "humanizing" their society, the mood alternated between bliss and doom. The most widely read vision of the future was Edgar Cayce's *The Sleeping Prophet,* which explained why the ancient technocracy of Atlantis came to an apocalyptic end. While the Commission on the Year 2000 lamented "great ruptures in moral temper," two films *(2001: A Space Odyssey* and *Barbarella)* revealed the future as a fantastic interplay of mind, body, and machine. From rainbow clothing to more supposed honesty about nudity and obscenity on Broadway, Americans of all ages participated in what Charles Reich called the *Greening of America,* the elevation of bell-bottomed self over gray-flannel community. In 1968, the murders of Martin Luther King Jr. and Robert Kennedy completed an assassination trilogy that struck many as the tragic if natural outgrowth of an era of unstoppable passion and violence.

During four midsummer weeks in 1969, three landmark events—*Apollo 11,* Woodstock, and Chappaquiddick—dramatized the most poignant contradictions of Awakening-era America. The first moon landing was a sublime expression of man's technological grandeur, marking the ultimate in "mission control" for those who believed in science, teamwork, and the conquest of nature. It achieved what Ayn Rand called "concretization" of American "rationality." Yet, as the media reminded everyone, moon rockets also diverted resources from poor people. The capsule had barely returned when Woodstock coarsely challenged the social order that made it possible. Grandeur was passé; bigness now meant half-clad mobs, not uniformed phalanxes. Meanwhile, Ted Kennedy's Chappaquiddick misadventure exemplified Americans' declining standards of public decorum and private virtue—and their flight from the suffocating duties of family life and childraising. In between watching these news stories on TV, people went to the bookstore to buy *Portnoy's Complaint,* to the theater to see *Oh Calcutta!,* and to the movies to watch *Rosemary's Baby.* Jimmy Hendrix's siren song "Star Spangled Banner" marked America's cultural Rubicon. Nothing in the culture would ever again feel quite the same or, later, feel quite so spontaneous and *new.*

That same year—1969—was the bloodiest of the Vietnam War, the conflict that lay at the Awakening's epicenter. From the Generation Gap to mob violence to rock music to the final exhaustion of the Great Society, this war was inseparable from the Awakening itself. Perhaps Vietnam's civil war would have been a fixable foreign problem back in the High, but American intervention was doomed to failure in the Awakening. Scientifically managed, the war tried to prop up a morally questionable ally without slowing the pace of grand constructions at home. It didn't work. For the first time in living memory, America's leaders were forced to concede that big national problems both abroad and at home lay beyond their capacity to solve. Yet the Vietnam War was more symptom than cause of the deepening cultural upheaval. James Reston remarked that America's "internal crisis could not be explained by any decline in the fortunes of the war" that had become a "symbol of a far deeper dissatisfaction with a wider set of circumstances."

The nation's domestic planners voiced the same hubris that afflicted the Pentagon. In 1966, LBJ's poverty chief, Sargent Shriver, predicted that the War on Poverty would be won in "about ten years." By the early 1970s, even as the Vietnam War effort sputtered, the goal of "Guns and Butter" plus a "guaranteed income" was considered achievable for a nation then landing men on the moon twice a year. By the time Saigon fell, both political parties were agreeing to spend the new "peace dividend" on middle-class elder benefits. Richard Nixon, Wilbur Mills, George McGovern and other G.I. leaders realized that, while the future cost of these benefits was vast, they were nonetheless affordable because younger generations would someday be richer than Croesus. What they didn't realize was that the High-era cornucopia was already a broken-down machine running on fumes.

Many Americans stopped believing in (or even caring about) economic progress. As people started looking at the future more inwardly, opinion leaders began to question whether further abundance would make Americans better people or simply corrupt them with greed. From the first Earth Day in April 1970 to the last *Apollo* launch in December 1972, cutting-edge America made the break from a Think Big to a Small Is Beautiful mind-set. Then in 1973 and 1974 the institutional order—and prosperity—broke down. With Watergate and its coincident recession, the forces of individualism had triumphed. Jimmy Carter was elected by a nation fed up with public grandiosity.

During the 1970s, which John Updike derided as "a slum of a decade," distrust of all large institutions (from governments to businesses to families) became rampant. As *The Late Great Planet Earth* led nonfiction best-seller lists, environmentalists called on Americans to consume less energy and build fewer big things. By living in a more passive harmony with outer nature, it was thought, Americans could reach truer harmony with their inner natures. This declinism sapped the nation's workplace productivity—without, however, quelling any thirst for goods. Combined with two inflationary oil price shocks, the result was a growthless stagflation. Even today, more than two decades later, America's average real take-home wage has yet to regain its 1973 level.

Late in the Awakening, the nation reeled from blows that would have been inconceivable in the High: gas lines, the Iran hostage crisis, and a plummeting dollar. As Jimmy Carter declared that America was suffering a national malaise, the World Symposium on Humanity declared a "Manifesto of the Person," proclaiming a "sovereign right of self-discovery" in which "the journey is the destination." Americans were now fully absorbed into what Christopher Lasch called the "Culture of Narcissism," feeling that the best way to approach life was not (as in the High) to start with the community and move in, but to start with the self and move out. The Awakening's last act was for ideological conservatives to reach the same conclusion and thereby launch a huge political revival. During the tax-cut fever of the late 1970s and the rise of Ronald Reagan in 1980, conservatives at last gave up on the Establishment. Agreeing with the post-Woodstock view that, yes, the individual is infinitely more virtuous than the state, they discovered to their delight that a society full of autonomous individualists was the perfect soil for a reenergized Republican Party.

By the end of Reagan's first term, the Awakening had run its course. Between 1964 and 1984, America's inner yearnings surged and its outer discipline decayed. As veteran pollster Daniel Yankelovich documented in his early 1980s mood scan, *New Rules: Searching for Self-Fulfillment in a World Turned Upside Down,* the Consciousness Revolution had transformed how the American people thought about themselves in relation to the larger community.

Anyone who was then an adult can recall how shifting generational currents influenced the history of those years. Indeed, memories of the Awakening follow generational lines. For G.I.s, the Consciousness Revolution was a time of disappointment, humiliation, and angry division. For the Silent, these were times of personal "passages" when their lives became more turbulent and adventuresome. For Boomers (who recall this era the most favorably), the Awakening laid out a lifetime agenda. For 13ers, this was, as the young writer Julie Phillips puts it, "like one of those stories where nobody laughs and you say, 'I guess you had to be there.' "

The mood of the American High was unsustainable, like a bubble in history. With or without the assassinations, the Vietnam War, and Watergate, the saeculum had to have its Awakening.

SECOND TURNINGS AND ARCHETYPES

Including this most recent era, Anglo-American history has had six Second Turnings (Awakenings), dating back to the sixteenth century:

- *Protestant Reformation* (1517–1542), Reformation Saeculum
- *Puritan Awakening* (1621–1649), New World Saeculum
- *Great Awakening* (1727–1746), Revolutionary Saeculum
- *Transcendental Awakening* (1822–1844), Civil War Saeculum
- *Third Great Awakening* (1886–1908), Great Power Saeculum
- *Consciousness Revolution* (1964–1984), Millennial Saeculum

An Awakening is an era of cultural upheaval and spiritual renewal. It begins when the waxing social discipline of the High suddenly seems tiresome, unfulfilling, illegitimate, and unjust—and when people begin to defy it in the name of spiritual authenticity. By now, memories of the last Crisis are buffered by the High's calm and comfort, and the core High virtues are regarded as outmoded, even unnecessary. The Awakening climaxes just after civilized progress reaches a saecular high tide—and just before that progress is overwhelmed by the liberating passions of reform and protest. The Awakening ends when the new consciousness converts its enemies and the new values regime overwhelms its oppressors.

This is the saecular solstice, the era of maximum light. The supply of social order reaches its apex, but the demand for order is now falling. The summer season begins, says Shakespeare, when "rough winds do shake the darling buds of May." Next come the canicular days and hot nights, when order relaxes and spirits rise. Thunder booms and electricity fills the air, as storms come and go with little warning. The season is inseparable from the passions of youth, when Emerson suggests that "we clothe ourselves with rainbows, and go as brave as the zodiac." As the midsummer fairies appear, life thickens, greens deepen, and paths get harder to find. At summer's end, nature creates a mood of satiation. Like Joseph Wood Krutch's month of August, the end of an Awakening "creates as she slumbers, replete and satisfied."

When a society moves from a High to an Awakening, the mood shift is deceptive. At first, people regard it as a minor (if refreshing) fillip to trusted institutions. Then the new passions gain force, laying siege against an old order that doesn't know how to stop building. As society's inner life strengthens, its outer life weakens. People exalt rights over duties, self over society, ideals over institutions, creativity over conformism. However blithely Awakenings begin, they gradually develop a dark edge. Besieged institutions no longer deliver the order and prosperity previously taken for granted. A new specter of apocalypse fans the intensity and hardens the ideology of the reformist agenda—often triggering violence, social chaos, and political convulsion. "Reformation must be universal," announced a member of Parliament in 1641. "Reform all places, all persons and callings. . . . Reform the universities, reform the cities, reform the counties. . . . You have more work to do that I can speak. . . . Every plant which my heavenly Father hath not planted shall be rooted up." By its end, an Awakening propels a broadening consensus that people's individual lives are in better condition than their collective social order.

At a distance, Awakening eras are memorable for their images of contrasting extremes—the triumph of power, wealth, and knowledge side by side with the passionate outcry of the spirit. Typically, the former reflects the achievements of the ruling generation, the latter the voice of the rising generation. Picture Cardinal Wolsey presiding over his sumptuous palaces next to collegians straining to learn about Luther's protest. Picture Francis Bacon completing his *Advancement of Learning* in the face of scornful Puritan converts insisting on salvation through faith alone. Picture Governor De Witt Clinton opening the stately Erie Canal next to the swooning young workers creating an evangelical Burned-Over District along its route. Or picture President Grover Cleveland turning on the electrified White City of Chicago's Columbian Exposition across town from anarchists and populists denouncing the new industrial America. Awakenings bear witness to history's noisiest showdowns between the kingdoms of Caesar and God.

Awakenings produce this mood because of the archetypes then entering a new life-cycle phase: Heroes into elderhood, Artists into midlife, Prophets into young adulthood, and Nomads into childhood. Generational differences come into sharp relief, as Prophets come of age assaulting the Heroes' constructions.

▪ As expansive *Heroes* replace Nomads in *elderhood,* they orchestrate ever-grander secular constructions, setting the stage for the spiritual goals of the young.

At last unconstrained by the caution of older Nomads, aging Hero generations enter the Awakening at their height of public power. The threshold of old age does not slow down their energy and collective purpose; instead, it spurs them to ever grander constructions. When their hubris is attacked by young zealots, they first battle against the new values, then accede to them. Afterward, they retain institutional power, through which they seek and receive economic reward from the young. During the latter stages of an Awakening, public coffers shower benefits on the war veterans who once sacrificed themselves for posterity. Aging Heroes are associated with optimism, teamwork, and civic trust at a time when younger generations appear to lack those qualities.

The Glorious elders of the Great Awakening perceived themselves to be what Benjamin Colman termed America's first "men of this world." Still marking GDs (for good deeds) in the margins of his diary, Cotton Mather felt his "patience . . . tried by the contempt" of young zealots "going the way of ecstasy" rather than "repentance." At the dawn of the Transcendental Awakening, old Republicans basked in acclaim as the New World's greatest generation ever. Yet even as Jefferson hailed "the great march of progress" and "general spread of the light of science," youthful critics spurned his generation's Masonic brotherhood and scorned its secure and palladian rationalism. "We will leave this scene not for a tittering generation who wish to push us from it," fulminated old David Humphreys. Beware "your worst passions," Albert Gallatin presciently warned the young. After hearing the bitter early debates over slavery, Jefferson despaired that "the useless sacrifice of themselves by the generation of 1776, to acquire self-government and happiness to their country, is to be thrown away by the unwise and unworthy passions of their sons."

■ As indecisive *Artists* replace Heroes in *midlife,* they apply
  expertise and process to improve society while calming the
  passions of the young.

Caught in a generational whipsaw, torn between the inner mission of younger Prophets and the outer mission of older Heroes, Artist generations carve out a mediator's role. They mentor new youth movements while sensitizing and pluralizing their elders' constructions. As they patch together a midlife pastiche out of fragments of the Hero and Prophet personas, they compensate for their earlier conformism by engaging in high-risk institutional and family behavior. Tolerant of discord, Artists deflect argument by compromising or postponing unpleasant choices.

Entering the Great Awakening just too old to join the youth protest, the Enlighteners warned (like Benjamin Doolittle) against "too much boldness," preferring instead to focus (like Nathaniel Appleton) on "pointing out those middle and peaceable ways" while seeking equipoise. "I have studied to preserve a due moderation," admitted Edward Wigglesworth, "and if any expressions have happened to slip from me, that may seem a little too warm or harsh, I shall be sorry for it." During the Transcendental Awakening, middle-aged Compromisers built their reputation as a "post-heroic generation." Like William Wirt, they tried "to assume the exterior of composure and self-collectedness, whatever riot and confusion may be within." Their destiny lay in solutions that split the difference. At the close of the nineteenth century, midlife Progressives searched through what Henry James called "the confusion of life" to find "the close connection of bliss and bale, of the things that help with the things that hurt." Such instinctive moderation helped keep the Third Great Awakening from deteriorating into social chaos.

■ As self-absorbed *Prophets* replace Artists in *young adulthood,*
  they challenge the moral failure of elder-built institutions,
  sparking a societywide spiritual awakening.

Having known firsthand only the High and not the Crisis, young-adult Prophet generations take for granted the comforts and indulgences of the new secular order. Nurtured to be creative thinkers, they cultivate a strong inner life. They burst forth with angry challenges to the older Heroes' grand constructions, which they regard as intolerably deficient in moral worth. Young Prophets look upon themselves (and their culture) as beacons of a new spiritual authority and arbiters of a new values regime. Eventually, they persuade others to join the pursuit of individual autonomy at the expense of social cooperation. They thereby launch the entire society into a fever of renewal.

Amid the Jacobean prosperity of the Puritan Awakening, John Winthrop exhorted his fellow Puritan "saints" to reject the "common corruptions" of "these so evil and declining times" and join him in founding a New Jerusalem. During the Great Awakening, young preachers fulminated against the "spirit-dead," demanding "New Light" faith over "Old Light" works, denouncing "those of another generation" who (in Gilbert Tennent's words) "imagine happiness is to be had in wealth and riches" amid all their "driving, driving to duty, duty!" When his Awakener peers were coming of age, "It seemed as if all the world were growing religious," Benjamin Franklin later recalled. At the climax of the Transcendental Awakening, William Lloyd Garrison vowed "to wake up a nation slumbering in the lap of moral death." As youth movements spread, Margaret Fuller's *Dial* magazine heralded "the unfolding of the individual man, into every form of perfection, without let or hindrance, according to the inward nature of each." The post–Civil War Missionary Generation assaulted the complacency of the Gilded Age. In 1889, George Herron, the twenty-seven-year-old "Prophet of Iowa College," electrified the Midwest and energized his peers when he lashed out at "the wicked moral blindness of our industrialism." The Third Great Awakening was under way.

■ As *Nomads* replace Prophets in *childhood,* they are left underprotected at a time of social convulsion and adult self-discovery.

Nomad generations have the misfortune to be children in an era when adults are persuading each other to shed social discipline and rediscover their deeper selves. Struggling to cope with the harsh underside of cultural upheaval, Nomad children acquire a cynicism about moral crusades and a fatalism about weak adults apparently unable to make simple things work. They are expected to grow up fast and learn to be independent, resourceful, and competitive at an early age. As they do, however, these qualities earn their fledgling generation a negative reputation among adults. By the end of the Awakening, as adults survey the damage done to the child's world, young Nomads become metaphors of society's newfound pessimism about the future.

Cavalier children grew up hearing disappointed elders like Richard Mather refer to "the sad face of the rising generation." "Are we not," asked Richard's son Eleazar, "a generation . . . in danger to sink and perish in the waters?" The rest of their lives, the Cavaliers marked the greatest one-generation backstep in years of education and life expectancy in American history. During the Great Awakening, clergymen observed how religious fervor

"frequently frights the little children, and sets them screaming," with enduring consequences for the Liberty Generation's skeptical temperament. During the Transcendental Awakening, Gilded youths were described as
practicing self-dependence, prompting a foreign visitor to remark that "children are commercial before they get out of their petticoats." Reflecting on
his own childhood, Thomas Wolfe wondered "what has happened to the
spontaneous gaiety of youth" among a Lost generation raised "without innocence, born old and stale and dull and empty, . . . suckled on darkness,
and weaned on violence and noise."

Throughout history, this layering of archetypes has produced Awakenings. The years between 1964 and 1984—the Consciousness Revolution—
were no exception.

G.I.s ENTERING ELDERHOOD: SENIOR CITIZENS

"Americans today bear themselves like victory-addicted champions," proclaimed *Look* magazine in 1965. "They've won their wars and survived their
depressions. They are accustomed to meeting, and beating, tests." For the
generation then reaching peak power, one such test was to demonstrate that
John Kennedy's assassination, however tragic, had not undermined its collective energy. Civil rights legislation provided the first trial. Through
Kennedy's term, Lost Generation leaders like Everett Dirksen and Dixiecrat
Richard Russell had succeeded in derailing integration, but now LBJ began
muscling laws through.

That was only the beginning. Lyndon Johnson's 1964 landslide trampled
what remained of Lost resistance. By 1966, the majority-G.I. Congress was
spending nearly as much money on education and health care in one year as
earlier Congresses had spent throughout the whole of American history. In
just a few months, the nation created everything from new transportation
and housing departments to new civil rights agencies to Medicare and Medicaid: The "Great 89th Congress" confirmed the G.I.s' collective ability to
build a Great Society, fight two wars, one cold and one hot, and reach the
moon, too. As Eric Hoffer said of the *Apollo* program, these generational
achievements marked "the triumph of the squares."

To work as intended, though, the G.I. edifices required beneficiaries to
behave as "squarishly" as they—but, as the Awakening progressed, younger
people did not. Like B. F. Skinner, G.I.s sought to create a "technology of
behavior," to design and build their way to social bliss. Yet while G.I.s envisioned a well-behaved *Walden Two,* the young insisted on acting out the
more Thoreau-like original. Model Cities public housing became hotbeds of
youth crime, welfare subsidized teen pregnancies, and tuition grants enabled
students to riot when they might otherwise have had to hold down jobs.

The launching of the Awakening produced a values clash then known as the Generation Gap. From hair to clothes to sex to music to tone of voice, everything about the new youth movement struck G.I. eyes and ears as divisive, passionate, and selfish—just the opposite of the qualities this aging generation had come to admire in itself. If the late 1960s were thrilling for young resisters, they were intensely frustrating for G.I. leaders, many of whom had children in the resistance: "Everything seemed to come unhinged" (James MacGregor Burns); "Something has gone sour, in teaching and in learning" (George Wald); "I use the phrase soberly: The nation disintegrates" (John Gardner).

Having conquered half the globe as young footsoldiers, G.I. leaders never imagined that a small regional war would pose much of a problem. The only two votes against the Tonkin Gulf Resolution came from older Lost Generation skeptics (Senators Morse and Gruening). But once the war was on, neither the troops nor the home front behaved in a way that pleased Lyndon Johnson's generation, and quarrels between parents and children (between G.I. fathers and Boomer sons, especially) worsened by the year. As Vietnam wore on, this generation despaired that their prized federal government had become, in Nixon's words, "a pitiless, helpless giant" no longer capable of doing great things. The old G.I. optimism began to ring hollow. Ultimately, the Bundy-Rusk-Rostow-McNamara "controlled-response" strategy culminated in a controlled *defeat,* alias Nixon's Vietnamization. Ever since, polls have shown that G.I.s are more likely than Boomers to despise Vietnam's memory.

The full price of G.I. hubris was still to be paid. Watergate became the Awakening's Thermidor, as two Boomers (Woodward and Bernstein) exacted the Generation Gap's biggest trophy: Nixon's resignation in disgrace. The power was thus sapped from the national government, even if the White House would long remain the property of this aging generation. The ensuing congressional election led to the ouster of powerful G.I. committee chairmen and the enactment of countless new procedural entanglements that made big new G.I.-style programs impossible. Nor was this limited to government: After Watergate, G.I. industrialists constantly heard themselves accused of moral outrages against nature, women, minorities, the poor, and the deepest needs of the human soul. By decade's end, petroleum had twice come into shortage. Energy was something young G.I.s had spent many a sweaty Depression-era day unleashing; now they heard constant complaints from youth that life would be better if only people used less of what those old G.I.-built dams and power plants produced.

Gradually G.I.s gave up arguing with the young, some agreeing with Milton Mayer that "we were wrong, and the new generation is right." The Awakening values regime flew in the face of their lifelong credo of optimism, teamwork, and community, but as G.I.s entered old age, agreeing with their kids could be construed as a sign of victory. Like George Bush later declared, this generation was inclined to "see life in terms of missions—missions defined, missions completed." Once the Awakening appeared irre-versible, G.I.s could lean back and admit that they had indeed made life pretty comfortable, and that maybe it *was* time to let go a little. Together, G.I.s had lifted America out of the Depression and built a magnificent pros-perity machine. Now, mission completed, it was time to claim a few tro-phies. As aging parents and bosses heard their children deride whatever remained of the High-era culture, G.I.s saw no point in holding their ground. And so, bit by bit, they acquiesced in a pan-generational ethos of self-in-dulgence.

The generation gap between G.I.s and their Boomer children thus reached a lopsided truce: Boomers won the values debate and control over the culture, while G.I.s continued to preside over the institutional firmament and gathered a vast public reward. "You've already paid most of your dues. Now start collecting the benefits," advised a brochure of AARP, an organi-zation which, having shed its Lost-era reticence, now emerged as leader of what *Newsweek* called "the single most powerful lobbying bloc on the planet." From the early 1960s to the late 1970s, the membership of elder or-ganizations (and the circulation of elder periodicals) grew sixtyfold, and their message shifted from the Lost's High-era self-reliance to a new notion of entitlement. After its beneficiaries began applying Awakening-era tactics that Gray Panthers called the "life style of outrage," Social Security attained its present-day status as the "third rail" of national politics. Meanwhile, ag-ing G.I.s provided the core of California's Proposition 13 and other local re-volts demanding—and winning—reductions in school taxes. Where Lost elders once preferred to attack public spending and leave revenues alone, G.I. seniors wanted the opposite. Where Lost elders had been overwhelm-ingly Republican, most G.I. elders were reliably Democratic.

Fueled by the new senior lobby, the last G.I. Congresses spent the entire post-Vietnam fiscal peace dividend on their own peers. By the late 1970s, transfer payments from younger generations to G.I.s towered (by a ten-to-one ratio) over what remained of Great Society poverty programs. This sud-den elder affluence was an extraordinary G.I. achievement. Through the High, when the Lost were old, elder benefits had fallen 20 percent behind wages; now, what seniors received from the U.S. government rose fifteen times faster than average wages. Where Lost elders had been the poorest generation of the High, G.I. seniors became the *least* poor generation of the Awakening. From 1957 to 1976, the proportion of persons scoring "very high" on a test of anxiety fell by one-third for elders while rising sharply for all other age brackets. Seven of eight G.I. seniors said they were faring bet-ter than their parents had, while other polls revealed them as the Awakening era's happiest and financially least-troubled generation.

Younger generations didn't much object to paying taxes to support extra benefits for seniors, because the money financed the latter's separation—culturally, geographically, and familially. The new subsidies also induced

G.I.s to vacate the workplace, voluntarily, as the youngest retirees in U.S. history. For the Lost, the word *retirement* had connoted something you did with a worn-out horse; for G.I.s, it came to mean a two-decade-long leisure world in relatively good health. Millions of retiring G.I.s separated into seniors-only communities, often far from where their grown children lived. Once there, they began showing a vigor and cheerfulness reminiscent of the High-era suburbs they had built in midlife. In Arizona's Sun City, observed Boomer gerontologist Ken Dychtwald, "it's hard to find time to talk to people; they're too active and busy." In their new communities, seniors could wall out the encroachments of Awakening-era culture. "Sun City is secure," said Dychtwald. "A resident may stroll the streets without fear of surprise, of unpleasantness, or unsightliness."

A powerful generational hubris underlay this vast new senior edifice no less than it did Vietnam or the Great Society. Where a G.I. Tomorrowland had once meant monorails and moon walks, it now meant space-age medicine in the intensive-care unit. As America's first elders to call themselves "senior citizens," most G.I.s believed that their collective choices were necessarily good for all generations—that whatever they did to improve their own old age would also improve it for those who followed, if only the young would stay optimistic and be patient. But as often happened during the Awakening, G.I.s persisted in the earlier civic habits without the earlier focus on the future. Senior benefits exploded upward at exactly the same time worker incomes started sputtering. The senior poverty rate plunged during the 1970s, exactly when the child poverty rate skyrocketed. Having inherited from their own parents an economy with vast excess capacity just waiting for youth to harness it, G.I.s began to pass on to their own children a fiscally overloaded economy unable to afford a new public agenda.

Even as they let go, G.I.s continued to sustain their reputation (and their self-image) as active and competent achievers. In this, they were assisted by a new consensus about aging. Back in the High, an era that valued physical energy, most health experts believed that old people's bodily decline made them different, and less productive, than the young. That view had helped propel G.I. efforts to accelerate the elder Lost's exit from the workforce. In the Awakening, G.I. psychoanalyst Erik Erikson suggested that the correct elder role lay in *generativity,* as though old age were a productive (even procreative) phase of life—what Betty Friedan later described as a "Fountain of Age." With an upbeat new emphasis on successful aging, *Modern Maturity* refused to accept ads that suggested physical decline, and Robert Butler led an assault against "ageist" employers who associated elderhood with physical decline.

By the Awakening's end, G.I.s had recoined the currency of old age: Never in living memory did America have an elder generation so politically and economically powerful—yet so invisible in the realm of culture and values. While G.I. senior citizens remained conspicuous as executives and treasurers for national institutions, they began having trouble with what George Bush would later call "the vision thing." Their formative impact on youth was nearly nil, seldom extending beyond replays of the past (like old *Honeymooner* reruns or monaural big band sounds on AM radio stations). Hardly any seniors produced films, wrote essays, composed music, or delivered homilies for the benefit of younger audiences. In the G.I.s' later years, even as the nation celebrated their heroic deeds in numerous World War II anniversaries, their irrelevance in the new values debate prompted the *New York Times* to ask, in large bold type, "Is anyone listening to the World War II generation?"

As their less-affluent children struggled in the economy, G.I.s continued in their accustomed roles as their families' financial backstops. With the aging of G.I.s, cash transfers from elders to adult children nearly tripled (after adjusting for inflation) and today account for an estimated 10 percent of all Boomer wealth. But the grown kids who often asked them for practical help seldom sought their advice on basic life directions. Many seniors grew troubled by what Dychtwald described as a "lack of respect and appreciation," in contrast to the deferential reverence they had once extended to their own Missionary parents. "In our time as children, grandparents were the teachers, advisors, counselors," roles from which Leshan said her G.I. peers were "robbed completely." Erik Erikson's wife, Joan, observed that "when we looked at the lifecycle in our forties, we looked to old people for wisdom." In the G.I.s' own turn, she lamented, "lots of old people don't get wise."

In their final reflections, prominent G.I.s like George Kennan, Lillian Hellman, Eric Sevareid, and Theodore White voiced distress over the steady loss in the American sense of community. Back in the High, when their generation ran the "general issue" culture, everything seemed to fit together constructively. Now, deep into the Awakening, it didn't.

In *It's a Wonderful Life,* Jimmy Stewart despairs at the worthlessness of his life until an angel reminds him how, had he never lived, his town would have sunk into a corrupt, pleasure-seeking abyss. Returning home, Stewart saves his government-subsidized savings and loan thanks to gifts from young and old, repaying him for all the wonderful deeds he once did. Like Jimmy Stewart, Awakening-era G.I.s were receiving their public rewards, yet unlike him they had to watch the society they so painstakingly cleaned up transform into something they didn't much like. The deal the G.I.s struck in the 1970s looked good then, but as the 1980s dawned the long-term price became clearer. "Despair comes hard to us," admitted Leshan, "because it was unfamiliar in our growing." Yet by the end of the Awakening, amid the golf courses and hospitals of their gleaming, youth-supported Sun Cities, despair was precisely what many G.I.s began to feel.

SILENT ENTERING MIDLIFE: VICARS OF VACILLATION

During John Kennedy's funeral, Theodore White noticed that "wherever one moved in Washington to participate in the grieving, one met young people . . . in their 20s, in their 30s." Polls confirm that this tragedy left a larger mark on the Silent than on any other generation. Three months before, a quarter million Americans, mostly young adults, had marched to the Lincoln Monument to hear thirty-four-year-old Martin Luther King Jr. speak eloquently of the dreams many of them shared. King, like Kennedy, enchanted a generation whose artists and intellectuals were just beginning to question the system to which they had so compliantly acquiesced.

The loss of President Kennedy prodded the Silent to demand more from what they then called "the powers that be." From the nonviolent activism of Medgar Evers to the folk songs of Joan Baez and the Kingston Trio, what some (correctly) label the "civil rights generation" tugged on the nation's conscience. Inspired, millions of Silent helpmates lent their expertise to the expanding G.I. edifice and their sympathy to burgeoning youth movements. Soon, two more tragedies brought tears to this generation. This time, the two fallen leaders were the Silent's own: King and Robert Kennedy, whom many felt then (and now) were the two best they had to offer. Afterward, there would be less residual hope and more regrets about what might have been. This generation would never again feel quite as uplifted by public life.

During the Awakening, the Silent had few economic problems. Their prime-of-life incomes rose without interruption, spurred by a relentless demand for skilled careerists throughout government and business. By the late 1970s, the Silent were old enough to ride out stagflation with relatively little consequence, and the S&L-financed runup in housing prices reaped huge windfalls for many of them. Except for divorced women who never remarried, every Silent demographic category joined in the bonanza, making theirs the most upwardly mobile generation in American history. Yet their outer good fortune masked an inner turmoil, a search for catharsis, a sense of having missed out on the life-cycle challenges faced by others.

During the Awakening, the Silent became the stuffings of a generational sandwich, just younger than the can-do G.I. yet just older than self-absorbed Boomers. Looking up the age ladder, the Silent felt more the faceless technocrat than a G.I.-style Superman with what Tom Wolfe admired as the "right stuff." Like Neil Armstrong, they made the "small step" enabled by the "giant leap" of their predecessors. Looking down the age ladder, they found themselves (in Howard Junker's words) "grown up just as the world's gone teen-age." The Silent felt tugged by the contradictory agendas of two quarreling generational neighbors. "During the ferment of the '60s, a period of the famous Generation Gap, we occupied, unnoticed as usual, the gap itself," Wade Greene recalled. Lacking an independent voice, middle-aged people adopted the moral relativism of the arbitrator, mediating arguments between others—and reaching out to people of all cultures, races, incomes, ages, and disabilities. The tensions they felt helped them become America's greatest generation of song writers, comedians, and therapists.

The Awakening's sexual revolution hit the Silent at an awkward phase of life, just when they had kids at home. This transformed them into *Bob and Carol and Ted and Alice,* what Rose Franzblau described as "a generation of jealousies and role reversals." Silent men felt claustrophobic, Silent women resentful. Both sexes found ways to break free after asking what Benita Eisler termed "the question that signals the end of every marriage: 'Is this all there is?' " From 1969 through 1975, as the Silent surged into state legislatures, the number of states with no-fault divorce laws jumped from zero to forty-five. While all generations joined the divorce epidemic, the Silent showed the steepest age bracket rise and emerged with the deepest residual guilt.

The midlife Silent discovered eros with the zest that comes to those who have missed it in their own youth. Fortyish men studied to become expert lovers, and "liberated" males pursued what John Updike called a "Post-Pill Paradise." Barrier-busting impresarios launched Playboy clubs, R-rated movies, and nude plays on Broadway. Looking up and down the age ladder for cues, Silent men assembled a composite definition of masculinity. The result was a hodgepodge of role models who combined G.I. confidence with Boomer sensitivity (Merlin Olsen, Carl Sagan), G.I. machismo with Boomer judgmentalism (Clint Eastwood, Charles Bronson), or a neurotic muddle (Alan Alda, Woody Allen). Others became America's first "out of the closet" gay politicians (Harvey Milk, Barney Frank) and celebrity transvestites (Christine Jorgensen, Renée Richards). Thus whipsawed, many Silent felt like one of Gail Sheehy's subjects who wished "somebody would let me be what I am, tender sometimes, and dependent, too, but also vain and greedy and jealous and competitive."

Many Silent women resented having allowed themselves to become *Stepford Wives,* limited to household chores and child care while their husbands' careers soared. And many looked more skeptically upon vows of fealty in an era when many a midlife married man succumbed to what Barbara Gordon called "Jennifer Fever," an attraction to sexually liberated younger women. The youngest- and most-married female generation in U.S. history began prefixing themselves with Gloria Steinem's status-cloaking "Ms." while fortyish divorcees began commanding media attention, demanding legal equality, and starting midlife careers. Adopting the younger Boomers' assaultive oratory, Silent feminists like Kate Millett, Susan Brownmiller, and Ti-Grace Atkinson attacked "man the oppressor" for being a "natural predator" driven by "metaphysical cannibalism." The gender-role partnership that had once satisfied midlife G.I.s was now in total shambles.

As middle-aged men and women began shattering conventions and taking more career and family risks—switching spouses, changing careers, dabbling in therapy—the "midlife passage" entered the pop lexicon. Ever since Silent authors Daniel Levinson and Gail Sheehy discovered what the latter called this "refreshing" life-cycle event, nearly everyone who has written about it has belonged to their generation. By the height of the Awakening, many Silent looked back on the High and felt, with Bob Dylan, "Ah, but I was so much older then, / I'm younger than that now." As William Styron remarked in 1968, "I think that the best of my generation—those in their late thirties or early forties—have reversed the customary rules of the game and have grown more radical as they have gotten older, a disconcerting but healthy sign." In *Future Shock,* Alvin Toffler developed a new "transience index" that quantified the breaking up of human relationships. Thanks to Toffler's own peers, that index shot upward through the latter half of the Awakening. While Daniel Ellsberg and Joyce Brothers pushed to get more secrets out, Phil Donahue and Ruth Westheimer pushed to get more talk going, all in the hope that more data and dialogue would somehow build a better society.

As rock stars, graduate students, and draft counselors, the Silent mentored the Awakening culture and founded the dissent groups Boomers would later radicalize. Like attorney Sam Yasgur, who coaxed his farmer father to lease their family property at Woodstock for a youth festival, the Silent drove the magic bus while the Boomer kids frolicked. Yet for all their sympathy, the Silent never felt fully welcome in the raging youth culture. The phrase "never trust anyone over thirty" was coined by Jack Weinberg, a Berkeley postgraduate who was himself approaching that age. *It's Hard to Be Hip Over Thirty,* mused Judith Viorst, writing poetic odes for a generation that had once felt born too late but now felt born too soon.

Still craving respect from G.I. elders, the Silent tried to convince Boomers that they understood them and could help channel their anger. From the exhortations of Stokely Carmichael and Malcolm X to the lyrics of Simon and Garfunkel to the psychedelic art of Peter Max to the Motown sound of Berry Gordy, Silent activists and artists lent expression to youth fury. As Abbie Hoffman and Jerry Rubin became the pied pipers of revolt ("We knew we couldn't get Archie Bunker, so we went for Archie Bunker's kids," said Hoffman), the Silent began lamenting their own missed opportunities in youth and rethinking their capitulation to G.I. culture. The new academic stars heard themselves derided by George Wallace as "pointy-headed professors who can't ride a bicycle straight," by Spiro Agnew as "nattering nabobs of negativism" and "vicars of vacillation." Yet if the Silent lacked the G.I.s' punch, they knew how to press the procedural buttons that would bring G.I. authority to its knees. The Chicago Seven, Harrisburg Seven, Camden Seventeen, Seattle Seven, Kansas City Four, Evanston Four, Gainesville Eight, the *Pentagon Papers* Four: From one trial to the next, these mostly Silent defendants and lawyers kept beating the system on technicalities and walking away to argue again.

By the mid-1970s, many a middle-aging ex-helpmate was sabotaging the G.I.-built civic order with what Russell Baker termed "a giant and progressive power failure." Ralph Nader launched the opening salvo against G.I.-style mass production by attacking American autos as *Unsafe at Any Speed,* having delivered "death, injury, and the most inestimable sorrow and deprivation to millions of people." Silent legislatures enacted new layers of process that Silent lawyers skillfully used to snare corporations or governments in new definitions of wrongdoing. From 1969 to 1975, the number of American public interest law centers quintupled. During those same years, the Silent began dominating jury boxes and awarding huge pain-and-suffering damage awards, creating chaos in the old G.I. insurance paradigm. Whatever the verdict, then came the appeal. In the Silent midlife mindset, nothing could be declared final; any outcome was subject to doubt or reinterpretation. All across American society, the midlife Silent wanted to make life like football's new instant replay, where anybody could check upstairs to get any decision reviewed or any contract renegotiated. Down on the field, a generation that had once manned the last clean-cut sports dynasties (Packers, Yankees, Celtics) now provided the lonely challengers (John Mackey, Curt Flood) and lawyer-agents who taught younger players how to assert their rights against older owners.

Having reached the age when G.I.s had earlier taken charge, the Silent now resisted the idea that *anybody* could or should assume G.I.-style leadership. Instead, they applied a lower-key brand of civic skill. They plumbed inner wellsprings older G.I.s seldom felt while maintaining a sense of social obligation Boomers seldom shared. Their solutions—fairness, openness, due process—reflected a keen sense of how and why humans fell short of grand civic plans or ideal moral standards. Toffler said America was in the midst of a "historic crisis of adaptation" and called for "the moderation and regulation of change" with "exact scientific knowledge, expertly applied to the crucial, most sensitive points of social control." Silent appeals for adaptation did not arise from G.I.-style secular power or Boomer-style spiritual fury, but rather from a self-conscious humanity and a well-informed social conscience.

In politics, other-directedness made this a generation Paul Tsongas describes as "much more questioning" than its predecessor. As Silent legislators displaced G.I.s in the latter half of the Awakening, they produced (says William Schneider) "a highly intellectualized political culture that respects expertise and competence." The Silent swept into office in the Watergate Baby election of 1974, a year remembered by Tim Wirth as the pivot-point when America entered the post-industrial era, the Information Age, and the era of "human capital" when states (rather than the nation) would be "laboratories of democracy." After they attained a majority of America's Congressmen and governors (in 1977), the main preoccupation was to prevent big institutions from doing bad things to everyday people. They did this by writing impact statements, reviewing market externalities, designing flow-charts, holding hearings, setting up oversight committees, and airing government secrets. In the business world, the Silent similarly challenged the G.I.-style pyramidal structure with a newly decentralized M-form corporation.

Where midlife G.I.s had disliked diversity, the Silent resonated to "different strokes for different folks." In the eyes of this least-immigrant generation in New World history, America was less a melting pot than a "salad" of unblended ingredients. Multilateralism and interdependence came to dominate foreign policy debates. The new academic elite, applying the counter-chauvinist Pogo Principle ("We have met the enemy, and they are us"), concluded that America might have more to learn from other societies than the other way around. Meanwhile, life became more complex and gourmet, much to the delight of a generation that had grown up with three-network TV and Wonder Bread.

Thanks to this Silent-spawned ambivalence, uncertainty, and complexity, building powerful new things (like a Three Mile Island nuclear reactor) became difficult or impossible. Once productivity stagnated, any response was rendered problematic by Silent thinkers who, like Lester Thurow in *Zero-Sum Society,* observed that improving the condition of one group now had to come at the expense of another. As the Club of Rome called for "limits to growth," Jerry Brown announced that America was "reaching the outer limit of our potential." The Age of Limits became what William Schneider termed "the *Zeitgeist* theme" of his generation.

Where midlife G.I.s had done great things and felt astride history, where young Boomers were satisfied to look within themselves, the Silent took great things for granted and looked *beyond* themselves, while worrying that history was passing them by. They became keen on manufacturing points of life-cycle reference around personal (not historical) markers, transitions having little connection to the larger flow of events. Like Elvis, a generation now squarely in midlife was still wondering if "I've spent a lifetime / Waiting for the right time." Struggling to break free from their early life conformity, the Silent wanted to turn themselves loose—not to build big things or preach big truths, but to get themselves and others to open up, mingle, relax, relate, express, and just *unwind* a little.

BOOMERS ENTERING YOUNG ADULTHOOD: MYSTICAL MILITANTS

"I Am a Student! Do Not Fold, Spindle, or Mutilate!" read the signs of picketers outside Berkeley's Sproul Hall in 1964, mocking the computer-punch-card treatment the faculty was supposedly giving them. Where earlier student movements had been the work of a lonely (and polite) few, this one swarmed and raged. The Free Speech movement rioters despised the life of "sterilized, automated contentment" that America's "intellectual and moral wastelands" were preparing for young graduates. As Barry McGuire's "Eve of Destruction" shot to the top of the pop charts, students at Berkeley resolved to "throw our bodies on the gears" to stop the G.I. machine.

Within a few years, America's finest universities were, like its inner cities and military depots, awash in youth violence. Often, the trouble started when administrators tried to clear a park or erect a building that would benefit students. Instead of praise, the G.I.s heard screams like Jacob Brackman's: "You build it up, mother, we gonna tear it down." Wealthy kids dressed down, donned unisex styles, and became self-declared "freaks" as if to reject the affluence and civic order of their elders. Back in 1962, the Silent-founded Students for a Democratic Society promoted social "interchange" and considered violence "abhorrent." By the late 1960s, a radicalized SDS screamed at the "pigs" who tried to keep order, while youth violence became what Rap Brown called "as American as apple pie." In 1970, 44 percent of college students believed that violence was justified to bring about change. The clenched fist became the emblem, T-shirts and jeans the uniform, and corporate liberalism the enemy. "Who are these people?" asked Daniel Moynihan, then on Harvard's faculty. "I suggest to you they are Christians arrived on the scene of Second Century Rome."

In *Do You Believe in Magic?* Annie Gottlieb declared the Boomers "a tribe with its roots in a time, rather than place or race." For her peers, that time was the 1960s, alias the Awakening. Born as the inheritors of G.I. triumph, Boomers came of age as what Michael Harrington termed "mystical militants" whose mission was neither to build nor to improve institutions but rather to purify them with righteous fire. America's new youths, observed Erik Erikson, were engaged in a "search for resacralization." Where Silent youths had come of age eager to fine-tune the system, cutting-edge Boomers wanted it to "burn, baby, burn." They had been raised to ask fundamental questions and apply fundamental principles. Among young radicals, Keniston noted the "great intensification of largely self-generated religious feelings, often despite a relatively nonreligious childhood." This search for spiritual perfection was often aided by mind-altering drugs, which *The Aquarian Conspiracy*'s Marilyn Ferguson described as "a pass to Xanadu" for "spontaneous, imaginative, right-brained youths."

Boomers sought to be "together" people—not together like the G.I. uniformed corps of the 1930s, but together as in a synchronous "good vibration." Boomers perceived their generational kinship as what Jonathan Cott called "the necklace of Shiva in which every diamond reflects every other and is itself reflected." Where Silent beatniks had expressed angst in poetry, earnestly seeking audiences, Boomer hippies megaphoned their "nonnegotiable demands" without much caring who listened. In the new youth culture, purity of moral position counted most, and "verbal terrorism" silenced those who dared to dissent from dissent. Organization counted for little. Keniston noted how the young radicals of the late 1960s, having grown up with "feelings of loneliness, solitude, and isolation," were profoundly mature by measures of ego strength, yet childlike in their social skills.

Where Silent nonconformists had feared blotches on their permanent records, Boomers perceived few real risks. Amnesty was often the student strikers' first demand, and—usually—it was granted. More important, a supercharged economy was offering careers to all comers. Most campus rioters assumed that the instant they deigned to do so, they could drop back into the American Dream machine. Planning for tomorrow was no big deal. Did Boomers expect to find better jobs, make more money, and live in better houses than their parents? "Certainly," recalls Robert Reich of his student activist days—that is, if Boomers wished it, and maybe they didn't. Pervasive affluence also meant that class conflict counted for little. Unlike the socialist Old Left, the Boomer New Left pressed moral and cultural (not political and economic) causes. As Irving Howe noted, Boomer radicals differed from the G.I.s' 1930s-era facsimiles in that they asked "how to live individually within this society, rather than how to change it collectively." Given how little the youth rage hinged on economics, many leading radicals were themselves children of the elite—a "Patty Hearst syndrome" that terrified elder G.I.s. Nor was the thirst for confrontation limited to the student elite or radical left. Arrayed against the Ivy Leaguers who occupied administration buildings and young blacks who set cities afire were the like-aged police who clubbed them and the like-aged National Guardsmen who fired on them. In the 1968 election, noncollege white Boomers were twice as likely as their older counterparts to vote for George Wallace.

The Generation Gap was fundamentally a Boomer revolt against G.I. fathers. Most sociologists who studied Awakening-era student radicals were struck by their attachment to mothers and their "ambivalence" (Keniston), "Oedipal rebellion" (Malcolm), or attitude of "parricide" (Lewis Feuer) toward male authority. The most memorable youth symbols were direct affronts against the constructions of G.I. men—from the two-fingered peace taunt (adapted from the old G.I. V-for-victory) to the defiant wearing of khaki (the G.I. color of uniformed teamwork) and the desecration of the American flag. The emerging Boomer agenda was a deliberate antithesis to everything the prototypical G.I. male had stressed during the High: spiritualism over science, gratification over patience, fractiousness over conformity, rage over friendliness, negativism over positivism—and, especially, self over community. "One wanted the young to be idealistic," Irving Kristol wrote at the time, "perhaps even somewhat radical, possibly even a bit militant—but not like this!"

The most overt cause of youth frenzy was the Vietnam War, a threat that was generally avoidable for those who actively sought a way out. Only one of every sixteen male Boomers ever saw combat, and ten times as many committed draft law felonies (mostly failure to register) as were killed in the war. The war's dodgeable draft created festering class and race divisions between Boomers who fought in Vietnam and those who didn't. Combat offered little glory for young soldiers. The most celebrated war heroes were G.I. POWs like Jeremiah Denton, while the most publicized Boomer soldier was the murderous William Calley. On film, John Wayne's get-it-done *Green Beret* fit the G.I.s' Vietnam fantasy, while Sylvester Stallone's blow-it-up *Rambo* fit the Boomers'. Coming home, young vets faced more opprobrium from peers than any other ex-soldiers in U.S. history. Yet until the May 1970 shooting of four Kent State students, most Boomers did not believe the Vietnam War was wrong, only that it was badly led. After Kent State, though, youths nationwide erupted into the Days of Rage, as students at hundreds of colleges went on strike. Campus unrest led the polls as America's number one problem, leading older generations to give Boomer views a bigger hearing: Prior to the 1972 election, eighteen-year-olds were awarded the vote, and the number of under-thirty delegates quadrupled at the two parties' political conventions.

Having hounded Lyndon Johnson out of office and having poisoned the campaign of his chosen successor Hubert Humphrey, Boomer zealots proceeded to turn on Richard Nixon. Even the presidential candidates who courted young supporters invariably saw their campaigns get wrecked on the shoals of this generation's weak civic instincts; in one antiestablishment election challenge after another, Boomer interest surged briefly before weakening by election day. In 1972, a year in which nearly twenty-five million newly eligible Boomers were expected to turn the tide, they did not. Half failed to vote, and Nixon outpolled McGovern among Boomers who did. By then, the war was winding down, the new draft lottery was kicking in, and Boomers began heeding their Beatle mentors' "simple words of wisdom: Let it be." The rest of the 1970s were studded with successful candidates (like Ronald Reagan and S. I. Hayakawa) who launched their political careers by running against the youth culture.

As the anti-Vietnam fever cooled, the economy became an issue with Boomers for the first time. In and after the 1973 recession, entry-level jobs became hard to find, and the euphoria of the early Awakening disappeared in a drizzle of sex, drugs, underemployment, and what Lansing Lamont called a "lost civility" on campus. The G.I.-built world suited Boomers no more now than it had in the heyday of Vietnam—and, with the economy souring, many Boomer post-antiwarriors found new reasons why money-making was beneath them. "I have made no plans because I have found no plans worth making," a Dartmouth valedictorian declared to the cheers of his peers. Like Mitch Snyder, who abandoned his own children before leading a crusade for the homeless, many a Boomer spent the 1970s believing "if it doesn't work, I just kind of move on." This manifested itself in a sudden sharp resistance against permanent linkages to mates, children, and professions. Like Katharine Ross in *The Graduate,* Boomers approached the altar (or corporate ladder) and heard something inside scream, "STOP!" Having jammed the gears of the Silent-era treadmill, Boomers wandered off to do what they wanted to do.

The self-absorption of young Boomers lent their generation—male and female—a hermaphroditic, pistil-and-stamen quality. In *The Singular Generation,* Wanda Urbanska exalted their "self-sexuality." Having grown up when gender-role distinctions had reached a zenith, Boomers set to work narrowing them. Men ventured into values domains that in the High had belonged to G.I. mothers and teachers, while Boomer women invaded the careerist roles once reserved for their G.I. fathers and providers. This made Boomers more independent of social bonds, yet also more open to emotional isolation and economic insecurity. Unlike Silent women, many Boomer women worried from the outset that early marriage might actually depress their future household standard of living.

Through the latter half of the Awakening, Boomers actively crafted new concepts of self-religion. Secularists heralded the New Age and asserted a "sovereign right of self-discovery." In the Human Potential movement, billed as a "reaction to industrialized, mechanized thinking," large numbers of Boomers dabbled in psychic phenomena and experiments in communal living. Meanwhile, a new breed of "Jesus freaks" and born-agains returned the Calvinist notion of calling to its original emphasis on an inspirational rebirth. From New Age fellowships to Southern Baptist churches, believers no longer had to spend a lifetime engaged in G.I. works to achieve salvation.

In their daily lives, young-adult Boomers began testing their powerful inner concepts on the outer world. As they retooled the American economy by insisting on meaningful (read: un-G.I.) careers and products, America's decades-long productivity surge came to an end. Boomers had little desire to produce or purchase the cars or furniture that looked like their neighbor's. In pro sports, free spirits like Kareem Abdul-Jabbar, Reggie Jackson, and Joe Namath introduced the inner athlete—and an era of declining loyalties among athletes, teams, cities, and fans. In their hobbies, Boomers did everything with an intensity others found obsessive—from exercise faddists looking for the runner's high to diet faddists looking for alpha waves. In the marketplace, consumer brand loyalties weakened, and Made in the USA became passé among the cognoscenti. By the early 1980s, *Times-Mirror* surveys developed a new "Values and Life Styles" typology to help advertisers reach such new Boomer types as the "I-Am-Me" consumer. Toward the end of the Awakening, when Boomers began reaching the higher councils of governance, they immediately asserted a new inner-world agenda. Hamilton Jordan and Jody Powell helped equip Jimmy Carter with a revivalist's vocabulary, and David Stockman, Ronald Reagan's principled budgetary executioner, was the first of many Boomers to enter public life after a stint at a seminary or theology school.

Rock promoter Bill Graham once recollected that, among the young radicals of his era, "there was very little *doing*." Instead of building or improving things, like the G.I.s or Silent at like age, Boomers pursued more of an expressive agenda. Like Hillary Clinton in her Wellesley valedictory speech, they were intent on "choosing a way to live that will demonstrate the way we feel and the way we know." Or, as the Beatles put it, Boomers were content to "say" that they "want a revolution." If inside their heads they had already succeeded, outside they had barely started.

When the tempest of the Awakening began to calm, aspects of life Boomers had once deemed spiritually empty—consumption, careerism, family formation—were now temptingly available, having at last been re-sacralized by their new values. Older and younger generations guffawed at their pick-and-choose idealism, but Boomers were too focused on their own drummer to notice what others thought. Where Snoopy and Woodstock had once plumbed the inner life of youth, they now were captioned, "Get Met, It Pays." Todd Gitlin recalls how, as the Awakening neared its end, "it was time to go straight, . . . from marijuana to white wine, from hip communes to summers on Cape Cod." Boomers couldn't forever linger in a state of suspended animation. By now, this generation had come to believe in the credo of *The Whole Earth Catalog:* "We are as gods, and might as well get good at it."

13ERS ENTERING CHILDHOOD: ROSEMARY'S BABY

Amid the gathering turbulence of 1964, baby making abruptly fell out of favor. In the spring of that year, American women were still giving birth at a record pace. But in the months that followed, conceptions plummeted—and by mid-1965 the U.S. fertility rate was entering its steep post-Boom decline. A national fertility study confirmed that a third of all mothers now admitted having at least one unwanted child. Stay-at-home moms began wearing buttons that read "Stop At One," "None Is Fun," and "Jesus Was an Only Child." The reasons for this sudden turn included birth control pills, nascent feminism, and a new societywide hostility toward children.

America's new antichild attitude revealed itself most clearly in the media. By the mid-1960s, the production of smart-kid family sitcoms and creative-kid Disney movies slowed to a trickle. Replacing them was a new genre featuring unwanted, unlikable, or simply horrifying children. *Rosemary's Baby,* a thriller about a woman pregnant with an evil demon, anchored a twenty-year period in which Hollywood filmed one bad-kid movie after another *(The Exorcist, It's Alive, The Omen, Halloween).* Most came with sequels, since audiences couldn't seem to get enough of these cine-matic monsters. Moviegoers also lined up to see kids who were savages *(Lord of the Flies)*, hucksters *(Paper Moon)*, prostitutes *(Taxi Driver)*, emo-tional misfits *(Ordinary People)*, spoiled brats *(Willie Wonka)*, and barriers to adult self-discovery *(Kramer vs. Kramer)*. Meanwhile, Hollywood made far fewer films *for* children. The proportion of G-rated films fell from 41 percent to just 13 percent, and the new R-rated films soon became Holly-wood's most profitable. Disney laid off cartoonists for the only time in its history.

Throughout the 13ers' childhood era, the adult media battered their col-lective reputation and, over time, began to portray this generation as having absorbed the negative message. "We're rotten to the core," sang the preteen thug-boys in *Bugsy Malone*. "We're the very worst—each of us con-temptible, criticized, and cursed." As the 1970s gave way to the 1980s, teenagers began repeating this line, as when one student mockingly tells his friends in *River's Edge:* "You young people are a disgrace to all living things, to plants even. You shouldn't even be seen in the same room as a cac-tus."

America's new consciousness celebrated childhood as an ideal, but it ne-glected childhood as an actual living experience. The nation moved from what Leslie Fiedler called a 1950s-era "cult of the child" to what Landon Jones called a 1970s-era "cult of the adult." With older G.I.s still smarting from attacks by their own kids, with the Silent now reconsidering their High-era family choices, and with fertile Boomers taking voyages to the in-terior, the very image of more children provoked widespread anxiety. Par-ents were shunned if they tried to bring small children into restaurants or theaters. Many rental apartments started banning children. The ascendant Zero Population Growth movement declared each extra child to be "pollu-tion," a burden on scarce resources.

Sacrificing one's own career or conjugal happiness for the sake of the kids became passé—even, by the logic of the era, bad for kids themselves. A flurry of popular books chronicled the resentment, despair, and physical discomfort women now said they endured when bearing and raising 13er children. As the cost of raising a child became a hot topic, adults ranked au-tos ahead of children as necessary for the "good life." The abortion rate sky-rocketed; by the late 1970s, would-be mothers aborted one fetus in three. In *Ourselves and Our Children*, a committee of Silent authors ranked "consid-ering yourself" ahead of "benefiting our children" as a principle of sound parenting. Parental guides began emphasizing why-to-dos over what-to-dos. The popular *Parental Effectiveness Training* urged adults to teach small tots about consequences rather than about right and wrong. As Marie Winn noted, an "early-childhood determinism" enabled parents to assume their kids could cope with later trauma, "given how carefully they had been tended as tots." Thus reassured, Awakening-era parents spent 40 percent less of their time on child raising than parents had spent in the High.

The Awakening's casual sex, nontraditional families, and mind-altering drugs left a large imprint on this child generation, an imprint reflected in much of today's 13er music and prose. In the late 1960s, sings Susan Werner, "There were some people smokin' weed, there were some others doin' speed / But I was way big into raisins at the time." "I remember wall-papering my younger brother's room with *Playboy* centerfolds," recalls Adriene Jenik. "I remember bongs and pipes and art and music among my parents greatest artifacts and my mother's vibrator and reading my father's *Penthouse* forums." As novelist Ian Williams writes, "We could play truth or dare with our parents' sex lives if we wanted to." By the late 1970s, once 13ers began practicing what they had learned, adults grew accustomed to seeing kids dress and talk as knowingly as Brooke Shields in ads or Jodie Foster in film.

As the media standard for the typical American family changed from *My Three Sons* to *My Two Dads,* divorce struck 13ers harder than any other child generation in U.S. history. Where Boomers had once been worth the parental sacrifice of prolonging an unhappy marriage, 13ers were not. At the end of the High, half of all adult women believed that parents in bad marriages should stay together for the sake of the children, but by the end of the Awakening, only one in five thought so. Best-selling youth books like *It's Not the End of the World* tried to show that parental divorce wasn't so bad, but left children with the impression that any family could burst apart at any time. In *The Nurturing Father: Journey Toward the Complete Man,* Kyle Pruett promised that family dissolution "freed" parent and child to have "better" and "less-constricted" time together. By 1980, just 56 percent of all 13er children lived with two once-married parents, and today this gen-eration's novels and screenplays bristle with hostile references to parents who didn't tough it out. Polls have since shown 13ers far more inclined than older Americans to believe current divorce laws are too lax.

In homes, schools, and courtrooms, America's style of child nurture completed a two-decade transition from *Father Knows Best* to Bill Cosby's *Fatherhood:* "Was I making a mistake now? If so, it would just be mistake number nine thousand seven hundred and sixty-three." "If anything has changed in the last generation," Ellen Goodman later admitted, it was the "erosion of confidence" among "openly uncertain" mothers and fathers. Alvin Poussaint noted the dominant media image of parents as pals who were "always understanding; they never get very angry. There are no bound-aries or limits set. Parents are shown as bungling, not in charge, floundering as much as the children."

Parents who admit they are "many-dimensioned, imperfect human be-ings," reassured *Ourselves and Our Children,* "are able to give children a more realistic picture of what being a person is all about." At best, the new model parents were, like Cosby's Cliff Huxtable, gentle and communicative; at worst, they undermined trust and expressed ambivalence where children sought guidance. Like father and son in *Close Encounters of the Third Kind,* adults became more childlike and children more adultlike.

This antiauthoritarian nurture fit the iconoclastic mood of the Awakening. Older generations went out of their way to tell children (in the words of *Mad*'s Al Feldstein) that "there's a lot of garbage out in the world and you've got to be aware of it." Silent parents, recalling their own closeted Crisis-era childhood, were especially eager to expose their kids to everything. Judy Blume exhorted parents to expose their children to every possible human catastrophe. "They live in the same world we do," she insisted. She and other Silent authors launched a New Realism bookshelf for children, targeting subjects (like abortion, adolescent cohabitation, child abuse, family-friend rapists, and suicide) that prior child generations had never encountered. After absorbing the books, movies, and TV shows the Awakening-era culture offered them, and after observing adults carefully and emulating how they behave, many 13ers began resembling Tatum O'Neal in *Paper Moon,* the kind of kid adults have a hard time finding adorable.

The events of the Awakening reinforced the impression that grown-ups were neither powerful nor virtuous. To the child's eye, adults were simply not in control, either of their own personal lives or (during the years of Vietnam, Watergate, and gas lines) of the larger world. Instead of preventing danger or teaching by example, adults were more apt to hand out self-care guides that told kids about everything that might happen and how to handle it on their own. As Neil Postman observed in *The Disappearance of Childhood,* 13er children were given "answers to questions they never asked." It was an era in which everyone and everything had to be liberated, whether it was good for them or not. In *Escape from Childhood,* John Holt urged freeing children from the vise of adult oppression, while Hillary Clinton published articles on children's rights.

Nowhere were 13er children liberated more than in Awakening-era schools, where High-era education now stood accused of having dehumanized little Boomers. Each child should be "left to himself without adult suggestion of any kind," urged Open Education advocate A. S. Neill, who suggested that facts and rules and grades and walls be replaced with "tools and clay and sports and theater and paint and freedom." Reformers tried to boost child self-esteem through "person-centered" education that stressed feelings over reason, empirical experience over logical deduction. Rather than ask students to evaluate a book's universal quality or message, teachers began probing students about how a reading assignment made them feel. Grammar was downplayed, phonics frowned on, and arithmetic decimals replaced by the relativistic parameters of New Math. Textbooks emphasized sensitivity and accessibility. Standards were weakened, in line with reformer Roland Barthes's theory that "there is no minimum body of knowledge which it is essential for everyone to know." The average time children spent on homework fell to half what it had been in the High era, and grade inflation ran rampant. As the Awakening progressed, the percentage of high school graduates who described themselves as straight A students nearly tripled.

Back in the High, being a good adult had meant staying married and providing children with a wholesome culture and supportive community. Now it meant festooning the child's world with self-esteem smiley buttons while the fundamentals (and media image) of a child's life grew more troubled by the year. Increasing numbers of children were born to unmarried teen mothers. While underfunded foster-home systems buckled in state after state, the media began referring to latchkey, abandoned, runaway, and throwaway kids. In the middle 1970s, the distinction of occupying America's most poverty-prone age bracket passed directly from the (elder) Lost to the (child) 13th without ever touching the three generations in between. By the late 1970s, the child suicide rate broke the Lost's previous turn-of-the-century record. Through the Awakening, the homicide rate for infants and small children rose by half, and the number of reported cases of child abuse jumped fourfold.

The Awakening's new hostility to power, authority, and secrecy had one meaning for forty-five-year-olds seeking a nuanced view of a complicating world, but another for ten-year-olds trying to build dreams. For the Silent, taught to Think Big as Crisis-era children, Thinking Small was a midlife tonic. But never having had their own chance to Think Big, preadolescent 13ers heard a new message: America's best days were over. Like the child of divorce writ large, this generation wondered if it was only a coincidence that they came along at just the moment in history when older people started complaining that everything in America was falling to pieces.

Ask today's young adults how they were raised, and many will tell you that they raised themselves—that they made their own meals, washed their own clothes, decided for themselves whether to do homework or make money after school, and chose which parent to spend time with on weekends (or side with in court). They grew up less as members of family teams, looking forward to joining adult teams, than as free agents, looking forward to dealing and maneuvering their way through life's endless options. In their childhood memory, the individual always trumped the group. During the Consciousness Revolution, as older generations stripped away the barriers that had previously sheltered childhood, 13ers were denied a positive vision of the future—denied, indeed, any reassurance that their nation had any *collective* future at all.

TOWARD THE THIRD TURNING

In 1983, a twentieth anniversary March on Washington drew roughly as many participants as had come to hear King's epic speech at the end of the High. Yet the old wistfulness had been replaced by a new sense of consolidation—as if some giant museum should now be built to memorialize the dream and the movement. The time for grand social movements had passed. That same year also produced heightened public alarm over the deadly AIDS virus. The days of euphoric experimentation had taken a grim turn.

America would see no more wild oscillations between utopian and dystopian visions of the future. That was not because the Awakening had subsided, but because it had triumphed. By the early 1980s, the anti-institutional shouts that had originated in the pot-laced dronings of Haight-Ashbury hippies could be heard in the free-market chatter of Wall Street brokers and Main Street merchants. From coast to heartland, inner city to edge city, Americans everywhere were listening to what *Habits of the Heart* coauthor Steven Tipton described as "their own little church in their own little mind."

By end of Reagan's first term, the Awakening had run its course. A new agenda had been set, and the old enthusiasm could not last. Each generation now filled the phase of life it had spent the prior two decades entering, and each was about to break ground into the next. As was the case around 1963, none of the generational archetypes showed signs of matching the role its predecessor had carried into the prior era. How could the Silent project anywhere near the hubris of the aging conquerors, building their Great Society and demanding their entitlement? How could the Boomers possibly emerge as midlife mediators, looking beyond themselves for procedural solutions? How could 13ers come of age preaching about moral perfection? How could American parents tolerate yet another underattended child generation? None of that had any chance of happening.

Toward the end of any Awakening, generational strains begin to show:

- The *elder Heroes,* still leading institutions while vacating the culture, now worry about a society whose new spiritualism they find alien.
- The *midlife Artists,* sensing that the old order has been repudiated, now plan to cast off community discipline and expand the realm of personal choice.
- The *young-adult Prophets,* inspired by the discovery of personal truth, now want to change society from the inside out.
- The *child Nomads,* cynical youths in a world of powerless adults, learn to distrust the rules and prepare to make their own way.

By the early 1980s, these generational archetypes were all primed for new directions. When the Silent began edging into elderhood, Boomers into midlife, and 13ers into young adulthood, their prior social roles could not continue.

The Awakening was over. As Roland Stromberg had predicted in the middle 1970s, eventually the mood of that era "will be revealed as simply one more exhausted option. And so a new one will have to be invented." The Second Turning necessarily had to give way to the Third.

CHAPTER 8

■

The Third Turning:
Culture Wars (1984–2005?)

"IT'S MORNING IN AMERICA," EXUDED PRESIDENT REAGAN
in his State of the Union message on January 15, 1984. "America is back,
standing tall, looking to the eighties with courage, confidence, and hope."
As California's governor during the prior era, Reagan had stood firm against
the Consciousness Revolution and symbolized the primacy of the Establishment. Now he symbolized the defeat of that Establishment and the primacy
of the self. Reagan detested the rules and taxes and penalties of the very system he ran—and, buoyed by the feel-good veneer of the economy and moment, people loved it. From "Hail to the Chief" to Springsteen's "Born in
the U.S.A.," the national tune had changed. The Awakening was over, and
people discovered they were comfortable with what America had become.

While watching the Super Bowl three days before Reagan's speech, TV
viewers saw an Apple Computer ad in which a young woman sledgeham-
mered an enormous video display of dull-faced, vintage-1950s men. "Nineteen eighty-four won't be like 1984," proclaimed the voice over, heralding
the supremacy of personal computers over Big Blue mainframes. The year's
four digits recalled George Orwell's famous High-era forecast that all modern society would now tremble under a soul-crushing Big Brother. Instead,
America smiled at the crushing of Big Brother.

At the deepest social level, the Awakening had triumphed. The new values regime was no longer controversial. Having accepted the obsolescence
of the old civic order, Americans found they could still lead inwardly fulfilling lives as individuals. During the Awakening, when the rebels had attacked the fortress, everyone expected that the victors would end up
ruling—over either a utopia (if the right side won) or a dystopia (if the
wrong side won). Now the rebels were inside the gates, the defenders had
fled, and nobody knew how the old fortress worked. No one ruled, so it no

longer mattered who won. Sensing this, people stopped believing that a fortress of any kind, especially one run by ex-rebels, could serve important social ends.

Civic attitudes had transformed into the opposite of what they had been in the High. Where America had once experienced what Barbara Whitehead called "an economy of abundance and a psychology of scarcity," the nation now had "an economy of scarcity and a psychology of abundance." Despite the popularity of the president, broad measures of public trust sank to new lows; only one American in five counted on the president or Congress to act responsibly. Yet polls also showed Americans awash in self-esteem. Not trusting government, people *did* trust the individual—as expressed through the marketplace, cultural diversity, interactive technologies, New Age spirituality, and evangelicalism. The old focus on policies and programs had receded, but the public vacuum was gradually being filled by a new politics of personal rootedness, inner values, and empathic gesture.

From TV talk shows to dependency groups to church basements, the search for personal meaning started with the direct experience of the individual. These self-discovered meanings were then ratified by others attracted to the individual's own niche group, people whose views had been authenticated by similar experiences. The niche could involve sex, race, religion, occupation, income, even—as with gun ownership—a hobby. As niche groups strengthened, they began erasing old (universal) worldviews and constructing new (particular) ones. Any argument or observation coming from outside the group became suspect because it lacked the torch of pure belief. Every act thus had a meaning, every meaning a right and wrong, every wrong a victim, every victim a victimizer. From one niche to the next, this logic led to different sets of wrongs, victims, and victimizers. Unlike in the High, there was no such thing as "normal" public opinion.

With America thus denormed, the center could not hold. As Senator Moynihan suggested, deviancy kept getting redefined downward. The people who in the Awakening had comprised the Silent Majority of Middle America now felt themselves engulfed in *Blade Runner* chaos and variance. On race, for example, polls showed Americans vastly *over*estimating the size and discontent of minorities and niche groups and *under*estimating the size and well-being of the majority. Fed by paranoia, public discourse became more tribal and less cordial with each passing year. Even mainstream Americans began to feel like Michael Douglas in *Falling Down*—that is, like an embittered minority. National parties weakened, incumbents were derided, and attack ads proliferated. Suspicion began to creep into dealings with strangers, with only three people in ten believing that "most people can be trusted," eight in ten that "civility in America has declined in the past ten years." As the 1980s ended, personal security became one of America's biggest growth industries.

By the early 1990s, America's niche group conflict came to be known as the Culture Wars, defined by Irving Kristol as a "profound division over what kind of country we are, what kind of people we are, and what we mean by 'The American Way of Life.' " Three basic battlegrounds emerged: multiculturalists against traditionalists (the Sheldon Hackneys versus the William Bennetts), media secularists against evangelicals (the Murphy Browns versus the Dan Quayles), and public planners against libertarians (the Robert Reichs versus the Charles Murrays). The Culture Wars had as many combatants as America had niches, from the Nation of Islam to the Internet. As each group exalted its own authenticity, it defined its adversary's values as indecent, stupid, obscene, or (a suddenly popular word) evil.

The new lexicon of the Culture Wars allowed America's post-Awakening ideals to be elevated into ideologies. In the 1994 election, voters split more ideologically than ever in the history of polling. Meanwhile, growing numbers of Americans either declared themselves independent or chose not to vote. Voting behavior gaps widened between genders, races, religions, generations, and (especially) between those who had children and those who didn't. Leaders who sought to assemble niches into coalitions met with little or no success. Old political alliances lay in ruins.

As this "politics of meaning" spread, Americans in every niche came to one common conclusion: The institutional order was not working and was not worth defending. No one felt responsible for things as they now stood or functioned—not even the leaders. President Clinton, presiding over big government, could proclaim in 1996 that "the era of big government is over." By then, top public officials were freely admitting that their own agencies had become bureaucratic nightmares. From courts to campuses, medicine to media, institutional America bathed in a self-criticism that corroborated the external critiques of the prior era.

Americans turned cynical, viewing every social arrangement as unworthy of long-term loyalty, deserving only of short-term exploitation. The attitude infected CEOs and temp workers, old and young, whites and blacks, family heads and single people, born-agains and gays, rural militias and urban juries. Conspiracy theories abounded, whether about FBI helicopters buzzing over Idaho or the CIA spreading AIDS in inner cities. The sense of civic decay developed a powerful momentum; the discrediting of each feature of the civic landscape made the other features look all the more dysfunctional. As institutions adapted to this changing mood, they became more finely tuned to individual needs but worse at meeting (or even pretending to meet) community needs. In the wake of the Simpson trial and multimillion-dollar verdicts for coffee spills, the justice system began striking people as more system than justice. In the Awakening, the system had looked corrupt from the outside; now it looked that way from the inside too.

Lacking a central direction in civic life, Americans began searching for it in narrower spheres. Despairing over the numbing complexity of what Cornel West calls "a decaying civilization," Americans avidly began talking about new ideals of total social cooperation and trying them out on small scales. For many, these ideals fell under the rubric of a growing "communitarian" or "civic republican" movement, dedicated to reconstructing public life from the bottom up. For others, they grew out of spiritual cosmologies, from evangelical rankings of angels to New Age numberings of planetary houses. Americans everywhere were mesmerized by visions of a universal moral order that they comprehended within themselves. Meanwhile, nine of ten people agreed that "there was a time when people in this country felt they had more in common and shared more values than Americans do today."

By the mid-1990s, pundits agreed that America was deep into a new era of lost purpose and shattered consensus. Robert Samuelson called it a "fragmenting"; *Commentary,* a "balkanization"; Thomas Byrne Edsall, an "era of bad feelings"; and William Raspberry, an "unraveling."

Now half over, this Unraveling has darkened the quality of American life in ways no one ever predicted. Looking back, Americans can see 1984 as a threshold year when several new trends emerged that defined the era to come. At first, these items seemed no more than passing curiosities. By the mid-1990s, however, they became overwhelming and seemingly ineradicable features of American life.

In 1984, the electorate decisively endorsed an economic policy of large deficits, unchecked growth in entitlements spending, falling national savings rates, and heavy borrowing from foreigners—amid talk that this "riverboat gamble" would either cure the economy or force policy makers to reverse course. A decade later, fiscal excess had become a political way of life and sluggish productivity an economic fact of life.

In 1984, with Mario Cuomo's "Two Americas" speech and Charles Murray's *Losing Ground,* the public first learned that the gap between rich and poor was widening. A decade later, the gap had grown to yawning proportions, yet liberals joined conservatives in doubting that much could be done about it.

In 1984, Jesse Jackson launched the Rainbow Coalition, declaring America to be "a quilt of many patches, many pieces, many colors, various textures." A decade later, after multiculturalism had swept the country, America seemed less a quilt than a ragrug of splitting strands.

In 1984, Americans were first noticing that the conventional family was no longer the norm and premarital teen sex no longer a rarity. A decade later, married couples with children had shrunk to only 26 percent of all households (versus 40 percent in 1970), and the share of sexually active fifteen-year-old girls had swollen to 26 percent (versus 5 percent in 1970).

In 1984, Hollywood had just invented the tech-enhanced violent action movie, and automatic weapons were still uncommon in inner cities. Ten years later, the typical child had seen ten thousand acts of TV mayhem by age eighteen, and the national rate of death by gunfire for children under eighteen had tripled.

In 1984, Peter Ueberroth turned a profit on the L.A. Olympiad, a few athletes earned more than the U.S. president, and Michael Jackson introduced America to a new *Thriller*-style megastar. A decade later, the Olympics were fully professional, some NFL players were making more in one game than the U.S. president makes in a year, and Kato Kaelin defined the celebrity circus.

In 1984, capital was just starting to cross national boundaries in large quantities, most corporations still dreaded debt-heavy balance sheets, and investment banking was a hot new career. A decade later, transnational capital rocked the American economy, billion-dollar leveraged buyouts reshuffled entire corporations, and the more long-time workers a company laid off, the more its stock seemed to rise.

In 1984, a new crack cocaine epidemic was propelling youth gangs in Los Angeles, and a *Chicago Tribune* columnist coined the acronym *NIMBY* ("not in my backyard") to refer to public resistance against public works. A decade later, the Crips and Bloods had spread to Utah and overseas military bases, and the NIMBY movement reached from walled-in suburbanites to small-town cyberpunks and rural militias.

In 1984, a surge in deinstitutionalized (homeless) vagrants prompted local governments to set up special shelters. A decade later, citing "compassion fatigue," many localities were evicting vagrants from public areas and building prisons at the fastest clip in history.

In 1984, as states were experimenting with legalized gambling, seventeen states had lotteries, two states had casinos, and none allowed video poker or gambling on Native American lands. Ten years later, those four numbers had risen to thirty-six, ten, six and twenty-four, respectively. By the mid-1990s, more Americans visited legal casinos than attended Major League baseball, NFL football, symphony concerts, and Broadway shows combined.

In 1984, the nation was awash in practical self-help movements, and a *Times-Mirror* survey tallied as many "upbeats" as "moralists" (roughly 10 percent of the U.S. population). A decade later, the nation was awash in spiritual movements, the *Times-Mirror*'s proportion of moralists had doubled, and the upbeat category had become so rare it was no longer used.

Early in the Unraveling, as people attached the prefixes *post-* and *neo-* to trends like these, the postmodern complexities of life struck neoliberals and neoconservatives as exciting new challenges. But in time the nation mirrored the 1980s book title, *Doing Better and Feeling Worse*. By the mid-1990s, amid an extended economic boom, three in four adults believed the United States to be "in moral and spiritual decline." Daily life had literally darkened to black, the color of the newest sports logos and luxury autos. Political rhetoric sank to the nastiest level in living memory, while sin and death metaphors crept into the national dialogue. Dan Quayle diagnosed "an ethical cancer that has metastasized through all levels of society." Hillary Clinton (quoting Lee Atwater) lamented a nationwide "tumor of the soul."

A series of jolts propelled this new mood. The 1987 stock crash and ensuing Wall Street scandals cut short the jovial talk about the greed-is-good yuppie. The Cold War and Desert Storm victories produced a New World Order that felt ephemeral and disquieting. The collapse of health care reform confirmed that America no longer had faith that big institutional solutions could solve public problems. The whipsaw elections of 1992 through 1996 accelerated the *de*alignment of national politics. The Oklahoma City bombing revealed maniacal passions seething just beneath the surface. The Simpson trial and Million Man March evoked a sullen new racialism. With each jolt, yet another piece of the old order lay in disrepute, its workings less respected, its directions less tolerable, its outcomes less predictable.

The 1990s are generating plenty of what in other eras would pass for good news: The economy perks along, and the stock market roars. School achievement is going up, the crime rate down. While the U.S. reigns as the sole superpower in a multilateral world, American culture is spreading all over the globe. The big hand on the atomic scientists' Doomsday Clock, which hit three minutes to midnight in 1984, has since retreated. Yet Americans are more pessimistic than ever. They are inclined to believe that any good news (like a roaring stock market) comes with a sinister edge (big layoffs) for which a price will someday be paid.

The new declinism has become unshakable. Where the Awakening's occasional talk of apocalypse had simply framed the era's euphoric urgency, the new declinism is more despondent—as though history were not hurtling toward a climax, just staggering toward exhaustion. Polls show that a majority of Americans, young adults especially, believe that the nation's best years have passed. A popular poll about recent decades showed that the best-liked ones were the furthest away—and the 1990s was least-liked of all. In 1995, *USA Weekend* held a readers' contest to name the 1990s. The vast majority of responses were gloomy, as in the "negative nineties," the "whiney nineties," the "denial decade," the "down decade," or the "decade of despair." Keynoted by Paul Kennedy's *The Rise and Fall of the Great Powers*, a list of more than two dozen "end of" books came into print by the mid-1990s, including *End of Affluence, End of Science, End of Culture, End of Marriage, End of Evolution, End of History, End of the Future,* and *End of the World.*

Yet as civic life dissolved, private life adhered. Both realms headed in exactly the opposite directions from where they had gone back in the High. In 1960, visions of a post-1984 America had been of either a benevolent Tomorrowland or a malign Big Brother, but the specter of communal chaos and rampant individualism was unimaginable. That explains why Americans old enough to remember the High feel so alarmed by the Unraveling, and why those too young to remember the High find so little meaning in America's pre-Awakening history.

The Unraveling mood shift is a natural consequence of the life-cycle transitions taking place among today's generations. The confident, team-playing G.I.s are weakening. The other-focused, compromise-minded Silent are vacating midlife. Boomers are exiting young adulthood after having embroiled it in self-discovery, argument, and new social pathologies. The departure of 13ers from childhood leaves people of all ages, themselves included, wondering what went wrong there. New Millennial babies are being born. America is moving into an archetypal constellation that is reaching an apogee of inner (private) power and a nadir of outer (public) power.

Like other eras, an Unraveling is a natural phase of human history. Now is the time a society clears away institutional detritus. With the Awakening over and no Crisis yet on the horizon, an Unraveling enables people to live life to the fullest, consume off the past, and pursue individual ends. Human civilization would be far poorer without such an opportunity, once per saeculum, to explore the private realms of self-fulfillment, even if it brings public pessimism. In many ways, a Third Turning can be the most personally enjoyable of the saecular seasons.

So too is an Unraveling a *necessary* phase: By empowering the ideals of the Awakening, it lays the agenda for the Crisis to follow.

THIRD TURNINGS AND ARCHETYPES

There have been seven Third Turnings (or Unravelings) dating back to the fifteenth century.

- *Retreat from France* (1435–1459), Late Medieval Saeculum
- *Intolerance and Martyrdom* (1542–1569), Reformation Saeculum
- *Reaction and Restoration* (1649–1675), New World Saeculum
- *French and Indian Wars* (1746–1773), Revolutionary Saeculum
- *Mexican War and Sectionalism* (1844–1860), Civil War Saeculum
- *World War I and Prohibition* (1908–1929), Great Power Saeculum
- *Culture Wars* (1984–2005?), Millennial Saeculum

All seven Third Turnings have followed a similar path of social entropy and disintegration. The Awakening complete, people are now fully immersed in their own purposes. The new social priority is to atomize, not to gather; people are harvesting, not sowing. Underneath, a new values regime grows and spreads. As large official entities continue to weaken, small informal ones (families, neighborhoods, small enterprises, volunteer groups, cultural niches) revitalize.

The Unraveling is an equinox era, a transition toward shorter days and longer nights. Both the demand and supply of social order are falling. This is the autumnal quadrant of the saeculum, when vines luxuriate, fruit spoils, leaves fall, and respect for life's fundamentals reappears. It is when Richard Wilbur's "hot summer has exhausted her intent. . . . Like a love-letter that's no longer meant." People reap prior plantings while wondering what to do with the seeds. (Eat them? Horde them? Leave them to the winds?) "For man," declared Edwin Way Teale, "autumn is a time of harvest, of gathering together. For nature, it is time of sowing, of scattering abroad." The pleasure of the harvest mingles with the shudder of approaching vulnerability. "All things on earth point home in old October," wrote Thomas Wolfe, "travelers to walls and fences, hunters to field and hollow and the long voice of the hounds, the lover to the love he has forsaken."

Just as a High begins with a political treaty that concludes the Crisis, an Unraveling era begins with a cultural treaty that concludes the Awakening. The society has settled the core issues that caused the turbulence: The new self-defined values have triumphed over the old group-defined values. Life can now go on—without apocalypse or utopia yet also without any overall social direction. An Unraveling often opens on a note of good cheer and renewed confidence, but the mood invariably sours. Satisfaction with private (and spiritual) life remains high, while trust in public (and secular) life declines—which further erodes the habits, rules, and manners that the Awakening has already delegitimized. This social entropy builds its own momentum. Stripping each layer from the old order makes the remnant look ever more corrupt and useless. This prompts even more cynicism and further calls to destroy what remains. The era nears its end amid a grim new expectation that the trend toward personal autonomy and institutional overthrow will persist indefinitely.

The best-known Unraveling decades (the 1550s, 1660s, 1760s, 1850s, and 1920s) bring to mind risk taking, bad manners, and a sobering of the social mood. These decades produced few strong leaders or enduring public works but many artists, moralists, enterprisers, and reckless celebrities of enduring fame, people whom we remember for what they did alone, not in groups. Unraveling eras reflect a social mood that has become newly personal, pragmatic, and insecure. These are times of buccaneers and barnstormers, of courtly intrigue and treacherous alliances, of civil unrest and boom-and-bust markets. Contrasts abound—between the rich and the poor, the garish and the sober, the sacred and the profane. People act out, welcoming conflict while disdaining consensus. All relationships seem in flux, all loyalties in doubt, all outcomes chancy. Society fragments into centrifugal parts, with small-scale loyalties rising amid the sinking tangle of civilization. The pace of life quickens, and time horizons shorten. Mounting secular problems are either deferred or deemed insoluble.

As in other turnings, the mood of an Unraveling results from the gradual aging of the generational archetypes: Artists entering elderhood, Prophets entering midlife, Nomads coming of age, and Heroes being born. Here is what happens across the life cycle.

- As empathic *Artists* replace Heroes in *elderhood,* they quicken the pace of social change, shunning the old order in favor of complexity and sensitivity.

Entering old age, Artists remain as other-directed as before—institutionally flexible, culturally sensitive,.and committed to process and expertise. They seldom produce strong, decisive leaders. Just as they once took cues from Hero elders, they now adopt the agenda of younger Prophets while wishing to be accepted as full partners in the new values regime. Tolerant of diversity and discord, elder Artists generally accept (even celebrate) centrifugal social forces. Hesitant to impose their judgment, they prefer to let events take their course—sometimes regretting the consequences. Frustrated yet resilient, old Artists retain their sentimentalism, social conscience, and liberal belief in second chances.

The Enlightenment elders of the French and Indian Wars were the most self-questioning and directionless in American colonial history, remembered for their "endless doubts, scruples, uncertainties, and perplexities of mind" (Samuel Johnson) and their "impartial yet pacific, firm yet conciliatory" manner (Nathaniel Appleton). A century later, during the era of sectionalism before the Civil War, the peers of Zachary Taylor went to their deathbeds admitting their mistakes while still seeking "such measures of conciliation as would harmonize conflicting interests." "Life itself is but a compromise," insisted old Henry Clay, who lamented that his generation of Compromisers could not stop the approaching collision between Abolitionism and King Cotton. In the years after World War I, as Woodrow Wilson pursued his Fourteen Points in vain, his aging generation was less concerned with real-world outcomes than with the fairness of the process by which competing ideals are reconciled. "If my convictions have any validity," Wilson declared, "opinion ultimately governs the world." Historian Mark Sullivan notes how, "reversing custom," in the 1920s "elders strove earnestly to act like their children, in many cases their grandchildren."

- As judgmental *Prophets* replace Artists in *midlife,* they preach a downbeat, values-fixated ethic of moral conviction.

Entering midlife, Prophet generations display first a reflective distance and gradually a sober severity in a phase of life previously known for tolerance. In their own eyes, they are pillars of rectitude. To others, they are ineffective hypocrites—though they are also begrudgingly respected for their capacity to focus on core issues of right and wrong. Midlife Prophets begin reshaping institutions from the inside out, taking the insights they had earlier cultivated in private life and projecting them into public life. They come to political power slowly but resolutely, beginning with relatively weak leaders tolerant of their peers' self-immersed impulses. As they resacralize institutions not in line with their values, passionate splits emerge between factions with competing moral positions.

By the time the first Puritan Generation of New England settlers reached midlife, their original law of love transformed into a love of law—especially when applied to unconverted younger adults. John Winthrop advised his followers to "submit unto that authority which is set over you," which granted "a liberty to that only which is good, just, and honest." A century later, the midlife peers of Sam Adams, Jonathan Edwards, and John Witherspoon expressed horror over growing moral decadence, sparking what historian Michael Kammen calls "an awakening of civic consciousness." In the 1850s, foreign visitors remarked on the "seriousness" and "absence of reverence for authority" of America's "busy generation of the present hour," that is, the Transcendentals. Just after World War I, Missionary crusaders joined the Holy Trinity of populism, fundamentalism, and feminism to win the day for women's suffrage and temperance. While a younger writer lampooned them as pompous Babbitts, middle-aged people slapped a new Code of Decency on movies, slammed the door on immigration, meted out tough sentences to criminals, and battled to impose a severe New Humanism on a society that felt out of control.

- As alienated *Nomads* replace Prophets in *young adulthood,* they become brazen free agents, lending their pragmatism and independence to an era of growing social turmoil.

Nomads come of age in a society strong in choices and judgments but weak in structure, guidance, or any sense of collective mission for young people. Lacking a generational core, they are defined by their very social and cultural divergence. Aware that elder leaders don't expect much from them as a group, they feel little collective mission or power. Yet their accelerated contact with the real world gives them strong survival skills and expectations of personal success. Acting as individuals, they take entrepreneurial risks and begin sorting themselves into winners and losers. Their culture develops a frenetic, hardened quality, provoking next-elder Prophets to accuse them of lacking a principled inner life. Young Nomads shake off these criticisms and do what they must to get by.

"A wicked and perverse generation" is how the young Quaker Josiah Coale described New England's renegade youths during the 1650s. To older immigrants, writes historian Oscar Handlin, "the second generation seemed a ruder, less cultivated, and wilder people." During the French and Indian Wars, George Washington's peers registered a seismic jump in drinking, gambling, crime, begging, and bankruptcy, prompting historian William Pencak to describe the Liberty as "young people with nothing to do and nowhere to go." A century later, in an era of declining college enrollments, the targets of elder critics were Mark Twain's gold rush boys, in whom George Templeton Strong was struck by "so much gross dissipation redeemed by so little culture." Historian Richard Hofstadter remarks that the Gilded grew up as "a whole generation of Americans who wanted things dreadfully, and took them." Just after World War I, Stephen Carter admitted that "magazines have been crowded with pessimistic descriptions of the younger generation." Randolph Bourne defended his Lost peers from elder moralists by noting that they were the "logical reaction" to parental neglect. While "it is true that we do not fuss and fume about our souls," he explained, "we have retained from childhood the propensity to see through things, and tell the truth with startling frankness."

■ As *Heroes* replace Nomads in *childhood,* they are nurtured with increasing protection by pessimistic adults in an insecure environment.

The Hero archetype is made, not born, and the making begins in childhood at the hands of parents gripped with spiritual confidence and secular anxiety. Newly perceived as dangerous, the child environment is pushed back toward greater protection and structure. Children are urged to be obedient achievers and team players. They form more conspicuous bonds with fathers (their main link to civic deeds) than with mothers (their main link to personal values). To older Prophet parents, Hero children are instruments through which their inner visions can someday be achieved. To younger Nomad parents, they are beneficiaries of a hard-fought effort to rediscover and reclaim a close family life.

When the Glorious were children, colonial parents came under attack for what Increase Mather labeled "cruel usage" and "neglect." Soon assemblies were building primary schools, and churches were teaching good works and "preparation of salvation" rather than passive conversion. The era of the French and Indian Wars produced a sea change in colonial attitudes toward children—away from the prior neglect and toward a new protectiveness, which benefited the emerging Republican Generation. "By 1750," observes historian Jay Fliegelman, "irresponsible parents became the nation's scapegoat." Afterward, notes historian Kenneth Lynn, "in no other period of our past can we find the top leaders of American society speaking as gratefully as these patriots did about the fathering they received." Similarly, Progressive-era adults succeeded in cleaning up the child's world. This produced, according to sociologist Leonard Cain, a "generational watershed" at roughly the year 1900: Children born after that year were much more favored than those born before and became a father-respecting generation that, as Bing Crosby sang, would "follow the old man wherever he wants to go."

America is now more than a decade into the current Unraveling, with roughly another decade remaining. Over the next ten years or so, the usual linear forecasts will prove to be correct: Into the new millennium, today's generations will display much the same persona as they now do, except in more exaggerated (and slightly older) form. But in so doing, they will be traveling to the threshold of yet another transformation whose nature and consequences the linearists cannot fathom.

SILENT ENTERING ELDERHOOD: HIGH-FLEX NEOSENIORS

As the 1984 election approached, David Broder announced that his "Fit Fifties" generation was ready to take over. No other U.S. generation had ever grown so old without winning a major-party presidential nomination. That year the Silent Generation finally did, only to see Walter Mondale and Geraldine Ferraro carry just one state. Four years later, a Silent veteran ran against a G.I. veteran, but when Michael Dukakis sat atop a tank, people laughed. Call the roll of failed candidacies: Lamar Alexander, Bruce Babbitt, Pat Buchanan, Jerry Brown, Bob Dornan, Pete Du Pont, Dick Gephardt, Phil Gramm, Tom Harkin, Gary Hart, Jesse Jackson, Jack Kemp, Richard Lamm, Ross Perot, Pat Robertson, Pat Schroeder, Paul Simon, Arlen Specter, Paul Tsongas, and Pete Wilson. By the late 1980s, pundits talked of "dwarves" who lacked "gravitas." Come the 1990s, Broder described a "Fractured Generation" that kept succumbing to a "flip-flopping inconsistency, pandering to special constituencies, riding pet hobbyhorse issues, having questionable values or just seeming strange." In the five presidential elections from 1980 through 1996, an era when the Silent should have dominated American politics, they earned only four of twenty spots on major-party tickets.

The Silent are well on the way to becoming the first generation in U.S. history never to produce a president. They have only had one vice president. Yet they have established themselves as a preeminent *helpmate* generation, with three First Ladies (Jackie Kennedy, Rosalynn Carter, and Barbara Bush) and an unprecedented four decades of behind-the-scenes prominence on

White House staffs (from Pierre Salinger, Joe Califano, and Bill Moyers in the 1960s to Dave Gergen, Mack McLarty, and Leon Panetta in the 1990s).

During the Awakening, the Silent helped an older generation run the nation and a younger generation challenge them. During the Unraveling, when the Silent should have taken charge, they have helped G.I.s linger and Boomers pass them by. Back in the 1980s, pundits coined the term "stature gap" to distinguish Silent contenders from aging G.I. statesmen like Reagan and Tip O'Neill to whom the public still looked for a confident hand on the tiller. A decade later, the Silent displayed a new "passion gap" with the more focused and passionate Boomers. Like the *Washington Post*'s description of Richard Lugar, this generation now presents itself less as leaders than as a collective "resumé in search of rhetoric." Having spent a lifetime looking beyond themselves, the Silent reached their turn at leadership only to find others looking beyond them too.

Their elder accomplishments—adding new definitions of fairness, new layers of process, new levels of expertise, and new categories of diversity—have enhanced amenities but done little to address the nation's core challenges. Like the law many Silent deem their greatest achievement, the Americans with Disabilities Act, their best efforts have helped some people out but tied others in knots. Now, as the Unraveling deepens and power drifts away, this generation feels a post-midlife passage that Daniel Levinson has described as "a silent despair, a pressing fear of becoming irrelevant."

"One of our most perplexing mysteries is why the quality of people in Congress is going up and the quality of performance is going down," David Gergen said in 1991. No other generation in U.S. history has entered old age addressing so many public wants and complaints but with so few results. In the mid-1980s, when the Silent held more then two-thirds of all legislative seats, Congress convened twice as many hearings, hired four times as many staff, mailed six times as many letters to constituents, and enacted one-third as many laws as G.I.s did back in the mid-1960s. In two decades of Silent plurality, from 1977 to 1996, Congress balanced not a single budget and added eight times as much to the national debt as all earlier American generations combined. Where the G.I.s had the Great 89th Congress in 1965, the Silent put "The Can't Do Government" on a 1989 cover of *Time*.

In their hands, America has become what Michael Sandel calls "the procedural republic." Beginning with the Budget Act and War Powers Act, Silent Congresses have installed endless budget and peace processes, usually making institutions fairer, kinder, and more responsive but never simply replacing them. "Issues come and go," says Colin Powell. "Process is always important." Much of what this generation values most is perceived by other generations as lying at the periphery of what makes a nation work. As Harvey Silvergate said of Justice Stephen Breyer's legal writings, Silent governance brings to mind "a finely tuned watch that is a mechanical wonder in its smooth and logical operation. The only problem is that, in the real world, it fails to keep time." As Bush said of Dukakis, this makes the Silent appear to others like "the technocrat who makes the gears mesh but doesn't understand the magic of the machine."

Through the Unraveling, America's style of elder leadership has gone (in *Fortune*'s words) from "macho to maestro." Like Dukakis's 1988 lectern, the Silent have recast G.I. red, white, and blue as salmon, gray, and mauve. They have offered a nuanced, ever-questioning perspective that Meg Greenfield praises as the "continuing reinspection of our inherited historical certitudes. . . . When all this is properly in play our understanding will be expanded, refined; elements of ambiguity or complexity or doubt will be admitted to the picture." As other-directed as ever, the Silent have turned against peers (like Robert Bork, Pat Buchanan, or Joycelin Elders) who are seen as rigid or abrasive but have embraced others who (like David Souter) plead that their own convictions would play "absolutely no role" on divisive issues like abortion.

In every realm of life, aging Silent try to solve problems by getting people to talk to one another—from weekend T-groups to corporate sensitivity seminars, from Ted Koppel's National Town Meetings to Sheldon Hackney's National Conversation in which "all participants will show respect for the views expressed by others." "We don't arrive with ready-made answers so much as a honed capacity to ask and to listen," says newspaperman Wade Greene, who touts his generation's ability "to bridge gaps, at a time of immense, extraordinarily complicated and potentially divisive changes." Silent-led governments have nudged every person and group to participate. In California, ballots carry so many initiatives that in 1990 they required a 230-page voters' guide, while new school textbooks required the assent of four committees, one with ninety members. Foreign policy has embarked on a new era of multilateralism and deference to international law—what Harvard's Joseph Nye terms "soft power, the complex machinery of interdependence." Under Silent command, even computers have started talking to each other: Space shuttles began carrying three, whose disagreements were resolved by two-to-one votes.

Where the G.I.s had reached the brink of elderhood pursuing a small number of large missions, the Silent reached theirs pursuing a large number of small ones. In the mid-1980s, the Union of International Associations cataloged ten thousand world problems requiring solutions. "Rather than painting the broad landscape," William Cohen says his Senate peers "engaged in a pointillist approach—each little aspect of the dots" lending fine detail to a world that had felt oversimple in their High-era youth. William Raspberry laments that "hardly anyone speaks convincingly to the national interest," instead just to countless "components."

Where the word *liberal* once referred to a G.I.-style energizer with a constructive and unifying national agenda that involved bulldozers and factories, the Silent have transformed liberals into enervators who prevent the bulldozers and factories from hurting anybody. Gary Hart boasted that "we're not a bunch of little Hubert Humphreys." Meanwhile, the definition of elder conservative has evolved from the Lost's cautious High-era stewardship to the hip, high-rolling optimism of Silent supply-siders, full of Unraveling-era zest and swagger. Like Phil Gramm (and unlike Boomers), they "ain't running for preacher" and don't like "simply moralizing." Across the ideologies, the Silent have sought what David Osborne describes as a neo-progressive "synthesis": "If the thesis was government as solution and the antithesis was government as problem, the synthesis is government as partner." Regardless of ideology, the Silent generally agree that policy decisions are best left to experts. In defense of his peers, Tom Foley fought Boomer-led term limit initiatives by hiring expert lawyers to keep expert incumbents in office.

From the culture to the economy, the aging Silent have been hard at work clearing away all the smothering societal restraints they recall from their youth. Aided by their elder cadre of ACLU-style civil libertarians, they have resisted curfews, school uniforms, and anti-panhandling laws. They have added risk to the economy with leveraged buyouts, derivatives, state-approved casinos, zero-coupon bonds, and "dynamic projections." They have opened every imaginable cultural door, broken every taboo, provided every peep show. Where High-era Silent hipsters had once toyed with on-the-edge naughtiness, the Unraveling's corporate chairmen put the Time-Warner logo behind the overt profanity of Nine Inch Nails. "There are no gatekeepers left at the networks," announces *Advertising Age*. "Aside from the F-word and saying that Advil is better than aspirin, you can get away with anything now." The elder Silent tend to undermine any social arrangement that requires social discipline or informal restraint to keep it going. From pop music to fashion, journalism to literature, the graying generation of Dick Clark, Calvin Klein, Hunter Thompson, and Gore Vidal pretends to scoff at the rules of the very realms they now rule.

Unlike the G.I. elders who came before, the Silent believe in options, negotiation, diversity, mobility, complexity—what Pat Choate calls the *High Flex Society*. In the Awakening, Silent microeconomists had defended market choice against macro-minded G.I.s. Now, the president's older economic advisers defend markets while his younger ones disagree. Through the Unraveling, G.I. industrialists have been replaced by Silent technocrats who manage financial holding companies long on flexibility and short on product identity or worker loyalty, and who take cues from books like Tom Peters's *Liberation Management: Necessary Disorganization for the Nanosecond Nineties*. The old vertical command structure has given way to the horizontal or even disintegrative. As labor unions, sports leagues, and oligopolies have weakened, antitrust policy has become less of a public priority because no one expects the Silent Jerry Joneses to collude like G.I.s used to do. So long as everyone avoids technical violations, Silent boards of directors presume that anything their companies do is acceptable—whether incentivizing CEOs with huge stock options or right-sizing employees onto the streets.

To guide them and the nation to right answers, this generation trusts *affect* above all else, what John Leo describes as "an unembarrassed relativism based mostly on feeling." The result of large doses of John Naisbitt's "high-tech/high-touch" strategy can be seen in Mario Cuomo's "compassionate" liberalism, Jack Kemp's "bleeding heart conservatism," or Ross Perot's deflective proposals to "engineer" reforms by taking more and better polls to see what everybody feels should be done. In Silent hands, the Ford Foundation's grand priorities have shifted from the underwriting of large public constructions to the support of special projects designed to "promote tolerance and social understanding" and ensure "access and equity." When Americans feel bad about some foreign situation they see on TV, U.S. troops go on overseas missions with few clear goals other than adhering to multilateral agreements and keeping everybody from getting hurt. Under generals like Norman Schwarzkopf and John Shalikashvili, military tactics are shifting toward the use of stand-off weapons that save lives but are extremely expensive to build yet leave the final outcome in doubt. The era of Silent generalship is the first in U.S. history in which more soldiers have died in training than in action.

The Silent take justifiable pride in their lifetime civil rights record. They have succeeded in producing more black and Hispanic members of Congress than all prior American generations put together. Racial understanding is perhaps the noblest legacy of a generation that, as Russell Means said of himself, "came to understand that life is not about race or culture or pigmentation or bone structure—it's about feelings. That's what makes us human beings." Yet the end game of that legacy includes a new resegregation of college dorms, public schools, and Congressional districts—and an *unfeeling* new tangle of social pathology that makes youths of all races less trusting of each other and less hopeful about racial progress than the Silent were when young.

Wincing at younger generations' troubles with the Unraveling-era economy, the Silent are embarking on old age feeling a vague dissatisfaction about their supposed luck as an inheritor generation grown old. They comprise America's wealthiest-ever elders, completing a stunning two-generation rags-to-riches transformation of American old age. Where the High-era Lost watched their growing offspring whiz past them economically, the Silent tower over the living standards of their children. In 1955, most thirty-five-year-olds typically lived in bigger houses and drove better cars than their sixty-year-old parents. Now the opposite is the case. As entry-level pay and benefits have shrunk for young workers, top-level pay has skyrocketed for their aging bosses: Where a G.I. CEO earned 41 times the pay of an average worker, a Silent CEO earns 225 times as much. "In 1940," recalls Russell Baker, "only an opium eater could have imagined the soft, lush future in which we now wallow." Yet with this prosperity has come a susceptibility to scandal. From Bob Packwood's sex-laced diaries to United Way's apologies for William Aramony's "lack of sensitivity to perceptions," the Silent pay a price for what the Teflon G.I.s more easily shrugged off.

Today, the Silent have become the "Establishment" but still feel like outsiders. Charles Reich wrote *Opposing the System* as if the hated system were in the hands of strangers. Silent legislators have enacted sunshine laws and inundated the nation with data for the purpose of enabling everyone to second-guess them. Yet a person can file Freedom of Information Act petitions, read through reams of expert depositions, and still have no clue who makes any choices or bears any responsibility. Behind this generation's evasive accountability lies a sense that, unlike in the Trumanesque High, the buck does *not* stop with them. Having prospered as a smallish generation in the shadow of powerful institutions, the Silent have felt collectively exempt from the consequences of failure, as though they just weren't numerous or strong enough to matter. Like Calvin Trillin's hero-victim in *Remembering Denny,* they suffer from an impostor complex, an anguish over an anointed success for which they never had to struggle.

Much as David Broder closes each year with a column acknowledging his gaffes, the Silent are closing their careers by reflecting on their mistakes and how they might make amends. Retired public officials admit easily to past errors yet are annoyed to hear their legislative artifacts of tolerance, compassion, and due process come under sharp attack from younger politicians. So this generation's decorous Miss Mannerses keep defending politeness, its erudite Paul Fussells keep protesting *The Dumbing of America,* and its sensible William Cohens keep dissenting from the view that "those who seek compromise and consensus" are "a 'mushy middle' that is weak and unprincipled." "Unfortunately," lamented Pat Schroeder upon announcing her retirement, "the Washington I'm leaving is meaner than it was when I arrived." "We have let the New Puritans take over," said Russell Baker, "spreading a layer of foreboding across the land."

What "chills the blood" of aging liberals like Daniel Moynihan is the realization that, in their youth, "the old bastards were the conservatives. Now the young people are becoming the conservatives and we are the old bastards." As more Silent incumbents retire rather than persevere, this generation's core of expertise is becoming ever more irrelevant. "Even the vocabulary of our lives faces extinction," despaired Baker, realizing that the very phrase " 'Soviet Union' may soon sound as antique as 'Third Reich.' " Late in life, many are feeling what Kevin Phillips calls an "end of empire frustration" and an anxiety about the flimsiness of a prosperity bought by decades of economic and cultural risk taking. When the Silent begin to convert their life story into gallery pieces like the Korean War Monument and the Rock and Roll Museum, they construct artworks more than landmarks, appealing more to aesthetic than to civic or moral sensibilities. And they fear that many of their lifelong achievements could turn out to be like Jackie Onassis collectibles: precious to them, but incomprehensible (and perhaps unaffordable) to others.

"Most of the time, we've been reeling, suffering from cultural and technological vertigo, off balance with an inner ear reverberating to the sounds of both Patti Page and the Rolling Stones," says Richard Cohen of his generation's late-life confusion. "We were raised for one era and had to live in another, and now, tragically, we've been discounted altogether, forgotten like some lost civilization or Tiny Tim. We're accused, I suspect, of having done nothing. That, however, is not the case. We've been in therapy."

Into the New Millennium: Rabbit at Rest

"Surprise!" gushes Gail Sheehy in *New Passages,* which describes the years from fifty on up as a series of zigzags one reviewer likened to a miniature golf course. "The second half of life is NOT the stagnant, depressing downward slide we have always assumed it to be," says Sheehy. In their "second adulthood," the Silent can, "without limits," make "all sorts of choices." Retiring men can learn to talk, politicians to be peacemakers, generals to cry, and businessmen to emote—while graying feminists come into full bloom. Elderhood will become a time for pleasure palaces and an un-hung-up aesthetic sensibility climaxing in what Sheehy calls the "Uninhibited Eighties," which the eldest in her generation will reach in the year 2005. Sheehy's peers will indeed combine a denial of age with a better-late-than-never search for catharsis. They will keep trying to think, act, and look young, conforming their wardrobes to mainstream fashions, undergoing many a face-lift and tummy tuck, and occasionally infuriating their children by succumbing to sexual dalliances and experimental urges. As Woody Allen said of his affair with his common-law wife's adopted daughter, "The heart wants what the heart wants."

The Silent may think they're aging imperceptibly, but the culture is noticing. *Funny, You Don't Look Like a Grandmother* is the title of Lois Wyse's peer-directed book; and indeed, America is just getting acquainted with a hip new elder batch that doesn't fit (or like) the familiar old G.I. senior citizen label. The Silent prefer to think of themselves more as high-flex neoseniors, iconoclastic connoisseurs who savor subtleties, subtexts, and art for its own sake—deft relativists who lace their thinking with "on the other hands" and appreciate all points of view. Disappearing are the Cadillac owners, bridge players, Moose, Masons, and members of gray power groups. In their place are the SeniorNet surfers (self-styled "Kids over 60"), Common Cause members, the Peace Corps' "older volunteers," museum docents, opera ushers, and unpaid aides to social workers and park rangers. In the child's book *My Grandma Has Black Hair,* Grandma does aerobics, buzzes about in a red sports car, and engages in cross-cultural conversations with young people. Golden America senior networks are giving way to Norman Lear's Act III Communications, huge luxury autos to snappier world-class sedans, vigorous big band music to maudlin oldies but goodies. A new genre of films about aging *(Grumpy Old Men, How to Make an American Quilt)* depict elder lives as a pastiche of sexual and family mistakes.

"I just found out I'm somebody's grandfather. And somebody's father. Maybe I'm somebody's friend in the bargain," said Paul Newman in *Nobody's Fool,* a 1994 embodiment of the Unraveling's sensitive and self-deprecating grand-daddio. Many Silent are finding their links with grand-children weakened by their own (and their children's) divorces, but now they're battling to rebuild broken relationships. Before the 1990s, America had few grandparent support groups; now there are more than 150. Since the end of the Awakening, the number of children living with grandparents has risen by 40 percent, as young parents boomerang back to their own affluent moms or dads living in large empty-nest homes.

Through the rest of the Unraveling, the Silent will rejuvenate what it means to be old in America. Leisure World and Sun City will lose popular-ity, as Silent tastemakers prefer townhomes within reach of restaurants, the-aters, and sports arenas populated by younger people. After the 13er master bedroom coup d'état, boomerang households will mature into extended families that can endure. Older people with hopelessly fractured families will experiment with nontraditional living arrangements. Many will be old "goofballs," more childlike than their grandchildren; others will become ex-pert at what they dabbled in when young. Long charter tours will lose ground to shorter but pricier adventure vacations and "grandtravel" trips with grandkids. Silent "elderhostelers" who once did Europe on five dollars a day will do it again at five hundred per. Keeping checklists of everything they still want to do, many will try anything that tingles with risk: scale mountains, ride rapids, hack through jungles, and ski across polar ice caps. They will travel to national parks with their smocks and berets, easels and paints. They will ante up to Chautauquas and Disney Institute resorts to lis-ten to big-name lecturers. They will turn their basements into photo labs or recording studios or computer workshops.

"What you need are more choices," says James Earl Jones's AT&T ad. Where retirement once meant a vanilla-flavored G.I. public reward, the Silent see it as full of options, including that of *un*retirement or *counter*re-tirement, as the Silent yearn to stay involved with what everybody else is do-ing. By style and habit, they will put new pressure on the cost of elder health care. "Mod gets Medicare" says the *Washington Post,* as Dr. Joyce Brothers urges her peers to be "expert patients." Many of them will download vast data about care options and special benefits, advise doctors about their preferred medications, and request the most complex treatments available. When their health fails, the Silent will be more loath than G.I.s to enter group living arrangements, spurring a surge in individualized home care. All this will add substantially to federal spending on elder health.

In the early 1990s, just as the Silent started collecting Medicare and Social Security, the long-term viability and intergenerational fairness of those programs began coming under attack, often from the Silent themselves. Many of what gerontologists call the "young old" were touched by guilt about receiving money from harder-pressed young workers—a guilt G.I.s never collectively felt. While articles about pampering the elderly began to appear in national publications, the aging elite began sharing demographer Frances Goldscheider's view that "the flip side of the poverty of the young is the affluence of the elderly." Silent senators like Warren Rudman, John Danforth, and Alan Simpson quit public life expressing anguish that, having left entitlements on autopilot during their own era of power, their generation allowed public advantage to tip too far in favor of elders and against youth. Richard Lamm feels "haunted by the fact that I am a member of the most fiscally irresponsible generation in America," and Paul Tsongas has launched a grass-roots Silent fight for "generational justice" that (in a reverse twist on the old G.I. agenda) would take money *out* of their own pockets.

In recent years, the Silent have begun to transform the once-monolithic senior lobby, making it more fractious, other-directed, and ineffective. By the mid-1990s, when AARP summoned members to support pro-senior benefit law changes, some members of Congress began receiving more anti- than pro-AARP letters from constituents in their sixties. Unlike its predecessors, the 1995 White House Conference on Aging stressed intergenerational themes and issued so many complex, polysyllabic resolutions that scant attention was paid to any of them. Meanwhile, AARP's *Modern Maturity* magazine has adopted a sleek new look, with high-brow cultural features, articles about youth trends, and columns offering diverse points of view.

In the decade ahead, the Silent will find themselves the unwitting fulcrum of a sweeping turn in America's attitudes about old-age public dependency. By the Oh-Ohs, America's rising familiarity with the Silent elder persona will erode today's support for across-the-board senior benefits. Unlike G.I.s, the Silent will not feel entitled. They came of age in the careerist 1950s, not in the do-without 1930s or the global-war 1940s. Their prior public deeds will not inspire them (or others) to lobby for a vast elder reward. Moreover, younger people will ask why government treats elderhood as a perennial dependency if so many Unraveling-era golden oldies are able to live such aesthetically fulfilling lives in such gorgeous pleasure palaces.

Given the diverging economic fortunes of the low-benefit McJobs worker and the early retiring and golden-parachuted pensioner, many young people will express resentment at seeing their large FICA taxes going to pay for *A Year in Provence* or a master bedroom Jacuzzi.

The Silent would be easy targets for generational war, except that their open-mindedness and un-G.I.-like fascination with youth will make them elders whom younger people enjoy being around. To deflect the inevitable youth criticisms, the Silent will play to the heart and suggest intergenerational co-caretaking, personalizing the reciprocal duties between young and old. Their sense of guilt and instinct for compromise will compel them to give in some, relax their claims on young workers, and drain the electricity out of the third rail of Social Security politics. As the Silent offer to accept a modest but important measure of sacrifice, they will succeed in completing their lives without ever having had a major quarrel with another generation, cementing their reputation as the most other-directed generation of their time.

In *Rabbit at Rest,* the last of John Updike's four novels about the life of Harry "Rabbit" Angstrom, Harry's death is described as a tangle of tubes and wires. Harry realizes that his past is "strewn with emotional wreckage," leaving nothing but "table scraps" for the "kids coming up." He recalls how different his own life had been. In Updike's High-era *Rabbit Run,* Harry questioned a married, careerist life he found stultifying. In the Awakening, Harry rejuvenated *(Rabbit Redux)* and then cashed in *(Rabbit Is Rich)*. Throughout their adventures, Updike's characters feel internally adrift as they "search for good sex, final sex, absolute sex. Sex that will enable them to be at rest." They can't figure out what to strive for in an America that keeps giving them plenty but promises to give their children less.

By the middle Oh-Ohs, the residual Silent world will bring to mind the reshuffling of international acronyms that are much-discussed on PBS but have little to do with the lives of most younger people. Whatever the unmet social need, the Silent inclination will be to propose a better process (a new budget amendment, a new incentive tax rate, a new review board, or what Raspberry calls "some latter-day Missouri Compromise" on abortion) rather than the pain-for-gain approach favored by their successors. Aging columnists and news anchors will lament what Theodore Roszak now calls "a war against kindness" while pleading, to ever fewer listeners, that the world is too complicated to permit anything other than gradual change.

Long a reliable generation of donors, the Silent will be legendary philanthropists in their final years. This will reflect a last urge to set things right, like the club that passes on members' Social Security checks to needy young people, or Ralph Nader's effort to reignite the "suppressed crusades" of his Princeton peers. In 1995, the median age of donors to America's liberal causes was sixty-eight (a dozen years older than for donors to conservative causes), and 43 percent of these donors are expected to die by the year 2005. Generous Silent bequests will feel like a final infusion of hope for many American symphonies, art museums, dance companies, jazz societies, and opera houses. Today's polls show the younger half of this generation to be the nation's leading benefactors and ticket-buying patrons. America's fine arts industry will worry, with reason, that after the Silent pass on, things will never be the same.

As time inexorably thins their numbers, even their deaths will be offbeat, iconoclastic, and extremely *un*silent. Ellen Goodman imagines a "dying process" of doctors who listen and obituaries that list "the way of death as well as the cause of death," and she asks, "Would that make a difference?" Nontraditional funerals are already on the rise, with cutting-edge decedents attaching personalized spins by prehiring speakers, poets, and musicians to bring less sobriety and more warmth to their final passage. No matter how sad the testimonials, no matter how mean and coarse civic life gets, this generation of Mark Russell and Bill Cosby will find the ironies and explore the lighter side to the very end.

Into the Oh-Ohs, the elder Silent will devote their last years trying to bring shattered families back together, getting angry political ideologues to listen to each other, making life fairer around the edges, and elevating the exquisite from the humdrum of life. Whatever fate may yield, they will keep yearning to help out—without being too judgmental, of course. Down to their last days, the old Silent will still believe, with Barbra Streisand, that "people who need people are the luckiest people in the world."

BOOMERS ENTERING MIDLIFE: THE CULTURAL ELITE

On March 25, 1984, the *New York Times* declared the "Year of the Yuppie," the surprising transmogrification of the Awakening-era hippie. America was awash in fads, diets, and jokes about Perrier-drinking sellouts engaged in what *Newsweek* described as "a state of transcendental acquisition." Literally, the word *yuppie* meant "young urban professional." Only 5 percent of the generation matched those demographics, but a much larger proportion fit the subjective definition: self-immersion, cultural perfectionism, and weak civic instincts.

Everything yuppies ate, drank, drove, watched, or listened to was an implicit rebuke of the G.I.'s High-era Wonder Bread culture. In their apparent quest for the perfect three-dollar chocolate-chip cookie, yuppies were needled for hypocrisy but didn't mind, since they set the new cultural standard by which hypocrisy now had to be measured. Having reformed the inner world, they were engaging the outer at their own pace: a jog. In 1984, Gary Hart tried in vain to mobilize yuppies as a political force, mistakenly thinking they still had an Awakening-era mind-set. But instead, yuppies were content to dabble, disperse, and leave affairs of state to an old G.I. president who shrewdly appealed to their new attitude.

Yuppiemania lasted less than four years. The stock crash of 1987 doused the media interest, and two years later the cultural accoutrements disappeared as well. This generation was moving on to something else, something more revealing of its true midlife persona. Come the new decade, the *Wall Street Journal* noted that "deferring gratification has suddenly become fashionable," talk of family values filled the airwaves, and new churches (and prisons) sprang up everywhere. Three intensely generational mid-1990s elections produced much talk about God and children, along with a surge in what media pundits called "conviction politicians," "prophets with attitude," "rhetorical Robespierres," or worse.

By the middle of the Unraveling, America was mesmerized by a midlife pastiche that included the nation's leading talk show host, "chosen by God" to explain *The Way Things Ought to Be;* a U.S. president who insisted he never inhaled hosting a White House conference teaching character; a House Speaker chided for his "blabby, effervescent, messianic" persona; a vice president who held evening seminars on "the role of metaphor" while accusing opponents of a Jihad against the environment; academic enforcers of political correctness who punished "inappropriately directed laughter"; think-tank luminaries at competing Renaissance and Dark Ages retreats holding seminars on shame; the former SDS radical turned culture warrior whose *Book of Virtues* vaunted "moral literacy"; the ex-Black Panther juror who judged everybody in the courtroom, not just the famous defendant; and the Operation Rescue leader who declared hate to be sacred.

"We all know these types," grumbles a prominent (Silent) critic of the U.S. Senate's youngest member: "critical of everything, impossible to please, indifferent to nuance, incapable of compromise. They laud perfection, but oddly never see it in anybody but themselves." President Clinton is "stereotypical" of them all, observes demographer William Dunn: "a little self-indulgent and pretty much convinced that he and his generation are smarter than everyone else."

Still the distracted perfectionists, America's new inhabitants of midlife are handling their new phase of life the way they have thus far handled so much else: They apply a light hand, then (once they start paying attention) a crushingly heavy one. They graze on munchies until they figure it's time to diet, after which they don ashes and sackcloth—and expect others to do the same.

"We aren't baby killers," declares the leader of the Michigan militia movement. "We're baby boomers."

When the G.I. Lloyd Bentsen told Dan Quayle, "You're no Jack Kennedy," the insult was partly generational: In midlife, Boomers are not G.I.s. They are not as eager to take JFK-style "long strides" or "get America moving again" as they are to think deep thoughts or get America to tend its soul. Offering themselves as America's midlife magistrates of morality, Boomers are stirring to defend values (monogamy, thrift, continence) that other generations do not easily associate with them.

The Boomers' midlife fire-and-brimstone judgmentalism is more noticeable when they're outside the fortress of power, storming its gates, and taking their first look around from the inside. But once their conquest is no longer news, once they have to manage the fortress themselves, their stern persona gives way to a wry philosophical detachment. Many of their best-known politicians have tended to treat civic responsibility the way David Letterman might treat a guest, dabbling and gesturing, never committing too much, spurning whatever isn't quite up to their lofty standards, spending more energy on discussing how power feels than on actually doing anything with it. When challenges grow too hard, they back off, as though not yet ready to take full charge of the nation's direction. In the mid-1990s, *Newsweek* magazine pointed out a "critical mass of baby boomers in the contemplative afternoon of life"—a comment no one would have made of the two prior generations in midlife.

Through the Unraveling, Boomers have been busy respiritualizing American culture and resacralizing its institutions. Even as they wreck old notions of teamwork, loyalty, and fraternal association (a trend Robert Putnam chides as "bowling alone"), they are trying to restore a new foundation for public virtue. A host of new Boomer magazines and newsletters are inserting terms like *communitarian, citizen,* and *public virtue* (or renorming words like *standard* and *paradigm)* into their titles. "Interestingly," writes Evan Thomas, "the people who seem most desperate to create a new civil society are baby boomers, the generation that was largely responsible for trashing the old one." "It was great to be young in the '60s, when everyone threw responsibility to the winds," says John Leo, "but what's even better is that the very same people get to be middle aged in the '90s, which is shaping up as a great decade for stuffiness."

Today's Boomer-style values politics had its roots in the Awakening. The temperament of the Boomer-dominated Congress has a recognizable link to the 1960s' kids in jeans with bullhorns. To Newt Gingrich, "values" are first "a way of dividing America." John Kasich views the national debt "almost like I look on the Vietnam War." What the *New York Times* calls "the new churlishness" echoes what once occurred on radicalized Awakening-era campuses. Now as before, the advantage goes to whomever yells the loudest and has the best conversation enders. Everything gets hyperbolized: An offensive touching becomes assault, which becomes rape, which becomes murder, which becomes genocide. In Boomer battles over symbols, polarization is easy, compromise hard.

In 1992, when Americans elected their first Boomer president, his campaign slogan ("It's the Economy, Stupid") and governance showed a distinctly generational flavor. Bill Clinton is smart but distractible, habitually late to an event or issue, after which he focuses "like a laser beam." Gifted in gestures of empathy, Clinton can persuasively flaunt his inner self to enhance his popularity. Yet Clinton generally polls worse among peers than among older voters. As Michael Barone has observed, Clinton can seduce fellow Boomers but can't marry them: His values preaching has never quite felt authentic to many people who share his life-cycle connections. As a candidate and president, Clinton has reminded many people (including his own peers) of his generation's best and worst qualities.

The 1994 Republican onslaught was the first election determined by Boomer votes, and the twentieth century's largest generational landslide. In the states, Boomer governorships rose from eighteen to twenty-eight, empowering a new peer-driven movement to devolve power to the states. In the House, Boomers gained the speaker's chair and a solid majority. Only the U.S. Senate remained in Silent hands as an island of politeness and moderation. As Boomers stoked the talk shows, their first Congress drowned out consensus-seekers, talked openly of default, and demanded that the government be reformed or closed. Thus has the American government, from G.I. to Silent to Boom, gone from moon walk to gridlock to train wreck.

By 1996, the Clinton-Dole race (talker versus doer, "comeback kid" versus "comeback adult") updated the old Boomer-G.I. Generation Gap. Eight years had passed since Bentsen's old quip, and the two generations had moved along in life: Bob Dole was no Dan Quayle. He was a standard-issue G.I. on "one last mission for my generation"—not a credentialed Culture Warrior, not a person who could *grok* values in the now-dominant Boomer tongue. Dole's peers had earlier turned over leadership to their grown children; now, said Al Gore, "it's not fair to take back the reins." The mere nomination of Dole was a slap in the face to a generation that (he implied) lacked the character to exercise power responsibly. In his convention speech, Dole blasted a Boomer elite "who never grew up, never did anything real, never suffered, and never learned."

In the 1996 election as elsewhere, the old Generation Gap found new Unraveling-era expression, despite Boomers' frequent encomia about how grandly G.I.s once ran the nation. Where middle-aged G.I.s came to Washington striving to fix the economics of everything, intent on curing poverty and building power plants (like a *Time Marches On* newsreel), middle-aged Boomers want to change the culture of everything, intent on altering minds and calming the spirit (like Steve Martin contemplating the *Grand Canyon*).

Where midlife G.I.s believed that public money was an earth-moving answer to social problems, Boomers are more likely to see it as a narcotic that makes social problems worse. In 1995, the National Taxpayers Union reported that two-thirds of Congress's fifty thriftiest members were Boomers (six of them Democrats), versus only one-third of the fifty biggest spenders.

Where G.I.s believed in The End of Ideology and the power of technocracy, Boomers are rediscovering ideology and the power of spirituality. Instead of the best and brightest, they would just as soon let a *Dave* or *Forrest Gump* rule. Instead of a New Deal Coalition, they're building a Christian Coalition. G.I.s had a reputation as better doers than talkers, Boomers as the reverse.

Where the G.I.s' midlife Power Elite included scientists and manufacturers adept at inventing and refabricating things, the Boomer elite comprise what *Newsweek* calls the Cultural Elite, a new Overclass studded with "talking heads" and "symbolic analysts" adept at inventing and refabricating thoughts.

Where G.I.s "ac-cent-tchu-ated the positive," Boomers are constantly "going negative." Defending against their attack ads has been shown to be futile; politicians who stay positive only get torn up worse. Where G.I. political adversaries used to be friends after hours, Boomer enemies are not.

Where G.I. voters have been habitual party loyalists, Boomers are slow to embrace candidates, quick to discard them, and disinclined to vote when uninspired. In the voting booth, they have leaned toward candidates who are preachers (Jesse Jackson, Pat Robertson) or apostles of gloom (Jerry Brown, Paul Tsongas, Pat Buchanan), all of whom fared poorly among G.I.s.

Before the early 1990s, when Boomers finally wrested national power from G.I.s, most of those who wanted to turn the status quo upside down had argued with (but mostly voted for) Democrats; since then, those who felt like revolutionaries argued with (but mostly voted for) Republicans. Between 1987 and 1994, the Times-Mirror survey recorded a doubling of "moralist types" as a share of all voters, two-thirds of the increase coming from Boomers alone. By the mid-1990s, more than twice as many Boomers came to call themselves conservatives than liberals, a difference that said less about their politics than about their self-perception as totally rooted and self-secure, beyond the reach of opinion or edict or even sociability.

"He's got a new way of walking. . . . He's getting back to his roots," sings Alan Jackson of Boomers who are "Goin' Country." In the Awakening, the Boomers' political voice had been mostly coastal, urban, and secular. In the Unraveling, Clinton, Gore, Gingrich, and many of the freshman Republicans are displaying a southern, rural, and evangelical bent. "Values" are not "add-ons," insists Bennett. "They are the very enterprise." Add to that a new preoccupation with families, and the words *family values* have become a catchall for the new midlife Boomer agenda. By pushing society toward an attitudinal conversion, Boomers are convinced that an institutional rebirth will follow. "The key is leading the culture, not leading the government," says Gingrich. "Because if you change the direction of the entire dialogue, everything else falls in place behind it."

This midlife obsession with values is propelling a huge growth of evangelical and New Age believers. Two Boomers in three say they've been touched by a supernatural power. (Among their elders, less than half do.) Back in the High, G.I. atheist Madalyn Murray O'Hair had battled to get prayer out of the public schools; now her born-again son William is battling to put it back. Only 1 percent of Boomers say they definitely do not believe in God, but 80 percent believe that attending church is unnecessary. Amid all the spiritual talk, church going has declined for Boomer age brackets, whereas among G.I.s and Silent it has held steady. America's middle-aged believers are fleeing mainline churches for fast-growing fundamentalist, charismatic, and breakaway redeemer sects that dress casually or ethnically, sing lively songs, listen to guitar-and-brimstone homilies, erupt in periodic applause, and engage in other rites drawn from the recovery movement. Boomers are adding new chic to old "S words" like sacred, spiritual, soul, sin, shame, and satan. Books on heaven, hell, and out-of-body experiences have become best-sellers. Angel books sold five million copies in 1993 alone. By the mid-1990s, *Utne Reader* described how "shamanic journeys" were becoming "for people in their 30s and 40s and 50s what rock concerts are for people in their teens." Gradually, the two main spiritual camps are converging: Evangelicals are turning to "devotional" therapy, while the New Age is discovering family values.

Middle-aged spiritualists are retooling America's commercial culture. By the mid-1990s, half of all small businesspeople claimed they were born again, and large corporations began pursuing what Saturn's Skip Lefauve describes as "more of a cultural revolution than a product revolution." *Value* (traditional workmanship, enduring quality, correct politics) has become the 1990s marketing buzzword. Boomer-led companies are mixing politics with products, applying *The Seven Spiritual Laws of Success* and tending to what Thomas Chappell calls *The Soul of a Business*. "To do well you must do good," advised Stephen Covey, "and to do good you must first be good." As Boomer corporatists read *Jesus: CEO* and accumulate *Money of the Mind,* their peers seek products believed to *be* good because they are made by good people. A virtuous company can gain a listing in the *Shepherd's Guide*'s religious yellow pages, while a bad company can end up on the *National Boycott News'* 124-page target list.

Many of America's largest corporations are replacing *The Man in the Gray Flannel Suit* with a Boomer facsimile the *Christian Science Monitor* has dubbed "The Man in the Cotton Twill Slacks." These new executives pride themselves on fostering a healthy corporate culture and managing through shared values. Even so, the Unraveling era's erosion of corporate loyalty has left many midlife "open collar" workers feeling more loyal to their calling than to their bosses. Laid off professionals often mask underemployment by becoming self-employed contractors or consultants. Whatever the cover, Boomers are looking for simpler careers and home-based work so they can spend more time with children or just slow down.

The Unraveling's Boomer-led family is predicated on a rebirth, and blending, of gender roles. Midlife women recall their G.I. mothers as not assertive enough; midlife men recall their fathers as not reflective enough. Both are taking steps to correct this in themselves—and others.

Midlife Boomer women admire what Clarissa Pinkola Estés calls the "wild woman" who "comes ahead, claws out and fighting." These include "mother lion" antimedia crusaders; lesbians and ecofeminists; a surge of female gun owners and hunters; heartland spouses who comprise roughly a third of radical militia membership; and authors of countless books about menopause, goddesses, and "sage women." New Victorians in women's studies programs show less interest in liberation than in punishment—and in censoring porn, regarded by Catherine MacKinnon as "the root of all women's woes." What the *New Yorker* calls ultrafeminists have moved beyond the Silent crusade for sexual equality to the belief that women, being closer to nature, are superior to men. Midlife women have emerged as a political juggernaut, writing big checks for both parties and quadrupling the female share of state legislators. At times, the wives of Boomer male candidates make voters think they should run instead of their husbands. Polls of middle-aged voters generally show women significantly more liberal than men—but just as disapproving of the old institutional order.

Boomer men have largely accepted their female peers' incursions. Without a second income, most of their households would fall below the living standards of the Silent at like age. Many Boomer wives have steadier and higher-paying jobs than their husbands'—a situation that would have mortified G.I. males. Half of all Boomer fathers describe themselves as better dads than their own dads were—evidence (says the National Fatherhood Initiative's Don Eberly) of a "regret bordering on anger" that reveals a "substantial gulf between the Boomer Generation and their fathers." Crafting a post-Awakening masculinity as suitable for churches as for homes, Boomer males are rejecting G.I. man's-manliness and Silent angst for a new gender definition *Newsweek* calls "the Godly man." They are massing in wilderness retreats, the Million Man March, and evangelical Promise Keepers rallies where men hold hands in football stadia. The new men's literature extends from Dave Barry's "guy" culture to mythopoetic tales of gender spirituality.

On race, Boomers are rerooting a traditional ethnic consciousness and asserting an intense new spirituality. From Muslims to the NAACP's Benjamin Chavis and Kweisi Mfume, Boomers are refusing to be what Ntozake Shange describes as "trees white people walk through." While values liberals like Stephen Carter attack *The Culture of Disbelief,* values conservatives like Clarence Thomas, Armstrong Williams, and Alan Keyes demand a fresh examination of what Shelby Steele calls *The Content of Our Character.* Across ideologies, Boomer blacks agree that Awakening-era laws and programs helped them as individuals but also engendered a culture of poverty that damaged their communities. They are more likely than their white peers to be born again and favor school prayer—and often voice regret that the core of African American leadership has passed from churches to government. As they back away from traditional civil rights organizations, Boomer blacks are less likely than the Silent to stress pluralism or solicit money from white taxpayers or private donors; instead, says one Muslim, they are intent on "replacing the integrated head on the civil rights movement's black body—with a black head." Much of the new race talk is moving away from procedural rights and equal opportunity and toward strengthening families, stopping crime, and saving children.

If rectifying civic virtue requires harsh new restrictions on child freedoms, Boomers everywhere—from inner cities to walled suburbs—are fully prepared for that. To date, the child's world is the one place where this middle-aged generation has fully focused. The severe, intrusive, perfectionist approach Boomers have applied here is a sure sign of what will gradually happen elsewhere as the Unraveling continues.

Into the New Millennium: Virtuecrats

As Boomers move more deeply into midlife, their collective mindset will grow more judgmental, snobbish, and severe. By nurture and habit, they will remain disinclined to do the regular or polite things that facilitate community life. Yet by midlife conviction, they will become what E. J. Dionne describes as "civic liberals" and "civic conservatives," obsessed with restoring shared values. This will pose a conundrum for Boomer parents and leaders as they traverse the millennium: How can a generation that can't march in a row tell others to do so? Graying Boomers will respond by tying their Awakening-era credos about personal growth and authenticity ever more tightly to new imperatives of social altruism. Many will redefine their jobs to stress the inspirational or preaching role. America will see more of what Newt Gingrich calls "didactic politicians," public crafters of what Bennett calls "the architecture of the soul."

Come the Oh-Ohs, Boomers will begin to find new uses for government. Where the first half of the Unraveling saw the rerooting of Boomer conservatives, the second half will see the rerooting of Boomer *anti*-conservatives. From the mid-1980s through the mid-1990s, as Democrats lingered to defend vast public institutions that had not been resacralized, Republicans made big inroads among Boomers. To the extent Republicans in power have to defend those same institutions, a new Boomer-led opposition will mobilize a rejuvenated alliance of "Duty Democrats" opposed to the Christian Coalition. Like Mickey Kaus in *End of Equality,* Boomer liberals will propose replacing the remnants of the Great Society with something less materially promising but more morally exacting. Yet no matter who gains high office, liberals or conservatives, many backers of the winning faction will wonder if high office in an era of ideological rage and train-wrecked government is where they really want to be—and if a tactical loss might not prove to be a strategic victory. For Boomer partisans who are out of power, the late Unraveling will mainly be an occasion to retool and jockey for long-range advantage.

On the Culture Wars front, Boomer communitarians—liberal *and* conservative—will gradually prevail over the libertarians in the Culture Wars. The dittohead Rush Limbaughs will lose listeners to the shame therapist Laura Schlessingers, and the free-enterprising Steve Forbeses will be overwhelmed by the family-minded Gary Bauers who insist that "the marketplace unleavened by virtue" produces "junk." The new Boomer ascendants will zero in on what Martha Bayles terms the *Hole in Our Soul,* "the loss of beauty and meaning" in America's Unraveling culturama. What John Leo calls "hair-trigger puritans" will attack licentiousness in the belief that the whole community is threatened by misdirected private pleasures. To galvanize the community to save itself against the darkness of human evil, Boomers will continue to allude to cleansing catastrophes, like the impending birthing pains predicted by the Earth Changes movement. Back in the Awakening, any bout of unusual weather prompted Boomers to predict the new Ice Age; today, it prompts them to predict global warming. Charles Krauthammer asks, "Is there a primitive religion that can match 'environmentalism' for attributing natural calamity to the transgressions of man?"

Boomer virtuecrats of all ideologies will increasingly distrust any path that doesn't hurt. Their prescription will not be a sugar-coated cure, but a purgative tonic. Addressing America's unmet social needs, Boomers will insist (with Karl Zinsmeister) that "we forego the comfortable, and ever so easier, responses of softness" and (with Texas governor George Bush Jr.) that "discipline and love go hand in hand." From chain gangs to "diet loaf" prison food to courtrooms where victims confront criminals, Boomers will re-stigmatize crime and emphasize "expressive justice" that judges the sinner along with the sin. According to the *Economist,* "Many of those baby-boomers, who once marched for peace and love, now want to see murderers injected, shot, or fried." They will seek to cleanse rather than comfort the poor, applying what John Kester suggests will be "blunt instruments" and "crude solutions." "Amputation is a tough treatment," he says, "but it does get rid of gangrene."

Boomer rhetoric will offer many polarizing arguments but few big institutional changes. National politics will become an arena for fierce arguments about new proposals that even the strongest partisans will know can't yet be enacted or enforced. As the Overclass argues for a flat tax (stressing the virtue of simplicity and moral desert), it will be stymied by less affluent recusants who will say they have "chosen" not to pursue a life of wealth. Similarly, Boomer Congresses will find ways to separate arguments about the federal budget from the budget itself, which will grind away without fundamental change. Not able to decide who is worse, the rich or the poor, Boomers will censure them both and impose symbolic (but minor) punishments: Some supposedly excessive income will be taxed from the one side, undeserved welfare slashed from the other. The result will be a vast and rusted-out public sector stripped of an engine—but with nothing yet ready to replace it.

Influencing these policy debates will be new stock figures: the roving philosopher-professionals, their careers held together only by the twisting thread of their own personality. The cutting-edge idea prescriptors will be author-politicians like Al Gore, William Bennett, or Bill Bradley, people who fuse spirituality with grass-roots activism. Questing after the elemental, primitive, and austere, Boomers with means will travel to abbeys and convents, kayak with aborigines, and backpack in orangutan sanctuaries. Those without means will retreat to a farmhouse or take a sabbatical teaching inner-city children. Upon their return, they will declare themselves renewed and issue stirring appeals to the national conscience. Many Boomers who preach honesty and sacrifice will remain personally self-indulgent. Like Bill Gates (whose ecofriendly mansion has a garage for twenty cars), the Cultural Elite will consume heavily while pretending otherwise.

Aided by the Internet and other media inventions, Boomers will carve new concepts of community within mental and moral rather than physical and institutional boundaries. In affluent suburbs, Boomer homes will buzz with offices, day care co-ops, food delivery, phone shopping, and other infrastructure around which will grow a new civic life, at times behind security gates. Those who live far from their parents and childhood homes will struggle toward their own definition of real community. Surveys show that Boomers today value neatness less than older or younger people. In the Oh-Ohs, their preferred style will lean toward the organic, the genuine, the unordered. They will reject Oldsmobiles, pavement, face-front garages, big lawns, and suburban sprawl for sturdy 4×4s, gravel driveways, front porches, spreading oaks, and rural hamlets (what some call "oldfangled new towns"). They will not mind letting age show on their homes or in their cities, where they will let parkland once cleared and mowed by G.I.s revert to native grasses and wildflowers.

Boomer values will increasingly be driven by a profound antipathy for much that is modern in American life. Where G.I.s once liked to surround themselves with regular and rational and progressive things, Boomers will prefer the unique and sacred and traditional. Elements of today's Luddite Congress will make a mark on the Oh-Ohs' U.S. Congress, as Boomers struggle to redefine what progress means. Already, they are attacking such old G.I. yardsticks as the Gross Domestic Product on the grounds that they *over*measure the mere payment of money (since divorce lawyers and industrial pollution technically add to GDP) and *under*measure what truly matters (since saving a species or teaching values to children count as zero). To replace these, Bennett has crafted his Index of Leading Cultural Indicators; the Clinton Commerce Department, a Gross National Welfare measure; and a liberal think tank, a Genuine Progress Index, which concludes that the quality of American life has *declined* by 40 percent since the mid-1970s.

Materially, most Boomers freely concede that they're not living much better in middle age than their parents did. At age forty, where a typical G.I. worker (during the High) enjoyed a two-thirds rise in real pay over the prior generation at the same age, a typical Boomer worker has shown no real improvement. Yet their self-esteem remains indomitable: By a five to one ratio, 1990s-era Boomers consider their careers better than their parents', and by nine to one, their lives more meaningful. By the Oh-Ohs, those views will harden. Downwardly mobile Boomers will "face the truth about the way they live now with some dignity and grace," writes Katy Butler. "If it's by choice and it's not overwhelming, having no money can be a way of entering more deeply into your life." Boomer recusants who choose not to achieve by any worldly standard will have second thoughts about Information Age technology. Spurred by magazines like *Simple Living* and *The Tightwad Gazette,* and by the Miserly Moms and Use Less Stuff movements, Boomers will find spirituality in what *Fortune* calls "non-ism," exalting whatever it is they will *not* be consuming, from no-nitrate meat to no-color gasoline. For many, the Oh-Ohs will be time to shed the tech toys, abandon workaholism, and "downshift."

In family and financial affairs, the late Unraveling will be a sobering time. Boomers will have to say farewell to most of their remaining G.I. parents, often after a geographic separation dating back to the Awakening era and fumbled efforts at reconciliation that betray mixed motives on both sides—as in Bud Lite's "I *love* you man!" commercial. Parental death will confront Boomers with an embarrassing reality for people their age: that the providers they had somehow counted on are gone and that what's left (in inheritance) is somehow not as much as they had imagined. *Thrift* will become a big late-Unraveling buzzword among Boomers as they make a big deal out of all the income they are diverting into mutual funds. But, as always, this generation will have trouble following through. Some will resist the notion of disciplining themselves for the sake of lucre. Others, looking at the runup in stock and bond prices caused by their sheer midlife numbers, will assume the market boom will last forever—and they will cut back on savings accordingly. Boomers will continue to support Social Security and Medicare for their own parents while also believing that both will be bankrupt by the time they retire. Into the Oh-Ohs, their leaders will talk constantly but do very little about this looming threat to the material security of their own age—a threat that will loom ever closer.

Gradually, the old wry detachment will give way to a jarring new focus. Boomers will at long last be ready to accept full responsibility for their own old age—and for the hard choices facing their nation. Increasingly, graying

Boomers will "muster the will to remake ourselves into altruists and as-cetics," as *Rolling Stone* urged in 1990. "But let's not fake it," the magazine warned, the yuppie persona still in its rearview mirror. Or at the very least, advises Hillary Clinton, "fake it until you make it." By the Oh-Ohs, this gen-eration will be of no mind to fake anything. "There is no way to avoid the coming confrontation," the *Catholic Eye* declared in 1992. "Fasten your seat belts—it's going to be a rough ride."

13ERS ENTERING YOUNG ADULTHOOD: TOP GUNS

America's college class of 1983 came with a new label, the first official wel-come of their coming-of-age generation. Around the time of their gradua-tion, the U.S. Office of Education published *A Nation at Risk,* describing the nation's student population as "a rising tide of mediocrity" whose learning "will not surpass, will not equal, will not even approach, those of their par-ents." This diatribe became the first in a flurry of reports, studies, and books (keynoted by Allan Bloom's *The Closing of the American Mind)* that casti-gated America's new youth as mindless, soulless, and dumb. In their caustic *What Do Seventeen-Year-Olds Know?,* Diane Ravitch and Chester Finn an-swered: not much. Grading youths in twenty-nine subjects, they dished out twenty F's, eight D's, and one C minus.

Through the early Unraveling years, recent graduates heard older writers and columnists call them a "nowhere generation," a "tired generation," a "generation of animals," a "high-expectation, low-sweat generation," and "an army of Bart Simpsons, armed and possibly dangerous." Russell Baker decried their "herky-jerky brain" and "indifference to practically everything on the planet that is interesting, infuriating, maddening, exhilarating, fasci-nating, amusing, and nutty." Youth-targeted films *(Breakfast Club, St. Elmo's Fire, Ferris Bueller's Day Off, Fast Times at Ridgmont High)* scripted adolescents to confirm these elder judgments. In *Pump Up the Volume,* Christian Slater's Hard Harry dismissed his peers as a "Why Bother Gener-ation." As novelist David Leavitt has observed, "Mine is a generation per-fectly willing to admit its contemptible qualities."

In the early 1990s, as Wayne and Garth chanted "We're not worthy!" and Beck sang "I'm a loser, baby," America's twentysomethings begrudgingly settled on the label *Generation X.* Like so much of the new youth culture, this term was a pop derivative: Somebody wrote a book about 1960s-era British mod teenagers, Billy Idol named his band for the book, the term be-came a Canadian youth cachet, and along came Doug Coupland's defining title. After the 1992 film *Malcolm X* landed X logo merchandise on black kids' caps and shirts, southern white kids began wearing T-shirts to match ("You wear your X and I'll wear mine"). Soon the letter was everywhere.

Seizing the new generational discovery, a barrage of media began portraying everything X as frenetic and garbagey. In their own lyrics and manuscripts, young people maintained the facade of self-denigration they had already learned in childhood—with a touch of ironic malice. "Our generation is probably the worst since the Protestant Reformation," said a college graduate in *Metropolitan*. When Subaru showed an ersatz grunger selling supposedly punk rock cars, the ads failed. Asked to buy a car decked out in their own culture, young people refused. "Whatcha gonna do when they come for you?" sang the theme song of *Cops*. "*Bad* boys! *Bad* boys!" *Bad as I Wanna Be*, Dennis Rodman chimed in.

"Nobody's really got it figured out just yet," Alanis Morissette sings in her album *Jagged Little Pill*, and indeed, many of her peers resist any effort to define their generation. Today's youths often regard their own circles of friends as too diverse to be thought of in collective terms. To them, *X* stands for nothing, or everything, or (as Kurt Cobain sang) "oh well, whatever, never mind." Compared to any other generation born this century, theirs is less cohesive, its experiences wider, its ethnicity more polyglot, and its culture more splintery. Yet all this is central to their collective persona. From music to politics to academics to income, today's young adults define themselves by sheer divergence, a generation less knowable for its core than by its bits and pieces.

As the 1990s have progressed, young adults have asserted more control over their own image. The generational TV shows have taken X from the glitzy *Beverly Hills 90210* to the atomized *Melrose Place* to the ersatz community of *Friends*, whose cast resembles the people who watched those other shows. Many of the story lines depict youths as noncommittal, unattached, brazen about sex and work, obsessed with trivial things, and isolated from the worlds of older people or children. In film, young directors explore their peers' disjointed alienation *(sex, lies, and videotape; Bodies, Rest, and Motion)* in a disappointing youth economy *(Clerks, Reality Bites)* and a life that seems to lead nowhere *(Slacker, Singles, Dazed and Confused)* amid a culturally splintered world *(Boyz 'n' the Hood, El Mariachi, Just Another Girl on the I.R.T.)* full of exploitive sexuality *(Kids, My Own Private Idaho)* and remorseless violence *(Natural Born Killers, Pulp Fiction, Menace II Society, Doom Generation)*. These films often have no beginnings or endings, or any "right" things to do, or older mentors who aren't cartoons, or any environment that isn't what Robert Rodrigues calls "spare and tough." What they do have is lots of drugs, alcohol, violence, moving around, boredom, meaningless sex, social chaos, and personal directionlessness.

Older generations mostly avoid these movies, so their impression of X mainly arises through mainstream media *(Newsweek,* Fox's sports broadcasts) that aggressively pursue young-adult psychographics and, especially, through advertising. Marketers zero in on young adults less because they have spendable money—of all adult age brackets, they have the least, per capita—than because they dominate the margins of product choice. Today's young adults have thin loyalties, what Coupland calls "microallegiances." "With them, once the fizz is gone, that's it," says a Shearson-Lehman pump-sneakers analyst. As advertisers search for the right fizz formula, shocked elders see constant thirty-second snippets of hyperkinetic, inarticulate young body-worshipers trampling the Tetons in pursuit of raw pleasure. Young adults may buy the beer, but the image leaves a hangover.

"X got hypermarketed," declared Coupland in 1995. "And now I'm here to say that X is over." *Generation Ecch!* declared one parody, as polls showed only 10 percent of youth willing to embrace the letter label. From Coupland to Pearl Jam's Eddie Vedder, putative leaders of the youth culture declare no interest in speaking for anybody, except perhaps to share writer Jennifer Lynch's realization that "maybe I have nothing really to say." The whole X persona has come to be perceived as such a mess that nobody wants to identify with it, as if to cut all connection with a loser.

Often, talk of X has degenerated into pretentious putdowns by a Boomer-dominated media bent on confirming the superior authenticity of their own Awakening-era youth. The 1994 Woodstock revival produced much Boomer talk about how much nobler and less commercial the original had been. In return, the bombast of middle-aged narcissists has provided a ripe target for this younger generation of survivors. "Boomers are finally growing up," says Kate Fillion, "and we don't hold it against them that they forced so many of us to beat them to it." To hear many 13ers tell it, following Boomers into youth is like entering a theme park after a mob has trashed the place and some distant CEO has turned every idea into a commercial logo. "Make love not war / Sounds so absurd to me," sings Extreme, confirming America's latest generation gap.

To get a fix on the today's young-adult generation, forget the X, look beyond the pop media, and skip the Boomers. Focus instead on their place in American history—number 13—and how different 13ers are at this age from the generation that nurtured them: the Silent.

Where Silent youth felt the need to break free from a gravitational conformism, 13ers feel the need to ground themselves out of a centrifugal chaos. The Silent were America's *least* immigrant generation and yearned for more diversity; 13ers are the twentieth century's *most* immigrant generation and yearn for more common ground. Where the Silent inhabited the most uniform youth culture in living memory, 13ers dwell in the most diverse minicultures.

Where the Silent were the youngest-marrying generation in U.S. history, with low rates of premarital sex, abortion, and venereal disease, 13ers are the oldest marrying, with the highest-ever rates of teen sex, abortion, and venereal disease (including AIDS).

Where the Silent's worst high school discipline problems were gum chewing and cutting in line, the image of troubled 13ers is *Kids,* in which the adult world is invisible amid a numbing youth search for violence and drugs and sex and money. Where the Silent had an annual young-adult arrest rate of 13 per 1,000, the 13er arrest rate is 117 per 1,000. One 13er student in six knows somebody who has been shot.

Where Silent youths came of age believing in sweet sentimentality, as kids who (sang Elvis) "just want to be your teddy bear," 13ers came of age believing in rock-hard reality, as kids who (writes Bret Easton Ellis) want to be "unambiguous winners . . . Tom Cruise characters." Where the young Silent wanted a *Heartbreak Hotel,* 13ers would rather be *Top Gun.*

"How could such wonderful parents as ourselves have produced such awful children?" asks William Raspberry. Try this: Where the Silent were children of a Crisis who came of age in a High, 13ers were children of an Awakening who came of age in an Unraveling.

Where the Silent grew up just when a hungry society wanted to invest, 13ers grew up just when satiated society wanted to cash out. Where the Silent came of age in an era when individualism was discouraged but economic success guaranteed, 13ers are coming of age when individualism is celebrated but economic success is up for grabs. Where the young Silent climbed the corporate ladder and flocked to Washington to staff the New Frontier and Great Society, twice as many 13ers say they would rather own their own businesses than be corporate CEOs, and four times as many would rather be entrepreneurs than hold a top job in government. With the Silent, prosperity and institutional stability gradually exceeded expectations, allowing them to turn their focus to affect and detail. With 13ers, the opposite happened, and expectations were betrayed. Where the Silent came of age with *How to Succeed in Business Without Really Trying,* 13ers have the stark declinism of *Rent,* riveting them on the bottom lines of life.

Generational economics bear this out. Unraveling-era 13ers, males especially, have been hit with a one-generation depression. From 1973 to 1992, the real median income for young-adult males fell by 28 percent, more than it did for the entire nation from peak to trough of the Great Depression. (During those same two decades in which youth incomes were plunging, real median income for seniors *rose* by 26 percent.) In 1969, the median earnings of full-time working men under age twenty-five was 74 percent of the median for all older full-time men; since 1986, that figure has never risen above 55 percent. In the Awakening, only 8 percent of young employed household heads lived in poverty; now 18 percent do. Notwithstanding this harsh youth economy, the image of *Beverly Hills 90210*-style wealth (cars, TVs, CD players, leather logo jackets) has wrapped itself tightly around 13ers. Yet what sociologist Jerald Bachman calls "premature affluence" has done more harm than good: It has accustomed youths to parentally subsidized luxuries they cannot possibly afford on their own, and it has persuaded older generations that if some young people aren't doing well, they have only themselves to blame. "The poor stay poor, the rich get rich," sings Concrete Blonde. "That's how it goes, everybody knows."

For a generation that struggles so much in economic and public life, fatalism is a survival skill, comforting those who are not doing so well. They apply it to wall off each fragment of life—work, family, friends, culture, fun—from the rest and thereby contain any damage from spreading. Unlike Boomers, 13ers can't spare the energy to be "together" people, linking every act to a core self. Instead, they tend to be modular people, dealing with each situation on its own terms. Nowhere is fatalism more rampant than in 13er views on crime. The Unraveling's youth crime rate has ebbed below its Awakening-era (Boomer) peak, but the public tolerates it far less. Where the Boomers were the most alibied and excused criminal generation in U.S. history, 13ers have become the most incarcerated. Roughly one-third of all 13er black males are either in prison, on probation, or under court supervision. Today's convicts are perceived as incorrigible, deserving not of rehabilitation but of pure punishment—from butt-caning to merciless execution. Yet of all Unraveling-era generations, 13ers are the toughest on criminals. If you're guilty and get caught, so the thinking goes, don't complain about what's coming to you.

Taking risks comes naturally to what is far and away America's most active generation of gamblers. As on-line sports bettors, lottery-ticket regulars, and avid bar bingo players, 13ers fill the age brackets that are now (but were not previously) most at risk to compulsive gambling. Lacking any guarantee that slow-but-steady, follow-the-rules, and trust-in-the-future behavior will ever pay off, 13ers tend to view the world as run by lottery markets in which a person either lands the one big win or goes nowhere. They have constructed a flinty ethos of self-determination in which being rich or poor has less to do with virtue than with timing, salesmanship, and luck. What people get is simply what they get and is not necessarily related to what they may or may not deserve.

Their dating and mating reflects much the same quest for risk amid decline, for modularity amid chaos, for doing what works amid constant elder judgments about right and wrong. Where the young Silent looked at sex as euphoric, marriage as romantic, and feminism as a thrilling breakthrough, 13ers look at sex as dangerous, marriage as what a *St. Elmo's Fire* character calls "all financial," and gender equality as a necessary survival tool in a world of wrecked courtship rituals, splintered families, and unreliable husbands. As older feminists debate what Deanna Rexe calls "problems of affluence and success, rather than serious ones," their 13er successors are more concerned about immediate self-defense (against AIDS, date rape, and street crime) and longer-term self-defense (against potential spouses who might be unreliable providers or abandon their families).

As the youngest-copulating and oldest-marrying generation ever recorded, 13ers maneuver through an unusually long span of sexually active singlehood, with the threat of AIDS ever lingering in the background. They have always been the physical center of the abortion debate—first as the surviving fetuses of the most aborted generation in U.S. history, later as the pregnant unmarried woman faced with the "choice" of what to do. Small wonder 13ers have such split feelings about the Consciousness Revolution. They fantasize about how the 1960s and 1970s supposedly offered Boomers easy sex without consequence, while resenting the lasting damage done by an era in which they now realize *they* were the babies adults were trying so much not to have.

A similar alertness to the hard truths—and anxiety about danger—informs the 13er view of race. They are coming of age in an Unraveling era that allows institutions, but not individuals, to discriminate on the basis of race, exactly the opposite of what the Silent encountered in the High. To the young Silent, affirmative action in schooling, college, and job selection was a goal of conscience. They didn't confront it themselves, but later on declared it fitting and just for their children to do so. To many 13ers, racial quotas are just another game in a larger institutional casino: They like it if it helps them, but not if it doesn't. At best, 13ers defend quotas as a sort of blood law. "Two wrongs don't make it right," says Sister Souljah, "but it damn sure makes it even."

Though often accused of rising racism and hate crimes, including many of the mid-1990s bombings of black churches, 13ers are by any measure the *least* racist of today's generations. Certainly none other in U.S. history has been as amenable to working for, voting for, living next to, dating, marrying, or adopting people of other races. America's black-white marriages have quadrupled over the span of just one generation. Yet the 13ers' greater colorblindedness doesn't necessarily bring bring them together as a generation. Their real diversity problem is less racial or ethnic than economic and familial: Young black professionals are faring almost as well as white peers, while uneducated 13er blacks are doing worse than one or two generations before. Nearly half of all young black males in the inner city do not hold full-time jobs.

Political surveys show 13ers to be somewhat more conservative, considerably less liberal, and far more independent than older generations are today or were at like age. "In a dramatic shift," writes James Glassman, "young people now constitute the majority of Republicans, while Democrats have become the party of the old." Never knowing anything except institutional decline, 13ers are deeply skeptical about grand policy visions they assume will somehow only add to America's fiscal debt and social chaos. From criminal justice to tort law, from public schools to the federal bureaucracy, government is viewed by many 13ers as a morass that is far too complex, far too tied to special interests, and far too enmeshed in ideology to get simple things done. Having grown up in an era of rising political cynicism,

Ian Williams notes how "we are moving beyond cynicism to apathy." As MTV airs *Like We Care* in a fruitless effort to show that Tabitha Soren's peers somehow do, millions are reaching voting age as what that network calls the "Unplugged"—total nonparticipants in public life. For many, *non*-voting has become an acceptable social choice.

More than three 13ers in four do not trust government to look after their basic interests. As they see it, other people get benefits, while they pay the bills. In California, thanks to Proposition 13, young new homeowners can pay several times as much in property taxes as their elder neighbors with identical homes. In Virginia, a thirty-year-old couple with a thirty-thousand-dollar income and a hundred-thousand-dollar house pays more than eight thousand dollars in major local, state, and federal taxes, while the typical sixty-five-year-old couple with the same income and house pays nothing at all. Nearly every major Unraveling-era policy proposal on taxes, health care, and Social Security has proposed transferring more money from youth to elders. And 13ers are even less inclined than Boomers to believe that paying now will benefit them later, when they grow old in their own turn. A Third Millennium survey found that more 13ers believe in UFOs than in Social Security lasting until they retire. Thus has arisen the downward spiral of 13er civic interest: They tune out, so they don't vote, so their interests are trampled, so they tune out, and on it goes.

Many 13ers prefer to express their community spirit less by voting than by hands-on volunteering. They believe that society is changed not by presidential orders or Million Man Marches, but by the day-to-day acts of ordinary people. When 13ers pick up a newspaper (which they do a third less often than the Silent, at like age), many skip the national news for the local and personal. When asked if they look at their world as "a global village" and not just as the town where they live, only 38 percent of Americans under age thirty say they strongly agree, versus 54 percent of those age forty-five and over. Today's youth voluntarism comes less through big institutional philanthropies than through small local charities that have no crusading figureheads or profiteering middlemen. More than older generations, 13ers believe in doing small acts of kindness as individuals, without caring if anybody applauds or even notices. The president of MIT has likened their civic attitude to that of the Lone Ranger: Do a good deed, leave a silver bullet, and move on.

Into the New Millennium: Generation Exhausted

His "Great Goal" for the twenty-first century, says *Wayne's World*'s Mike Myers, is "to have fun rather than not to have fun." His generation will, but only by continuing to wall off the money problems and elder criticisms.

Economics will continue to tell the 13er story. By the early twenty-first century, young-adult incomes will be lower, their poverty rate higher, and their safety nets skimpier than was true for Boomers in the early 1980s—confirming the 13th as the only U.S. generation (aside from the Gilded) ever to suffer a lifelong economic slide. Many will be kicked off welfare. Others will buffer their downward mobility by working multiple jobs, living in multiple-income households, or moving in with their parents.

An Unraveling that began unfriendly to entry-level job seekers will close unfriendly to promotion seekers. From professional partnerships to store manager positions, 13ers will find their paths blocked by institutions that aren't expanding and by older generations who aren't leaving. This is already the first generation born in this century to be less certifiably professional than its predecessors. By the Oh-Ohs, many forty-year-olds will remain permanent temps, no-benefit contractors, second-tier careerists, and lesser-paid replacements. Since the Awakening, young adults have shown by far the greatest rise in income inequality (while elderly incomes have actually become more equal). The share of young workers with benefit cushions—health insurance, unemployment compensation, pension plans, collective bargaining—has fallen (while the public and private cushions for the elderly have grown substantially more generous).

Into the Oh-Ohs, the 13er reputation will be no better than now. Whatever thirty-to-fortyish people do will be criticized by elders—not just for failing to meet the prior standard, but also for being a bad influence on children. This generation will personify what America will dislike about the widening gap between haves and have-nots. Its failures will be perceived as deserved, its successes less so. High-flying youths will be condemned as economic predators and appropriate targets of luxury taxation, while low-lifers will be assailed as incorrigible and unworthy of public aid. By the end of the Unraveling, the American social category with the greatest reputation for virtue will be the one to which relatively few young adults will belong: the middle class.

The 13er high-risk mind-set will come under attack as a national affliction. High-stakes entrepreneurs will be busy arbitraging deals and acquiring U.S. assets for foreign interests. They will be making markets more fluid, leveraging more risk, establishing more distance and anonymity in the links between debtors and their creditors, and flooding the world with American pop culture. In cyberspace, they will be hacking, spamming, code breaking, and tax evading. For all this, they will come under heavy criticism, prompting urgent new calls for government regulation.

At the same time, what the *Wall Street Journal* calls "high-tech nomads" will be the fungible workers of the Unraveling's globalized economy. They will barnstorm the marketplace, exploring its every cranny, seeking every edge, exploiting every point of advantage. They will talk about jobs rather than careers, emphasizing what can get totally done by the end of the day rather than potentially done later in life. Where the Silent believed in the building blocks of success and inhabited a corporate world of stable pay and benefits, 13ers will believe in the quick strike and inhabit an economy of erratic pay, no benefits, and little loyalty. Where young Silent workers let others negotiate for them, 13ers will strike their own deals, stressing near-term incentives like piece work or commissions. Where the typical Silent expected to stay with a first employer for decades, the typical 13er will expect a rapid turnover of employers and work situations.

The 13er low-sweat, task-efficient work style will be extremely good for U.S. profitability—one enterprise at a time. Economists have long said this sort of worker is what an ever-changing global economy needs, but once America acquires a whole generation of them, older managers won't be so pleased. The perceived problem won't be whether 13ers work enough, which they will, but rather their distance from corporate culture. Young workers will follow the contract: When it's time to work, they will focus; but when it's quitting time, they will disengage. Ersatz social arrangements (often a platoon of friends) will provide them with the life-support functions for which their parents once looked to employers.

Many 13ers will skip the institutional economy entirely and go it alone or with friends, outpacing and underpricing older rivals, playing crafty high-tech games with and against elder-built systems. What Saren Sakurai calls "countercommerce" will steal markets from big corporate rivals, undermine rule-encrusted state enterprises (mail, education, security), and mount gray-market challenges to credentialed professions (law, insurance, finance). Whenever governments privatize or big companies restructure, 13ers will benefit. In the military, 13er officers will flaunt a spartanlike warrior ethos. On campus, their laconic libertarianism will clash with the voluble liberalism of aging tenured professors.

By the Oh-Ohs, fortyish novelists, filmmakers, and pop stars will be pushing every niche, every extravagance, every Xtreme sport, every technology, every shock (sex, violence, profanity, apathy, self-mutilation) to the maximum, prompting Boomer calls for boycotts and censorship. As young-adult attendance sags at national parks, historic sites, museums, and classical concerts, a clear demarcation will exist between the 13er fun culture and the Boomer "classic" alternative. Sports and celebrity entertainments will acquire a brassy quality, more akin to gladiatorial than civic ritual. Athletes and entertainers will raise sports and media to new heights of commercial glitz. Star salaries will skyrocket ever higher, but journeymen will lose ground. Their individual exploits will be applauded, their team spirit condemned. Fan loyalties will weaken, as parents urge children to look elsewhere for role models. Eventually, the 13er youth culture will come to feel, like Kurt Cobain before his suicide, "bored and old."

Near the end of the Unraveling, 13ers will start tiring of all the motion and options. Feeling less Generation X than a generation exhausted, they will want to reverse their life direction.

Their attitude toward risk will change. Those who are doing well will reveal a young-fogey siege mentality that discourages further risk taking. High-achieving married 13ers will push family life toward a pragmatic form of social conservatism. Restoring the single-earner home will be a male priority; restoring the reliability of marriage will be a feminist priority. Late-born 13ers will start marrying and having babies younger, partly to avoid the risks of serial sex and harassment at work, but also to get a head start on saving and homeowning. By the end of the Unraveling, the median age at first marriage will be lower than it is today.

In time, even 13ers without good jobs will take comfort in their toeholds on the American Dream. On the whole, they will appreciate the worth and precariousness of whatever good fortune they have achieved and will fear how far they could fall if they ever lost it. Many will scrupulously avoid risk in their personal lives, even if they still have no choice but to keep taking long shots in their work lives. They will become intensely frugal, loyal to kin, faithful to spouses, and protective of children. They will not take a close and supportive family for granted; building one will be an achievement in which they will take great pride. "Been there, done that" will be their parental attitude toward sex, whose dangers they will be determined to shield from children. As 13ers cordon off their self-contained lives, older critics will find fault with a home life that will strike some as too much family and not enough values. Modular-minded young parents will go out in the evening and enjoy Quentin Tarantino films, and then come home and tuck toddlers snugly into bed, much to the amazed disapproval of older people.

By the Oh-Ohs, 13ers will comfortably inhabit a world of unprecedented diversity. Few will share the High-era view that race in America is simply a problem of black versus white. Asian and Hispanic Americans will make 13er race issues a more multivariate equation. As those ethnicities catapult into the cultural mainstream, they will be greeted with demands for a clampdown on immigration. A small but significant share of young adults (including whites) will gravitate toward organizations touting racial or ethnic separatism. From poverty to crime to making families work again, 13ers will redefine old civil rights issues into problems independent of race. Many will come to associate the phrase *civil rights* with elder ministers, teachers, and bureaucrats whom they won't want meddling in their lives. Their goal will be to stop all the racial game-playing, and they will be skeptical that the solution is simply to get everybody to understand one another.

As more 13ers form families, they will finally start voting in respectable numbers. By 1998, they will comprise America's largest potential generational voting bloc and, by the end of the Unraveling, the largest actual bloc. Once they discover the voting booth, their prior partisan detachment will work to their advantage. Come the Oh-Ohs, 13ers will occupy the critical margins of politics, capable of deciding who wins and loses. They will apply their "Pop and Politics" Internet skills for the benefit of candidates who avoid hype, who do what it takes to get a job done, and who promise not to make their problems worse.

The first prominent 13er politicians will detach positions from principles, simplify the complex, and strip issue debates to their fundamentals. To their mind-set, no program will be untouchable, no promise inviolable, no budget incapable of balance. They will propose bold new remedies to crack down on the Unraveling era's most elusive targets, from trial lawyers to wealthy seniors to corporations at the public trough. Among their first political goals will be to eliminate no-fault divorce and racial quotas. Their no-nonsense pragmatism will be criticized—by the Silent as uninformed, by Boomers as unprincipled. Few of their proposals will be enacted—not yet, anyway.

As the Unraveling nears an end, the public image of a worn-out era will fuse with the image of a worn-out and unraveled generation. By the mid-Oh-Ohs, the 13er persona will be thrown into relief not just by very different older generations but also, now, by a very different younger generation. As always, 13ers will handle it with a shrug before going ahead and doing what they must, knowing that, as a generation, they are not getting anything except older. As these forty-year-olds buy and collect pop culture junk from the 1970s, their childhood anchor-decade, they will sense the irony of their situation.

Whatever their elders may think of them, America's 13er Generation will be around for the usual duration. "They are our children, and we should love them," says Mario Cuomo, "but even if we don't love them, we need them, because they are our future."

MILLENNIALS ENTERING CHILDHOOD: FRIENDS OF BARNEY

Around Christmastime of 1983, adult America fell in love with a precious new doll, harvested from nature, so wrinkly and cuddly that everybody thought it cute. By the hundreds of thousands, Cabbage Patch Kids decorated the playpens of a new Millennial Generation of babies. A year earlier, a *Newsweek* cover story had heralded these toddlers as the past-due offspring of Boomers who had spent the prior two decades celebrating childlessness. Now Boomers were making a fuss over the life-cycle choice to give birth.

As bright yellow signs proclaimed Baby on Board in car windows across America, Hollywood quickly picked up the trend. In the early 1980s, movies about demon children *(Firestarter, Children of the Corn)* suddenly flopped at the box office, soon to be replaced by wanted-baby stories like *Raising Arizona, Three Men and a Baby,* and *Baby Boom.* By the end of the 1980s, pop-culture families still had punkish teenagers, but now the younger six- to eight-year-olds were as virtuous as Bart Simpson's younger sister, and their parents were heeding *Fatal Attraction* warnings against Awakening-era family behavior. By the middle 1990s, cinematic ten- to twelve-year-olds were literally angels (like *The Piano*'s winged Anna Paquin, or the inner-city kids in *Angels in the Outfield*) whose mere presence inspired older people to be and do better. "Was there ever a bad child in the world—a spiteful, stubborn, domineering sapper of his parents' spirit?" asked a *Time* reviewer in 1993. "There is rarely one in a Hollywood movie."

Through the Unraveling, these Cabbage Patch babies have grown into Power Ranger preteens, riding the crest of a protective wave of adult concern. As they entered preschool, adults experienced what Harvard's Arthur Miller termed a "national hysteria" about child abuse, and polls reported a three-year tripling in the popularity of "staying home with family." When the first Millennials reached elementary school, children's issues topped the agenda in the 1988 and 1992 presidential election races, and the United Way launched a huge new children's agenda. As they reached junior high, proposals were made for a new V-chip that would enable parents to screen out violent programming, three-quarters of the nation's largest cities enacted youth curfews, and state legislatures pursued deadbeat dads and changed custody rules for the welfare of children, not (as in the Awakening era) for the convenience of parents. By the time the first Millennials reached high school, the 1990s had become what Mario Cuomo termed "the Decade of the Child." From crime to welfare, from technology to gun control, health care to balanced budgets, nearly every policy issue has been recast in terms of what journalists called *kinderpolitics*. Both parties began crafting their messages around the need to save children (whether from deficits or spending cuts). By the 1996 campaign season, Clinton's focus on protecting children grew so overt that Silent critic Ellen Goodman quipped, "If this is Thursday, it must be Curfews. If this is Friday, it must be School Uniforms. V-Chips on Monday, Smoking on Tuesday."

Millennials are emerging as something of a generational public property. Where child 13ers had once been the castoffs of Awakening-era euphoria, Millennials have become symbols of an Unraveling-era need to prevent the social hemorrhaging before it could damage another new generation. The "only way" to stop the cycle of dependency and crime, warned Ohio governor George Voinovich, "is to pick one generation of children, draw a line in the sand, and say to all 'This is where it stops.' " When George Bush spoke of "weed and seed," he was implicitly drawing a line between 13ers and Millennials. Much of the Unraveling era's attack against welfare spending has reflected the judgment that many of the grown 13er children of Awakening-era family decay are unfit parents. Courts have become increasingly inclined to punish parents for child misbehavior—or to take the kids away. Serious talk has arisen about "breaking the poverty cycle" by raising children in orphanages.

This new adult focus has not yet reversed the Awakening-era damage to the child's world. The child poverty rate is still high. The crack babies of the 1980s are growing up with severe emotional disabilities. Dysfunctional families are still a terrible problem, and ten-year-old victims (or murderers) still make the news. TV sex and violence have receded only slightly. In the Awakening, all this prompted few complaints from adults. But now, in the Unraveling, it infuriates them.

As the beneficiaries of moral outrage, Millennial children have come to personify America's Unraveling-era rediscovery of moral standards and spiritualism. The natural child represents absolute good, the abused child the victim of absolute evil. Many Boomer evangelicals report that their born-again moment arrived with the birth of their first Millennial child. From evangelical Christians to Pentecostals to Muslims, many of today's new religious currents revolve around parishioners' protective urges toward small children. And in the secular culture, the little Jonahs provide the magic by which *Sleepless in Seattle* adults find the right paths.

Through the Unraveling, a solid adult consensus has emerged that Millennial children warrant more protection than 13ers received. Where the cutting-edge fertility issues of the Awakening pertained to taking pills or undergoing surgery to avoid unwanted children, the Unraveling is marked by advances in fertility medicine, preemie care, and other technologies to produce desperately *wanted* children. Where the circa-1970s natural childbirth fad focused on the richness of the experience for parents, the circa-1990s priority became longer hospital stays for the sake of the baby. An expanded child safety industry that focused on I-See-U car mirrors in the 1980s started emphasizing child-athlete injury prevention in the 1990s. The Unraveling began with new laws requiring infant restraints in automobiles; now, new laws mandate bicycle helmets.

As Boomers have come to lead the institutions that dominate a child's life, they have combined two ascendant words—*family values*—to capture the gist of Millennial nurture. What David Blankenhorn calls the "new familism" has begun to reverse the Awakening's rise in divorce and abortion rates. The stay-at-home parent is reviving as a popular choice among families able to afford it. In sharp contrast to the Awakening, a majority of working women now say they would "consider giving up work indefinitely" if they "no longer needed the money." Spurred by the new Fatherhood movement, record numbers of American men are stay-at-home nurturers. When fathers divorce, they now often demand joint (or sole) custody. From the Million Man March to its Promise Keepers white equivalent, men are seeking atonement for past child neglect and are vowing to become better role models. Two of every three parents say they would accept a pay cut in return for more family time. Thanks to such new workplace trends as job sharing, telecommuting, and career sequencing, parents are putting away the latchkeys and reconstructing an adult presence after school. Unlike circa-

1980 13ers, the high-tech child of the 1990s is less a home-alone game freak than a pen pal on the Internet with a parent peering over the shoulder.

Adult nagging has returned to the child's world. Wincing at their own coming-of-age behavior, Boomers have become what the *New York Times* has dubbed a "Do As I Say, Not As I Did" generation of parents. In the High, parents generally loosened the rules from one child to the next; now the reverse is true, with parents tightening the rules from one child to the next. Good habits are newly demanded, poor attitude less tolerated. When a much-touted Pepsi ad showed a small child uttering its new "Gotta Have It" slogan, the parental reaction was, "If that's how you ask for it, then you're not going to get it!" (The campaign failed.) In the Little League World Series, a Texas twelve-year-old boy was rebuked for celebrating his home run while his team was losing. In Youth League football, kids get yellow flags for moon walking in the end zone.

Boomers on all sides of the Culture Wars agree that Millennial children must be shielded better than 13ers were from media sex, violence, and profanity. Having grown up in a High-era culture in which nearly everything on the TV dial was all right for children to watch, many Boomers take cues from the author of *Not with My Child You Don't* and guard the hearth against the Unraveling's far less kid-friendly culture. According to *Raising Children in a Socially Toxic Environment,* renting kids a random video or buying them an unfamiliar CD could be the cultural equivalent of dioxin. When William Bennett says, "There are, after all, some things that children simply should not see," he delivers a message that his own generation laughed off in the *All in the Family* Awakening years. Responding to Bennett, Tipper Gore, Michael Medved, and others, Boomer scriptwriters are crafting plots with stronger moral lessons and less ambivalent messages about drugs, alcohol, and teenage sex. In TV sitcoms, parents are now depicted as more in charge, children as more dutiful. Children's books and magazines are returning to simple stories and traditional themes, while New Realism books are being removed from child shelves.

In their new attitudes toward children, Boomers are playing out a psychodrama about how undisciplined they themselves have become. "By intuition or design," writes Michael Sandel, "Clinton has discovered a solution: Don't impose moral restraints on adults; impose them on children."

The new values nurture is starting to produce a fledgling civic virtue. Since the Awakening's end, the child savings rate has nearly tripled. More children are doing community deeds under adult supervision. Child sports teams have never been more popular. A dozen states have launched Trial by Peers programs, letting children judge one another. In Kids Voting USA, children discuss issues, register, campaign, and vote in mock elections. "It's created political monsters among Arizona kids," said the head of Phoenix's program. "We couldn't stop them." *Newsweek* has called "the peer group" a potential "magic bullet for academic success," citing a 1996 study that found that "the influence of friends" boosted school achievement even more than "the influence of parents."

As Boomers seek to standardize the culture and values of this child generation, they see advantage in uniform clothing. In Washington, D.C., this trend began in the fall of 1988, when inner-city kindergartners at Burville Elementary sported green and yellow coats, ties, blouses, and skirts. The contrast could not have been starker between these daffodil-colored younger kids and their older siblings with their X caps, logo shirts, baggy pants, and Day-Glo sneakers. Within three years, thirty-one D.C. schools encouraged uniforms; by 1995, the idea was spreading rapidly across the nation. In districts that require uniforms, four in five parents support uniforms, in the belief (said the *Washington Post)* that children who wore standard clothes "would become more productive, disciplined, law-abiding citizens." In 1996, much to the nation's applause, President Clinton added his own support for school uniforms and for child curfews—notions that would have enraged most of his peers in their youth.

Nearly all school systems are trying to heed Rudolph Giuliani's demand that schools "once again train citizens." The new 1990s educational buzzwords call for *collaborative* (rather than independent) learning for *regular* (rather than ability-grouped) kids who must be taught *core values,* do *good works,* and meet *standards,* with *zero tolerance* for misbehavior. The new three R's are rules, respect, and responsibility. Some inner-city schools are returning to old-style direct instruction, requiring children to recite their lessons in unison. Calls are mounting for more objective grades, separation of boys and girls, abstinence-only sex education, and school prayer—along with longer school days, year-round schooling, and stiffer truancy laws. Like Hillary Clinton, many Boomers who once believed in liberating the child from the community are discovering that *It Takes a Village* and now support a strong and protective child-community bond.

In public schools, surveys indicate that teachers are feeling much better about their own profession and are staying with it longer than at the start of the Unraveling. Since the early 1980s, the share of teachers with more than twenty years' experience has nearly doubled. Parents have reversed the Awakening-era decline in PTA membership, where they are now raising money at a record clip. Many Boomers are demanding that public funds be redirected to charter schools and vouchers to allow parent choice, a threat intended to compel underperforming public schools to improve. Through the Unraveling, the number of U.S. children taught at home—mostly by Boomers who believe the public schools have been corrupted—has risen from fifteen thousand to half a million.

Parents are slowing down the developmental clock, letting Millennials linger longer in childhood, reversing what Richard Riley terms the "hurry-hustle" of the Awakening. From *Sesame Street* to *Barney and His Friends,* the most popular TV programming for kids has gone from urban to pastoral, from kinetic to lyrical, from wry to sweet, from discovering the self to sharing with others, from celebrating what makes kids different to celebrating what makes them the same. Many grown-ups find Barney mystifying, perhaps because it provides no adult subtext. One *Washington Post* TV writer called the show "so saccharine it can send adults into hypoglycemic shock." Anna Quindlen fears its utter simplicity: "What they're learning is that life is black and white," which she sees as "the primary colors of censure." Parents are stressing a values nurture, aided by a huge new bookshelf on the subject. Bennett's *Book of Virtues,* the Unraveling's best-selling children's book, has a medicinal cover, scant humor, and eleven teachable virtues that do *not* include individuality or creativity. Millennials are not being raised to explore the inner world (Boomers figure they can handle that just fine) but rather to achieve and excel in the outer.

Like any child generation, Millennials are undergoing a mid-turning transition in the generational composition of their parents. The Cabbage Patch babies, born in the 1980s, are mostly the offspring of Boomers. Their parents' overt pride in them rankles Silent observers like Jonathan Yardley who chide these kids as "Baby Boom trophies"—an implicit concession that the Silent's own (13er) kids weren't anyone's trophies. Born in the early 1990s, Barney's kids are about equally divided between Boomers and 13ers. The rest of America's Unraveling-era babies will mostly be born to 13ers. Polls show 13er married couples with children to be far more culturally conservative than their peers who (for now) remain childless. Younger 13er parents seem less interested than Boomers in political discourse about the child's world, but they show signs of being even more protective within their families.

Into the New Millennium: Junior Citizens

From their birth through their arrival in junior high, a national spotlight has followed those first Cabbage Patch Millennials. Where the first half of the Unraveling was marked by rising alarm over the children's problems, the remainder will be marked by rising satisfaction in their achievements. Meanwhile, the cutting-edge of initial concern will move on to adolescents and, as the Oh-Ohs progress, to collegians and young workers.

In the years ahead, the well-being of the Millennial Generation will become a focal point for the renewal of America's civic culture. Organized public places—athletic stadia, cinemas, parks, malls—will be newly segmented, isolating kid-friendly havens from coarser fare elsewhere. The Internet will start teaching "netiquette" and will help parents shield adolescents from chat rooms with misbehaving adults. Hollywood will make movies about wholesome teenagers doing good things for their communities. Suggestive teen ads and magazines will draw adult condemnation, as Boomers aggressively scrutinize and chaperone the teen culture.

Millennials will provide a focal point for the renewal of the American family. Thanks to a growing presence of telecommuting parents and live-in Silent grandparents, neighborhoods will retain more daytime adults, whose supervision will grow more assertive. Boomers will follow Hillary Clinton's demand that adolescent behavior be monitored and constrained. The rates of divorce will decline—in part, because new state laws will make divorce harder for couples with children. Judges will not so freely grant separations in families with children and will punish deadbeat dads severely. This re-strengthened family will not be a replica of the 1950s. Children will not attach themselves so exclusively to mothers, many of whom will be working. Instead, they will attach themselves to a rotating array of substitute parents (often male) who represent the community. Like the offspring of well-run kibbutzim, Millennials will grow up to be sociable and team-oriented adolescents but will strike adults as somewhat bland, conformist, and dependent on others to reach judgments.

Children will enter their teens looking and behaving better than any in decades. In place of the late Awakening's "tragic freshmen" dressed in dark, dour colors, the late Unraveling's friendlier frosh will dress in bright, happy colors. The new impetus toward upbeat styles and behavior will come from *peer pressure*—words that by the Oh-Ohs will carry a newly positive connotation. Millennials will police themselves and force a sharp reduction in adolescent miscreance. Teen coupling will become less starkly physical and more romantic and friendly. As no-longer-*Clueless* teens will back away from early (and unprotected) sex, the adolescent abortion rate will fall, fewer teens will get pregnant, and adoption or marriage will become more prevalent among those who do. Binge drinking and teen gambling will decline. Just as today's twelve-year-olds are confounding experts by turning against the crime and crack cocaine habits of their 13er predecessors (with juvenile murders down 15 percent in 1995 alone), Millennial teens will prove false the consensus prediction among today's criminologists that America is in for a big new wave of youth violence. To the contrary, youth crime will decrease. Some youth gangs will gradually redirect their energy from criminal mayhem toward collegial enforcement of an ad hoc public order. Those Millennials who do step out of line will be dealt with swiftly. Unlike with aging 13er criminals (many of whom will be warehoused and forgotten), the purpose of punishing Millennials will be to shame them, shape them up, and get them back in line.

This generation will build a reputation for meeting and beating adult expectations. In 1990, America's third graders were issued three major challenges: Dr. Koop called on this Class of 2000 to be more drug-free, smoke-free, and sexual disease-free high school graduates than their predecessors; President Bush summoned them to graduate "first in the world in mathematics and science achievement"; and the African American Project 2000 called on school boys to grow up providing "consistent, positive, and literate black role models" for the children who follow. Millennial kids will do all that, and more. Around the year 2000, America's news weeklies will run cover stories singing the praise of American youth—commending them for their growing interest in current affairs, rising aptitude scores, good community deeds, and a more wholesome (and standardized) new teen culture.

By the end of the Unraveling, adult Americans will view twenty-year-olds as smart and forty-year-olds as wasted—the inverse of the perception at the end of the Awakening. Impediments against this generation's current and future well-being will be not be tolerated. To the extent Millennial kids appear to be losers in the free marketplace, adults will demand redress. Youth poverty will fuel a new class politics. Colleges will be pressured into holding the line on tuitions and student indebtedness, faculties into putting teaching ahead of research, employers into creating apprenticeships, older workers into making room for the young.

Graying Boomers will see in Millennials a powerful tool for realizing their values and visions deep into the twenty-first century. "My great hope," says *Greater Expectations* author William Damon, "is that we can actually rebuild our communities in this country around our kids." Democrats will point to youth as reasons for expanding government, Republicans as reasons for cleaning up the culture. Calls will rise for a spare-no-expense national program of compulsory youth service. The dwindling defenders of public borrowing (and of public spending that benefits the old over the young) will hear themselves accused of fiscal abuse of a glorious new generation of junior citizens. Old federal budget arguments will feel all the more urgent.

Where Boomer children came to the conclusion that the adult world was culturally deficient but well run, Millennial children will come to the opposite discovery: that adults understand values well enough, but don't know how to apply them to public life. They will reach voting age acutely aware of their own potential power to meet this need. They will organize huge youth rallies and produce vast voter turnouts. A new breed of college activists will band together not to resist national leaders, but to prod them into taking bolder steps. Starting with the election of 2000, when the first Millennials will vote, anything perceived to be a barrier to their future will provoke heated political argument.

Each day, adult optimism is building about this generation. Aerospace commercials plug Millennial kids as the astronauts who will build and run the first big space stations. In a mid-1990s global competition, U.S. elementary school students placed second (and U.S. girls first) in reading skills, prompting Hillary Clinton to praise these kids as "the smartest in the world." In 1995, *National Geographic* launched a brand-new Kids' Hall of Fame (for children age fourteen and under) that "celebrates the good news, recognizing and rewarding some of the great things that kids have done"—praise Americans seldom offered to 13ers back in the Awakening.

By the Oh-Ohs, Americans will hear constant talk about the budding heroism of youth. A 1996 TV ad for Kohler faucets showed a bearded Boomer father pulling his wet tot from a bathtub, anointing him with bath oil, and proclaiming him "king." In future TV ads, the father's beard will be grayer, and the child will be stepping off a graduation podium, but the proclamations will be much the same. The *Arizona Republic* recently asked elementary school students how they expect to improve the world. "We should start now," said an eleven-year-old boy. "Plant a tree every day. Get groups together." Can they make a difference? "I know it. I just feel it," said one cheerful young girl. "I believe in myself because my parents and teachers do."

TOWARD THE FOURTH TURNING

Years in advance, plans are afoot for an epic revelry to celebrate the dawning of the year 2000. Some revelers will hear the scrolls of Nostradamus recited in the shadows of the pyramids of Giza. Others will board a chartered Concorde just after midnight and zoom back through time from the third millennium to the second. But once the gaudy doings are over and the bags unpacked, Americans will reach a distressing realization: The first days of the new millennium will look and feel like the last days of the old one.

A year later the trumpets will blare Zarathustra to mark the dawn of 2001, the true start of history's new millennial epoch. Then, too, the ensuing year will produce the same old news about Culture Wars, social chaos, and political gridlock. Not much will change.

The mood of the early Oh-Ohs will be much like today's, except a lot more jittery. These will be years of the reality check, of worries about a looming national payback as Americans of all ages begin focusing on how poorly they and their government have prepared for the future. People will no longer deny that the Unraveling's individual empowerment has led to antisocial behavior and a dangerous degree of institutional decay. The harms (especially to youth) will now be perceived to have accumulated to such a grievous extent that truly fundamental change will be required to get the nation back on course. Today's talk about America's inability to mobilize except for emergencies—what some call the "Pearl Harbor syndrome"—will have become a tired cliché. More people will start rooting for something big to happen, something bad enough to shock the society out of its civic ennui. The political party in power will stress the ample good news and insist that things have never been better—but the party out of power (and any niche group that senses it is losing the Culture Wars) will warn against, and show signs of welcoming, a catastrophe on the horizon.

The late Unraveling mood will feel much the opposite of the closing (New Frontier) years of the American High. Back then, institutions were at their point of maximum strength. Whether curing poverty or landing men on the moon, the nation's grandest conceptions felt entirely achievable. Yet circa-1960 Americans, in the shadow of their Establishment, were starting to chafe at the staleness of their culture. By the middle Oh-Ohs, institutions will reach a point of maximum weakness, individualism of maximum strength, and even the simplest public task will feel beyond the ability of government. As niche walls rise ever higher, people will complain endlessly about how bad all the other niches are. Wide chasms will separate rich from poor, whites from blacks, immigrants from native borns, seculars from born-agains, technophiles from technophobes. America will feel more tribal. Indeed, many will be asking whether fifty states and so many dozens of ethnic cultures make sense any more as a nation—and, if they do, whether that nation has a future.

In the early Oh-Ohs, institutions will seem hypercomplex and fastidiously interconnected at the periphery, but empty at the core. Individuals will feel exquisitely exempt from the day-to-day random vagaries of nature and civil authority, yet rawly vulnerable to the greatest disasters fate can mete out. With soft finger strokes from their home-based tech-centers, millions of people will be commanding pizza deliveries, masterminding financial transactions, and securing hard-disk secrets. But they will be acutely aware that the Unraveling era's "empowered individual" survives on the flimsiest of foundations—that, with just one tsunami, the whole archipelago of little human islands could sink into a sea of social chaos. The better the economy performs, the more people will feel they have to lose, and the worse will be the national case of nerves.

Meanwhile, the Unraveling-era culture carnival will race along, ever faster, ever more splintery and frenetic, with more jewelry and tattoos and trash talk and loud Lollapaloozas. The public will plunge ever further into what Tom Peters calls *The Pursuit of Wow!* until, eventually, the remaining enthusiasm will be summed up in two words: *yeah, right.*

People young and old will puzzle over what it felt like for their parents and grandparents, in a distantly remembered era, to have lived in a society that felt like one national community. They will yearn to recreate this, to put America back together again. But no one will know how.

As the Fourth Turning approaches, each generation will view events from its own life-cycle perspective. The Silent, approaching eighty, will be deeply anguished. Sixtyish Boomers will brood over their institutional powerlessness to impose a cleansing agenda. Broken into shards, 13ers will privately find ways of making small things work in disordered environments. The first Millennials will come of age amid the adulation of elders to whom they will embody the hopes for civic renewal. The problems of childhood now fixed, a new batch of babies will start arriving to hardly a ripple of notice.

Each generation will show clear signs of changing. As each approaches the brink of its next phase of life, it will not want to behave like its next-elders did. Boomers will be of no mind to carry on an other-directed, self-doubting sentimentalism. The 13ers will have no desire to be argumentative and judgmental. Millennials will earnestly want to shed the cynical alien-ation of youth. Parents will be disinclined to make any further changes in what will now be deemed an acceptably protective style of nurture.

Toward the end of an Unraveling, each archetype's phase-of-life role reaches a point of new strain:

- The *elder Artists,* now appearing less flexible than indecisive, begin impeding the Prophets' values agenda.
- The *midlife Prophets,* now filled with righteousness of conviction, grow impatient to lead society toward ever-deeper spiritual conversion.
- The *young-adult Nomads,* now tiring of an unrewarding self-sufficiency, yearn to settle down and shore up social barriers.
- The *child Heroes,* protected by adults who are fearful of their future, begin sensing a dire secular challenge at the heart of the Prophets' visions.

By the early Oh-Ohs, when the four generational archetypes fully occupy these life-cycle phases, they will be poised to assert new social roles. Their Unraveling-era behavior cannot and will not continue. The public mood will feel stale, used up, primed for something else. Americans will have had quite enough of glitz and roar, of celebrity circuses, of living as though there were no tomorrow. Forebodings will deepen, and spiritual currents will darken. Whether we realize it or not, we will be ready for a dramatic event to shock the nation out of its complacency and decay.

The Fourth Turning will be at hand.

CHAPTER 9

◾

Fourth Turnings
in History

"SOMETHING HAPPENED TO AMERICA AT THAT TIME," RE-
called U.S. senator Daniel Inouye on V-J Day in 1995, the last of the fifty-
year commemoratives of World War II. "I'm not wise enough to know what
it was. But it was the strange, strange power that our founding fathers experienced in those early, uncertain days. Let's call it the Spirit of America, a
spirit that united and galvanized our people." Inouye went on to reflect wist-
fully on an era when the nation considered no obstacle too big, no challenge
too great, no goal too distant, no sacrifice too deep. A half century later, that
old spirit had long since dissipated, and nobody under age seventy remembered what it felt like. When Joe Dawson reenacted his D-Day parachute
drop over Normandy, he said he did it "to show our country that there was a
time when our nation moved forward as one unit."

In the climactic years between Pearl Harbor and V-J Day, arguments were
forgotten, ideals energized, and creaky institutions resuscitated for urgent
new purposes. At home or in the military, teamwork and discipline were unusually strong. Anybody who doubted or complained or bent the rules drew
the wrath of fellow soldiers, coworkers, or neighbors. People looked on their
elected representatives as moral exemplars. In 1943, the author of *The Hero
in History* described the current age as brimming with leaders who qualified
for the title "great man in history." People were also full of hope, even in the
face of terrible adversity. "During the summer of 1940, with France crushed
and England hanging by a thread," writes David Gelernter, a Roper poll
found that "a handsome plurality, 43 percent to 36, was optimistic about 'the
future of civilization.' " Energized by visionary leadership and hopeful fol-
lowership, America attained a stunning triumph.

With the people thus united, that era established a powerful new civic order replete with new public institutions, economic arrangements, political

alliances, and global treaties, many of which have lasted to this day. That era also produced a grim acceptance of destruction as a necessary concomitant to human progress. Quite unlike today, that was a time when wars were fought to the finish, when a president could command a prized young generation to march off with the warning that one in three would not come home, when America's wisest and smartest scientists built weapons of mass destruction, when imagined domestic enemies were rounded up in snowy camps, and when enemy armies were destroyed and their leaders hanged. Indeed, while this beloved Spirit of America resonates with warm reminiscences from a distance of a half century, it was also a time of blunt, cruel, even lethal forms of social change.

Today's elder veterans recall that era fondly but selectively: They would like to restore its unity and selflessness, but without the carnage. Yet how? The only way they can see is a *way back,* what Bob Dole calls a "bridge" to a better past—an America stripped of the family damage, cultural decay, and loss of civic purpose that has settled in over the intervening five decades. Such a task feels hopeless because it is.

Like nature, history is full of processes that cannot happen in reverse. Just as the laws of entropy do not allow a bird to fly backward, or droplets to regroup at the top of a waterfall, history has no rewind button. Like the seasons of nature, it moves only forward. Saecular entropy cannot be reversed. An Unraveling cannot lead back to an Awakening, or forward to a High, without a Crisis in between.

The spirit of America comes once a saeculum, only through what the ancients called *ekpyrosis,* nature's fiery moment of death and discontinuity. History's periodic eras of Crisis combust the old social order and give birth to a new.

A Fourth Turning is a solstice era of maximum darkness, in which the supply of social order is still falling but the demand for order is now rising. It is the saeculum's hibernal, its time of trial. In winter, writes William Cullen Bryant, "The melancholy days are come, the saddest of the year, / Of wailing winds, and naked woods, and meadows brown and sere." Nature exacts its fatal payment and pitilessly sorts out the survivors and the doomed. Pleasures recede, tempests hurt, pretense is exposed, and toughness rewarded—all in a season (says Victor Hugo) that "changes into stone the water of heaven and the heart of man." These are times of fire and ice, of polar darkness and brilliantly pale horizons. What it doesn't kill, it reminds of death. What it doesn't wound, it reminds of pain. In Swinburne's "season of snows," it is "The light that loses, the night that wins."

Like natural winter, which reaches its solstice early, the Fourth Turning passes the nadir of public order right at its beginning. Just as the coldest days of winter are days of lengthening sun, the harsh (and less hopeful) years of a Crisis are years of renascent public authority. This involves a fundamental shift in social momentum: In the Unraveling, the removal of each civic layer brought demands for the removal of more layers; in the Crisis era, each new exercise of civic authority creates a perceived need for the *adding* of layers.

As the community instinct regenerates, people resolve to do more than just relieve the symptoms of pending traumas. Intent on addressing root causes, they rediscover the value of unity, teamwork, and social discipline. Far more than before, people comply with authority, accept the need for public sacrifice, and shed anything extraneous to the survival needs of their community. This is a critical threshold: People either coalesce as a nation and culture—or rip hopelessly and permanently apart.

A MORPHOLOGY OF CRISIS ERAS

Fourth Turnings have provided the great pivot points of the Anglo-American legacy. Dating back to the fifteenth century, there have been six. Each produced its own Crisis and its own facsimile of the halcyon spirit today's aging World War II veterans remember so vividly. From the similarities of these eras, a morphology can be constructed:

- A Crisis era begins with a *catalyst*—a startling event (or sequence of events) that produces a sudden shift in mood.
- Once catalyzed, a society achieves a *regeneracy*—a new counterentropy that reunifies and reenergizes civic life.
- The regenerated society propels toward a *climax*—a crucial moment that confirms the death of the old order and birth of the new.
- The climax culminates in a *resolution*—a triumphant or tragic conclusion that separates the winners from losers, resolves the big public questions, and establishes the new order.

This Crisis morphology occurs over the span of one turning, which (except for the U.S. Civil War) means that around fifteen to twenty-five years elapse between the catalyst and the resolution. The regeneracy usually occurs one to five years after the era begins, the climax one to five years before it ends.

Every Fourth Turning starts with a *catalyst* event that terminates the mood of Unraveling and unleashes one of Crisis. Chapter 4 explained how sparks of history—sudden and startling events—can arise in any turning. Some sparks ignite nothing. Some flare briefly and then extinguish. Some have important effects but leave underlying problems unresolved. Others ignite epic conflagrations. Which ones ignite? Studying the sparks of history themselves won't help answer this question, because what they are is far less important than how a society reacts to them. That reaction is substantially determined by the season of the saeculum—in other words, by the turning in which they are located. Sparks in a High tend to reinforce feelings of security; in an Awakening, argument; in an Unraveling, anxiety. Come the Fourth Turning, sparks of history trigger a fierce new dynamic of public synergy.

The catalyst can be one spark or, more commonly, a series of sparks that self-ignite like the firecrackers traditionally used by the Chinese to mark their own breaks in the circle of time. Each of these sparks is linked to a specific threat about which society had been fully informed but against which it had left itself poorly protected. Afterward, the fact that these sparks were *foreseeable* but poorly *foreseen* gives rise to a new sense of urgency about institutional dysfunction and civic vulnerability. This marks the beginning of the vertiginous spiral of Crisis.

Once this new mood is fully catalyzed, a society begins a process of *regeneracy,* a drawing together into whatever definition of community is available at the time. Out of the debris of the Unraveling, a new civic ethos arises. One set of post-Awakening ideals prevails over the others. People stop tolerating the weakening of institutions, the splintering of the culture, and the individualizing of daily behavior. Spiritual curiosity abates, manners traditionalize, and the culture is harnessed as propaganda for the purpose of overtly reinforcing good conduct. History teaches that, roughly one to three years after the initial catalyst, people begin acknowledging this new synergy in community life and begin deputizing government to enforce it. Collective action is now seen as vital to solving the society's most fundamental problems.

With the civic ethos now capable of producing civic deeds, a new dynamic of threat and response takes hold. Instead of downplaying problems, leaders start exaggerating them. Instead of deferring solutions, they accelerate them. Instead of tolerating diversity, they demand consensus. Instead of coaxing people with promises of minimal sacrifice, they summon them with warnings of maximal sacrifice. Leaders energize every available institution and direct them toward community survival. Thus invigorated, society starts propelling itself on a trajectory that nobody had foreseen before the catalyzing event. Societal problems that, in the Unraveling, posed insuperable dilemmas now appear to have simple if demanding solutions. A new resolve about urgent public goals crowds out qualms about questionable public means.

A Crisis mood does not guarantee that the new governing policies will be well designed or will work as intended. To the contrary: Crisis eras are studded with faulty leadership and inept management—from President Lincoln's poor record of choosing generals to President Roosevelt's colossal blunders with such alphabet soup agencies as the AAA, NRA, and WPA.

What makes a Crisis special is the public's willingness to let leaders lead even when they falter and to let authorities be authoritative even when they make mistakes. Amid this civic solidarity, mediocre leaders can gain immense popular following; bad policies can be made to work (or, at least, be perceived as working); and, as at Pearl Harbor, even a spectacular failure does not undermine public support. Good policy choices pay off quickly. (In an Awakening, by contrast, even the best leaders and plans can fail, and one misstep can destroy public confidence.)

Private life also transforms beyond prior recognition. Now less important than the team, individuals are expected to comply with new Fourth Turning standards of virtue. Family order strengthens, and personal violence and substance abuse decline. Those who persist in free-wheeling self-oriented behavior now face implacable public stigma, even punishment. Winner-take-all arrangements give way to enforceable new mechanisms of social sharing. Questions about who does what are settled on grounds of survival, not fairness. This leads to a renewed social division of labor by age and sex. In the realm of public activity, elders are expected to step aside for the young, women for men. When danger looms, children are expected to be protected before parents, mothers before fathers. All social arrangements are evaluated anew; pre-Crisis promises and expectations count for little. Where the Unraveling had been an era of fast-paced personal lives against a background of public gridlock, in the Crisis the pace of daily life will seem to slow down just as political and social change accelerates.

When society approaches the *climax* of a Crisis, it reaches a point of maximum civic power. Where the new values regime had once justified individual fury, it now justifies public fury. Wars become more likely and are fought with efficacy and finality. The risk of revolution is high—as is the risk of civil war, since the community that commands the greatest loyalty does not necessarily coincide with political (or geographic) boundaries. Leaders become more inclined to define enemies in moral terms, to enforce virtue militarily, to refuse all compromise, to commit large forces in that effort, to impose heavy sacrifices on the battlefield and home front, to build the most destructive weapons contemporary minds can imagine, and to deploy those weapons if needed to obtain an enduring victory.

The Crisis climax is human history's equivalent to nature's raging typhoon, the kind that sucks all surrounding matter into a single swirl of ferocious energy. Anything not lashed down goes flying; anything standing in the way gets flattened. Normally occurring late in the Fourth Turning, the climax gathers energy from an accumulation of unmet needs, unpaid bills, and unresolved problems. It then spends that energy on an upheaval whose direction and dimension were beyond comprehension during the prior Unraveling era. The climax shakes a society to its roots, transforms its institutions, redirects its purposes, and marks its people (and its generations) for life. The climax can end in triumph, or tragedy, or some combination of both. Whatever the event and whatever the outcome, a society passes through a great gate of history, fundamentally altering the course of civilization.

Soon thereafter, this great gate is sealed by the Crisis *resolution,* when victors are rewarded and enemies punished; when empires or nations are forged or destroyed; when treaties are signed and boundaries redrawn; and when peace is accepted, troops repatriated, and life begun anew.

One large chapter of history ends, and another starts. In a very real sense, one society dies—and another is born.

FROM UNRAVELING TO CRISIS

To understand how a Fourth Turning might arise early in the next century, it is useful to look at how Unravelings end and Crises begin.

There have been six prior Fourth Turnings in the Anglo-American lineage, dating back to the fifteenth century:

- *Wars of the Roses* (1459–1487), Late Medieval Saeculum
- *Armada Crisis* (1569–1594), Reformation Saeculum
- *Glorious Revolution* (1675–1704), New World Saeculum
- *American Revolution* (1773–1794), Revolutionary Saeculum
- *Civil War* (1860–1865), Civil War Saeculum
- *Great Depression and World War II* (1929–1946), Great Power Saeculum

With the partial exception of the U.S. Civil War, each Fourth Turning followed a similar morphology.

Great Power Saeculum

Up until the fall of 1929, America still inhabited a decade then known as "an era of wonderful nonsense." Through the 1920s, America felt increasingly wild, its daily life propelled ever faster by a stream of thrilling and innovative technologies, its government increasingly discredited and irrelevant, its culture hopelessly cleaved between the Prohibitionist "booboisie" and jaded pleasure seekers, its public captivated by what Hemingway called a "movable feast" of celebrities and trifles. "The shows were broader, the buildings were higher, the morals were looser, and the liquor was cheaper, . . . but all these did not really minister to much delight," Fitzgerald remarked in 1926. "The city was bloated, glutted, stupid with cakes and circuses, and a new expression, 'O yeah?' summed up all the enthusiasm." By decade's end, Frederick Lewis Allen described the "public spirit" as having reached "a low ebb." Everyone knew the fun and frolic couldn't last forever, but no one had reason to believe the end would come soon.

The catalyst came on Black Tuesday, October 29, 1929. A market come-uppance was foreseen by some, but the public reaction caught everybody by surprise. In a mood shift historian Allen described as "bewilderingly rapid," Americans now realized that "an old order was giving place to the new," that the 1930s "would not be a repetition" of the 1920s, that there would be no more "aching disillusionment of the hard-boiled era, its oily scandals, its spiritual paralysis, the harshness of its gaiety." As Shipwreck Kelly descended from his flagpole, the ballyhoo that once entertained was now viewed as irrelevant, ridiculous, even shameful. The descent into depression produced what Allen called "an armistice" in "the revolution in manners and morals." As Prohibition reached its weary end, "The wages of sin had become stabilized at a lower level. . . . What had departed was the excited sense that taboos were going to smash, that morals were being made over or annihilated, and that the whole code of behavior was in flux." According to *The New Yorker,* sex was now "as tiresome as the Old Mortgage." By 1931, with life's problems now growing distressingly real, the 1920s-style litera-ture of alienation—and the economics and politics of fragmentation—felt totally outdated.

By the time of FDR's Hundred Days in the Spring of 1933, the regener-acy was in full swing. The national economic output had declined by one-third, unemployment had swelled to over 20 percent, many banks had been closed—yet people (and their leaders) insisted on principles and policies that only made the emergency worse. In his somber first inaugural address, Roosevelt warned his countrymen that "the only thing we have to fear is fear itself," a comment that would have been incomprehensible just four years before. America was poised to build a new order, one that would inspire the president to proclaim "nationwide thinking, nationwide planning, and na-tionwide action" the "three great essentials" of public life. By the middle 1930s, America was awash in FDR's New Deal, a political revolution whose ethical roots lay in the Social Gospel of decades past. A half decade later, Pearl Harbor redirected the new national unity overseas, as the same youths who had recently worn CCC uniforms now marched off against Hitler and Tōjō.

This story of depression and global war has become so familiar to Amer-icans that people lose sight of how suddenly the nation regrouped and how unexpected and fundamental the mood shift was.

Civil War Saeculum

The Civil War arrived more abruptly than today's Americans might think. Up until 1860, a war of union was at best only dimly foretold, and no one imagined a tragedy on the scale of what subsequently occurred. For many decades, most free Americans had counted on legislators to craft clever deals, keep the slavery issue defused, and prevent sectional hard feelings from boiling over. By the early 1850s, this confidence began to wane as the great Compromise Generation (led by the triumvirate of Clay, Calhoun, and Webster) began to pass from public life. In their place came a more acerbic and spiritual crop of public figures who were much less willing to go along to get along. "The age is dull and mean. Men creep, not walk," complained John Greenleaf Whittier of the 1850s. Yet outside the radical abolitionist circle, the mood did not become inflammatory through the end of that decade. Bleeding Kansas was a skirmish, not a war. In the spring of 1857, even the *Dred Scott* decision brought what seemed to be a dry issue of property law—not an issue of potential war—to the nation's attention.

That summer Hinton Helper, a young North Carolinian who opposed slavery, published *The Impending Crisis of the South*. It was the first major warning that danger lay ahead, but its arguments were shrouded in statistics and its predictions were unspecific. The next year brought sharper words, as William Seward became the first Republican to foresee "an irrepressible conflict between opposing and enduring forces." But that view was still considered alarmist. When Abraham Lincoln issued his famous warning that "a house divided against itself cannot stand," he answered the question "whither we are tending" by predicting that "I do not expect the union to be dissolved." A year later, in 1859, John Brown's raid at Harpers Ferry (and especially his subsequent trial and execution) touched off a paroxysm of abolitionist fervor. "How vast the change in men's hearts!" cried Wendell Phillips. "Unborn deeds, things soon to be, project their shapes around me," mused Walt Whitman of "this incredible rush and heat, this strange ecstatic fever of dreams." Even so, Brown's uprising did not polarize opinion as much as his aging backers had hoped. Afterward, the nation settled back into the sullen brooding for which the 1850s were notorious.

The point of no return came the next year. As 1860 dawned, Edmund Ruffin's book *Anticipations of the Future* forecast a bloody civil war (beginning with an armed assault on Fort Sumter!), but he predicted that this war would not start until Christmas Eve 1867—*seven years later.* Actually, it started just one year later. The spark came with the November presidential election, which gave Abraham Lincoln 40 percent of the popular vote, enough to defeat several candidates belonging to the other broken political parties. Here at last was the "Redeemer President" Whitman had envisioned. The two halves of the nation thereupon prepared for a war Lincoln now insisted "no mortal could stay."

The next summer, following the Union debacle at Bull Run, the Crisis reached regeneracy. When Lincoln declared that day Black Monday and ordered the immediate enlistment of half a million soldiers, Americans realized that the struggle would be neither glamorous nor painless. Government authority (Union and Confederate) began assuming entirely unprecedented powers of taxation, compulsory service, suspension of due process, and martial law amid a catastrophic spiral of organized butchery. The climax came swiftly and savagely, with Gettysburg and Sherman's swath of destruction. The resolution was equally swift and savage: The five days from Appomattox to Lincoln's assassination marked the single most convulsive week in U.S. history. The nation reunited and corrected the core problem of slavery that had divided it, but otherwise the resolution felt as much like defeat as like victory.

In the Civil War Saeculum, the Third and Fourth Turnings together covered the span of just one generation and produced no Hero archetype. By the usual pattern of history, the Civil War Crisis catalyst occurred four or five years ahead of schedule and its resolution nearly a generation too soon. This prompts the question, What would have happened if tempers had cooled for a few years, postponing the Crisis for another presidential election and slowing it down thereafter? In all likelihood, there would still have been a crisis of union and emancipation. There might still have been a war. But the generational dynamics and the archetypal behavior would have been somewhat different. The gridlocked elder Compromisers would have passed from the scene altogether. The apocalyptic passions of the Transcendentals would have cooled a bit as they aged. And the Gilded would have been quicker to see war as danger rather than adventure. Imagine what might have happened differently in the South (which was devastated), in race relations (which reverted to Jim Crow), in the women's movement (which collapsed), and to the Gilded and Progressive Generations (both heavily damaged by war). Such a Crisis scenario might well have led to a more constructive outcome.

The Civil War experience thus offers two lessons: first, that the Fourth Turning morphology admits to acceleration, and second, that acceleration can add to the tragedy of the outcome.

Revolutionary Saeculum

The revolutionary mood did not strike the American colonists until the winter of 1773 to 1774, when the whirlwind of independence was nearly upon them. Back in 1765, during the short-lived Stamp Act tempest, even the stormy James Otis warned that "none but rebels, fools, or madmen" would urge separation from the mother country. Tensions rose again in 1767, when Parliament's Townshend Duties prompted colonists to start organizing their (ostensibly) nonviolent resistance and embargoing British luxury goods. But three years later, Parliament backed down and wiped out most of the duties, leaving just one symbolic duty on tea. Despite the prevailing fatalism about the wildness and degeneracy of social life in the colonies (which had yet to be attributed to the "corruption" of "vile Albion"), many colonists greeted the new decade feeling that maybe the unpleasantness had blown over. In the early 1770s, Americans still widely referred to England as the Mother Country. As late as 1773, the speeches and writings of colonial leaders showed scant desire for (much less prediction of) the rupture that was coming.

Then, in December of that year, came the Boston Tea Party, which catalyzed a dramatic change in the colonial mood. Event now followed event in a fast-moving chain reaction. In March 1774, an out-of-patience British Parliament approved the punitive Coercive Acts. In the spring and fall, the colonists drafted plans of union, organized politically and militarily, and convened the First Continental Congress. Abigail Adams's diary (which until then had been conciliatory) now agonized over whether "redress by the Sword" should sever the "three fold cord of Duty, interest and filial affection" binding the colonies to the throne. Die-hard patriots (whom Adams called "those men" of "contagious Ambition") began hinting that there might be no alternative to total separation. Early in the next year, after what her diary termed "the terrible 19 of April" (the British raid on Concord and Lexington), all hope for reconciliation was lost: "Tyranny, oppression and Murder," she wrote, had now "plunged her Sword into our Bosoms." As lines were being drawn and sides taken, the colonial patriots embarked on a course of action that a few years earlier would have been deemed (even by most Americans) as blatantly treasonous.

In 1776, the Crisis reached its regeneracy. Everywhere in the colonies, the call for group solidarity and action was inspired by brave words and coerced, if necessary, with tar and feathers. An armed struggle on behalf of liberty and virtue now seemed utterly unavoidable, even if the melding of quarreling colonies into a constitutional republic remained a distant fantasy.

New World Saeculum

The Glorious Revolution came as a similarly massive surprise. In the early spring of 1675, American colonists viewed their long-term future with foreboding. Many worried about the uncontrolled competition over land between immigrants and natives; few trusted the restored monarchy in England. But there was no cause for immediate concern. At that time, the colonists' relations with Native Americans were improving, their trade prospering, and their political liberties secure.

Then came the fatal spark of history: Twenty-four months that turned their world upside down. It began with several simultaneous (and deadly) wars between natives and settlers, which led directly to rebellions in Virginia and Maryland together with parliamentary efforts to void most of New England's liberties. "It was in 1676, more than any year since 'the starving times,' the beachhead years of the European invasion of North America, that the English came closest to being driven from the continent," writes historian Stephen Saunders Webb. "Just the fighting in 1676—not to mention human casualties from 'cousin german to the plague,' crop failures, and livestock losses—cost more in lives, in proportion to the population, than any other war in American history. In 1676 was wiped out an entire generation of settlement."

Decimated but resolute, the colonists now perceived that the very social and political future of their world was in peril and that they had been sucked into a collective maelstrom beyond their control. Over the next few years, the Crisis reached its regeneracy. The colonists forged the community ties that would enable them to withstand the absolutist machinations of the duke of York, the Stuart heir. The climax came with the political revolution of 1689, the resolution with the advent of global war between England and France. But in 1676 the American colonists did not yet know of all the trials to come—nor of the sunny peace to be born of such hardship.

Reformation Saeculum

In the late 1560s, the English people were anxious about the specter of religious conflict and civil unrest. They had suffered both in recent decades and worried that the future could eventually bring worse. But they had no reason to fear a serious threat from abroad, and the immediate prospects for the kingdom never looked better. By then a decade on the throne, Queen Elizabeth I was proving herself a popular and able Tudor monarch. She was restoking the royal treasury, patching up things with Scotland, and proving herself a master diplomat and administrator on all fronts.

In the fall of 1569, there came sudden news of a Catholic uprising led by the most powerful peer of the realm. Within months, the queen found herself excommunicated by the pope and, a year after that, the target of a Spanish attempt to assassinate her. In the fall of 1572, the Spanish-allied Catholic League slaughtered thousands of French Protestants in the St. Bartholomew's Day Massacre, and the duke of Alba's troops crushed a Protestant revolt in the Netherlands. From the Mediterranean came word that Spain had annihilated the Turkish fleet. Everywhere on earth, Spanish troops, ships, and gold seemed indomitable. From behind the walls of El Escorial, King Philip II (former husband of Elizabeth's predecessor, Queen Mary) began to regard Elizabeth as a removable annoyance.

Feeling itself encircled by the armed might of a Catholic Empire, the English Parliament convened later that year to unite behind their queen. The mood was grim. Petty politics were forgotten, new taxes levied, new regiments raised, new trade laws enacted, and new punishments imposed. The regeneracy thus under way, England rallied and gathered. The Crisis mood would not climax and ease for another sixteen years—not until Philip II's great fleet lay at the bottom of the sea.

Late Medieval Saeculum

In the 1450s, a twilight decade of medieval beliefs and usages, the English people were despondent. In recent years, their kingdom had lost virtually all of its vast acquisitions in France. They also suffered from a weak king who lapsed into periodic insanity, conniving royal relatives, a corrupt court, and a pandemic of social disorder—spread by armed and unemployed veterans returning from the mainland. Even so, England remained a relatively wealthy kingdom at peace, and there was no immediate reason to suspect the strength of the ruling House of Lancaster.

Then came the rush of events of autumn 1459. The mighty houses of York and Lancaster—which had been alternately feuding, skirmishing, and negotiating for many years—fell at last into a worsening chain of open battles. The catalyst arrived in November, when a Lancaster-packed Parliament of Devils condemned most of the Yorkist leaders for high treason. Fleeing England in December, these leaders now perceived they had no choice but to return and initiate the all-out warfare that engulfed the realm over the next eighteen months. Come the spring of 1460, the two sides had abandoned the medieval custom of parleying before battle. By autumn, fallen knights were routinely slain on the field. Next spring, the Yorkists routed the Lancastrians at the battle of Towton. With nearly forty thousand fallen, this battle may rank as the most lethal (as a share of the population) ever fought by the English people anywhere in the world.

With the victory of young Edward York, the regeneracy began—but the violence was far from over. For the next quarter century, as the ruling families chased a crown that changed heads six times, England reverted to anarchy. The Wars of the Roses witnessed the casual slaughter of nobles, the expropriation of vast landed wealth, the murder of princes and kings, and emergency experiments in expanded central authority—none of which became permanent until the Crisis climax in 1485, when Henry Tudor established a new royal dynasty.

CRISIS AND THE LOOKING GLASS

Human history seems logical in afterthought but a mystery in forethought. Writers of history have a way of describing interwar societies as coursing from postwar to prewar as though people alive at the time knew when that transition occurred. It is a useful exercise to picture yourself midway through each earlier Third Turning, roughly eight to ten years before its end—in other words, approximately where America is now, deep into the 1990s. What could a person reasonably have foreseen?

In 1920, Americans had polarized into competing moral camps, and a mood of alienated pleasure-seeking was settling in. Could people have envisioned the economy crashing down on the heads of a shortsighted, risk-taking public? *Possibly.* What about global depression, political upheaval, and another world war worse than the last? *No.*

In 1850, a new north-south compromise had just been worked out and the Republican Party did not exist. Could people have envisioned an incipient abolitionist party seizing the White House? *Possibly.* What about a horrifying national hemorrhage, a Civil War bloodier than any known war in the history of mankind? *No.*

In 1764, England still pampered its New World colonies and forebore from making their habitants pay the full cost of their wars and governance. Could people have envisioned heavy new taxes and an armed crushing of popular resistance? *Possibly.* What about a war for independence, the coalescence of thirteen quarreling colonies into one new nation, and the creation of a constitutional republic? *No.*

The same pattern applied in the three prior Unravelings. Around 1660, 1550, or 1450, people could have envisioned the opening skirmishes, but not the ultimate upheavals.

In every prior Fourth Turning, *the catalyst was foreseeable but the climax was not.* Had those alive at the time applied the above morphology, they would have had nothing much to say about the ultimate direction the Crisis would take, or about its resolution, or about the kind of world that would result. But they could have issued cogent warnings about where the gateway to Crisis might lie—and about the timing, nature, and dimension of what lay ahead.

FOURTH TURNINGS AND ARCHETYPES

If the Spirit of America is poised for a revival a full saeculum after its last appearance, we should ask, Why? How? What is it that causes a society to ignite into conflagrations?

The key lies in the ingredients of the catalyst. In chemistry, a catalytic agent is a reaction enabler, an ingredient that lowers the energy threshold required to produce a chain reaction. Imagine a test tube full of chemicals whose mass, temperature, and pressure remain constant (or, perhaps, are rising gradually) but which cannot alone produce an explosion no matter how often you stick a flame into it. For that, there must be a slight change in chemical composition, something that, combined with those other variables, can lower the energy threshold for ignition.

History leaves no doubt about the reaction enabler of a Crisis: the Fourth Turning constellation of generational archetypes. Once every saeculum, the archetypes reach a combustible combination, dramatically lowering the threshold for a spark of history to ignite a Crisis.

Since the dawn of the modern world, there has been but one Fourth Turning constellation: elder Prophets, midlife Nomads, young-adult Heroes, and child Artists. For half a millennium, that constellation has recurred exactly the same way five times, and a sixth time with a slight variation in timing and consequence. This archetypal lineup has been one of the great constants of Anglo-American history.

- The indulged *Prophet* children of Highs, born in the aftermath of one Crisis, foment the next Crisis upon entering elderhood.
- The abandoned *Nomad* children of Awakenings become the pragmatic midlife managers of Crisis.
- The protected *Hero* children of Unravelings provide the powerful young-adult soldiers of Crisis.
- The suffocated children of Crises come of age afterward as *Artist* youths.

Earlier chapters explained how Crisis eras shape generations; now you see how generations shape Crises. This explains the underlying link between the cycles of history and the rhythms of the saeculum.

While all generational transitions are important to create a Fourth Turning constellation, the aging of the Prophet is critical. A Crisis catalyst occurs shortly after the old Prophet archetype reaches its apex of societal leadership, when its inclinations are *least* checked by others. A regeneracy comes as the Prophet abandons any idea of deferral or retreat and binds the society to a Crisis course. A climax occurs when the Prophet expends its last burst of passion, just before descending rapidly from power. A resolution comes, with the Prophet's symbolic assistance, at a time when the Nomad is asserting full control.

Except for Nomads and Heroes during the Civil War, every prior Crisis era witnessed each generational archetype entering the following phase of life: Prophets into elderhood, Nomads into midlife, Heroes into young adulthood, and Artists into childhood. Here is what history teaches about the four life-cycle phases (and archetypes) in turn.

- As visionary *Prophets* replace Artists in *elderhood,* they push to resolve ever-deepening moral choices, setting the stage for the secular goals of the young.

As Prophet generations enter elderhood, their passion for principle leads beyond the point of no return. No longer are their crusades mostly symbolic; now they acquire a last-act urgency. As the Crisis erupts, their cultural arguments coalesce around a new vision of community. In families, they redefine elderhood as spiritual stewardship. In the larger society, they trade material security for moral authority and translate their lifelong values agenda into commandments that exact sacrifice from themselves and others. From the young, they seek personal obedience and respect; to the young, they offer the opportunity for heroism and achievement unlike anything they themselves had known at like age.

Ever since the late sixteenth century, aging Prophets have provided the torch of conviction for younger generations during their times of trials. The aging Puritan Generation faced death with what historian Perry Miller describes as "cosmic optimism." They knew their world was heading for catastrophe. But as they looked down on what they perceived to be the shallow souls of their grown children, their last acts were to set unyielding examples—against rebels, kings, and (above all) unbelievers. As the American Revolution catalyzed, die-hard elder Awakeners briefly surged into governors' posts to inspire heroism and curse treachery. "Let us act like . . . wise men," declared Sam Adams in 1772. Praying while others fought, this generation produced the first two presidents of the Continental Congress, which enacted blue laws to make "true religion and good morals" the national credo. Through the Civil War Crisis, the Transcendental Generation dominated the leadership in both Richmond and Washington. "Instruments of war are not selected on account of their harmlessness," thundered Thaddeus Stevens as he urged Union armies to "lay waste to the whole South." And so they did, finding redemption in what the aging minister Albert Barnes called *The Peaceful Death of the Righteous*. Afterward, the younger Henry Adams recalled the elder trumpets of war and bitterly observed "It's always the good men who do the most harm in the world."

- As pragmatic *Nomads* replace Prophets in *midlife,* they apply toughness and resolution to defend society while safeguarding the interests of the young.

Playing to win but half-expecting to lose, Nomad generations enter midlife with a sense of exhaustion. Still forced to take hit-or-miss risks in their work and public lives, they become increasingly cautious in their family lives. By now they take for granted widening gaps between classes, ethnicities, regions, and gender roles. The ablest among them emerge as cunning, pragmatic, and colorful public figures. When the Crisis hits, they find their lives painfully split between the old order and new. But they rise fiercely (and sacrificially) to the occasion, able to make hard and fast choices without fretting much about what others think. Exalting the workable over the ideal, midlife Nomads forge an effective alliance with the elder Prophets. Yet people of other ages are quick to criticize them and slow to give them praise.

Through the centuries, Nomads have starred in the role of midlife marauder, of the graying, picaresque, and (sometimes) corruptible adventurer who always finds a way to get the job done: Francis Drake and John Hawkins; Benjamin Church and Jacob Leisler; Robert Rogers and Daniel Boone; Ulysses Grant and Boss Tweed; Huey Long and George Patton. In the Glorious Revolution Crisis, the Cavalier Generation displayed both courage and generosity. Leaving the fulminations to their elders, they staged the rebellions and bore the crushing war-era taxation necessary to deliver the colonies through their darkest hour. In the American Revolution, the Liberty peers of George Washington expected to be hanged if the rebellion failed. They fought as the canny patriots who (as the British charged of "Swamp Fox" Francis Marion) "would not fight like a Christian or a gentleman." They won the hardest victories, committed the worst war-era treacheries, and later anchored the new nation with a cautious realism. The Gilded peers of Andrew Carnegie, George Armstrong Custer, and John D. Rockefeller, who (anomalously) entered midlife just *after* the Civil War, proved themselves to be a generation of metal and muscle both during the Crisis and afterward. By the time they became what historian Daniel Boorstin calls "the Go-Getters" of the late 1860s, a few had made fortunes, while millions had paid an unrecoverable price in ruined bodies, families, and farms.

■ As teamworking *Heroes* replace Nomads in *young adulthood,* they challenge the political failure of elder-led crusades, fueling a societywide secular crisis.

Coming of age, Hero generations develop a strong ethos of constructive activity, a peer-enforced code of dutiful conduct, and an overwhelming sense of generational community. Instinctive doers and team players, they gravitate toward social goals and human relationships that can be clearly defined. They expect and receive challenges from older generations. They band together on command. At the Crisis climax, their heroism seemingly makes the difference between bright and dark futures for all of posterity. "Fire is the test of gold," Seneca once observed, "adversity, of strong men." Young men enter battle because, like their society, they perceive they have no other choice.

Hero generations provide the fulcrum for the most celebrated turning points of modern history, whether the charge of young Henry Tudor at Bosworth Field or the charge of young G.I.s at Omaha Beach. Cotton Mather called the Glorious Revolution "a happy revolution." According to historian T. H. Breen, that colonial Crisis "released long-suppressed generational tensions" and triggered a seismic shift in political power from old to young. "All gaming, tricking, swearing, lying, / Is grown quite out of fashion," intoned a popular ballad of the American Revolution, "For modern youth's so self-denying, / It flies all lawless passion." In elder eyes, nothing but magnificence could come of the young Caesars who penned the great documents, won the great battles, and energized the great constitutional conventions. "All human greatness shall in us be found," exuded young David Humphreys after Yorktown. The contrast with the prior youth generation, now their hardscrabble generals, could not have been more striking.

- As *Artists* replace the Heroes in *childhood,* they are overprotected at a time of political convulsion and adult self-sacrifice.

Artists enter childhood surrounded by no-nonsense adults who fiercely protect, even envelop them at a time when mighty events are deciding the fate of nations. Children are expected to be obedient, stay out of harm's way, and let adults do important work. And they do, though they earn less praise for it than the prior generation. Though assured of their collective worth, they are constantly reminded that their individual needs take a low priority as long as the community is struggling for survival. This fosters an anxiety about how (or if) they can ever live up to the expectation of powerful elders who are sacrificing so much on their behalf.

From the peers of Thomas More and Desiderius Erasmus onward, the generations that have added the most refinement, nuance, and openness to civilization have been those whose childhoods were simple, basic, and closed. "You can't be too careful in these matters," said Cotton Mather of the need to "restrain your children" during a Glorious Revolution Crisis in which towns appointed tithing men "to attend to disorder of every kind in the families under their charge." Spending his childhood watching adults revolt against the Crown, Henry Clay felt "rocked in the cradle of the Revolution." The young John Quincy Adams held his mother's hand as he watched the Battle of Bunker Hill from safety, and young William Henry Harrison watched the Redcoats use the family cattle for target practice. As the Constitution was being drafted, educators molded the first "national children." During the Civil War, the small children were so well behaved that one foreigner remarked how—in sharp contrast to prior decades—"the most absolute obedience and the most rigid discipline prevail in all American schools." This implosion of family life reflected what youth historian Joseph Kett calls the midcentury "desire of middle-class Americans to seal their lives off from the howling storm outside."

As these archetypes reveal, a Fourth Turning harnesses the seasons of life to bring about a renewal in the seasons of time. In so doing, it provides passage through the great discontinuities of history and closes the full circle of the saeculum.

The Fourth Turning is when the Spirit of America reappears, rousting courage and fortitude from the people. Another Crisis era is coming—and soon. With history as our guide, there is much that we can foresee about what may happen.

CHAPTER 10

∎

A Fourth Turning
Prophecy

SOMETIME AROUND THE YEAR 2005, PERHAPS A FEW YEARS
before or after, America will enter the Fourth Turning.

In the middle Oh-Ohs, America will be a very different society than in
the late 1920s, when the last Crisis catalyzed. The nation will be more affluent, enjoy better health, possess more technology, encompass a larger and
more diverse population, and command more powerful weapons—but the
same could be said about every other Unraveling era society compared to its
predecessor. They were not exempt from the saeculum; nor will we be.

A spark will ignite a new mood. Today, the same spark would flame
briefly but then extinguish, its last flicker merely confirming and deepening
the Unraveling-era mind-set. This time, though, it will catalyze a Crisis. In
retrospect, the spark might seem as ominous as a financial crash, as ordinary
as a national election, or as trivial as a Tea Party. It could be a rapid succession of small events in which the ominous, the ordinary, and the trivial are
commingled.

Recall that a Crisis catalyst involves scenarios distinctly imaginable eight
or ten years in advance. Based on recent Unraveling-era trends, the following circa-2005 scenarios might seem plausible:

- Beset by a fiscal crisis, a state lays claim to its residents' federal
  tax monies. Declaring this an act of secession, the president
  obtains a federal injunction. The governor refuses to back down.
  Federal marshals enforce the court order. Similar tax rebellions
  spring up in other states. Treasury bill auctions are suspended.
  Militia violence breaks out. Cyberterrorists destroy IRS
  databases. U.S. special forces are put on alert. Demands issue for
  a new Constitutional Convention.

- A global terrorist group blows up an aircraft and announces it possesses portable nuclear weapons. The United States and its allies launch a preemptive strike. The terrorists threaten to retaliate against an American city. Congress declares war and authorizes unlimited house-to-house searches. Opponents charge that the president concocted the emergency for political purposes. A nationwide strike is declared. Foreign capital flees the U.S.

- An impasse over the federal budget reaches a stalemate. The president and Congress both refuse to back down, triggering a near-total government shutdown. The president declares emergency powers. Congress rescinds his authority. Dollar and bond prices plummet. The president threatens to stop Social Security checks. Congress refuses to raise the debt ceiling. Default looms. Wall Street panics.

- The Centers for Disease Control and Prevention announce the spread of a new communicable virus. The disease reaches densely populated areas, killing some. Congress enacts mandatory quarantine measures. The president orders the National Guard to throw prophylactic cordons around unsafe neighborhoods. Mayors resist. Urban gangs battle suburban militias. Calls mount for the president to declare martial law.

- Growing anarchy throughout the former Soviet republics prompts Russia to conduct training exercises around its borders. Lithuania erupts in civil war. Negotiations break down. U.S. diplomats are captured and publicly taunted. The president airlifts troops to rescue them and orders ships into the Black Sea. Iran declares its alliance with Russia. Gold and oil prices soar. Congress debates restoring the draft.

It's highly unlikely that any one of these scenarios will actually happen. What *is* likely, however, is that the catalyst will unfold according to a basic Crisis dynamic that underlies all of these scenarios: An initial spark will trigger a chain reaction of unyielding responses and further emergencies. The core elements of these scenarios (debt, civic decay, global disorder) will matter more than the details, which the catalyst will juxtapose and connect in some unknowable way. If foreign societies are also entering a Fourth Turning, this could accelerate the chain reaction.

At home and abroad, these events will reflect the tearing of the civic fabric at points of extreme vulnerability—problem areas where, during the Unraveling, America will have neglected, denied, or delayed needed action. Anger at "mistakes we made" will translate into calls for action, regardless of the heightened public risk. It is unlikely that the catalyst will worsen into a full-fledged catastrophe, since the nation will probably find a way to avert the initial danger and stabilize the situation for a while. The local rebellions will probably be quelled, terrorists foiled, fiscal crisis averted, disease halted, or war fever cooled. Yet even if dire consequences are temporarily averted, America will have entered the Fourth Turning.

The new mood and its jarring new problems will provide a natural end point for the Unraveling-era decline in civic confidence. In the pre-Crisis years, fears about the flimsiness of the social contract will have been subliminal but rising. As the Crisis catalyzes, these fears will rush to the surface, jagged and exposed. Distrustful of some things, individuals will feel that their survival requires them to distrust more things. This behavior could cascade into a sudden downward spiral, an implosion of societal trust.

If so, this implosion will strike financial markets—and, with that, the economy. Aggressive individualism, institutional decay, and long-term pessimism can proceed only so far before a society loses the level of dependability needed to sustain the division of labor and long-term promises on which a market economy must rest. Through the Unraveling, people will have preferred (or, at least, tolerated) the exciting if bewildering trend toward social complexity. But as the Crisis mood congeals, people will come to the jarring realization that they have grown helplessly dependent on a teetering edifice of anonymous transactions and paper guarantees. Many Americans won't know where their savings are, who their employer is, what their pension is, or how their government works. The era will have left the financial world arbitraged and tentacled: Debtors won't know who holds their notes, homeowners who owns their mortgages, and shareholders who runs their equities—and vice versa.

At about the same time, each generation's approach to its new phase of life will set off loud economic alarms, reminding people how weakly their Unraveling-era nation prepared for the future. The Boomers' old age will loom, exposing the thinness in private savings and the unsustainability of public promises. The 13ers will reach their make-or-break peak earning years, realizing at last that they can't all be lucky exceptions to their stagnating average income. Millennials will come of age facing debts, tax burdens, and two-tier wage structures that older generations will now declare intolerable. As all these generations enter their Crisis constellation, the Unraveling will have left the government so fiscally overcommitted to sustaining everyone's expectations that initial official responses to these new concerns will lack credibility. Subliminal fears will now become urgent. The Unraveling era's wry acceptance that people might never get much back from Social Security will crystallize into a jolting new fear that everything from Treasury bills to remortgage instruments to mutual funds could become just as suspect.

At some point, America's short-term Crisis psychology will catch up to the long-term post-Unraveling fundamentals. This might result in a Great

Devaluation, a severe drop in the market price of most financial and real assets. This devaluation could be a short but horrific panic, a free-falling price in a market with no buyers. Or it could be a series of downward ratchets linked to political events that sequentially knock the supports out from under the residual popular trust in the system. As assets devalue, trust will further disintegrate, which will cause assets to devalue further, and so on. Every slide in asset prices, employment, and production will give every generation cause to grow more alarmed. With savings worth less, the new elders will become more dependent on government, just as government becomes less able to pay benefits to them. With taxes hiked, the new midlifers will get to pocket even less of their peak-year incomes. With job offers dwindling, the new youth will face even taller barricades against their future.

Before long, America's old civic order will seem ruined beyond repair. People will feel like a magnet has passed over society's disk drive, blanking out the social contract, wiping out old deals, clearing the books of vast unpayable promises to which people had once felt entitled. The economy could reach a trough that may look to be the start of a depression. With American weaknesses newly exposed, foreign dangers could erupt.

From this trough and from these dangers, the makings of a new social contract and new civic order will arise. In the initial, jerry-built stages, people will not be entitled, but *authorized* to receive whatever they get from government. This will lead to conflict, as people do battle to establish where, how, and by whom this authority is to be exercised. This battle could be peaceful, involving political processes—or violent, involving public and private militias. Public needs will assume a new shape and urgency. Old political alliances will be broken and new ones forged, and debates will commence on laws that radically shift the balance between individual rights and duties. National issues will break clear of the Unraveling-era circus and cast a clear and immediate shadow over the everyday shape of American life. The Unraveling-era culture warriors will no longer be attacking national institutions mostly from the outside. Come the Fourth Turning, they will be fully in charge.

Soon after the catalyst, a national election will produce a sweeping political realignment, as one faction or coalition capitalizes on a new public demand for decisive action. Republicans, Democrats, or perhaps a new party will decisively win the long partisan tug-of-war, ending the era of split government that had lasted through four decades of Awakening and Unraveling. The winners will now have the power to pursue the more potent, less incrementalist agenda about which they had long dreamed and against which their adversaries had darkly warned. This new regime will enthrone itself for the duration of the Crisis. Regardless of its ideology, that new leadership will assert public authority and demand private sacrifice. Where leaders had once been inclined to alleviate societal pressures, they will now *aggravate* them to command the nation's attention. The regeneracy will be solidly under way.

In foreign affairs, America's initial Fourth Turning instinct will be to look away from other countries and focus total energy on the domestic birth of a new order. Later, provoked by real or imagined outside provocations, the society will turn newly martial. America will become *more* isolationist than today in its unwillingness to coordinate its affairs with other countries but *less* isolationist in its insistence that vital national interests not be compromised. The Crisis mood will dim expectations that multilateral diplomacy and expanding global democracy can keep the world out of trouble. Even before any conflicts arise, people will feel less anxiety over the prospect of casualties. Old Unraveling-era strategies (flexibility, stealth, elite expertise, stand-off weaponry, and surgical goals) will all be replaced by new Crisis-era strategies (mass, intimidation, universal conscription, frontal assault, and total victory) more suitable to a fight for civic survival. By then, people will look back on the Unraveling as the time when America evolved from a postwar to a prewar era.

The economy will in time recover from its early and vertiginous reversals. Late in the Crisis, with trust and hope and urgency growing fast, it may even achieve unprecedented levels of efficiency and production. But, by then, the economy will have changed fundamentally. Compared to today, it will be less globally dependent, with smaller cross-border trade and capital flows. Its businesses will be more cartelized and its workers more unionized, perhaps under the shadow of overt government direction. And it will devote a much larger share of its income to saving and investing. Fourth Turning America will begin to lay out the next saeculum's infrastructure grid—some higher-tech facsimile of turnpikes, railroads, or highways. The economic role of government will shift toward far more spending on survival and future promises (defense, public works) and far less on amenities and past promises (elder care, debt service). The organization of both business and government will be simpler and more centralized, with fewer administrative layers, fewer job titles, and fewer *types* of goods and services transacted.

Meanwhile, Americans will correct the Unraveling's social and cultural fragmentation by demanding the choice that era never offered: the choice not to be burdened by choice. As people again begin to trust institutional authority, they will expect that authority to simplify the options of daily life—at the store (with more standardized products), on TV (with fewer media channels), at the office (with one pay scale and benefit package), and in the voting booth (with one dominant party). Institutions will be increasingly bossy, limiting personal freedoms, chastising bad manners, and cleansing the culture. Powerful new civic organizations will make judgments about which individual rights deserve respect and which do not. Criminal justice will become swift and rough, trampling on some innocents to protect an endangered and desperate society from those feared to be guilty. Vagrants will be rounded up, the mentally ill recommitted, criminal appeals short-circuited, executions hastened.

Time will pass, perhaps another decade, before the surging mood propels America to the Fourth Turning's grave moment of opportunity and danger: the climax of the Crisis. What will this be? Recall from Chapter 9 that a climax takes a form wholly unforeseeable from the advance distance of twenty-five years. Imagine some national (and probably global) volcanic eruption, initially flowing along channels of distress that were created during the Unraveling era and further widened by the catalyst. Trying to foresee where the eruption will go once it bursts free of the channels is like trying to predict the exact fault line of an earthquake. All you know in advance is something about the molten ingredients of the climax, which could include the following:

- *Economic distress,* with public debt in default, entitlement trust funds in bankruptcy, mounting poverty and unemployment, trade wars, collapsing financial markets, and hyperinflation (or deflation)
- *Social distress,* with violence fueled by class, race, nativism, or religion and abetted by armed gangs, underground militias, and mercenaries hired by walled communities
- *Cultural distress,* with the media plunging into a dizzying decay, and a decency backlash in favor of state censorship
- *Technological distress,* with cryptoanarchy, high-tech oligarchy, and biogenetic chaos
- *Ecological distress,* with atmospheric damage, energy or water shortages, and new diseases
- *Political distress,* with institutional collapse, open tax revolts, one-party hegemony, major constitutional change, secessionism, authoritarianism, and altered national borders
- *Military distress,* with war against terrorists or foreign regimes equipped with weapons of mass destruction

During the coming Fourth Turning, some of these climax ingredients will play little or no role at all; others will shoot along channels that swell, diverge, and reconnect in wholly unforeseeable ways. Eventually, all of America's lesser problems will combine into one giant problem. The very survival of the society will feel at stake, as leaders lead and people follow. Public issues will be newly simple, fitting within the contours of crisp yes-no choices. People will leave niches to join interlocking teams, each team dependent on (and trusting of) work done by other teams. People will share similar hopes and sacrifices—and a new sense of social equality. The splinterings, complexities, and cynicisms of the Unraveling will be but distant memories. The first glimpses of a new golden age will appear beyond: *if only this one big problem can be fixed.*

Decisive events will occur—events so vast, powerful, and unique that they lie beyond today's wildest hypotheses. These events will inspire great documents and speeches, visions of a new political order being framed. People will discover a hitherto unimagined capacity to fight and die, and to let their children fight and die, for a communal cause. The Spirit of America will return, because there will be no other choice.

Thus will Americans reenact the great ancient myth of the *ekpyrosis.* Thus will we achieve our next rendezvous with destiny.

Emerging in this Crisis climax will be a great entropy reversal, that miracle of human history in which *trust* is reborn. Through the Fourth Turning, the old order will die, but only after having produced the seed containing the new civic order within it. In the moment of maximum danger, that seed will implant, and a new social contract will take root. For a brief time, the American firmament will be malleable in ways that would stagger the today's Unraveling-era mindset. "Everything is new and yielding," enthused Benjamin Rush to his friends at the climax of the American Revolution. So will everything be again.

The prospect for great civic achievement—or disintegration—will be high. New secessionist movements could spring from nowhere and achieve their ends with surprising speed. Even if the nation stays together, its geography could be fundamentally changed, its party structure altered, its Constitution and Bill of Rights amended beyond recognition. History offers even more sobering warnings: Armed confrontation usually occurs around the climax of Crisis. If there is confrontation, it is likely to lead to war. This could be any kind of war—class war, sectional war, war against global anarchists or terrorists, or superpower war. If there is war, it is likely to culminate in total war, fought until the losing side has been rendered nil—its will broken, territory taken, and leaders captured. And if there is total war, it is likely that the most destructive weapons available will be deployed.

With or without war, American society will be transformed into something different. The emergent society may be something better, a nation that sustains its Framers' visions with a robust new pride. Or it may be something unspeakably worse. The Fourth Turning will be a time of glory or ruin.

The Crisis resolution will establish the political, economic, and social institutions with which our children and heirs will live for decades thereafter. Fresh from the press of history, the new civic order will rigidify around all the new authorities, rules, boundaries, treaties, empires, and alliances. The Crisis climax will recede into the public memory—a heart-pounding memory to all who will recall it personally, a pivot point for those born in its aftermath, the stuff of myth and legend for later generations. And, for better or worse, everyone who survives will be left to live with the outcome.

What will propel these events? As the saeculum turns, each of today's generations will enter a new phase of life, producing a Crisis constellation of Boomer elders, midlife 13ers, young adult Millennials, and children from the New Silent Generation. Every generational transition will contribute to the shift in mood from Unraveling to Crisis.

As each archetype asserts its new social role, American society will reach its peak of potency. The natural order givers will be elder Prophets, the natural order takers young Heroes. The no-nonsense bosses will be midlife Nomads, the sensitive souls the child Artists. No archetypal constellation can match the gravitational capacity of this one—nor its power to congeal the natural dynamic of human history into new civic purpose. And none can match its potential power to condense countless arguments, anxieties, cynicisms, and pessimisms into one apocalyptic storm.

Think of all the Boomers, 13ers, and Millennials you know (or know about) today. Picture them ten to thirty years older, pursuing the archetypal paths of ancestral generations during prior Fourth Turnings. *This* will be America's next Crisis constellation, capable of propelling America into and through the next great gate in history.

BOOMERS ENTERING ELDERHOOD: GRAY CHAMPIONS

Back in 1886, "The Evangelization of the World in This Generation" had been the motto of America's post–Civil War youth. From youth into midlife, the Missionary Generation peers of FDR muckraked, preached an ascetic Social Gospel, proclaimed a spiritual Brotherhood of Man, and slapped prohibitions on the wayward in the culture wars of the 1920s. Nearing old age, they looked up at an elder Progressive Generation whose abiding trust was in expertise, complexity, and what Louis Brandeis called "the process of trial and error." Old Progressives battled constantly against the tolls of aging, G. Stanley Hall noting how his peers' "faculties and impulses which are denied legitimate expression during their nascent period . . . break out well into adult life—falsetto notes mingling with manly bass as strange puerilities."

As the Missionary Generation supplanted Progressives in old age, the persona of American old age shifted from friendly and yielding to stern and resolute. Following the Crash of 1929, the new elders dressed dark, filled churches and libraries, and sought by example to persuade the young, in Vachel Lindsay's words, that "a nation can be born in a day if the ideals of the people can be changed." As graying poets and novelists entered political life, elder Missionary presidents became stalwarts of first principles. Young people began looking to elders not for warmth and understanding, but for wisdom and guidance. Physically weak but cerebrally strong, Franklin Roosevelt became the leader whom "young men followed," writes historian Arthur M. Schlesinger Jr., "as they had followed no American since Lincoln." "God, God," remembered Lyndon Johnson. "How he could take it for us all." As the Crisis climaxed, this generation tried to deliver what the octogenarian art critic Bernard Berenson described, just after World War II, as "that humanistic society which under the name of Paradise, Elysium, Heaven, City of God, Millennium, has been the craving of all good men these last four thousand years or more."

This was the last time the Prophet archetype entered a Fourth Turning.

Picture veterans at a holiday parade in the late 2010s marking the Vietnam War's various fiftieth-year observances. Almost forgotten will be the Awakening era's crisp formations of Shriners in bright-colored scooters. Gone too will be the Unraveling era's personable Korean War vets with their modest We Fought Too buttons. In their place will be bearded old Aquarians in tattered camouflage, their step defiantly out of sync, their eyes piercing the crowd with moral rectitude.

"You and I are on our way to an unexpected harvest festival," says Craig Karpel to his fellow Boomers. In *The Retirement Myth,* he likens his generation's coming elderhood to a journey to "Owl Mountain," a "primordial sanctuary . . . preserved since the most ancient times," sustaining wisdom passed down from "villages in the middle of nowhere speaking to us across the millennia."

The bulk of today's gerontologists and demographers do not yet grasp what's coming. Ken Dychtwald's *Age Wave* and Cheryl Russell's *Master Trend* create the impression that Boomers will be much like today's busy senior citizens—except better-educated, more selfish, and (an easy prediction) much more numerous. This kind of forecast leads to the conclusion that early next century, younger generations will be overwhelmed by extravagantly doctored, expansively lobbying, age-denying old people. To support their consumptive Sharper Image lifestyles through old age, Boomers would have to impose confiscatory taxes on younger people. This would be an enormous dead weight, if it ever happens. It won't.

Clues of what old Boomers *will* be like can be glimpsed in the "conscious aging" movement. Cutting-edge books like *From Age-ing to Sage-ing* speak of new "spiritual eldering institutes" teaching people to engage in "vision quests." These new "elders of the tribe" see themselves as "wisdom keepers" who must apply "their dormant powers of intuition . . . [to] become seers who feed wisdom back into society and who guide the long-term reclamation project of healing our beleaguered planet." Boomer gerontologist

Harry Moody sees a twenty-first-century shift to a "contemplative old age" that eliminates today's focus on activity and instead "transcends doing, in favor of being." Elders will be defined as spiritually gifted over their juniors who "are too busy to cultivate the quietness and inwardness from which mystical experience is possible." Pain and bodily decline will be accepted, even honored as the necessary burning off of worldly dross for the purpose of acquiring higher insights. In sharp contrast to the youth-emulating "uninhibited octogenarians" of Gail Sheehy's Silent Generation, these new earth sages will want to be authentically *old* people, critical links in human civilization, without whose guidance the young might sink into Philistinism—but with whom the young can craft what gerontologist David Gutmann terms "the new myths on which reculturation can be based."

A New Age gerontology is similarly rediscovering the spiritualism of female aging. In *Goddesses in Everywoman,* Jean Bolen describes gatherings where postmenopausal women enter underground ritual caves. Sitting in a sacred circle in the "nourishing dark," they light candles to enable each participant to claim the traditional "wise woman" as her new self. There is talk of stripping negative connotations away from words like *crone* or *witch,* as though a withered female body (like Grandmother Willow's in *Pocahontas)* were a sign of magical knowledge.

Boomer evangelicals will join the search for a spiritual old age. Elder conservative Christians will sharpen their sermonizings about good and evil, implant God and prayer in public life, and demand more divine order in civic ritual. They will view as sacrilegious many of the Unraveling era's new pro-choice life-cycle laws, from genetically engineered births to nontraditional marriages to assisted suicides. They will desecularize birth, marriage, and death to reauthenticate the core transitions of human life.

Boomer-led niche cultures will cease much of their Unraveling-era quarreling and find new communitarian ground. Ethnocentrics will reveal new civic virtue in racial essences. The Fatherhood movement will become patriarchal (and feminism matriarchal), demanding and enforcing family and community standards. Active members of these cadres will comprise just a small minority of old Boomers, but like the hippies and yuppies of the Second and Third Turnings they will command the attention and set the tone for the Fourth. Those who dislike them—and there will be many—will be unable to avoid seeing and hearing their message.

At the onset of old age, Boomers will do what they have done with every earlier step of the aging process: They will resist it for a while, then dabble in it, and ultimately glorify it. Like old Transcendental men (who sprouted long beards as badges of wisdom), Boomers will establish elegant new insignia of advanced age—flaunting, not avoiding, the natural imprints of time. Rather than trying to impress the young with G.I.-style energy or Silent-style cool, old Boomers will do so with a Zen-like serenity, a heightened consciousness of time. Slow talking, walking, and driving will become badges of contemplation, not decline. The ideal of an advanced age will not be the active and leisured G.I. or the empathic and expert Silent, but rather the inner elder who thinks deeply, recalling Emerson's view that "As we grow old, . . . the beauty steals inward."

The very word *retirement* will acquire a new negative meaning, connoting selfish consumption and cultural irrelevance. The elder goal will not be to retire, but to *replenish* or *reflect* or *pray*. The very concept of any retirement will fade, as elders pursue new late-life careers, often in high-prestige but low- (or non-) paying emeritus positions. In academe, Boomers will become part professor and part spiritual guide in a reinvention of the university. In church, elders will deliver the fierce homilies while younger adults collect the money, the reverse of what is common today. Talk radio will be a bastion of elder reflection.

Aging Boomers will be drawn to the classic. Their late-life cultural questing will not evoke juvenescence, as it did in the Awakening era, but rather a preservation of values that will increasingly seem antiquated to others. Boomers will rail against pop culture detritus left over from the Unraveling: violent films, shopping malls, convenience stores, packaged throwaways. Under their stewardship, Hollywood will establish standards of taste while making definitive films of great literature, biography, and history. Old travelers will seek self-discovery and wisdom, preferring monastic retreats over cheery cruises, tai chi over shuffleboard. Elder enclaves will resemble Sedona more than Sun City, rural hamlets more than condo minicities. The gray elite will cluster in areas long associated with this generation: Northern California, the Pacific Northwest, New Mexico, New England.

Boomer elders will still make heavy demands of the young, but the nature of those demands will differ greatly from those imposed by today's elders. Where the Awakening-era G.I.s burdened the young fiscally, Crisis-era Boomers will burden the young culturally. They will reverse the coin of elderhood from what they will remember of the Awakening: Where G.I. elders once obtained secular reward in return for ceding moral authority, Boomers will seek the reverse. Accordingly, grandchildren will not look to them for financial advice (as per G.I. seniors) or emotional support (as per Silent seniors), but rather for guidance in the realm of ideals and values. To young eyes, old Boomers will appear highly eccentric. What Boomers feel as inner warmth will feel cold to others, and what they see as ethical perfectionism will sometimes strike others as hypocrisy.

In the Fourth Turning, Boomers are likely to occupy the vortex of a downward economic spiral. This will happen partly because of their numbers but mainly because of their location in history and collective persona. As financial expert David Barker observes, "the generation born in a K-Wave advance and inevitably spoiled by the wealth created by their parents' generation is sure to drive the system over the edge, without the experience of the past decline to provide financial and economic sobriety." Born to the High's new cornucopia, come of age with the Awakening's fiscal levers at full throttle, the national economy in the Boomers' old age will provide them with a very different end game. Consequently, this elder generation will get a comeuppance for a lifelong habit of preaching virtues its members have not themselves displayed—of talking more than doing. There will be a payback for the Boomers' tendency to graze on a problem until they finally decide to focus fully, at which point their sudden discovery becomes as much the issue as the original problem. Sooner or later, the truth will dawn on old Boomers that the money simply won't be there to support their accustomed consumption habits in old age. Neither they nor their nation will have saved enough.

From this sudden realization could issue the end game of Boomer life-cycle consumption and savings habits: the Great Devaluation. At long last, aging Boomers will focus on the hard fact that a newly endangered America truly cannot (and younger generations will not) make their old-age subsidies a top public priority. This realization will render Boomers jittery about preserving their remaining assets. Some unforeseeable happenstance could spark a precipitous market selloff, as old investors will want to liquidate their equities to a shrinking universe of buyers. The main domestic buyers would be 13ers, who will have lower incomes and far fewer assets than Boomers and who will be of no mind to take risks with wobbling markets. Foreigners will be hesitant to acquire more U.S. assets in a time of pending fiscal crisis, especially since so many of their own societies will be facing similar demographic problems. A brief but precipitous panic could ensue. Years of savings could vanish in a matter of days—or hours.

The Great Devaluation is likely to hit Boomers just as their first cohorts are reaching the official ages of retirement, long before Social Security is now projected to go into official bankruptcy. Indeed, the panic could be triggered in part by the crystallizing financial anxieties of leading-edge Boomers. The flash point may well occur when the new elder mindset (of the 1943 "victory baby" cohort) combines with the new demographic realities (of the large 1946 "baby boom" cohort) to reach a critical mass. This could occur a few years before or after 2005—perhaps between 2002 (when the 1943 cohort reaches the IRA distribution age of fifty-nine and a half) and 2008 (when the 1946 cohort reaches the initial Social Security eligibility age of sixty-two, the age at which over two-thirds of Americans now start receiving benefits).

Unlike their predecessors, Boomers will consider their old-age finances to be more a private than public concern. For G.I.s, Social Security has been a generational bond running through government, its monthly checks a standard-issue badge of senior-citizen equality. For the Silent, Social Security will have been a play-by-the-rules annuity, offering a mixture of delight (for sneaking through just in time) and guilt (for burdening their kids). For Boomers, Social Security will be the object of fatalism and sarcasm. Some will get it, and some won't. The typical Boomer will live on bits and pieces of SEP-IRAs, Keoghs, 401Ks, federal benefits, and assorted corporate pension scraps that will vary enormously from person to person. For many, this will add up to a lot; for many others, nearly nothing.

When the market hits bottom, millions of Boomers will find themselves at the brink of old age with far smaller nest eggs than they ever expected. They will immediately have to make do with steeply diminished material consumption. Many will have no choice but to live communally or with their adult children, while groping for ways to preserve a meaningful life on very little money. Some without kin will form "intentional families," while others who shunned neighbors all their lives will form "intentional communities."

Following the Great Devaluation, Boomers will find new ethical purpose in low consumption because, with America in Crisis, they will have no other choice. If the Crisis has not catalyzed before, it will now. With other urgent problems facing the nation, public spending on elder benefits will necessarily decline. All the old Unraveling-era promises about Social Security will now be known to be false, just as most Boomers had always presumed. This will create a moral rubric for breaking those promises. A debate will begin about which (if any) of the old promises should still be honored, and what new ones made, in a Next New Deal among the generations. Where Unraveling-era Congresses debated over one or two percentage point differences in rates of increase, Crisis-era Congresses will debate massive cuts. To maintain G.I.-style elder dependence on the young, Boomers would have to wage political war on their coming-of-age Millennial children. It is a war they will not wage—and would not win if they did.

Instead of political battles with other generations, Boomers will engage in moral battles among themselves. Those who retain assets will accuse those who don't of irresponsibility and lack of thrift. Those who don't have assets will accuse those who do of having battened off the corrupt old order. Younger generations will agree with both accusations. In the end, the Next New Deal will find all Boomers, rich and poor, paying a price. Many who spent a lifetime paying steep Social Security and Medicare taxes will be substantially excluded from benefits by an affluence test. Those who still qualify for public aid will receive a much worse deal than their G.I. parents did. The debate will rip apart whatever remains of the old senior citizen lobby built by G.I.s back in the Awakening. The AARP will survive only by reinventing itself as a council of elders committed to advancing the needs of posterity. *Modern Maturity* magazine will shift its style from Silent hip to Boomer classic and change its title to refer to aging in more traditional and less euphemistic terms.

The Next New Deal will render the Boomers' old-age health-care subsidies a tightly regulated social decision. Crafting necessity into virtue, Boomers will deem the postponement of death as *not* a public entitlement.

Many elders will eschew high-tech hospital care for homeopathy, minimalist self care, and the mind-body techniques Deepak Chopra calls "quantum healing." The G.I.-era of extended care facilities (with bodies kept busy but minds at rest) will be replaced by less expensive elder sanctuaries (with bodies at rest but minds kept busy). Despite the Boomers' larger numbers and longer life spans—and the costly end-of-life technologies that medicine might then offer—the share of Fourth Turning national income that will be spent on federally subsidized elder health care could fall below what it was in the Unraveling.

Old Boomers will construct a new social ethic of decline and death, much like they did in youth with sex and procreation. Where their youthful ethos hinged on self-indulgence, their elder ethos will hinge on self-denial. As they experience their own bodies coping naturally with decline and death, they will expect government to do the same. Old age will be seen as a time of transition and preparation for dying. With the same psychic energy with which they once probed *eros,* Boomers will now explore *thanatos,* the end-time, what the book *Aging As a Spiritual Journey* heralds as "the final night-sea journey" that lends an elder "the courage and insight to be profoundly wise for others." Their last Big Chills will not so much mourn journeyed friends as celebrate the after-death teaching their departed souls can still offer the young. Funeral homes will help predecedents prepare posthumous books and CD-ROMs to communicate with heirs in perpetuity.

As they fill the upper age brackets, Boomers will believe themselves to be elders who, in the words of anthropologist Joan Halifax, "function like old cobblers and dressmakers, sewing us back into the fabric of creation." They will feel a new transformative dimension of time, enabling them to craft myths and models that can resacralize the national community, heal its dysfunctions, and grant moral authority for the next Golden Age. The very other-worldliness that Boomers will regard so highly in themselves will strike younger generations as evidence of incompetence. Elder contempt for this world will strike younger people as dangerous. Yet regardless what youth think of these old messengers, they will respect their message and march to their banner.

Thus will the Gray Champion ride once more.

Eight or nine decades after his last appearance, America will be visited by the "figure of an ancient man . . . combining the leader and the saint (to) show the spirit of their sires." Again will appear the heir to the righteous Puritan who stood his ground against Governor Andros, the old colonial governors of the American Revolution who broke from England, the aging radicals of the Civil War who pitted brother against brother with a "fiery gospel writ in burnished rows of steel," and "the New Deal Isaiahs" who achieved their rendezvous with destiny.

Whence will come the Gray Champion? Picture the Boomer Overclass of the Unraveling, aged another twenty years. Picture William Bennett's "Consequence and Confrontation" missives; Al Gore predicting an environmental cataclysm; James Webb's summoning a "ruthless and overpowering" retaliation against foreign enemies; James Fallows rooting for a "7.0 magnitude diplo-economic shock"; "Apocalypse Darman" and "Default Newt" with their budget train wrecks; Earth First saboteurs, willing to sacrifice other people's lives to save trees; and Army of God antiabortionists summoning the terminally ill to "use your final months to torch clinics." Picture Boomers like these, older and harsher, uncalmed by anyone more senior, feeling their last full measure of strength, sensing their pending mortality, mounting their final crusade—all at a time of maximum public peril.

The full dimension of the Boomer persona will only emerge when today's better-known 1940s birth cohorts (whose youth was marked by relatively few social pathologies) are joined in public life by the tougher-willed, more evangelical 1950s cohorts (whose youth was marked by many more pathologies). *That* is the mix that will beget this generation's elder priest-warrior persona, vindicating the early Unraveling-era warning of Peter Collier and David Horowitz that Boomers are "a destructive generation whose work is not over yet."

As the Crisis deepens, Boomers will confront the end result of their life-long absorption with values. They will have laid a long trail of Unraveling-era rhetoric, much of it symbol and gesture, but now the words will matter. When James Redfield (or his elder equivalent) describes his peers as "a generation whose intuitions would help lead humanity toward a . . . great transformation," the summons will no longer be for pensive spiritual reflection but for decisive civic action. Boomers will comply with Cornel West's suggestion that "the mark of the prophet is to speak the truth in love with courage—come what may." Their habitual tendency to enunciate unyielding principles will now carry the duty of enforcement.

The final Boomer leaders—authoritarian, severe, unyielding—will command broad support from younger people who will see in them a wisdom beyond the reckoning of youth. In domestic matters, old Boomers will recast the old arguments of the Culture Wars into a new context of community needs. They will redefine and reauthenticate a civic expansion—crafted from some mix of Unraveling-era cultural conservatism and public-sector liberalism. In foreign matters, they will narrowly define the acceptable behavior of other nations and broadly define the appropriate use of American arms.

The same Boomers who in youth chanted "Hell no, we won't go!" will emerge as America's most martial elder generation in living memory. Whatever the elements of Crisis, old Boomer leaders will up the moral ante beyond the point of possible retreat or compromise. The same Boomers who once chanted "Ho Ho Ho Chi Minh, the NLF is gonna win!" will demand not just an enemy's defeat, but its utter destruction. They will risk enormous pain and consequence to command youth to fight and die in ways they themselves never would have tolerated in their own youth. They will believe, as did Cicero, that this moment in history assigns "young men for action, old men for counsel."

Old Boomers will find transcendence in the Crisis climax. As they battle time and nature to win their release from history, they will feel themselves in position to steward the nation, and perhaps the world, across several painful thresholds. It is easy to envision old Aquarians as pillars of fire leading to the Promised Land—but just as easy to see them as Charon-like monsters abducting doomed souls across the Styx to Hades. Either is possible.

As the Crisis resolves, elder Boomers will have not the last word, but the deep word. If they triumph, they will collectively deserve the eulogy Winston Churchill offered to Franklin Roosevelt: to die "an enviable death." If they fail, their misdeeds will cast a dark shadow over the entire twenty-first century, perhaps beyond. Whatever the outcome, posterity will remember the Boomers' Gray Champion persona long after the hippie and yuppie images have been forgotten to all but the historian.

13ERS ENTERING MIDLIFE: DOOM PLAYERS

"Now once more the belt is tight and we summon the proper expression of horror as we look back at our wasted youth," F. Scott Fitzgerald said after the crash that hit his peers at the cusp of what should have been their highest-earning years. "A generation with no second acts," he called his Lost peers—but they proved him wrong. They ended their frenzy and settled down, thus helping to unjangle the American mood. Where their Missionary predecessors had entered midlife believing in vast crusades, the post-Crash Lost skipped the moralisms and returned directly to the basics of life. "What is moral is what you feel good after," declared Ernest Hemingway, "what is immoral is what you feel bad after." "Everything depends on the use to which it is put," explained Reinhold Niebuhr on behalf of a generation that did useful things regardless of faith—a role the Missionaries chose not to play.

This "no second act" generation lent America the grit to survive dark global emergencies and, in the end, to triumph over them. In the Great Depression, the Lost were hard-hit but refused to ask for public favors. In World War II, they manned the draft boards, handed out the ration coupons, mapped the invasions, and dispatched the bomber fleets. They gave the orders that killed thousands but saved millions. From "blood and guts" generals to "give 'em hell" presidents, the Lost knew how to prevail over long odds and harsh criticism.

This was the last time the Nomad archetype entered a Fourth Turning.

In a recent genre of action films (from *War Games* and *Back to the Future* to *Terminator* and *Independence Day),* a stock drama unfolds. A young protagonist—alone, unprepared, and immersed in a junky culture—is chosen by chance to decide the fate of humanity. The situation looks dicey. The protagonist, too, has slim expectations of success. But at a pivotal moment, this lonely wayfarer challenges destiny, deals with the stress, zeroes in on what matters, does what is required, and comes out on top. The most popular video games, following the same script, stress one-on-one action and deft timing: Find a treasure, grab the tools, rescue a princess, save the kingdom, slay the enemy, and get out alive. Everything is yes-no, full of code words and secret places—in a style one TV executive calls "Indiana Jones meets a game show."

"I've glimpsed our future," warns a high school valedictorian in the film *Say Anything,* "and all I can say is—go back." The message to her classmates is understandable, because Nomad generations—what Christian Slater refers to as "a long list of dead, famous wild people"—have always been the ones who lose ground in wealth, education, security, longevity, and other measures of progress. Yet they have also been the generations who lay at the fulcrum between triumph and tragedy, the ones who hoist their society through the darkest days of Crisis.

The onset of the Fourth Turning will find 13ers retaining their troubled reputation, the only change being that America's troubled age bracket will then be perceived as more fortyish than twentyish. They will carry the reputation for having come of age at a time when good manners and civic habits were not emphasized in homes and schools. With their arrival, midlife will lose moral authority and gain toughness. Their culture will be a hodgepodge of unblending styles and polyethnic currents that will reflect the centrifugal impulse from which many Americans (including 13ers) will now be eager to escape.

In the economy, 13ers will fare significantly worse than Boomers did at like age back in the mid-1980s. They will fan out across an unusually wide range of money and career outcomes. A few will be wildly successful, a larger number will be destitute, while most will be losing ground but doing tolerably. The Crisis era's image of a middle-aged worker will be a modest-wage job hopper who retains the flexibility to change life directions at a snap. The prototype midlife success story will be the entrepreneur who excels at cunning, flexibility, and high-tech ingenuity. The prototype failure will be the ruined gambler, broke but still trying. The high-risk harbors where 13ers will have bet their stray cash during the Unraveling (from lottos to Indian casinos to derivative markets) will, like this generation, be stigmatized and left to rot.

As they confront their money problems amid a mood of deepening Crisis, 13ers will take pride in their ability to "have a life" and wall off their families from financial woes. Their divorce rate will be well below that of midlife Silent and Boomers. They will clamp down on children. In exchange for financial help, many will invite their better-off parents to live with them.

Surveying the Crisis-era detritus of the Unraveling, 13ers will see the opposite of what the midlife Silent saw in the Awakening-era wreckage of the High. Where the Silent felt claustrophobic, yearning to break free in a world that felt too closed, 13ers will feel agoraphobic, yearning to root in a world that feels too open. Where the Silent were torn between the socially necessary and the personally desirable, 13ers will be torn between the personally necessary and the socially desirable.

Gripped with deeply felt family obligations, 13ers will resist the idea of relaxing their survival instincts—yet will sense the need to restore a sense of community. They will widen the continuing dispersions of technology and culture—yet will vote for politicians who promise to reverse it. Middle-aged Hispanic-, Asian-, and Arab-Americans (among others) will embrace their racial or ethnic identities—yet will yearn for new ties to the communal core.

The Unraveling's initial 13er pop elite will lose influence as their peers tire of the old ways and seek something simpler and less frenzied. Those who persist in the discarded culturama will be chastised and perhaps even quarantined in the newly wholesome Millennial youth culture. A few aging outcasts will scatter around the world, feeling like those whom Doug Coupland calls "a White Russian aristocracy, exiled in Paris cafes, never to get what is due to us." Replacing them as the cutting edge of their generation will be a *Revenge of the Nerds,* slow-but-steady plodders (many of them ethnics) who will overtake the quick strikers who took one risk too many.

The 13er mind-set will be hardboiled and avuncular, the risk taking now mellowed by a Crisis-era need for security. Middle-aged people will mentor youth movements, lend stylishness to hard times, and add nuts-and-bolts workmanship to the resolute new mood. They will be begrudgingly respected for their proficiency in multimedia and various untutored skills to which old Boomers will be blind and young Millennials dismissive. Throughout the economy, 13ers will be associated with risk and dirty jobs. They will seek workable outcomes more than inner truths. "We won't have a bad backlash against our lost idealism," predicts *Slacker* filmmaker Richard Linklater, since his generation "never had that to begin with." Like Hemingway, their moral judgments will be situational, based on how everybody feels afterward.

As the Crisis deepens, 13ers will feel little stake in the old order, little sense that their names and signatures are on the social contract. They will have reached full adult maturity without ever having believed in either the American Dream or American exceptionalism. They will never have known a time when America felt good about itself, when its civic and cultural life didn't seem to be decaying. From childhood into midlife, they will have always sensed that the nation's core institutions mainly served the interests of people other than themselves. Not many of their classmates and friends will have built public-sector careers, apart from teaching and police work. Most 13ers will have oriented their lives around self-help networks of friends and other ersatz institutions that have nothing to do with government.

The "we're not worthy" 13er streak of weak collective esteem will define and enhance their new civic role. Where the Boomers' Unraveling-era narcissism interfered with America's ability to exact even minor sacrifice for the public good, the 13ers' ironic self-deprecation will render their claims unusually selfless. "We may not get what we want. We may not get what we need," chanted the young adults in *True Colors*. "Just so we don't get what we deserve." They will vote against their own short-term interests if persuaded that the community's long-term survival requires it. Where the Silent once agonized over procedural braking mechanisms, where Boomers had huge arguments over gesture and symbolism, 13er voters will disregard motive and ideology, and will simply ask if public programs get results that are worth the money.

In the Fourth Turning's Next New Deal, 13ers will be strategically located between moralistic old Boomers and cherished young Millennials. With 13ers occupying the margins of political choice, no intergenerational bargain will be enacted without their approval. In *The Breakfast Club,* a Boomer teacher despaired of "the thought that makes me get up in the middle of the night: That when I get older, these kids are gonna take care of me." As elder benefits hit the fiscal wall, Boomers and 13ers will, like siblings, half-remember and half-forget how they behaved toward each other in earlier decades. There will be some talk of ethnogenerational war, as non-Anglo 13ers attack Boomer benefits as what former Social Security Commissioner Dorcas Hardy has called "a mechanism by which the government robs their children of a better future, in order to support a group of elderly white people." Led by ethnic populists, 13ers will strike a hard bargain with elders they will collectively perceive as lifelong hypocrites with a weak claim on the public purse. So long as the Next New Deal hits Boomers hard, 13ers won't mind if it's projected to hit themselves even harder.

As the Crisis rages on, the era's stark new communitarianism will require 13ers to rivet new grids in place. New-breed mayors and governors will abandon old labels and alliances, patch together people and technology, and rekindle public support for community purpose. Having grown up in a time when walls were being dismantled, families dissolved, and loyalties discarded, 13er power brokers will reconstruct the social barriers that produce civic order. They will connive first to get the people behind them, next to bribe (or threaten) people into doing what's needed, and then to solidify those arrangements into something functional. They won't worry about the obviously insoluble and won't fuss over the merely annoying. Their politicians won't brim with compassion or nuance, and won't care if they have to win ugly. To them, the outcome will matter more than democracy's ritual aesthetics. Their hand strengthened by the demands of Crisis, 13ers will sweep aside procedural legalisms and promises legislated by old regimes, much to the anguish of the octogenarian Silent. They won't mind uttering— and listening to—the sound bite that seems to sum up a situation with eloquent efficiency. To critics, the new style of 13er urban leadership will appear unlearned, poorly rooted in values, even corrupt, but it will work.

This generation's institutional rootlessness will make its leaders and electorates highly volatile, capable of extreme crosscurrents. Lacking much stake in the old order, many 13ers might impulsively welcome the notion of watching it break into pieces. They won't regard the traditional safety nets as important to their lives. The real-life experience of their own circles will reinforce their view that when people lose jobs or money, they can find a way to cope, deal with it, and move on. Looking back on their own lives, they will conclude that many of the Awakening- and Unraveling-era trends that may have felt good to older generations didn't work so well for them— or for the nation. Come the Crisis, many 13ers will feel that emergency action is necessary to re-create the kind of secure world they will feel was denied them in childhood.

In this environment, 13ers could emerge as the leaders of a Crisis-era populism based on the notion of taking raw action now and justifying it later. A charismatic anti-intellectual demagogue could convert the ad slogans of the Third Turning into the political slogans of the Fourth: "No excuses." "Why ask why?" "Just do it." Start with a winner-take-all ethos that believes in action for action's sake, exalts strength, elevates impulse, and holds weakness and compassion in contempt. Add class desperation, antirationalism, and perceptions of national decline. The product, at its most extreme, could be a new American fascism.

The core feature of the 13ers' midlife will be the Crisis itself. Early in the era, the Great Devaluation could quash many a midlife career and cause real hardships to families under their protection. Like the Lost Generation in the 1920s, 13ers will have bought into the Unraveling-era boom market late and high—only to sell out late and low. At the same time, urgent necessity will lend new meaning to their lives. Many of the traits that were criticized for decades—their survivalism, realism, lack of affect—will now be recognized as vital national resources. The emergency will melt away much of the Unraveling era's old fuss about political correctness. Now 13ers will hear far less complaint about their soldiers being too much the warrior, their entrepreneurs too much the operator, their opinion leaders too much the blunt talker. As the Crisis catalyzes, they will recall the old Jesus Jones lyric, feel themselves "Right here, right now / Watching the world wake up from history," and know they are the generation on the spot. Though 13ers will have little ability to influence the elements and timing of the Boomer-propelled Crisis, they will provide the on-site tacticians and behind-the-scenes bosses whose decisions will determine its day-to-day course.

Middle-aged 13ers will be the only ones capable of deflecting the more dangerous Boomer tendencies. The Boomers won't check themselves, nor will Millennials, so the task will fall to 13ers to force the Boomer priest-warriors to *give it a rest* when the fervor gets too deep, to *get real* when the sacrifices outweigh the future reward. A 13er may indeed be the intrepid statesman, general, or presidential adviser who prevents some righteous old Aquarian from loosing the fateful lightning and turning the world's lights out.

At or just after the Crisis climax, 13ers will supplant Boomers in national leadership. History warns that they could quickly find themselves playing a real-world *Sim City,* facing quick triage choices about who and what to sacrifice, and when and how. They will need every bit of those old Doom player joystick skills—the deft timing, the instinctive sense of what counts and what doesn't, the ability always to move on from one problem to the next. Whatever they do, they will get more than their share of the blame and less than their share of the credit.

As the Crisis resolves, the society will be fully in 13er hands. If all ends well, their security-minded leadership will usher the society away from urgent crusades and into the next High. If not, 13ers will be left with no choice but to yank younger generations by the collar, appraise what's left of their society, and start anew.

MILLENNIALS ENTERING YOUNG ADULTHOOD: POWER RANGERS

"I promise as a good American to do my part," one hundred thousand young people chanted on Boston Commons in 1933. "I will help President Roosevelt bring back good times." These young G.I.s were touted by Malcolm Cowley as "brilliant college graduates" who "pictured a future in which everyone would be made secure by collective planning and social discipline"—whereas, at the same age, Cowley's own Lost peers had grown "disillusioned and weary" from hearing so much pessimism about their future. During the Lost's peak coming-of-age years, the youth suicide rate rose by half and the homicide rate by 700 percent, while American youth showed precious little improvement in rates of illiteracy or college entry.

A few years before the Crash of 1929, youth took the most dramatically positive change ever recorded. All of a sudden, young Americans turned away from cynicism, suicide, and crime and toward optimism, education, and civic fealty. A new vernacular spoke of trust and geometric order, of "level-headed" and "regular guys" who were "on the square," "fit in," and could be "counted on." "Underneath, we really thought we were all right," Gene Shuford recalled. If the souring economy dampened many a career and marriage plan, that only steeled the G.I. determination to act on the 4-H motto: Make the Best Better. Older people lent them direction and help. America "cannot always build the future for our youth," said FDR on the eve of World War II, "but we can build our youth for the future." Having received 80 percent of a huge youth vote in 1932 and 85 percent in 1936, by far the largest such mandates ever recorded, FDR proclaimed that "the very objectives of young people have changed" away from "the dream of the golden ladder—each individual for himself" and toward the dream of "a broad highway on which thousands of your fellow men and women are advancing with you." Before long, the highways and seaways were full of a generation now fully in uniform, heralded by General Marshall as "the best damn kids in the world"—a world they proceeded to conquer. "The difficult we do at once," their Seabees famously proclaimed. "The impossible takes a little longer."

This was the last time the Hero archetype entered a Fourth Turning.

Power Rangers are wholesome kid-soldiers in bright, primary-color uniforms. No relation to the junk-fed mutant turtles of the 13er child era, Power Rangers have provided the Unraveling's leading toy role models for children. When summoned, these ordinary youths transform themselves into thunderbolting evil fighters. Cheerful, confident, and energetic, Power Rangers are nurtured to succeed in the face of great odds. Whatever they do—from displaying martial arts to piloting high-tech weaponry—they do as a choreographed group. Their very motto, The Power of Teamwork Overcomes All, speaks of strength in cooperation, energy in conformity, virtue in duty. Their missions are not chosen by themselves, but by an incorporeal elder in whose vision and wisdom they have total trust. Come the Fourth Turning, coming-of-age Millennials will have a lot in common with these action toys.

In the next Crisis, Millennials will prove false the supposition, born of the recent Awakening and Unraveling eras, that youth is ever the age for rebellion, alienation, or cynicism. As they break into their twenties, Millennials will already be accustomed to meeting and beating adult expectations. Basking in praise, they will revive the ideal of the common man, whose virtue is defined less by self than from a collegial center of gravity. Rather than argue with elders, Millennials will seek out their advice—about the ought-to-dos from old Boomers and about the want-to-dos from 13ers. But their style will be distinct from either generation. From the youth perspective, most Boomers will seem too unworldly and most 13ers too undisciplined to be emulated.

New pop culture trends will be big, bland, and friendly. In film, young stars will be linked with positive themes, display more modesty in sex and language, and link new civic purpose to screen violence. In sports, players will become more coachable, more loyal to teams and fans, and less drawn to trash talk, in-your-face slam dunks, and end-zone taunts. In pop music, Millennials will resurrect the old ritual of happy group singing, from old campfire favorites to new tunes with simple melodies and upbeat lyrics. Whether in film, sports, or music, the first Millennial celebrities will win praise as good role models for children.

Every youth domain will become more mannerly, civic-spirited, and emotionally placid. In college, Millennials will lead a renaissance in student decorum and appearance, making profanity as out of date as the backward cap. On urban streets, young adults will begin sensing that their best path to prosperity is to follow their peers, not their families. In technology, they will carve out fresh concepts of public space—by designing fewer and more centralized paths of communication and by using information to empower groups rather than individuals. In social movements, they will (initially) seem pacifist, hard to ruffle, their civic power as yet untapped. The media will miss no opportunity to celebrate good deeds they do.

On the job, Millennials will be seekers of order and harmony. They will delight employers with their skills, work habits, and institutional loyalties. They will have a knack for organization and hierarchy more than creative entrepreneurship. Young workers will revitalize trade unions and treat co-workers as partners more than rivals. The Millennials' entry into the workforce, combined with the Boomers' exit, will produce a sudden surge in productivity—quite the opposite of the stagnation that arose from the Awakening's Boomer entry and G.I. exit.

The Great Devaluation may occur right around the time Millennials fill the twenties age bracket, just as they are emerging as a truly national generation, the pride of their elders. Whatever their new economic hardships (and they could be severe), Millennials will not rebel, but will instead mobilize for public purpose. Older people will be anguished to see these good kids suffer for the mistakes of others. Boomers and 13ers will together urgently resist the prospect that a second consecutive generation might be denied access to the American Dream. No matter how shattered the economy, no matter how fiscally stretched the government, places will be found for the rising generation. To accomplish this, the status of young workers will be standardized, their job titles shortened, and pay gaps narrowed. Millennials will respond with a cheerful patience reminiscent of Depression-era G.I.s. Government will play an important role in their lives, as people of all ages jointly resolve to remove any barrier to a bright Millennial future.

With youth coming of age so willing and energized, older leaders will be inspired to enlist them for public actions that in the Unraveling would have felt hopeless. Young adults will see politics as a tool for turning collegial purpose into civic progress. Millennial voters will confound pundits with huge youth turnouts, massing on behalf of favored candidates—especially elders who, like Lincoln or FDR, can translate spiritual resolve into public authority. They will reject the negativism and cloying affect of the political campaigning they witnessed as children. When young adults encounter leaders who cling to the old regime (and who keep propping up senior benefit programs that will by then be busting the budget), they will not tune out, 13er-style. Instead, they will get busy working to defeat or overcome their adversaries. Their success will lead some older critics to perceive real danger in a rising generation perceived as capable but naive.

This youthful hunger for social discipline and centralized authority could lead Millennial youth brigades to lend mass to dangerous demagogues. The risk of class warfare will be especially grave if the 20 percent of Millennials who were poor as children (50 percent in inner cities) come of age seeing their peer-bonded paths to generational progress blocked by elder inertia. Unraveling-era adults who are today chilled by school uniforms will be truly frightened by the Millennials' Crisis-era collectivism. As Sinclair Lewis warned of G.I.s in the 1930s, older Americans will look abroad at rigidly ordered societies and wonder whether, among youth with so much power and so little doubt, *It Can't Happen Here.*

Wherever their politics lead, Millennials will become identified with a new American mainstream, a fledgling middle class just waiting to assert itself. They will vex Hollywood's Unraveling-era elite with their cool rationalism. They will vex feminists by accepting a new mystique between the sexes. They will vex free marketeers with their demands for trade barriers, government regulation, labor standards, and public works.

Just as the Unraveling's political agenda centered around children, the agenda of the Next New Deal will center around young adults. In exchange, old Boomers will impose a new duty of compulsory service, notwithstanding those elders' own youthful draft resistance. Millennials will not oppose this because they will see in it a path to public achievement. If inducted for war, Millennials will cast aside any earlier pacifism and march to duty. Like Power Rangers, they will not be averse to militarized mass violence, just to uncontrolled *personal* violence—quite the opposite of Boomer youths back in the Awakening. National leaders will not hesitate to mobilize and deploy them in huge armies. Where Boomer youths once screamed against duty and discipline, Boomer elders will demand and receive both from Millennial troops.

Near the climax of Crisis, the full power of this rising generation will assert itself, providing their society with a highly effective instrument for imposing order on an unruly world. They will appear capable of glorious collective deeds, of conquering distant lands, of potently executing any command that may be issued. Quite the opposite of the Boomers' Awakening-era casualties in Vietnam, which weakened the public will to fight, the Millennials' heroic sacrifices will only add to the national resolve. As a Crisis-era president commits the society to clear a path for a bright future, the political juggernaut of Millennial youth will stand squarely with their beloved commander-in-chief. This generation of young heroes will follow wherever the Gray Champion leads, whether to triumph or disaster.

NEW SILENT ENTERING CHILDHOOD: SWEET INNOCENTS

"Overprotective was a word first used to describe our parents," Benita Eisler recalls of her Silent peers' Depression-era youth, when adults ruled the child's world with a stern hand. Back in the G.I. childhood years, no one spoke of overprotection, because the crusade to protect the child's world was then just getting started. As the *Literary Digest* demanded a "reassertion of parental authority," parents injected what historian Daniel Rodgers describes as "a new, explicit insistence on conformity into child life." Thus raised, G.I.s passed through childhood showing America's largest measurable one-generation improvement in health, size, and education—along with big reductions in youth crime and suicide.

By the time the Silent entered school, however, clean-cut behavior was taken for granted. The leading parenting books suggested a no-nonsense total situation parenting with behavioral rules that critics likened to the house-breaking of puppies. Whenever movie kids like Alfalfa or Shirley Temple encountered adults, they would "mind their manners." During the war years, America had perhaps the best-behaved teenagers in its history, but controversy simmered about whether the long absence of soldiering fathers would cause them to grow up a little uncertain of themselves. Times were indeed fearful for children, since any day could bring devastating news. Frank Conroy recalls having asked, as a boy, "what was in the newspapers when there wasn't a war going on."

This was the last time the Artist archetype entered a Fourth Turning.

"Many of the social conditions we think of as black problems are merely white problems a generation later," William Raspberry has observed. Early in the Awakening, the children in America's urban cores were the harbingers of new trends that afflicted the whole society by the start of the Unraveling: disintegrating families, absentee fathers, teen mothers, rising crime, falling performance in school. In today's Unraveling, America's urban children are once again bearing signposts. They have became shut-ins, tucked behind walls, sleeping in bulletproof bathtubs, escorted to school by anxious adults and swept off late-night streets by police curfews, even though the actual risk of violence, in many inner cities, is beginning to recede. Come the Fourth Turning, variants of these 1990s-era inner-city child swaddling trends will be visible all across America, from downtown to suburb to small town.

Imagine being a child living in a world surrounded by a concrete wall originally raised to ward off dangerous neighbors. The danger has receded (the enemies are now more distant), but the concrete remains. Adults don't bother to remove the wall because they're busy and find it an easy way to keep track of their kids. Come the Fourth Turning, the rules a child must follow will begin outlasting the original reasons for those rules. Picture high-rise children still barricaded behind walls in a time of reduced crime on the streets below. Picture compulsory kindergarten uniforms in a time of whole-some new trends in young-adult fashion. Picture a vigorous police presence in a time of generally compliant teenagers. What in the Unraveling felt like sensible protections will now, in the Crisis, reach a state of stifling suffoca-tion at the hands of parents and governments alike.

The babies of the Oh-Ohs will be America's next Artist archetype, the New Silent Generation. Their link to Crisis will be as the vulnerable seeds of society's future that must be saved while the emergency is overcome and the enemy defeated. They will be the Crisis era's fearful watchers, tiny helpers, and (if all goes well) lucky inheritors. Tethered close to home, they will do helpful little deeds like recycling, keyboarding, or tending to elders, the circa-2020 equivalents of planting World War II victory gardens or col-lecting scrap metal. The New Silent will look on adults as competent and in control. Crisp rights and wrongs will be a common adult message, unques-tioning compliance the expected response. New Silent kids will not be en-couraged to take chances or do things on their own. Naïveté and sweet innocence will be presumed to flow from those of tender age. In a reverse from the Unraveling, deviancy will be redefined *upwards*. Youth sex, abor-tion, and substance abuse will remain at low levels. Parental divorce will be restigmatized, and public talk about private matters will be newly taboo in the media. Unlike today, the bulk of the family disruptions will be involun-tary, the result not of personal choice or dysfunction but of Crisis-era forces utterly beyond the family's control.

Child welfare will be a settled priority, no longer anyone's crusade. Pro-tective nurture will be on autopilot. Few adults will dispute that children must be taught community norms, often by rote. Children who fall below standards will be warned that the community has ways of remembering, that a young person's reputation can be easy to harm but hard to repair. Good child behavior, academics, and civic deeds will win few kudos because all this will simply be expected.

Children's activities that felt new for Millennials will now feel well es-tablished. The child's world will be altered only to meet urgent community needs, not any new inklings of children's needs. In an America locked in

Crisis, no one will be particularly interested in the teen culture, except to chastise anything that offends. As nativism runs its course, the New Silent will be the least immigrant, most English-speaking generation in living memory. Growing up in a time of adult sacrifice and narrowing cultural horizons, the New Silent will develop an earnest and affective temperament, yet feel stuck in a stiflingly parochial social environment.

The New Silent will be treated this way because that will be how middle-aged 13ers will prefer it—and they will be America's dominant Crisis-era nurturers of children. As parents, teachers, and community leaders, 13ers will look back on their Awakening-era childhoods as chaotic, hurried, inse-cure, and underprotected. While 13ers take pride in the firmer, more reliable family life they will establish, New Silent kids will eventually look back on it as a smothering *over*correction. Later in life, they will recall their Crisis-era child's world as having been oversimple, overslowed, overprotected, too grounded in moral cement—and, like the Silent, they will loosen parental authority accordingly.

Like history's other inheritor or postheroic generations, the New Silent will endure constant reminders of what great sacrifices are being made on their behalf. As the Crisis rolls toward its resolution, they will cope with anxiety, fear, and powerlessness. For the rest of their lives, they will never forget these feelings.

TOWARD THE FIRST TURNING

In 1781, as the British troops surrendered at Yorktown, American pipers played the song "The World Turned Upside Down." That was indeed how history appeared to the patriot army phalanxed nearby—and, in later saec-ula, to forces massed at the McLean House in Appomattox or on the deck of the *Missouri*. Having witnessed incredible convulsions of history, these troops presented themselves for one final confirmation of a new dawn. Then it was over. Their society remained mobilized for Crisis, still bristling with war materiel, but now the troops were on their way home to chart different roles in what they hoped would be a calmer new era.

When final treaties were crafted, reparations assessed, punishments meted out, or regencies managed, elders remained to close out the era. Benjamin Franklin did this in Philadelphia and Paris, the radical Republicans in Richmond and Washington, Douglas MacArthur in Asia, and George Marshall in Europe. That much was expected—but if the old priest-warriors kept crusading (as Thaddeus Stevens tried to do with the impeachment of Andrew Johnson), they were ceremoniously but firmly nudged aside. It's an old story: Moses was not allowed to accompany Joshua into the Promised Land.

"No winter lasts forever," Hal Borland has written. "No Spring skips its turn." So is it with the final season of the saeculum. Of the four turnings, none spends its energy more completely than a Crisis, and none has its end more welcomed. In nature, the frigid darkness serves a vital purpose, but only to enable what follows. "Cold is agreeable," said Pascal, "that we may get warm."

If the Crisis catalyst comes on schedule, around the year 2005, then the climax will be due around 2020, the resolution around 2026.

What will America be like as it exits the Fourth Turning?

History offers no guarantees. Obviously, things could go horribly wrong—the possibilities ranging from a nuclear exchange to incurable plagues, from terrorist anarchy to high-tech dictatorship. We should not assume that Providence will always exempt our nation from the irreversible tragedies that have overtaken so many others: not just temporary hardship, but debasement and total ruin. Since Vietnam, many Americans suppose they know what it means to lose a war. Losing in the next Fourth Turning, however, could mean something incomparably worse. It could mean a lasting defeat from which our national innocence—and perhaps even our nation—might never recover. As many Americans know from their own ancestral backgrounds, history provides numerous examples of societies that have been wiped off the map, ground into submission, or beaten so badly they revert to barbarism.

The outcome of the next Fourth Turning will determine the enduring reputation of the Unraveling era in which we now live. In the 1930s, the 1920s were blamed for everything that had gone wrong. After World War II was won, however, Americans began to look back more fondly on those roaring good times. Imagine how the 1920s would have looked in 1950 had the Great Depression never lifted, the Axis prevailed, or both. Now imagine the pre-Crisis 1990s—all its O. J. Simpsons and Michigan militias, its Beavises and Buttheads and Crips and Bloods, its low voter turnouts and anguish over tiny cuts in Medicare's growth—all from the vantage point of America in the year 2030.

If America plunges into an era of depression or violence which by then has not lifted, we will likely look back on the 1990s as the decade when we valued all the wrong things and made all the wrong choices. If the Fourth Turning goes well, however, memories of the Unraveling will be laced with nostalgic fun. More important, a good ending will probably mean that America has taken individual freedoms that now seem socially corrosive and embedded them constructively in a new social order. After the next Fourth Turning has solved the historical problems of our saeculum, many of today's Unraveling-era social problems will be recognizable as worsening symptoms of what had to be—and was—fixed.

In every saeculum, the Awakening gives birth to a variety of individual and social ideals that are mutually incompatible within the framework of the old institutional order. In the Unraveling, the tension between wants and shoulds widens, sours, and polarizes. In the Crisis, a new social contract reconciles these competing principles on a new and potentially higher level of civilization. In the following High, this contract provides the secure platform on which a new social infrastructure can be hoisted. In the parlance of its time, each of the past three Crises resolved aggravating values struggles that had been building up over the prior saeculum. The American Revolution resolved the eighteenth-century struggle between commerce and citizenship. The Civil War resolved the early-nineteenth-century struggle between liberty and equality. The New Deal resolved the industrial-era struggle between capitalism and socialism.

What present-day tensions will the next Fourth Turning resolve? Most likely, they will be Culture Wars updates of the perennial struggle between the individual and the collective—with new labels dating back to our recent Consciousness Revolution. This time, the individual ideal goes under the rubric of "choice": from marketplace choice to lifestyle choice; from choice about manners, appearance, or association to the choice of expression and entertainment. The social ideal goes under the rubric of "community" and points to where all of the various choices must be curtailed if we wish to preserve strong families, secure borders, rising living standards, a healthy environment, and all the other building blocks of a sustainable civilization.

In today's Unraveling, with its mood of pessimism, a reconciliation between these opposing principles seems (and probably is) impossible. But come the Fourth Turning, in the white heat of society's *ekpyrosis* and rebirth, a grand solution may suddenly snap into place. Once a new social contract is written and a new civic order established, it could eradicate (or, at least, narrow) many of the today's seemingly insoluble contradictions—for example, between no-fault divorce and dependable families, poverty assistance and the work ethic, or gun control and personal defense. If the next Fourth Turning concludes successfully, some great leader may be credited with saving individual empowerment by making it compatible with higher ideals of social responsibility—much as FDR was credited with saving capitalism while forging the New Deal and Lincoln with extending liberty while redefining America's nationhood.

This is how a triumphant Fourth Turning can establish a new High, a new golden age, a new plane of American civilization, a workable twenty-first-century redefinition of life, liberty, and the pursuit of happiness.

However sober we must be about the dark possibilities of Crisis, the record of prior Fourth Turnings gives cause for optimism. With five of the past six Crises, it is hard to imagine more uplifting finales. Even after the Civil War, the American faith in progress returned with new robustness. As a people, we have always done best when challenged. The New World still stands as a beacon of hope and virtue for the Old, and we have every reason to believe this can continue.

Whatever the outcome of the Fourth Turning, whatever its *ekpyrosis* and new social contract, by its end the mood of grim determination will feel un-shakable. People will worry about what will happen once the storm clouds pass. As in the months after V-J Day, people will fear that their society might revert to its pre-Crisis chaos—that it could again become like the 1990s, with all that would then entail. But, on the brink of the new turning, they will be amazed at how ingrained their new civic habits have become.

By the mid-2020s, the generational archetypes will be ready for some-thing new. The Fourth Turning will be ready to expire when old Prophets weaken, Nomads tire of public urgency, and Heroes feel hubris. This occurs around the time each archetype stands on the brink of a new life phase:

- The *elder Prophets,* still leading the culture while vacating institutions, now worry about a society whose new materialism they find alien.
- The *midlife Nomads,* sensing that the old crusades have run their course, now plan to fortify community discipline and narrow the scope of personal choice.
- The *young-adult Heroes,* energized by the success of collective action, now want to change society from the outside in.
- The *child Artists,* credulous youths in a world of powerful adults, learn to trust conventions and prepare for ways to help others.

By the middle 2020s, the archetypal constellation will change, as each generation begins entering a new phase of life.

Once the Gray Champion recedes yet again into history, younger people may still respect but will no longer heed the old moral imperatives, having wearied of the cost of principle. If the Crisis ends badly, very old Boomers could be truly despised. If it ends well, they will bask in grand encomia in a new golden era that will resemble the very kind of ordered society in which they were raised as children. Many will seclude themselves deep in the woods or in dusty libraries, exploring ways to bequeath to posterity their fi-nal states of consciousness. Like the "four old men" (Holmes, Longfellow, Whittier, and Lowell) whose portraits graced countless Gilded Era school-rooms, the all-seeing eyes of old Boomer titans will stare down on yet an-other child generation. Recalling what old Susan B. Anthony did for the turn-of-the-century women's movement, a few Boomer antiques will exhort the young to rise against the post-Crisis order and launch another 1960s-style Awakening. Around the year 2050, to the delight of a few lingering ex-flower children straddling age 100, Pepperland will finally recur.

Come the next High, at long last freed of the weight of Boomers, 13ers will be America's new old fogeys, widely perceived as old-fashioned, the only generation still rooted in the mostly forgotten pre-Crisis past. If the Cri-sis ends badly, they might provide the demagogues, authoritarians, even the tribal warlords who try to pick up the pieces. If the Crisis goes well, its 13er generals may well become the U.S. presidents of the next high. Crusty conservatives, they will warn younger generations of the danger of rushing too swiftly in a world rigged with pitfalls. They will force the nation to produce more than it consumes, perhaps through stiff taxes and budget surpluses—exactly the opposite choices from the ones elders made in their own Unraveling-era youth. Under 13er leadership, America will concentrate on building infrastructure and institutions, not on cultural depth or spiritual fervor. In the High, a stingier public treatment of old people will be taken for granted. Despite a rough and neglected elderhood, 13ers will find solace in seeing their children shoot past them in affluence and education.

Of all today's generations, the Millennials probably have the most at stake in the coming Crisis. If it ends badly, they would bear the full burden of its consequence throughout their adult lives. If they come of age traumatized, like the Progressive youths of the Civil War, Millennials will thereafter attend to the details of suffering and healing as heirs to the Artist archetype. Yet if the Crisis ends well, Millennials will gain a triumphant reputation for virtue, valor, and competence. People of all ages will steer them vast fiscal rewards and build them grand monuments. Like the world-conquering G.I.s in midlife, Millennials will feel intensely modern in science and taste. They will construct large new things, establish a powerful social regimen, and indulge their children. When a new Awakening later erupts, the Millennials will for the first time discover a generation that refuses to celebrate them: their own kids, freshly come of age.

A positive ending to the Crisis will craft the New Silent into the romantics, technicians, and aesthetes of an exultant new order. Feeling the emotional strains of their cloistered childhood and postheroic youth, they will sing plaintive songs and tell ironic jokes about the brittle inequities of the new order. Though unable to match the Millennial standard, they will be their able helpmates. If a prosperous new High thrusts mankind deeper into space, the New Silent could well be the first to reach other planets in a rocket fleet launched by the next John Kennedys and piloted by the next Neil Armstrongs.

And if the Crisis ends in triumph, what will come of the splendid new Victory Generation born just after it ends? As children, they will be indulged. As youths, they will revolt against the Millennial-built world. In midlife, they will protect their children from civic decay. As elders, sometime around the year 2100, the Gray Champion will appear yet again among them.

History is seasonal, but its outcomes are not foreordained. Much will depend on how tall we stand in the trials to come. But there is more to do than just wait for that time to come. The course of our national and personal destinies will depend in large measure on what we do now, as a society and as individuals, to prepare.

PART THREE

·

Preparations

CHAPTER 11

■

Preparing for
the Fourth Turning

GIVEN THE GRAVITY OF THE COMING SAECULAR WINTER,
you may be asking, Can anybody do anything about it?

Saith the preacher: To every thing there is a season, and a time to every
purpose under the heaven. In each of the four seasons of life and nature,
there are things a person should and should not do. There is no single style
of behavior, no one maxim of right living, that is appropriate for all ages.
The spring of life can be carefree; its autumn should not be. With land, likewise, there is a time to sow, a time to reap, a time when almost anything will
grow, a time when almost nothing will. If you expect acorns to fall in spring,
or tulips to bloom in autumn, you condemn yourself to frustration.

The same seasonal principle applies to the saeculum. Cyclical time
teaches you not just to accept the rhythms of history, but to look for ways to
make use of them, to fulfill your role in those rhythms as best you can. It is
an antidote to fatalism. If you wish to get more out of life (or nature), you
have the power to do that, but it takes work. You and your society have the
power to influence history, but that takes work too—and, always, your efforts must be appropriate for the time. A common modern reaction is to seek
to avoid harsh seasons altogether. Whether facing old age or winter, many
of us look for a bridge or a wall or a cure, anything that can keep unwanted
seasons from interfering with our fixed purpose. That's the essence of linear thinking. If you follow that strategy, you had better be right; if not, you
could find yourself totally flattened when times turn hard.

The recent anxiety that America is "on the wrong track" reflects an un-
ease with linear thinking—and an instinctive sense that a saecular winter is
nearing. That instinct is sound, but seldom reflected by the popular pre-
scriptions or paradigms. Is new thinking required? On the contrary: To prepare for the Fourth Turning, America needs *old* thinking.

As with life or nature, the proper plan for the saeculum is to move with, not against, the seasons. We should

- Participate in *seasonal* activities, by taking advantage of the current turning
- Avoid *postseasonal* behavior, by terminating habits that were appropriate for the prior turning but are not for the current one
- Make *preseasonal* preparations, by trying to anticipate the needs and opportunities of the next turning

MOVING WITH THE SEASONS

To be *seasonal,* America should take maximum advantage of the current Unraveling.

At any phase of life, a person can attend to its needs and engage in its pleasures well or badly. Middle age can be the prime of life or a disappointment. Autumn can be a season of bounty and beauty or of waste and decay. Much as we can experience a good or bad midlife or autumn, a person (or society) can have a good or bad Unraveling.

This is certainly the case today. The diversity and complexity of 1990s-era America are thrilling when intelligently explored. The popular culture at its best is outstandingly creative. New personal technologies are challenging, exciting, and broadly affordable, lending unprecedented access to every crevasse of human knowledge, culture, and experience. Travel to distant lands is relatively safe and broadly permitted. Persons with talent and market leverage can earn and keep enormous sums of money. The economy offers vast quantities of interesting things to consume. We should enjoy and harness all that while we can, because much of it will be less available or feel less pleasurable in the Fourth Turning.

At the same time, there is plenty to guard against. Diversity is producing new racial enclaves. The pop culture at its worst is violent and debasing. New technologies are eroding traditional human interactions, manners, and civic duties. The gap between rich and poor is daunting. America consumes more than it produces and goes ever more deeply into debt. We should avoid and control these excesses now, while realizing that society will address them more fundamentally in the Fourth Turning.

We can try to make the current turning a splendid saecular autumn, but we can't change it into spring. We would be foolish to try to eradicate all the vices of an Unraveling while still in an Unraveling. We just can't do it.

To avoid being *postseasonal,* America should stop Awakening-era behavior.

In midlife, a person is expected to relinquish youth. The maxim "act your age" applies to middle-aged people who behave in ways that might be all right for younger people but not for them. A reckless naïveté can be charming in a twenty-five-year-old, but not in a person twice that age. In nature, a farmer should not let corn go unharvested past its time, because the rains are no longer nourishing and will now cause it to decay. Similarly, an Unraveling-era society must let go of old habits that made sense twenty years ago but no longer do.

The year 1997 is not 1979, and we should not pretend that it is. A stock joke of the 1990s is how ridiculous people look in photos taken in the 1970s. Beyond clothes and haircuts, most Americans have substantially redirected their lives since the Consciousness Revolution. If parents, professors, or employers try to treat children, students, or young workers in ways that made sense in the 1960s, they would succeed only in looking eccentric—and trigger perverse reactions. If today's Congress tried to behave like the "Great 89th," it would be greeted by hoots of derision from a public that today reserves the word *great* for few things other than a pro sports play-off.

Whenever public figures do something that conjures up the prior turning, they fail—often spectacularly. In the High, when MacArthur wanted to cross the Yalu and widen the Korean War, the president and public wanted none of it, because the time for total war had passed. Joe McCarthy was eventually censured by a citizenry that a decade earlier had tolerated the imprisonment without trial of Japanese-American pseudo-enemies. The same thing happened during the Awakening. LBJ's Vietnam brain trust pursued a global containment strategy and a Selective Service channeling policy that Americans supported in the High but now rejected. In the early 1950s, politicians could ruin people's careers by accusing them of disloyalty, but in the early 1970s Spiro Agnew's attacks on nonconformists only enhanced their careers and hastened the ruin of his. And consider President Nixon: From his constant appeals to a "Silent Majority" to his closet profanities to his famous image of walking on the beach in a suit, he was a saecular anachronism, a First Turning man trying to lead a Second Turning nation.

In the current Unraveling era, many people have paid dearly for postseasonal behavior. Gary Hart's political career ended over a dalliance far less serious than the Chappaquiddick incident that Ted Kennedy's career survived in 1969. Bob Packwood had to resign from the Senate when his critics applied Unraveling-era standards to revelations about his Awakening-era behavior. Joycelin Elders lost her surgeon generalship for comments many in the media would have praised two decades earlier. Calvin Klein had to withdraw jeans ads flaunting an adolescent sexuality that would have seemed tame in the 1970s. The Clintons' 1994 proposal to create a vast new federal health-care edifice conjured up Johnson's 1964 proposals for Medicare and Medicaid. LBJ's plans were seasonal and sailed through, but Clinton's were postseasonal and crashed.

To be *preseasonal,* America should prepare now for the Fourth Turning.

Wise fifty-five-year-olds save money and preserve good health habits. Realizing that old age must come, they do what they can to make it a good time of life, not a scourge of poverty and infirmity. In autumn, wise farmers prepare against an early and hard winter. They protect their harvest, gather their seeds, and stock their fuel. Similarly, a wise society begins in an Unraveling to guard against the dangers of the coming Crisis.

Even when people do not think seasonally, an instinctive feel for the cyclicality of time can prompt valuable pre-Crisis preparations. In the last Third Turning, amid the complexities of the 1910s and the circuses of the 1920s, the Missionary Generation launched preseasonal trends that greatly aided the nation in the ensuing depression and war. Parents, teachers, and scoutmasters restored order to a child's world. Culture czars cleaned up Hollywood and baseball. Preachers of divergent faiths issued parallel missives against civic decay. Local officials tested new social programs. World War I aside, national officials avoided new debt. None of this was done explicitly to prepare for bad times, but it had that effect—much to America's later advantage.

The Unraveling era prior to the Civil War illustrates how a society can fail to act preseasonally. Through the 1840s and 1850s, the moral preachings of midlife Transcendentals went beyond fixing families and protecting children to trying to win old arguments dating back to the 1830s (their equivalent of the 1960s). Transcendental opinion kept polarizing North and South, with little hint of a common values agenda. Politicians pursued what was quite literally a linear path of procedural compromise, as the slavery debate extended due westward from Missouri to Kansas to the Pacific. Meanwhile, spiritualists accelerated the linear Christian path, fervently proclaiming that the Second Coming was near, just as they did in 1844 when hundreds of thousands of Millerites donned ascension robes and climbed hills and rooftops to receive the Lord. By the late 1850s, aging fanatics of all stripes parlayed their Awakening-era passions into apocalyptic preachings. Thus did the Transcendentals take political and military action that many presumed would right all wrongs and prepare for Christ's rule. Riding under the postseasonal banner of the prior Awakening, the Civil War's Gray Champion rode early, rode hard, and rode destructively.

Preseasonality is as functional as postseasonality is dysfunctional. We admire preseasonal purpose when we see it in people. Indeed, America's best-remembered presidents displayed this in deed or oratory before they were elected. The Crisis-era steadfastness of Washington and Eisenhower foreshadowed the coming Highs, making both generals enormously popular choices for presiding over those eras. In manner and morals, John Kennedy anticipated the Consciousness Revolution. Nearly alone amid the late Awakening's nervous and hysterical clatter, Ronald Reagan had a feel for the self-assured and jaunty Unraveling mood he would later personify. America's two most beloved national saviors each augured Fourth Turnings before these eras arrived—Lincoln in his Douglas debates, FDR in his pre–New Deal policy experiments as governor of New York.

In recent years, many Americans have despaired that their nation no longer produces leaders who can galvanize and inspire. Yet it is the turning, not the nation, that elevates great people to the apex of power. Lincoln and FDR are both cases in point: Both had to wait for the Crisis to hit. An Unraveling is an era when most people of intelligence, vision, and integrity do not seek (much less get elected to) high public offices. Nor is it an era when people want leaders to lead them anywhere. Indeed, 1990s-era Americans seem to care very little about who leads and much more about making sure that we aren't led too fast or too far in any direction. Were candidates of Lincoln's mettle to emerge in a time like our own, they would strike people as odd, out of joint. Voters might admire them, but not enough to elect them—certainly not after the usual Unraveling-era media deconstructions.

Perhaps this is just as well. Were we to elect a Lincoln-like leader before the Fourth Turning is due, we would be following the ominous precedent of Lincoln's own election. Suppose some principled moralist ekes out a year 2000 presidential win in a four-way screaming match. An event like that could catalyze a Crisis early, casting Boomers and 13ers into the same destructive roles once played by the Transcendentals and Gilded. After the Fourth Turning arrives, however, a Lincoln-like leader will be more likely to seek office, and a Lincoln-like leader could be exactly what American needs, wants, and gets.

The national pastime—baseball—offers a similar lesson in seasonality. Each of the last four turnings produced an extraordinary player whose manner was much admired but, being preseasonal, did not yet define the rewarded norm. Lou Gehrig illustrated this before the last Crisis, Joe DiMaggio before the High, Jackie Robinson before the Awakening, Reggie Jackson before the Unraveling, and Cal Ripken now. Ripken's Gehrig-like virtue is distinctly Fourth Turning. Yet while it is admired by many people, it is not the kind of in-your-face, high-stepping, free-agent behavior that still sells most Unraveling-era tickets.

Just as no single style of leadership or hero worship is suitable for every turning, neither do any of today's familiar political philosophies offer the right answer for every turning. People who are for or against a particular policy seldom allow for changes in the saeculum. Whether they want big government or lower taxes, more regulation or less, they tend to hold that view regardless of the era, as though the correct prescription lies outside of time. The political and media elites abet this view. From liberalism and conservatism to socialism and libertarianism, all the popular ideologies are non-seasonal. To the extent their paradigms evolve, they do so linearly, carved around notions of American exceptionalism.

Yet the appeal of these ideologies is very cyclical. Nearly all political philosophies wax and wane with the saeculum. The belief in public-sector liberalism emerged in the last Crisis, rose in the High, crested in the Awakening, and is falling out of favor in the Unraveling. Cultural conservatism has followed the same pattern, though lagged by one turning. (It emerges in Unravelings and crests in Highs.) Interest-group pluralism and free-market libertarianism follow yet a different pattern. Since both of these -isms exalt rights over duties, they crested in the last Unraveling (1920s), fell out of favor in the last Crisis (1930s), reemerged in the High (1950s), rose in the Awakening (1970s), and are cresting again in the current Unraveling (1990s). Nearly every static ideology is likely to advance in one turning per saeculum (when what it offers is preseasonal and useful) and retreat in another (when what it offers is postseasonal and harmful).

In the current Unraveling, pluralism and free markets are both very popular. The seasonal rhythm implies that the popularity of both is now cresting. Were America back in the High, preseasonal thinking would suggest pushing for *more* of both. Today, however, preseasonal thinking suggests preparing for *less* of both—since, come the Fourth Turning, America will no longer be as hospitable to we-first lobbies and me-first free agents. As the saeculum turns, their day will ultimately come again, albeit not until the middle of the twenty-first century.

Seasonal blindness afflicts proponents of countless well-known causes. Whether feminists or right-to-lifers, the ACLU or NRA, supply siders or the civil rights establishment, single-issue champions persistently demand unilinear progress toward a fixed programmatic goal. In a seasonal world, such efforts lead to inevitable self-deception and frustration. In some eras these causes take credit for progress that was mostly due to come anyway. In other eras they despair over backsliding which really isn't their fault, either. Through the last three saecula, most liberationist social causes (like feminism or civil rights) tend to seed in a High, blossom in an Awakening, mature in an Unraveling, and decay in a Crisis. Yet today, many of their proponents keep struggling for postseasonal goals: They seek more Awakening-era passion in the midst of a gathering Unraveling-era cynicism. It is as though, by dint of sheer will, they could force tiger lilies to bloom in the November woods.

To cut through linear doctrines, Americans need to reappraise their opinions of the recent turnings. Many people bear grudges against a decade they recall unfavorably. For some this is the 1950s, for others the 1960s, for still others the 1980s. These unfavorable memories reflect a negative judgment of (respectively) the High, Awakening, or Unraveling—as though the era in question ought never to have happened. Such judgments are misplaced. None of those turnings (or decades) had to be exactly what it was, but each was a phase of history America had to transit. What we remember as the 1960s could have been altered—perhaps made better, perhaps worse. Yet even with the altering we would only have experienced a better or worse 1960s, not a repeat of the 1950s or a hastening of the 1980s. The American High did not require institutional racism or sexism, but it did require a social stasis. The Consciousness Revolution did not require a Vietnam War or Watergate, but it did require a youth revolt and cultural experimentation. Today's Unraveling does not require profane media or endless budget deficits, but it does require individualism and institutional decay. A Fourth Turning does not require economic depression or civil war, but it does require public sacrifice and political upheaval.

Neither of the two major political parties has been adept at seasonalist thinking. The Republicans were worse at figuring out what the early Awakening required, the Democrats worse at the early Unraveling. With the Fourth Turning roughly a decade away, each party now has it half right: Democrats have seized the saeculum's autumnal instinct to harvest, Republicans the instinct to prune and scatter. Each party is usefully pressing for some preseasonal policies: Democrats wish to close the gap between rich and poor, reverse the decline of the middle class, and expand children's programs—while Republicans want to de-fund time-encrusted bureaucracies, restore an ethic of personal responsibility, and promote traditional virtues.

Yet both parties are also harmfully postseasonal. In their quest for an ever bigger harvest, Democrats want to remove sacrifice ever further from the public lexicon. They seek entitlements for every victim, including the entire middle class, without caring whether all this guaranteed consumption is sustainable. If Democrats get their way, they would impose huge debts and future taxes on Millennial children. In their quest for ever more individualism, Republicans want to make public authority ever more dysfunctional. They seek to starve all government of revenue and are willing to shut down whole federal agencies to make their point. If Republicans get their way, they would prevent Millennials from forging a positive bond with government and limit the public resources directed toward the care and schooling of the neediest children.

Although both parties cater rhetorically to Millennial children, both are blind to what the saeculum reveals about them. Democrats who praise G.I. seniors' wartime heroism don't reflect on what example of sacrifice must be provided to infuse *team spirit* in a new generation, while Republicans who admire the G.I.s' senior citizenship don't reflect on what image of government must be reinforced to infuse *civic spirit* in the young.

Suppose both parties continue down their linear paths through what remains of the Unraveling. If so, Democrats will remain usefully linked with civic authority, but in a paradigm so oriented around a harvest mentality that it precludes any across-the-board sacrifice for a significant public purpose.

Picture them in charge when the Crisis catalyzes and an urgent need arises to shatter old consumption promises and ask voters to give up something. They would seem to be exactly the wrong party to command an imperiled citizenry. Alternatively, suppose Republicans keep to course, still usefully linked with sacrifice but in a paradigm so beset with individualism as to preclude effective civic mobilization for any purpose. Picture Republicans in charge when a sudden Crisis prompts an urgent need for rejuvenated public authority to achieve a new national purpose. If this happens, they would seem to be exactly the wrong party to command a strengthening government.

Come the Fourth Turning, America will need both personal sacrifice *and* public authority. The saeculum will favor whichever party moves more quickly and persuasively toward a paradigm that accommodates both. Both parties should lend seasonality to their thinking: Democrats a concept of civic duty that limits the harvest, Republicans a concept of civic authority that limits the scattering. If they do not, the opportunity will arise for a third party to fill the void—after which one or both of today's two dominant parties could go the way of the Whigs.

History warns that when a Crisis catalyzes, a previously dominant political party (or regime) can find itself directly blamed for perceived "mistakes" that led to the national emergency. Whoever holds power when the Fourth Turning arrives could join the unlucky roster of the circa 1470 Lancastrians, circa 1570 Catholics, circa 1680 Stuarts, circa 1770 Tories, circa 1860 Democrats, and circa 1929 Republicans. That party could find itself out of power for a generation. Key persons associated with it could find themselves defamed, stigmatized, harassed, economically ruined, personally punished—or worse.

HOW AMERICA SHOULD PREPARE

Complaints about the loss of civic virtue date back to the dawn of civilization. The most eloquent commentaries on the ideal of personal sacrifice to the community (whether a polis, a kingdom, or a superpower nation) typically arise just when people see the ideal slipping away. That much is well known. What's less well known is this: Such complaints nearly always specify that the steepest loss is of relatively recent origin. Read any of the great moralists, from Cicero and Cato the Elder to Burke and Bolingbroke, and notice how they all harken back to a time within living memory when civic giants strode the earth. American jeremiads on declining public spirit, whether voiced by a Daniel Webster or a Ross Perot, never identify the lost paragon with any era farther back than the critic's own childhood.

If civic virtue is so frequently lost, it must be just as frequently regained. This is what happens in a Fourth Turning. While a Crisis mood renders so-

cieties newly desperate, it also renders them newly capable, which is why a
saecular winter is to be welcomed as much as feared. As today's Americans
look ahead, the challenge is to marshal the coming season's new public energies to achieve positive, not destructive ends. The better we ready ourselves collectively, the more likely we will be not just to survive the Crisis
but to apply its fury for good and humane purposes.

To prepare for the Fourth Turning, America can apply the lessons of seasonality. The following suggestions distinguish between actions that the nation can act on now, in the Unraveling, and those that are simply not possible
before the Crisis catalyzes.

- *Prepare values:* Forge the consensus and uplift the culture, but
  don't expect near-term results.

America's culture warriors need not worry whether values will return to
public life. They always do in a Fourth Turning—with a vengeance.
Speeches will become public sermons; schools, civic churches; and art, mo-
tivational propaganda. The open questions are *which* values will reign and
whether America's cultural consensus will be broad and imaginative enough
to avoid a destructive polarization as the nation fights for its survival. People on all sides of the Culture Wars should cultivate pragmatic alliances with
niches possessing competing visions. Americans of all generations should
work to elevate moral and cultural standards. What we do now may not close
down many Unraveling-era carnivals, but will serve two critical longer-term
purposes: to help protect the world of childhood and to help resacralize public institutions and reinfuse them with a much-needed sense of public purpose. A decadent or nihilistic culture is a seedbed for fascism. The less
self-control the media or public exercises now, the more likely it becomes
that some outside authority will impose a despotic control tomorrow.

- *Prepare institutions:* Clear the debris and find out what works,
  but don't try building anything big.

The Fourth Turning will trigger a political upheaval beyond anything
Americans could today imagine. New civic authority will have to take root,
quickly and firmly—which won't be easy if the discredited rules and rituals
of the old regime remain fully in place. We should shed and simplify the
federal government in advance of the Crisis by cutting back sharply on its
size and scope, but without imperiling its core infrastructure. Meanwhile,
we should turn state and local governments into competitive policy labs that
test new solutions to vexing societal problems. Come the Crisis, local experiments will provide the experience base for swift national action. All levels of government should prune the legal, regulatory, and professional
thickets that stymie institutional change. They should also thin out the pro-

cedural requirements that could delay or weaken emergency measures. Courts should avoid erecting constitutional obstacles to legislative action or executive fiat; these would just get in the way when the mood becomes urgent. By delaying effective action, courts could in fact encourage an authoritarian overreaction.

- *Prepare politics:* Define challenges bluntly and stress duties over rights, but don't attempt reforms that can't now be accomplished.

When the Fourth Turning catalyzes, many Americans will regret having faced up to so few national problems during the Unraveling, when time and resources were so plentiful. At the same time, people will appreciate whatever modest progress we do make today. To prevent further civic decay, politicians should speak very candidly about the nation's future challenges and craft a new rhetoric of public purpose that emphasizes collective duties over personal rights. Politicians who do this will help stem the downward slide of cynicism, negative campaigning, and apathy. They will help expand voter turnout among the young, encourage better civic attitudes from the media, and keep the public at least minimally engaged in public life. Come the Crisis, these politicians will be best situated to take charge and become great leaders—however lukewarm their support will have been during the Unraveling. Meanwhile, we should accept that fundamental reforms are not now possible. We should not bother attempting vast civic projects in an Unraveling: If proposed, they will not pass; if passed, they will not work; and if forced upon the public, they will only breed further contempt for politics.

- *Prepare society:* Require community teamwork to solve local problems, but don't try this on a national scale.

Come the Fourth Turning, national survival will require a level of public teamwork and self-sacrifice far higher than Americans now provide. From urban graffiti to suburban NIMBYism, today's anticivic habits must either be discouraged piecemeal now or be broken violently on the wheel of history tomorrow. We must battle against civic dysfunction wherever it appears. Compulsory youth service is coming: Though we cannot enact it today, we should start experimenting in ways that allow liberals and conservatives to work toward a consensus on the civic apprenticeship of the young. Among people of all ages, we need to reinvent good citizenship at the local level. Communities should improve their own functions (schools, housing, transportation, safety, justice, social services) with their own resources, without expecting money from anywhere else. Towns and cities should create public spaces, hold public meetings, and expect citizens to attend. We should encourage ethnic integration and discourage group niching (from walled suburban enclaves to monoethnic college dorms). In the Crisis, national survival could depend on how well people of diverse backgrounds succeed in forging a new sense of civic community.

- *Prepare youth:* Treat children as the nation's highest priority, but don't do their work for them.

The outcome of the Fourth Turning may depend on the mettle of the generation then coming of age—and on whether, as children, this generation will have developed powerful team instincts, a positive connection to public activity, and a sense of optimism about its future. To raise youths who will be able and willing to do whatever is required, we must bear any expense to nurture them properly. The federal government should start now to shift its benefit budget away from the nonneedy old and toward the needy young. Local governments should forge a community consensus in generous support of schools. In cooperation with norm-setting youth groups and churches, school boards should set high standards of achievement and conduct, teach community values, enforce norms of appearance and manners, and empower the student mass by keeping high- and low-achievers with their fellows. Spending on safety nets and social services for children in need should increase, but the focus must be entirely on the welfare of the child; irresponsible parents must be called strictly to account. The Millennial Generation is Unraveling-era America's most important investment priority—and should be treated as such.

- *Prepare elders:* Tell future elders they will need to be more self-sufficient, but don't attempt deep cuts in benefits to current elders.

Not far into the Fourth Turning, today's long-term projections for Social Security, Medicare, and other elder benefits programs will lie in history's dust bin. The economy will not keep growing as smoothly as the actuaries now assume—and critical events will force the government to reshuffle all its spending priorities. At that point, no one will be entitled to anything; those in need will merely be *authorized* something. Public figures should alert today's working Americans to their vulnerability. People should be urged to save *much* more of their current income and be allowed to shift some of their FICA contributions into fully funded plans whose liabilities cannot burden future taxpayers. For employee pensions, all levels of government (including the military) should shift from defined benefits plans to defined contributions plans, ending the buildup of still more unfunded liabilities. Some public benefits (particularly in health care) will have to be trimmed even before the Crisis arrives. G.I. senior citizens should be largely spared from such cuts. But younger people (including the Silent who have yet to retire) should brace for a more self-reliant old age, with fewer subsidies from poorer younger workers.

■ *Prepare the economy:* Correct fundamentals, but don't try to fine
   tune current performance.

During the Crisis, the American economy will experience the most extreme shocks to asset values, production, employment, price levels, and industrial structure in living memory. The economy may also, at some point,
be pushed to the breaking point in order to produce the tools necessary to
save the nation and, later, the infrastructure that will underlie the next saeculum. During the rest of the Unraveling, we should encourage high-tech innovation and competition to develop the best technologies for ultimate
deployment. Now is not yet the time to deploy them—or to practice industrial policy by picking winners and losers. We must also try to raise the national savings rate. By foolishly overconsuming during a current era that
many demographers call a fiscal Indian Summer, America is now on track
to be overwhelmed by unfunded retirement obligations at just the worst moment—as the Crisis is closing in. To raise private-sector savings, we should
shift the tax base from income toward consumption and mandate personal
and portable pension plans for every worker. To raise public-sector savings,
we should aim not just for federal budget balance, but for budget surplus as
soon as possible. America would be wise to risk a Third Turning recession,
if need be, to help alleviate the risk (or at least mitigate the severity) of a
Fourth Turning depression.

■ *Prepare the defense:* Expect the worst and prepare to mobilize,
   but don't precommit to any one response.

It is typical of an Unraveling for a society to be complacent about the
threat of war—and to expect that isolation, diplomacy, massive superiority,
and simple goodwill can keep it (and the world) out of serious trouble. Today, America's prevailing military doctrine is shaped by the so-called
lessons of Vietnam, which presume all of the above. But before the Fourth
Turning catalyzes, America should gird for something else: a possible war
whose scale, cost, manpower, armaments, casualties, and homefront sacrifices far exceed anything the nation would tolerate now. In the trials to
come, we will receive scant help from transnational bureaucracies, but major help from allies who share our fundamental interests. Present-day diplomatic energies (and foreign aid) should be directed accordingly. We should
invest heavily in R&D oriented toward future dangers now only dimly foreseen, maintain diverse defense infrastructures in good function (capable of
expanding swiftly as the need arises), and retain the ability to remilitarize
surplus domestic properties and overseas bases. We should not overspecial-
ize manpower or overinvest in deployments (like robot weapons and extrav-
agant information technology) which, when the Crisis climaxes, could be

cheaply rendered as obsolete as the Maginot Line. Had America built a huge navy and air force in the 1920s, those procurements could have impaired the nation's ability to build newer and better forces after Pearl Harbor, thereby putting the entire war effort at risk.

Some of these suggestions may appear rather modest given the magnitude of the challenges America will soon face. But that is all the current season will allow. In an Unraveling, it would be pointless (indeed, even counter-productive) to try sounding the full-throated trumpet of national action. Yet we owe it to ourselves and our children to do our best to carry out those less glorious measures for which now *is* the season. To the extent we do not, the Crisis of the Fourth Turning will be that much more destructive.

The prospect that, as a nation, we might *not* prepare makes it all the more important for individuals to prepare on their own.

HOW YOU SHOULD PREPARE

Reflect on what happens when a terrible winter blizzard strikes. You hear the weather warning but probably fail to act on it. The sky darkens. Then the storm hits with full fury, and the air is a howling whiteness. One by one, your links to the machine age break down. Electricity flickers out, cutting off the TV. Batteries fade, cutting off the radio. Phones go dead. Roads become impassable, and cars get stuck. Food supplies dwindle. Day-to-day vestiges of modern civilization—bank machines, mutual funds, mass retailers, computers, satellites, airplanes, governments—all recede into irrelevance. The storm strips you bare, reducing your world to a small number of elemental forces—some bad, others good. On the bad side are the elements of nature. On the good are whatever scraps of social cohesion you can muster, from your own family's survival skills to neighbors who pitch in and share, to a family who lends you a truck-mounted plow because you once helped them out in a pinch.

Picture yourself and your loved ones in the midst of a howling blizzard that lasts for several years. Think about what you would need, who could help you, and why your fate might matter to anybody other than yourself. That is how to plan for a saecular winter.

Don't think you can escape the Fourth Turning the way you might today distance yourself from news, national politics, or even taxes you don't feel like paying. History warns that a Crisis will reshape the basic social and economic environment that you now take for granted. The Fourth Turning necessitates the death and rebirth of the social order. It is the ultimate rite of passage for an entire people, requiring a liminal state of sheer chaos whose nature and duration no one can predict in advance. It could involve episodes of social dislocation (and enforced migration), total mobilization (and youth conscription), economic breakdown (and mass joblessness), communications blackouts (and household isolation), or social breakdown (and committees of public safety). Most likely, it will involve more than one of these elements.

As in a blizzard, simple but fundamental verities will reemerge. These are the familiar elements of legend and myth that have endured over time simply because they are required in times of peril. Classic virtues that didn't necessarily pay off in an Unraveling (traits like trust, reliability, patience, perseverance, thrift, and selflessness) will become hard currency in a Crisis. Were history not seasonal, these virtues would have long since atrophied, vanished from memory as useless to humanity. They remain in our tradition because, once every saeculum, they are reaffirmed in full glory, rewarding those who embrace them and penalizing those who do not. In the epic sagas of social peril, from *Beowulf* to *Victory at Sea,* notice who prevails and what values they possess. Come the Crisis, *these* are the myths you will want to emulate, and *these* will be the values you will need to display.

To prepare yourself for the Fourth Turning, you would do well to apply the following lessons of seasonality.

■ *Rectify:* Return to the classic virtues.

In the coming Crisis, sharp distinctions will be drawn between people who can be counted on and those who cannot. Build a reputation as a person of honor and integrity who values self-restraint, family commitments, cultural decency, and mutual trust. Be a good citizen in your town, a good neighbor on your block, a good work partner on the job. Be mannerly and adhere to public standards of conduct. Expect your community reputation to matter far more than it does now. The Fourth Turning will not be kind to the free agent (or organization) with a reputation for discarding loyalties, revising settled deals, or pressing every point of leverage. The more your bottom line is interwoven with other people's (and your community's), the more helpful these other people (and public officials) will be in an emergency. Expect to be dealt with according to the reputation of your group. Regardless of your current institutional advantage, if your business is perceived as predatory, your profession as parasitical, or your influence as corrupting, then you will personally be at risk.

■ *Converge:* Heed emerging community norms.

In a Fourth Turning, the nation's core will matter more than its diversity. *Team, brand,* and *standard* will be new catchwords. Anyone and anything not describable in those terms could be shunted aside—or worse. Do not isolate yourself from community affairs. Being "unplugged" could penalize you at a time you might need to know what all levels of government are doing just to meet your most basic of needs. Appearances will matter. Justice will be rough, because society will require more order but have fewer resources and less time to impose it. As technicalities give way, innocent people will suffer. If you don't want to be misjudged, don't act in a way that might provoke Crisis-era authority to deem you guilty. If you belong to a racial or ethnic minority, brace for a nativist backlash from an assertive (and possibly authoritarian) majority. At the height of Crisis, you might have to choose between loyalty to the national community and loyalty to your own group. Isolating yourself from people of other races or ethnicities could be risky, because you may need emergency help from people you might now be able to avoid.

■ *Bond:* Build personal relationships of all kinds.

When the Crisis hits, anonymity will be associated with discredited Unraveling-era vices—and feared. Direct personal linkages will be newly valued. Know the people who can help you. In the Fourth Turning, having well-positioned friends could be very important. High-level (institutional) corruption may recede, but low-level (personal) dealing could flourish as people seek ad hoc official favors to meet the most basic and urgent of needs. The marketplace will apply similar rules. Face-to-face contacts with everyone (neighbors, bosses, employees, customers, suppliers, creditors, debtors, public officials, police) will become newly important. Expect a loss of personal privacy. Fourth Turnings can be dark times for the free spirit: Just as one kind of official may have new authority to do something *for* you, another kind—some hastily deputized magistrate—may have new authority to do something *to* you.

■ *Gather:* Prepare yourself (and your children) for teamwork.

In the Fourth Turning, the rewards will grow for people with a reputation for accepting authority and working well in teams. Integrate your skills, works, and pastimes with those of others. Stress less what sets you apart as an individual, and more what you have in common with others. In business, move toward structures that combine teams and hierarchies, using technology (including computers) as tools to bring people together. Raise children to excel at team virtues. Don't track kids out of the mainstream. Where public schools work, you should educate them there, so they can learn group skills among peers of diverse backgrounds and abilities. Expect children to develop a powerful connection with government. Your children may be inducted as they come of age, perhaps into circumstances of real danger. This is cause for worry, certainly—but given the uplifted status of youth, it should also be cause for pride and hope.

■ *Root:* Look to your family for support.

When the Fourth Turning arrives, your family will become your ultimate safety net. Maintain relationships of trust with your extended family, from grandparents to grandchildren, in-laws to distant cousins. As other supports weaken, your household will function best if it is multigenerational, with young and old caring for each other's special needs. At the height of Crisis, being a young retiree (or living far from other family members) could pose new hardships. A wealthy elder might consider transferring as many assets as possible to heirs during the Unraveling, thereby avoiding the risk of confiscatory estate taxation later on. If you have no spouse or children, you should develop an alternative family-like support network among friends, neighbors, and co-workers. The Fourth Turning will not be a good time to be, or feel, socially stranded.

■ *Brace:* Gird for the weakening or collapse of public support mechanisms.

During the Fourth Turning, today's generous government supply of senior benefits (cash, health, housing, and social services) could erode sharply. Youth, not age, will be the target of civic action and reward. Unless you expect your income and wealth to be low enough to pass a means test, you should discount U.S. government promises about the reliability of Social Security, Medicare, and Medicaid, and perhaps even public employee pensions. Any of these could turn out to be no more reliable than earlier promises about Continental and Confederate Dollars. You should start at once to build your own financial security. You should save plenty of money, even if that means cutting back on your current lifestyle. The best way to guarantee good health care in old age is to practice good health habits today. Expect a new triage in health care rules, and don't count on anybody else paying for the residue of your Unraveling-era bad habits. Discuss with your family how the burdens of old age would be shouldered if and when public assistance becomes unavailable. Prepare for the hard choices you could face in the Fourth Turning by reflecting on what your life (and death) will someday mean to others.

■ *Hedge:* Diversify everything you do.

Once the Crisis catalyzes, anything can happen. If you are starting a career now, realize that generalists with survival know-how will have the edge over specialists whose skills are useful only in an undamaged environment. Be fluent in as many languages, cultures, and technologies as you can. Your business could face a total alteration of market conditions: Expect public subsidies to vanish, the regulatory environment to change quickly, and new trade barriers to arise. Avoid leveraged investments or long-term debt, including massive student debt. Assume that all your external safety nets (pensions, Social Security, Medicare) could end up totally shredded. Invest heavily in equities to profit while you can during the remainder of the Unraveling, but stay alert to the public mood. Keep in mind that the closer we get to the Fourth Turning, the greater will be the risk of a Great Devaluation. Hedge your portfolio and include assets in foreign markets where the saecular rhythms do not appear to coincide with America's. Enter the Crisis with a reliable cash flow, diversified savings, and some liquid assets. Really *know* where your money is. Try to ensure that no one severe outcome (inflation, deflation, market crash, bank panic, default on the national debt) would destroy your entire asset base.

If you apply these lessons, you would be risking little. Suppose you're lucky, and the Crisis doesn't touch you much personally. By having prepared for it, you may have lost some short-term income or pleasure, but nothing of lasting consequence. Suppose you're not so lucky. If you haven't prepared, you will have put much at risk. History warns that saecular winters can be searing times for everyone, especially for those who are caught entirely by surprise. No matter what your age, sex, income, race, family status, or line of work, sensible choices today could help you avoid truly desperate choices in the Fourth Turning.

GENERATIONAL SCRIPTS

In ancient Rome, it was understood that most people could expect to witness the secular games once in a lifetime. Some would encounter it in *senectus,* others in *viritas, iuventus,* or *pueritia.* The phase of life in which people experienced the games permanently marked their location in Roman history.

The same is true of generations. Each archetype traverses the four saecular seasons along a path resembling a one-year voyage through the four natural seasons. Since the winter reaches each archetype at a different phase of life, it fits differently within each of their respective life-cycle dramas. Accordingly, the Fourth Turning lends each archetype its own script.

Within these scripts, each archetype confronts its shadow in the Crisis, and each finds itself in a position to provide society with an attribute that felt lacking in the turning of its own childhood. The Prophet, born in the

High, seeks vision; the Nomad, born in the Awakening, seeks realism; the Hero, born in the Unraveling, seeks power; and the Artist, born in the (prior or current) Crisis, seeks empathy.

Into and through the next Fourth Turning, America's generational constellation will change dramatically. Among today's living generations, important demographic changes can be expected to occur between 2005 and 2026. The *G.I.s* will be nearly gone, leaving them with a purely ancestral role. Of all the G.I.s who ever lived, only 1 in 8 will survive to see the Crisis catalyze, 1 in 250 (all centenarians) to see its resolution. The *Silent* will have the frustrating role of bearing incomplete witness to the epic event of their adult experience. Of all the Silent who ever lived, 3 in 5 will survive to see the Fourth Turning begin, only 1 in 5 to see it end. About 5 of 6 *Boomers* will be alive for the catalyst, 2 in 3 for the resolution. The overwhelming majority of *13ers* will live to witness the end of the Fourth Turning. They will enter the Crisis as America's largest generation, but leave it eclipsed by two others. By the end of the Crisis, the *Millennials* will be America's largest generation of voters.

If today's generations follow the historical pattern, the following national leadership changes can be expected: At the Crisis catalyst, the Silent will be out of authority, Boomers will be nearing their peak of power, 13ers will be rapidly ascending, and Millennials will be fledgling voters and soldiers. When the Crisis resolves, the Silent will have no power, Boomers on the brink of a steep descent, 13ers near their peak, Millennials rapidly ascending, and the New Silent just starting to vote and join the military.

As individuals, most of us have little power to help America weather the coming Crisis. Yet as members of generations, our power is far greater. Remember the core dynamic of the saeculum: *History shapes generations, and generations shape history.*

G.I. Script

The Hero does not look forward to passing on during an Unraveling, an era of disintegration for the social order he once constructed. It is the Hero's late-in-life frustration to see so many problems fester and younger people unable to fix them. The Hero must accept that he may never know what the next Crisis will be, nor how it will resolve. However, he can take solace in knowing it will happen when the Hero's shadow (the Prophet) plunges society into an era of emergency like the one in which the Hero himself once thrived. Yet the Hero gains no comfort from this. Finding the temperament of the younger Prophet too self-centered, he fails to understand how this temperament is needed to raise a child Hero whose power and virtue can someday match his own.

The G.I.s' script requires them to move beyond the residue of their old

Awakening-era quarrel with Boomers. G.I.s need to find in Boomers the spirit of their sires—and in Millennials the scoutlike virtue of their own child selves. G.I.s should welcome the Boomer style as necessary to raise children who can someday soldier a Crisis as well as they soldiered World War II. To do that, however, G.I.s must allow Boomers to secure a place in public life for Millennial children. That, in turn, requires the G.I.s to accept that the well-being of Millennials (and not of themselves) must be government's highest Unraveling-era priority.

Alone among the adult archetypes, G.I.s possess the civic virtue that America will need to triumph in the Fourth Turning. They know better than anyone else the degree of public sacrifice that will be required. However, their post-Awakening separation from the Boomer-led culture has diminished the G.I. reputation for selflessness, eroded the national memory of their youthful valor, and served as an excuse for them to shed their original notions of duty and sacrifice. To prepare America for the Fourth Turning, G.I.s must reestablish their reputation among the young by reverting to the old Depression-era substance of their civic virtue (the community-first attitude) and rejecting its late-life variant (the we-first attitude). Younger generations will never compel G.I.s to give up their Hero reward. By agreeing to relinquish some unneeded portion of it, however, G.I.s could transform themselves from senior citizens to *citizen seniors*, able to speak to the young with renewed authority about the need to arrest the current decay of civic behavior.

If G.I.s fail at this script, the America they once saved will be weakened. Lacking resources and civic nurture, Millennial children might not grow up with enough of that legendary "right stuff" to triumph in the Fourth Turning. The G.I.s, who put the sword back in the stone after V-J Day, have waited four generations for a child to arrive who could pull it out again. That time is nearing. If G.I.s see this and apply their script well, they can die believing, as Sir Thomas Malory wrote of King Arthur: *Hic Iacet Arthurus, Rex Quondam, Rexque Futurus* (Here lies Arthur, who was once King, and King will be again).

Silent Script

Having witnessed the last Crisis as an anxious child, the Artist will approach the next one as an anxious elder. He will see its catalyst and feel its mood shift but will probably pass away before learning how it turns out. In the Fourth Turning, therefore, the Artist must disengage and refrain from interfering as other archetypes do their necessary work. In an Unraveling, the old Artist sees little of his own empathic quality in the Nomad who (he fears) will ignorantly shatter his own achievements. The Artist may even worry that refinement and sensitivity are themselves dying with him. He is unaware that a new Artist archetype is soon to be reborn in the Fourth Turning, nurtured by the Nomad to possess exactly the traits the old Artist wishes to preserve.

In the Fourth Turning, the Silent will be fading from power, with less chance to act than to veto (or, as always, to entangle) the actions of others. Their vestigial powers will reside mainly in courtrooms. If they block the Next New Deal, Silent jurists would follow in the Crisis-aggravating saecular footsteps of Roger Taney in the 1850s and the "nine old men" in the 1930s. They should avoid intruding on the moral judgments of Boomer legislatures and avoid using detail, complexity, and delay to stifle the recrudescence of civic authority. Crisis-era antagonisms will not be amenable to being smoothed over, and warring sides will refuse mediation. Decisions will not be improved by adding new layers of procedure, and urgent problems will not await further study. The Silent should defer to the 13er view that experts can be dead wrong, that professional elites can stumble over simple choices, and that kind intentions do not always produce kind results. As the Crisis deepens, 13er-style survivalism will trump Silent-style procedural democracy every time.

Through the remainder of the Unraveling, however, a Silent dose of what the Progressive Generation's Ella Wheeler Wilcox called "just the art of being kind" could usefully help America prepare for the challenges ahead. With measured checks and balances, the Silent can artfully deflect Boomer anger and challenge 13er apathy, preventing those two generations from imprudently plunging America into dangerous rapids before the Fourth Turning arrives. At the turn of the Millennium, the election of an empathic Silent president might stretch out the Unraveling era just long enough to restrain Boomers and 13ers from engaging their worst instincts until both have had a chance to mature further. Once the Crisis catalyzes, however, the time for Silent leadership will expire.

Though eager to mentor youth personally, the Silent should realize that Millennials are not like 13ers and are even less like Boomers. The rising generation will not want to expand the frontier of individualism and introspection. They will want the opposite—teamwork and construction. The child's world is just now recovering from what Silent parents, educators, and pop-culture leaders did to it back in the Awakening in the name of reform. Millennial nurture depends on this change continuing. The kindest thing the Silent can do for Millennials is to be the helpmate. Perhaps, by dint of their smaller numbers, the Silent can sneak through unnoticed with a G.I.-style elder reward. But by acceding gracefully to requests that they relinquish some of their late-life public reward, the Silent could prove that good intentions *can* make a difference, that nice people *can* alter history.

If the Silent play their script badly, they will end their lives like Webster, Clay, and Calhoun, fearing that the national greatness hoisted by others in their childhood will pass away with them. If they apply their script well, however, they can go into history's good night like those who reached their eighties in the Great Depression, old Progressives like Louis Brandeis and John Dewey, who (in the latter's words) remained "committed to an end that is at once enduring and flexible."

Boomer Script

The Fourth Turning brings special meaning to the Prophet, because the seasons of the saeculum exactly match those of his own life. From spring to winter, history's seasons are those of his life cycle as well. Where the Prophet's shadow (the Hero) had his greatest trial young, the Prophet will find his in old age. To achieve late-life glory, the Prophet must harness the civic duty and skill of the old Hero (whom he rewards but does not honor) and child Hero (whose temperament he nurtures but does not understand). In the current Unraveling, though, the Prophet is damaging the civic culture created by the old Hero, thereby making it harder for the child Hero to thrive and pursue his destiny. It is the Prophet's challenge to confront his shadow, offer the old Hero respect as well as reward, and instill the old Hero's virtue in the child.

As the next Gray Champion, the Boom Generation will lead at a time of maximum danger—and opportunity. From here on, Boomers will face the unfamiliar challenge of self-restraint. Having grown up feeling that G.I.s could always step in and fix everything if trouble arose, Boomers have thus far pursued their crusades with a careless intensity. In the Fourth Turning, G.I.s will no longer be around as a backstop, and the young Millennials will follow the Gray Champion off a cliff. If Boomers make a wrong choice, history will be unforgiving.

The continued maturation of Boomers is vital for the Crisis to end in triumph. These one-time worshipers of youth must relinquish it entirely before they can demand from Millennials the civic virtue they themselves did not display during the Awakening. This will require a rectitude that will strike some as hypocritical, yet it will be no more than a natural progression of the Prophet's life-cycle persona. When the Crisis hits, Boomers will need to defuse the Culture Wars at once. Their pro-choice secularists and pro-life evangelicals will need to move beyond their Unraveling-era skirmishes and unite around an agenda of national survival, much as Missionary elders did during depression and war.

Boomers must also display a forbearance others have never associated with them. By nature, they will always tend toward self-indulgence in their personal lives—but if they allow this to overflow into public life and demand generous public benefits, they will bankrupt their children financially, themselves morally. Unlike the Silent, sneaking through unnoticed will not be an option. Worse, if Boomers become pointlessly argumentative and let their values back them into a corner, their current talk-show hyperbole about annihilating enemies could translate into orders to use real doomsday machines.

Come the Crisis, Boomers will face the utterly unyuppielike task of presiding over an era of public authority and personal sacrifice. This generation must squarely face the threat its unyielding moralism could pose to its own children, to the nation, indeed to the entire world. "When people repeat the slogan 'Make love not war,' " historian David McClelland has warned, "they should realize that love for others often sets the process in motion that ends in war." But if aging Boomers can control the dark side of their collective persona, they can look back on their role in the Fourth Turning the way old Ben Franklin looked back on his. When asked what image belonged on the national seal of the United States, the old man replied: the inspiring image of Moses, hands extended to heaven, parting the waters for his people.

13er Script

Survival skills are what a society needs most in a Fourth Turning, and those are precisely what the most criticized archetype—the Nomad—possesses in abundance. Through the natural corrective force of the saeculum, the Nomad was raised to excel in exactly those skills that history will require from him in midlife at a time of real public danger. His challenge will be to stop dispersing these skills for scattered purposes and start gathering them for one larger purpose. Through the Unraveling, the Nomad has been able to withdraw from civic life, but come the Crisis he cannot. It will be his duty to ensure that whatever choices society makes will work as intended. In public life, the Nomad must cut through the paralytic residue once built by his shadow, the old Artist. In private life, he must rebuild the family and community rituals once discarded by the old Artist. As he does this, the Nomad will nurture the new child Artist.

The Fourth Turning will find other generations with lives either mostly in the past or mostly in the future, but it will catch 13ers in "prime time," right at the midpoint of their adult years. They must step forward as the saeculum's repair generation, the one stuck with fixing the messes and cleaning up the debris left by others. Every tool 13ers acquired during a hardened childhood and individualist youth will be put to maximum test. If 13ers apply these tools for community purpose, they will become antidotes to pathologies remembered from their own Awakening-era childhood— from divorce and latchkeys to public debt and cultural decay.

The 13ers' gravest Fourth Turning duty will be their society's most important preseasonal task: to ensure that there can indeed be a new High, a new golden age of hope and prosperity. For the Crisis to end well, 13ers must keep Boomers from wreaking needless destruction and Millennials from marching too mindlessly under their elders' banner. They will not find it easy to restrain an older generation that will consider itself far wiser than they, and a younger one that will consider itself more deserving. For this, 13ers will require a keen eye, a deft touch, and a rejection of the wild risk taking associated with their youth.

From now through the end of the Fourth Turning, 13ers will constantly rise in power. From 1998 until around the Crisis climax, they will be America's largest *potential* generational voting bloc. As the years pass, their civic contributions will become increasingly essential to their nation's survival. They will have to vote more and participate more, if they want to contain the Boomers' zealotry. They will have that chance. Their own elected officials will surge into Congress as the Crisis catalyzes, eclipse Boomers around its climax, and totally dominate them by the time it resolves.

As they go one-on-one with history, 13ers should remember that history is counting on them to do whatever hard jobs may be necessary. If 13ers play their script weakly, old Boomers could wreak a horrible apocalypse, and 13er demagogues could impose a mind-numbing authoritarianism—or both. If 13ers play their script cleverly but safely, however, a new golden age will be their hard-won reward. As they age, 13ers should remember Hemingway's words: "Old men do not grow wise. They grow careful."

Millennial Script

For the child Hero, the Fourth Turning looms as a great coming-of-age trial. Whether the Crisis will be won or lost will depend in large measure on the Hero's teamwork, competence, and courage. By forever sealing his reputation for valor and glory, the Fourth Turning can energize the Hero for a lifetime of grand civic achievements.

Today's Millennial children should bask in adult hope, remain upbeat themselves, and reject the Unraveling-era cynicism that surrounds them. They should keep their innocence and avoid growing up too quickly. They should do small good deeds while dreaming of the day they will do greater ones. By applying peer pressure to positive purposes, they will be able to reconstruct a positive reputation for American adolescence. When older generations preach traditional values that they themselves failed to learn as children (and which are not yet common to the adult world), Millennials would do well to ignore the hypocrisy—and heed the lessons. The sooner today's children succeed in displaying these virtues, the more likely older people will be to treat them generously (by paying school taxes and relinquishing elder reward), thereby helping them prepare for their coming trial.

At the onset of the Great Depression, President Herbert Hoover demanded "a fair chance" for American youth: "If we could have but one generation of properly born, trained, educated, and healthy children," he predicted, "a thousand other problems of government would vanish." Events—and young G.I.s—proved him right. The Millennials' time is near. If they play their script well, perhaps the day will come when they sing in unison, as young patriots did in 1776, "The rising world shall sing of us a thousand years to come / And tell our children's children the wonders we have done."

These archetypal scripts recall the testament of the ancients, as restated in the carvings on Mount Rushmore: A society is best served by a quaternity of temperaments, kept in proper balance.

The great discontinuities of history are not like huge accidents, random collisions of four different personalities. Instead, the saecular winter follows a natural path of compensation, as each archetype confronts its shadow and offers its own contributions. From this, a Fourth Turning allows a society's survival instincts to emerge. It harnesses all the archetypal strengths to maximum advantage, enabling a society to work through problems that might otherwise destroy it.

In the Fourth Turning, as every generation reenacts the legends and myths of its ancestors, we can together establish new legends and myths—ones that can shape, and teach, posterity.

CHAPTER 12

■

The Eternal Return

ON THE EARTHEN FLOORS OF THEIR ROUNDED HOGANS, Navajo artists sift colored sand to depict the four seasons of life and time. Their ancestors have been doing this for centuries. They draw these sand circles in a counterclockwise progression, one quadrant at a time, with decorative icons for the challenges of each age and season. When they near the end of the fourth season, they stop the circle, leaving a small gap just to the right of its top. This signifies the moment of death and rebirth, what the Hellenics called *ekpyrosis*. By Navajo custom, this moment can be provided (and the circle closed) only by God, never by mortal man. All the artist can do is rub out the painting, in reverse seasonal order, after which a new circle can be begun. Thus, in the Navajo tradition, does seasonal time stage its eternal return.

Like most traditional peoples, the Navajo accept not just the circularity of life, but also its perpetuity. Each generation knows its ancestors have drawn similar circles in the sand—and each expects its heirs to keep drawing them. The Navajo ritually reenact the past while anticipating the future. Thus do they transcend time.

Modern societies too often reject circles for straight lines between starts and finishes. Believers in linear progress, we feel the need to keep moving forward. The more we endeavor to defeat nature, the more profoundly we land at the mercy of its deeper rhythms. Unlike the Navajo, we cannot withstand the temptation to try closing the circle ourselves and in the manner of our own liking. Yet we cannot avoid history's last quadrant. We cannot avoid the Fourth Turning, nor its *ekpyrosis*. Whether we welcome him or not, the Gray Champion will command our duty and sacrifice at a moment of Crisis. Whether we prepare wisely or not, we will complete the Millennial

Saeculum. The epoch that began with V-J Day will reach a natural climax—and come to an end.

An end of *what?*

The next Fourth Turning could mark the end of man. It could be an omnicidal Armageddon, destroying everything, leaving nothing. If mankind ever extinguishes itself, this will probably happen when its dominant civilization triggers a Fourth Turning that ends horribly. But this end, while possible, is not likely. Human life is not so easily extinguishable. One conceit of linear thinking is the confidence that we possess such godlike power that—at the mere push of a button—we can obliterate nature, destroy our own seed, and make ourselves the final generations of our species. Civilized (post-Neolithic) man has endured some five hundred generations, prehistoric (fire-using) man perhaps five thousand generations, and *Homo erectus* ten times that. For the next Fourth Turning to put an end to all this would require an extremely unlikely blend of social disaster, human malevolence, technological perfection, and bad luck. Only the worst pessimist can imagine that.

The Fourth Turning could mark the end of modernity. The Western saecular rhythm—which began in the mid-fifteenth century with the Renaissance—could come to an abrupt terminus. The seventh modern saeculum would be the last. This too could come from total war, terrible but not final. There could be a complete collapse of science, culture, politics, and society. The Western civilization of Toynbee and the Faustian culture of Spengler would come to the inexorable close their prophesiers foresaw. A New Dark Ages would settle in, until some new civilization could be cobbled together from the ruins. The cycle of generations would also end, replaced by an ancient cycle of tradition (and fixed social roles for each phase of life) that would not allow progress. As with an omnicide, such a dire result would probably happen only when a dominant nation (like today's America) lets a Fourth Turning *ekpyrosis* engulf the planet. But this outcome is well within the reach of foreseeable technology and malevolence.

The Fourth Turning could spare modernity but mark the end of our nation. It could close the book on the political constitution, popular culture, and moral standing that the word *America* has come to signify. This nation has endured for three saecula; Rome lasted twelve, Etruria ten, the Soviet Union (perhaps) only one. Fourth Turnings are critical thresholds for national survival. Each of the last three American Crises produced moments of extreme danger: In the Revolution, the very birth of the republic hung by a thread in more than one battle. In the Civil War, the union barely survived a four-year slaughter that in its own time was regarded as the most lethal war in history. In World War II, the nation destroyed an enemy of democracy that for a time was winning; had the enemy won, America might have itself been destroyed. In all likelihood, the next Crisis will present the nation with a threat and a consequence on a similar scale.

Or the Fourth Turning could simply mark the end of the Millennial Saeculum. Mankind, modernity, and America would all persevere. Afterward, there would be a new mood, a new High, and a new saeculum. America would be reborn. But, reborn, it would not be the same.

The new saeculum could find America a worse place. As Paul Kennedy has warned, it might no longer be a great power. Its global stature might be eclipsed by foreign rivals. Its geography might be smaller, its culture less dominant, its military less effective, its government less democratic, its Constitution less inspiring. Emerging from its millennial chrysalis, it might evoke nothing like the hope and respect of its American Century forbear. Abroad, people of goodwill and civilized taste might perceive this society as a newly dangerous place. Or they might see it as decayed, antiquated, an old New World less central to human progress than we now are. All this is plausible, and possible, in the natural turning of saecular time.

Alternatively, the new saeculum could find America, and the world, a much better place. Like England in the Reformation Saeculum, the Superpower America of the Millennial Saeculum might merely be a prelude to a higher plane of civilization. Its new civic life might more nearly resemble that "shining city on a hill" to which colonial ancestors aspired. Its ecology might be freshly repaired and newly sustainable, its economy rejuvenated, its politics functional and fair, its media elevated in tone, its culture creative and uplifting, its gender and race relations improved, its commonalities embraced and differences accepted, its institutions free of the corruptions that today seem entrenched beyond correction. People might enjoy new realms of personal, family, community, and national fulfillment. America's borders might be redrawn around an altered but more cogent geography of public community. Its influence on world peace could be more potent, on world culture more inspiring. All this is achievable as well.

If the Fourth Turning ends triumphantly, much of the modern world may follow the same saecular rhythm and share in the same saecular triumph. And if that happens, many might hope that the world could achieve an "end of history," a destination for mankind that Francis Fukuyama describes (with some irony) as "an end of wars and bloody revolutions" in which, "agreeing on ends, men would have no large causes for which to fight." Is such an outcome possible? Probably not. A Fourth Turning triumph of such colossal dimensions is much more likely to produce a very magnificent, but very impermanent, First Turning. The saeculum would endure. Indeed, the more magnificent the High, the more powerful would be resulting generational tectonics. The Millennials would be resplendent—and expansively hubristic—as world-shaping Heroes. Young Prophets would later trigger an Awakening to match, and the circle would continue.

We should not feel limited, but rather empowered by the knowledge that the Fourth Turning's *ekpyrosis* can have such decisive consequences. By lending structure to life and time, the saeculum makes human history all the more purposeful. A belief in foreseeable seasons and perceptible rhythms can inspire a society or an individual to do great things that might otherwise seem pointless. There is nothing ethically inhibiting in the notion that our behavior is, in some fundamental sense, a reenactment of the past. To the contrary: The ancients understood that to participate in cyclical time is to bear the responsibility for participating well or badly.

Were history pure chaos, every expression of human will could be undone at any time. Were there no intelligible connection between past intention and future result, we could do nothing to assist our children or posterity. We might as well drain the treasury, ruin the atmosphere, ravage the culture, and consume the seed corn of civilization.

Were history purely linear, humanity would also find itself degraded. Even the most noble of societies would become no more than a means to an end. Generations not present at the end of time would become mere building blocks, their members mere sacrifices on the altar of progress. Along the great highway of history, nothing would be eternal. The only free choice anyone might make would be to speed or slow a foreordained juggernaut. As linear history develops ever narrower standards of perfection, any generation not measuring up to that standard must look on itself (and be looked on by others) as a bad seed, useless to humanity except as a source of harm. The same would be true for any individual. Recent Western experiments with totalitarian regimes provide an object lesson: Societies that deify history's destination typically have no respect for the moral autonomy of the people making the journey.

When history is viewed as seasonal, by contrast, each generation can discover its own path across time, its own meaningful linkage to ancestors and heirs. Whoever we are—G.I.s, Silent, Boomers, 13ers, Millennials—we can locate our rendezvous with destiny, seize our script, make of it what we can, and evaluate our performance against the legendary myths and traditional standards of civilization. The seasons of time offer no guarantees. For modern societies, no less than for all forms of life, transformative change is discontinuous. For what seems an eternity, history goes nowhere—and then it suddenly flings us forward across some vast chaos that defies any mortal effort to plan our way there. The Fourth Turning will try our souls—and the saecular rhythm tells us that much will depend on how we face up to that trial. The saeculum does not reveal whether the story will have a happy ending, but it does tell us how and when our choices will make a difference.

Over the last century, the faith in progress has suffered many blows, perhaps none so devastating as Friedrich Nietzsche's early and devastating critique. Nietzsche believed that delusions about never-ending progress toward an unattainable standard had become a root malady of the Western psyche. This delusion, he believed, constituted a cruel vehicle of self-loathing, a spawning ground for hypocrisy, and a cage around the authentic human spirit. His invented prophet, Zarathustra, identifies the problem as "the spirit of revenge" against "time and its 'It was' "—meaning a resentment against history itself, against a one-way pilgrimage whose lofty goals keep proving mankind's actual condition to be one of contemptible insignificance. As an alternative, Zarathustra teaches the doctrine that every event is perpetually reenacted, that everything anyone does has been done before and will be done again forever. Every act therefore becomes an end in itself as well as a means to an end. Zarathustra calls this "the eternal return," the opportunity afforded everyone to share fully in what it means to be a human being.

The saeculum provides this same opportunity. Regardless of generation, every person who lives into deep old age experiences each of the four seasons of life once—*and* each of the four turnings of history once. The intersection of these two quaternities does more than just make our own generation unique among the living: It bonds us with every fourth generation that came before or will come after. We reenact the legends of our ancestors, just as our progeny will someday reenact our own. Through this, the depth and breadth of the human spirit expresses itself and endures over time.

Linear time tempts us moderns to believe that we are immeasurably better or contemptibly worse than our ancestors. By appealing to our pride or despair, unidirectional history relieves us of the challenge of proving ourselves worthy of their example. Yet relieved of the challenge, we are also relieved of the fulfillment. Commenting on the manners of Rome during the early empire, the great historian Tacitus disagreed with moralists who argued that the civic virtue of a great society can only change in one direction. "Indeed, it may well be that there is a kind of cycle in human affairs," he wrote, "and that morals alternate as do the seasons. Ancient times were not always better: Our generation too has produced many examples of honorable and civilized behavior for posterity to copy. One must hope this praiseworthy competition with our ancestors may long endure." And, two millennia after Tacitus, so must we share this hope.

Each of us communicates across a vast reach of time. Think back to your childhood. Recall the oldest person who influenced your life—maybe a grandparent, maybe an elderly neighbor. The distance between that person's birth year and the present is your memory span back in time. Now go in the other direction. Project the probable life span of the youngest person whose life you will someday influence—most likely, your youngest grandchild. If you are young, assume that at age thirty-five you will bear your last child, who also will bear a last child at thirty-five, who will in turn live to be eighty-five. The years between the present day and your last grandchild's death mark your memory span forward.

Now add these two periods together to calculate your total memory span, linking the lives of those who touched you with the lives of those who will be touched by you. For the authors of this book, the spans extend from 1881 to 2104 (Strauss) and from 1888 to 2114 (Howe)—223 and 226 years, respectively. That's longer than the American nation has been in existence. The memory spans of long-lived members of the Gilded Generation (John D. Rockefeller, Mother Jones, Oliver Wendell Holmes Jr.) extended from before the American Revolution through the present day. A child born in 1997 will anchor a memory span reaching from around the 1930s to the 2150s, a future remote beyond comprehension.

Or is it?

When you think of time seasonally, in terms of turnings, those vast spans of time become comprehensible, meaningful, shared. No matter what your age or generation, you knew or will know loved ones whose lives will cross nearly three full saecula. Together, you will experience three Fourth Turnings, three Crises, three *ekpyroses*. A memory span of this length is a fundamental vantage on history that you share with all Americans who ever lived or ever will live. It connects you personally with the ebb and flow of the lives of remembered ancestors. It acquaints you with the lives your own children and grandchildren are likely to lead.

If the saeculum continues, a girl born today will come of age just before the Fourth Turning's Crisis climax, enter midlife during the ensuing High, and reach old age during an Awakening. In all likelihood, she will live to glimpse another Unraveling. If health and history treat her well, she could (as a centenarian) witness another Crisis catalyze on the eve of the twenty-second century. She will have much to tell her youngest grandson—who, if he survives that circa-2100 Crisis, can teach the saeculum's lessons to his own grandson who, in time, could grow old as another in a long line of Gray Champions.

Perhaps that latter grandson will become a late-twenty-second century historian who will write a complete chronicle of American civilization, which by then will stretch back over ten saecula. Come the 2190s, he will be as far away from the 1990s as we today are from George Washington's presidency. Every schoolchild will know what happened next, from the Oh-Ohs to the 2020s, as the Fourth Turning unfolded—but academics will surely debate how and why it came to pass. In his history, this great-great-grandson of today's baby girl will reflect on what the Fourth Turning came to mean for his own time and generation.

His history is not yet written. What will it be?

To every thing there is a season,
and a time to every purpose under heaven:
a time to be born, and a time to die;
a time to plant, and a time to pluck up that which is planted;
a time to kill, and a time to heal;
a time to break down, and a time to build up;
a time to weep, and a time to laugh;
a time to mourn, and a time to dance;
a time to cast away stones, and a time to gather stones together;
a time to embrace, and a time to refrain from embracing;
a time to get, and a time to lose;
a time to keep, and a time to cast away;
a time to rend, and a time to sew;
a time to keep silent, and a time to speak;
a time to love, and a time to hate;
a time of war, and a time of peace.

—Ecclesiastes 3.1–8

Acknowledgments

Everyone has a stake in the next Fourth Turning, and the two of us are no exception. Between our two households, we have six children, three parents who spend much of the year living with us, and two parents who live elsewhere. Our children range in age from two to nineteen, our parents from sixty-nine to eighty-seven. The life ahead for our daughters and sons, the future memory of our parents, the old age we and our wives will face—all this was on our minds and in our hearts as we wrote this book. The birth of a son or high school graduation of a daughter can make a parent think long and hard about what can be known of, and done for, the future. We thank our families for their inspiration and patience—and, in the case of Simona Howe and Janie, Melanie, and Suzy Strauss, for their editorial suggestions as well.

Many who helped with this project share our generational membership. We were born in 1947 (Strauss) and 1951 (Howe), and it is with mixed emotion that we watch our peers retrace the life-cycle path of their archetypal ancestors. We thank our text readers Jim Coyne, Peter D'Epiro, Richard Jackson, Bill Lane, Rick Semiatin, and Jim Stone; Mike Tilford, whose voice graces the audio version of this book; Elaina Newport and other colleagues at the Capitol Steps, for the insight their humor lends to current events; Rafe Sagalyn, for being an advisor, advocate, and friend; and our editor and publisher at Broadway Books, John Sterling and Bill Shinker, for sharing our vision and helping us bring life to it.

However stark the omen may be to our peers, a Fourth Turning prophecy is even more consequential to younger people, who can expect to live beyond. We thank our text readers Arlynda Boyer, Scott and Susan Defife, and Anne Eakin; David Datelle, who tracked down some hard-to-find items; Third Millennium's Richard Thau; our gifted webmaster Nabeel Hyatt; and our research aide Matt Moore, who asked good questions and gave good help.

Over the years, many of our elders have inspired this project in important ways, from mentors like Charles Goodell, Charles Percy, Pete Peterson, and Paul Weaver, to family members like our parents Arthur and Suzy Strauss and Bert and Margot Howe, and our wives' parents Howard and Mary Kamps and Giorgio and Carla Massobrio. We thank our children Melanie, Victoria, Eric, and Rebecca Strauss and Giorgia and Nathaniel Howe, and our wives Janie and Simona for their loving patience and support.

The great German scholar Leopold Von Ranke studied the Old World over the annals of time and observed that "before God all the generations of humanity appear equally justified." In "any generation," he concluded, "real moral greatness is the same as in any other. . . ." To all the generations that have touched our lives and our book, we wish liberty and fulfillment in their own time and greatness in their later remembrance.

We must recognize our cycle-theory predecessors who, often in the face of harsh contemporary criticism, discovered the importance of generations and saecular rhythms. To Arnold Toynbee and Quincy Wright, Giuseppe Ferrari and Samuel Huntington, Peter Harris and George Modelski, Frank Klingberg and the two Arthur Schlesingers (to name just a few), we express our gratitude for their pathbreaking inspiration.

We would also like to acknowledge each other. Neither of us could possibly have discovered or written *The Fourth Turning* without the other. Our cycle theory has been the product of a fruitful decade-long collaboration that began back in the middle 1980s, when we together started writing *Generations*. Our interest in the subject originated in Strauss's prior books about the Vietnam-era draft and military and Howe's about America's long-term fiscal problems. In *Generations,* we wanted to explain how these two problems were related to each other—how, for example, the uneasy resolution of the 1960s-era generation gap helped give rise to the 1980s-era entitlement ethic. At the time, we presumed that the generational dynamics of our own era were unlike anything that had ever happened before. But the more deeply we reviewed American history, the more we realized that only the details were new. The underlying rhythms were not.

While we wrote *Generations* primarily as a history book, we also observed how generations come in cycles of four types. In a closing chapter, we applied this cycle to offer predictions about America's near-term future. We suspected that, amid all the buzz about Information Ages and New World Orders, the seasonal patterns observed by the ancients might be hardwired into the inner nature of our modern society. When the 1990s did in fact unfold as the cycle would suggest, we felt an urgent need to alert people about the Fourth Turning.

Lastly, we thank our readers for taking the time to hear us out—and for doing whatever you can do to help the future turn out well. For those who come upon this book in the future, we extend our greetings and best wishes from across the saeculum. It is you who will see the Fourth Turning in its full historical context. It is you who will craft the great myths and legends around whatever today's Americans do in the coming time of trial. We hope you craft them with pride.

—William Strauss and Neil Howe

Notes

The primary purpose of these notes is to flag important works that have proved to be useful to the authors and that may be helpful to readers who want to investigate further the issues raised in this book.

As a rule, specific references to individuals and to publications or other media are also sourced. In order to keep the notes manageably brief, however, the references do not include some recent quotations, citations, and media titles that serve as primary sources whenever these sources are either familiar or can be easily ascertained through an electronic word search. This exception applies mostly to Chapters 6, 7, and 8, where representative quotes and titles are used extensively to illustrate the current Millennial Saeculum.

The reader may also want to consult the quantitative and bibliographical appendices available (pp. 455–519) in William Strauss and Neil Howe, *Generations: A History of America's Future, 1584-2069* (1991), hereafter abbreviated as *Generations*. These appendices are especially helpful for background on any of America's historical generations, on quantitative indices of American political leadership by generation, and on the works of generations theorists.

All references marked *"op. cit."* refer to works denoted in full earlier in the notes to the same chapter. All biblical references are to the King James version (1611). The following abbreviations are used: *NYT, New York Times; WSJ, Wall Street Journal; WP, Washington Post; LT, Los Angeles Times; USNWR, U.S. News and World Reports; DHI,* Philip P. Wiener (ed.), *Dictionary of the History of Ideas* (1973); *EnS,* David L. Sills (ed.), *International Encyclopedia of the Social Sciences* (1968); *EAEH,* Glenn Porter (ed.), *Encyclopedia of American Economic History* (1980).

CHAPTER 1
BACKGROUND

On interpretations of how societies perceive historical time (and of the chaotic, cyclical, and linear approaches), see "Determinism in History," "Recurrence," "Cycles," "Periodization in History," "Progress in Classical Antiquity," and "Progress in the Modern Era" entries in *DHI;* "Periodization," entry in *EnS;* "Ages of the World" entry in Mircea Eliade (ed.), *The Encyclopedia of Religion* (1993); "Ages of the World" and "Cosmogony and Cosmology" entries in James Hastings (ed.), *Encyclopedia of Religion and Ethics* (1912); J. B. Bury, *The Idea of Progress* (1932); J. Baillie, *The Belief in Progress* (1950); Mircea Eliade, *The Myth of the Eternal Return* (trans. in 1954; orig. *Le Mythe de l'éternel retour: archétypes et répétition,* 1949); Petrim Sorokin, *Social and Cultural Dynamics* (revised, 1957); Norman Cohn, *The Pursuit of the Millennium* (1957); Georg G. Iggers, "The Idea of Progress in Recent Philosophies of History," *Journal of Modern History* (Sep 1958); Joseph Maier, "Cyclical Theories," Werner J. Cahnman and Alvin Boskoff (eds.), *Sociology and History: Theory and Research* (1964); S. G. F. Brandon, *History, Time, and Deity* (1965); Iggers, "The Idea of Progress: A Critical Reassessment," *American Historical Review,* 71,1 (Oct 1965); W. Warren Wagar, "Modern Views of the Origins of the Idea of Progress," *Journal of the History of Ideas* (Jan–Mar 1967); Charles Van Doren, *The Idea of Progress* (1967); Harry Levin, *The Myth of the Golden Age in the Renaissance* (1969); J. H. Plumb, *The Death of the Past* (1970); Grace E. Cairns, *Philosophies of History: Meeting of East and West in Cycle-Pattern Theories of History* (1971); Jan Dhondt, "Recurrent History," *Diogenes,* 75 (Fall 1971); Peter Munz, *The Shapes of Time* (1977); G. W. Trompf, *The Idea of Historical Recurrence in Western Thought: From Antiquity to the Reformation* (1979); Robert Nisbet, *History of the Idea of Progress* (1980); James Glieck, *Chaos: Making a New Science* (1987), ch. "Inner Rhythms"; and essays in Leo Howe and Alan Wain (eds.), *Predicting the Future* (1993); and Robert Heilbroner, *Visions of the Future* (1995). For the development of America's special sense of its own history and destiny, see Albert K. Weinberg, *Manifest Destiny* (1935); Howard Mumford Jones, *O Strange New World: American Culture, The Formative Years* (1952); Charles L. Sanford, *The Quest for Paradise: Europe and the American Moral Imagination* (1961); Ernest Lee Tuveson: *Redeemer Nation: The Idea of America's Millennial Role* (1968); Cushing Strout, *The New Heavens and New Earth: Political Religion in America* (1973); Edward Cornish, *Study of the Future* (1977); Gerard K. O'Neill, *2081: A Hopeful View of the Human Future* (1981); and W. Warren Wagar, *The Next Three Futures: Paradigms of Things to Come* (1991).

REFERENCES

Results of "Are you a very important person?" survey administered by the Mayo Clinic in 1940 and 1990, as reported in Cheryl Russell, *The Master Trend* (1993), 33. For surveys on attitudes toward Social Security and the economic future of today's young, see "Americans, Especially Baby Boomers, Voice Pessimism for Their Kids' Economic Future," *WSJ* 1/19/96; Floyd Norris, "Social Security: The Issue They Chose to Ignore," *NYT* 11/6/94; Mathew Greenwald & Associates, "Entitlement Survey" (Sep 1994, on behalf of the National Taxpayers Union Foundation and the Congressional Institute for the Future); and Frank Luntz, *The American Dream* (12/8/94, on behalf of the Hudson Institute).

It's All Happened Before
Walter Lippmann, *Drift and Mastery* (1914), 152–53. Benjamin Franklin calling the Paxton Boys "white savages," in Brooke Hindle, "The March of the Paxton Boys," *William and Mary Quarterly,* 3 (1946). President Franklin Roosevelt, in speech accepting renomination (Jun 27, 1936).

Theories of Time
Aeschylus, *The Eumenides* (458 B.C.). Lucien Lévy-Bruhl, *La Mentalité Primitive* (1922). Mircea Eliade (1954), *op. cit.,* 34. Carl L. Becker, *The Heavenly City of the Eighteenth-Century Philosophers* (1932). Editors' "Introduction," *Cambridge Modern History* (New York, 1902). Lord Acton, in Herbert Butterfield, *Man on his Past* (1955). Herbert Croly, *The Promise of American Life* (1909). James Truslow Adams, *The Epic of America* (1931), 174. Saint Augustine, explicating Psalm 12:8 in Book XII of *De civitate Dei* (426–413 B.C.). On the gender associated with numbers three and four, see relevant entries to Jean Chevalier and Alain Cheerbrant, *A Dictionary of Symbols* (orig. 1969, trans. in 1994); and Carl Gustav Jung, *Psychology and Alchemy* (orig. 1944; trans. in 1953; 2nd ed., 1968), part I; see also Edward F. Edinger, *Ego and Archetype* (1972), 179–193.

Overcoming Linearism
Mark Twain, *Life on the Mississippi* (1883). Mary McCarthy, "America the Beautiful: The Humanist in the Bathtub," *On the Contrary* (1961). W. W. Rostow, *The Stages of Economic Growth* (1960). Herman Kahn and Anthony J. Wiener, *The Year 2000* (1967). Charles Reich, *The Greening of America* (1970). Alvin Toffler and Heidi Toffler, *The Third Wave* (1980). Francis Fukuyama, *The End of History and the Last Man* (1992). John Naisbitt, *Megatrends: Ten New Directions Transforming Our Lives* (1982), 9. Aristotle, *Poetics,* 1451^{b}5. Arthur M. Schlesinger Jr., *The Cycles of American History* (1986), 27.

Rediscovering the Seasons
Winston S. Churchill, in Charles W. Kegley Jr., "Neo-Idealist Moment in International Studies? Realist Myths and the New International Realities," *International Studies Quarterly,* 37 (1993). Sir Arthur Wing Pinero, *The Second Mrs. Tanqueray* (1893), 4.

CHAPTER 2
BACKGROUND
On the Etruscans and their view of time, see Alain Hus, *The Etruscans* (trans. in 1975; orig. *Les Étrusques, peuple secret,* 1961); Agnes Carr Vaughan, *Those Mysterious Etruscans* (1964), esp. ch. XX; Otto-Wilhelm von Vacano, *The Etruscans in the Ancient World* (trans. in 1965; orig. *Die Etrusker in der Welt der Antike,* 1960); and Luisa Banti, *Etruscan Cities and Their Culture* (1973). On the Roman view of history and time, see Jean Hubaux, *Les Grands Myths de Rome* (Paris, 1945); Kenneth J. Reckford, "Some Appearances of the Golden Age," *The Classical Journal,*

54, 2 (Nov 1958); and H. J. Rose, "World Ages and the Body Politique," *Harvard Theological Review,* 54, 3 (Jul 1961). On cyclical time expressed in ritual and festival, see W. Lloyd Warner, *The Living and the Dead: A Study of the Symbolic Life of Americans* (1959); essays in Victor Turner (ed.), *Celebration: Studies in Festivity and Ritual* (1982); essays in Alessandro Felassi (ed.), *Time Out of Time: Essays on the Festival* (1987); and Jack Santino, *All Around the Year* (1994). On the concept of centuries and end-of-centuries from antiquity through modernity, see essays in Pierre Citti (ed.), *Fins de Siècle* (1990, Université de Bourdeaux); John Stokes, *Fin de Siècle/Fin du Globe: Fears and Fantasies of the Late Nineteenth Century* (1992); Shearer West, *Fin de Siècle* (1993); essays in Mikulas Teich and Roy Porter (eds.), *Fin de Siècle and Its Legacy* (1990); and essays in Elaine Scarry (ed.), *Fins de Siècles: English Poetry in 1590, 1690, 1790, 1890, 1990* (1995). On "long cycles" of war and peace, see Wright, Toynbee, Ferrar Jr., Modelski, Thompson, and Rosecrance (all cited below); for an extensive overview of the literature, see Joshua Goldstein, *Long Cycles: Prosperity and War in the Modern Age* (1988); see also the ongoing discussion and debate in such journals as *International Studies Quarterly, World Politics,* and *Journal of Conflict Resolution.* On "revolution," see entry in *DHI;* see also Melvin J. Lasky, "The Birth of a Metaphor," *Encounter* (Feb and Mar, 1970).

REFERENCES

Censorinus, *De die natali liber ad Q. Caerellium* (A.D. 238; trans. by the authors from the text edited by Nicolaus Sallmann, 1983), ch. 17. D. H. Lawrence, *Etruscan Places* (1932). On the numbering of the saecula by Varro, Lucan, Juvenal, and others, see Rose, *op. cit.*

The Wheels of Time
Tung Chung-shu (c. 179–104 B.C.), *Luxuriant Dew of the Spring and Autumn Annals* (as trans. and summarized by Cairns, *Philosophies of History* (1962, 1971), 171–186. R. G. Collingwood, *Essays in the Philosophy of History* (1965), 75, 89.

The Saeculum Rediscovered
Desiderius Erasmus in letter to Budaeus (Feb 21, 1517), in Jean Lafond, "Réflexions sur deux fins de siècle: les seizième et dix-septième siècles," in Citti, *op. cit.* Tommaso Campanella, in ibid. John Dryden, *The Secular Masque* (1700). Madame de Pompadour, reputed comment (Nov 5, 1757) to Louis XV after Frederick the Great's victory at Rossbach. Gustav Rümelin, "Über den Begriff und die Dauer einer Generation," in *Reden und Aufsätze* (1875). Ralph Waldo Emerson, "Considerations by the Way," in *The Conduct of Life* (1860). *Fin de Siècle,* by F. de Jouvenot and H. Micard, was performed first in Paris on April 17, 1888. Rémy de Gourmont, in Maurice Penaud, "Rémy de Gourmont et la notion de fin de siècle," in Citti, *op cit.* Benito Mussolini ("the twentieth century will be known in history as the century of fascism"), reputed comment in 1933 upon Hitler's seizing power; Henry Luce, "The American Century," editorial in *Life* (Feb 17, 1941); Henry Wallace, in "The Price of Free World Victory" (speech; May 8, 1942). Antoine-Augustin Cournot, *Considérations sur la marche des idées et des événements dans les temps modernes* (1872), 105. Arnold Toynbee, *Change and Habit* (1966), 20.

The Saeculum of War and Peace

Quincy Wright, *A Study of War* (1942). Wright, ibid., 223–32 and 380–87. Arnold Toynbee, *A Study of History* (twelve volumes; pub. 1934–1961). Toynbee, *A Study of History,* volume IX (1954), 220–347. For "human control," ibid., 348. L. L. Ferrar Jr., "Cycles of War: Historical Speculations on Future International Violence," *International Interactions,* 3 (1977). Richard Rosecrance, *International Relations: Peace or War?* (1973), 301–02; see also Rosecrance, "Long Cycle Theory and International Relations," *International Organization,* 41, 2 (1987). Ludwig Dehio, *The Precarious Balance: Four Centuries of the European Power Struggle* (1962). Terence Hopkins, Immanuel Wallerstein, and Associates, "Cyclical Rhythms and Secular Trends of the Capitalist World Economy: Some Premises, Hypotheses, and Questions," in Hopkins and Wallerstein (eds.), *World-Systems Analysis: Theory and Methodology* (1982). William R. Thompson, *On Global War: Historical-Structural Approaches to World Politics* (1988), 50. George Modelski, *Long Cycles in World Politics* (1987), 34. Nicolaus Copernicus, *De revolutionibus orbium coelestium, libri VI* (1543). Thomas Hobbes, *Behemoth, or an Epitome of the Civil Wars of England* (1679), end of Fourth Dialogue. Thomas Paine, *The American Crisis* (orig. pub. as fourteen pamphlets, 1776–1783). Gerhard Masur, "Crisis in History," *DHI.* Modelski, *op. cit.,* 118–20. Anthony F. C. Wallace, "Revitalization Movements," *American Anthropologist,* 58 (1956). Robert Wurthnow, "World Order and Religious Movements," in Albert Bergesen (ed.), *Studies of the Modern World-System* (1980).

The Saeculum in America

G. W. F. Hegel (in *Philosophy of History),* in Maier, *op. cit.* President Abraham Lincoln, "Gettysburg Address" (Nov 19, 1863). Thomas Paine, *Common Sense* (1776). Lincoln, *op. cit.* Walt Whitman, "O Captain! My Captain!" (1865). Charles and Mary Beard, *The Rise of American Civilization* (1927, 1933 ed.), vol. II, ch. 18. Carl Degler, "The Third American Revolution," in *Out of Our Past* (1970). Bruce Ackerman, *We the People: Foundations* (1991), 44. Michael Lind, *The Next American Nation: The New Nationalism and the Fourth American Revolution* (1995). Walter Dean Burnham, "The Fourth American Republic?" *WSJ* 10/16/95. Winston S. Churchill, *Marlborough: his Life and Times* (1934), vol. II, 478. Richard Maxwell Brown, "Violence and the American Revolution," in Stephen G. Kurtz and James H. Hutson (eds.), *Essays on the American Revolution* (1973). James M. McPherson, *Battle Cry of Freedom* (1988), 854. Richard L. Bushman, *From Puritan to Yankee: Character and the Social Order in Connecticut, 1690–1765* (1970); 187, and Bushman (ed.), *The Great Awakening* (1970), xi. Robert Bellah, *The Broken Covenant* (2nd ed., 1992), xvi. William G. McLoughlin, *Revivals, Awakenings, and Reform* (1978), ch. 1. Robert Fogel, "The Fourth Great Awakening" (Bradley Lecture at the American Enterprise Institute 9/11/95) and in *WSJ* 1/9/96; see also Irving Kristol, "Times of Transformation," *WSJ* 6/13/95; and George F. Will, "The Fourth Awakening," *Newsweek* 10/2/95. Henry Steele Commager, *The American Mind: An Interpretation of American Thought and Character Since the 1880s* (1950), 42. Richard Hofstadter, *Age of Reform* (1955), 166. Thompson, *op. cit.,*

p. 276. Modelski, "A Global Politics Scenario for the Year 2016," in Modelski (ed.), *Exploring Long Cycles* (1987). Ferrar Jr., *op. cit.* Goldstein, *op. cit.,* 353. "Chrono-macropolitics" in Modelski, "The Study of Long Cycles," in Modelski (1987), *op. cit.*

CHAPTER 3
BACKGROUND

On phases of the human life cycle, see Carl Gustav Jung, "The Stages of Life" (1933; orig. "Die Lebenswende," 1931); S. N. Eisenstadt, *From Generation to Generation* (1956); Erik H. Erikson, *Childhood and Society* (1950) and *The Life Cycle Completed* (1982); essays in Matilda W. Riley, et al., *Aging and Society* (1972); Daniel J. Levinson, *The Seasons of a Man's Life* (1978); essays in Robert H. Binstock and Ethel Shanas (eds.), *Handbook of Aging and the Social Sciences* (1985); and Thomas R. Cole and Mary G. Winkler (eds.), *The Oxford Book of Aging* (1994). On generations theory, see *Generations,* chs. 2–4 and appendix A; "Generations" entries (by Julián Marías and Marvin Rintala) in *EnS;* Julián Marías, *Generations: A Historical Method* (trans. in 1970; orig. *El metodo histórico de las generaciones,* 1967); Alan B. Spitzer, "The Historical Problem of Generations," *American Historical Review* (Dec 1973); essays in Richard J. Samuels (ed.), *Political Generations and Political Development* (1976), esp. chs. 1–2; essays in Stephen R. Graubard (ed.), *Generations* (1979); Anthony Esler, *Generations in History: An Introduction to the Concept* (1982); and Yves Renouard, "La notion de génération en histoire," *Revue Historique* (Jan–Mar 1953). On the Hellenic theory of elements, see "Biological Conceptions in Antiquity" entry in *DHI;* and F. M. Cornford, *From Religion to Philosophy* (1957). On the development of the theory of humors and temperaments, see G. E. R. Lloyd (ed.), *Hippocratic Writings* (trans. by J. Chadwick and W. N. Mann, 1978); see also "Temperance," "Health and Disease," "Macrocosm and Microcosm," "Pre-Platonic Conceptions of Human Nature," and "Psychological Ideas in Antiquity" entries in *DHI.* On the modern-day persistence of temperament theory, see Jerome Kagan, *Galen's Prophecy: Temperament in Human Nature* (1994). On Myers-Briggs "type testing," see David Keirsey and Marilyn Bates, *Please Understand Me: Character and Temperament Types* (1978); and Otto Kroeger and Janet M. Thuesen, *Type Talk* (1988). On myths and mythical archetypes, see Joseph Campbell, *The Power of Myth* (1988); Campbell, *The Hero with a Thousand Faces* (2nd ed., 1968); Robert Graves, *The Greek Myths* (1955), 2 vols.; Norma Lorre Goodrich, *Ancient Myths* (1960) and *Medieval Myths* (1961); Alexander Eliot, *The Universal Myths: Heroes, Gods, Tricksters and Others* (1976); see also Pierre Brunel, *Companion to Literary Myths, Heroes and Archetypes* (trans. in 1992; orig. *Dictionnaire des Mythes Littéraires,* 1988).

REFERENCES

Marcus Tullius Cicero (106–43 B.C.), *De senectute.* Lin Yü-t'ang, "Human Life a Poem," in *The Importance of Living* (1937). Levinson, *op. cit.,* 7. Jung (1933), *op. cit.*

The Fourscore Journey

Ralph Waldo Emerson, "History," in *Essays: First Series* (1841). For "the days of our years," see Psalm 90:10. Jung (1933), *op. cit.* For "tempestivitas," see Cole and Winkler (1994), *op. cit.,* 14; and entry in Oxford English Dictionary; see also Sir Thomas Browne (1605–82), *Christian Morals* (1716), pt. 3, sec. 8. John Schowalter, in "Childhood Circa 1995," *WSJ* 2/9/95; Levinson, *op. cit.,* p. 4. Henry Adams, *The Education of Henry Adams* (1907), 35. Thomas Hardy, *Jude the Obscure* (1895), pt. I, ch. 2. José Ortega y Gasset, *Man and Crisis* (orig., *En torno a Galileo,* 1933). Levinson, *op. cit.,* 29. For "individuation," see Jung, *Psychological Types* (orig., *Psychologische Typen,* 1921). For the age of midlife, Dante Alighieri, *Il convivio,* IV, 24; Browne, *op. cit.;* Aristotle, *Rhetoric,* 1390^{a}28; Jung (1933), *op. cit.;* Levinson, *op. cit.,* ch. 2. Ogden Nash, "Crossing the Boarder," in *Marriage Lines* (1964). For changes in labor force participation rates by age, see *Employment and Earnings* (monthly and historical), U.S. Dept. of Labor. For current median age of OASI retired-worker awards, see *Annual Statistical Supplement, 1995,* to the *Social Security Bulletin,* Social Security Administration.

Generations and History

Karl Mannheim, "Das Problem der Generationen" (1928). Philo (c. 20 B.C.–c. A.D. 50), *Cosmogony.* Herodotus (c. 484–c. 425 B.C.), *History.* "Generation of vipers," Matthew 3:7 and Luke 3:7. Hesiod (eighth century B.C.), *Theogony.* Thomas Jefferson, letter to James Madison in New York (Sep 6, 1789). Auguste Comte, *Cours de Philosophie Positive* (1869), 51^e leçon. John Stuart Mill, *A System of Logic, Ratiocinative and Inductive* (1840), II, X. Wilhelm Dilthey, *Über das Studium der Geschichte der Wissenschaften vom Menschen, der Gesellschaft und dem Staat* (1875), trans. here by Marías, *op. cit.,* 55. Giuseppe Ferrari, *Teoria dei periodi politici* (1874), 9–15. Mannheim, *op. cit.* Ortega, *The Modern Theme* (orig., *El tema de nuestro tiempo,* 1923). François Mentré, *Les générations sociales* (1920). Kurt Cobain, "Smells Like Teen Spirit" (song, from album, *Never Mind,* 1991). Esler, *op. cit.,* 152.

Identifying Generations

Thomas Wolfe, *You Can't Go Home Again* (1934), 715. Ferrari, *op. cit.,* 7–8. Ortega (1933), *op. cit.,* trans. in Marías, *op. cit.,* 98. Cheryl Merser, *"Grown Ups": A Generation in Search of Adulthood* (1987), 98. Marías, *op. cit.,* 101–02. On Vietnam-era draft eligibility, see Lawrence Baskir and William Strauss, *Chance and Circumstance* (1978). Comte, *op. cit.* Dilthey, *op. cit.* For attitudes of college freshman, see Alexander Astin, et al., *The American Freshman: Twenty-Five Year Trends, 1966–1990* (UCLA; 1991), plus more recent annual reports. For U.S. elections by generation, see *Generations,* appendix B. Marías, *op. cit.,* 106. Ortega, *The Modern Theme* (orig. *El tema de nuestro tiempo,* 1923), trans. in Marías, *op. cit.,* 94. Julius Peterson, "Die Literarischen Generationen," in Emil Ermatinger (ed.), *Philosophie der Literaturwissenschaft* (1930). Ortega (1923), *op. cit.,* trans. in Marías, *op. cit.,* 94. Mannheim, *op. cit.* Martin Heidegger, *Sein und Zeit* (1927), 384–85.

The Generational Panorama
Arthur M. Schlesinger, *New Viewpoints in American History* (1925, 1948), ch. 5. Morton Keller, "Reflections on Politics and Generations in America," in Graubard, *op. cit.* Henri Peyre, *Les Générations littéraires* (1948), ch. XIV. Samuel Huntington, "Paradigms of American Politics: Beyond the One, the Two, and the Many," *Political Science Quarterly* (Mar 1974).

The Four Archetypes
For Anaximander, see Cornford, *op. cit.,* 7–12. For Hippocrates, see Lloyd, *op. cit.* For Alcmaeon of Croton, see "Biological Conceptions in Antiquity" in *DHI.* E. Adickes, *Charakter und Weltanschauung* (1907). Eduard Spranger, *Lebensformen* (1914; trans. as *Types of Men,* 1928), pt. I. Ernst Kretschmer, *Körperbau und Charakter* (1920; trans. as *Physique and Character,* 1925). Jung (1921), *op. cit.* For Jung's concept of archetypes and the collective unconscious, see Jung, "Approaching the Unconscious," in Jung (ed.), *Man and his Symbols* (1964), and relevant entries in Andrew Samuels, Bani Shorter, and Fred Plant, *A Critical Dictionary of Jungian Analysis* (1986). Isabel Myers, *The Myers-Briggs Type Indicator* (1956). Robert Moore and Douglas Gillette, *King, Warrior, Magician, Lover: Rediscovering the Archetypes of the Mature Masculine* (1990). Carol S. Pearson, *Awakening the Heroes Within* (1991). William Irwin Thompson, *At the Edge of History* (1971), ch. 4. For "enantiodromia," see *The Collected Works of C. G. Jung* (trans. by R. F. C. Hull; 2nd ed., 1967), vol. 5 *(Symbols of Transformation),* 375; on link with Heraclitus, see Joseph Campbell, "Editor's Introduction," in Campbell (ed.), *The Portable Jung* (1971). Moore and Gillette, *op. cit.,* 118.

Archetypes and Myths
For Jung on the "hero myth," see Jung (1964), *op. cit.,* 68–71. Joseph Campbell, *The Power of Myth* (1988), 152. Campbell, *The Hero with a Thousand Faces* (2nd ed., 1968), 69. Igor Stravinsky, *Conversations with Igor Stravinsky* (1959). Margaret Mitchell, *Gone with the Wind* (1936), 680–81.

The Cycle of Archetypes
For the age at which U.S. generations reach their peak of political dominance, see *Generations,* appendix B. Benjamin Spock, *The Common Sense Book of Baby and Child Care* (1946), ch. 1, "The Parents' Part." Judy Blume, *Letters to Judy: What Your Kids Wish They Could Tell You* (1986), 273. J. Zvi Namenworth and Richard C. Bibbee, "Change within or of the System: An Example from the History of American Values," *Quality and Quantity,* 10 (1970).

Archetypes and History
For "twenty years old and upward, all that are able to go forth to war," see Numbers 1:3. For "there arose another generation after them," see Judges 2:10. For scholarship on four-stage narrative cycles in the Old Testament, see G. W. Trompf, *The Idea of Historical Recurrence in Western Thought* (1979), ch. 3. For "One generation passeth away . . . ," see Ecclesiastes 1:4. For "As is the generation of

leaves . . . ," see Homer, *Iliad,* VI, 146. Polybius (c. 208–c. 126 B.C.), *Histories,* bk. V, 5–9. Ibn Khaldun, *The Muqaddimah* (trans. by Franz Rosenthal, 1958), vol. I, ch. II, 14; ibid., vol. I, ch. III, 11–12; see also, Fuad Baali, *Society, State, and Urbanism: Ibn Khaldun's Sociological Thought* (1988), ch. 5–6. Paul-Émile Littré, *Paroles de philosophie positive* (1860), in Marías, *op. cit.,* 28. Ivan Turgenev, *Fathers and Sons* (1862). Giuseppe Ferrari, *Teoria dei periodi politici* (1874). Eduard Wechssler, *Die Generation als Jugendreihe und ihr Kampf um die Denkform* (1930), 137–248. Arnold Toynbee, *A Study of History,* volume IX (1954), 319–26. Marías, *op. cit.,* 170–88. Samuel Huntington, *American Politics: The Promise of Disharmony* (1981); see also the earlier Huntington (1974), *op. cit.* George Modelski, *Long Cycles in World Politics* (1987), 62–3 and 115–25. J. Zvi Namenworth, "Wheels of Time and the Interdependence of Value Change in America," *Journal of Interdisciplinary History,* III, 4 (Spring, 1973).

CHAPTER 4
BACKGROUND

On general cycle theories of American history, see Arthur M. Schlesinger, *Paths to the Present* (1949), ch. 4, "The Tides of National Politics"; P. M. G. Harris, "The Social Origins of American Leaders: The Demographic Foundations," *Perspectives in American History,* III (1969); J. Zvi Namenworth, "Wheels of Time and the Interdependence of Value Change in America," *Journal of Interdisciplinary History,* 3, 4 (Spring 1973); David C. McClelland, *Power: The Inner Experience* (1975); Samuel P. Huntington, *American Politics: The Promise of Disharmony* (1981); A. O. Hirschman, *Shifting Involvements: Private Interest and Public Action* (1982); and Arthur M. Schlesinger Jr., *The Cycles of American History* (1986), ch. 2. On Walter Dean Burham's theory of party systems and realignments, see Burnham, "Party Systems and the Political Process," in Burnham and William Nisbet Chambers (eds.), *The American Party Systems: Stages of Political Development* (1967); Burnham, *Critical Elections and the Mainsprings of American Politics* (1970); Burnham, "Revitalization and Decay: Looking Toward the Third Century of American Electoral Politics," *Journal of Politics* (Aug 1976). For landmarks in the development of this perspective, see Samuel Lubell, *The Future of American Politics* (1952); V. O. Key Jr., "A Theory of Critical Elections," *Journal of Politics,* XVII (1955); Angus Campbell, et al., *The American Voter* (1960); Gerald Pomper, "Classification of Presidential Elections," *Journal of Politics,* XXIX (1967); Charles Sellers, "The Equilibrium Cycle in Two-Party Politics," *Public Opinion Quarterly,* XXIX (1965); Kevin Phillips, *The Emerging Republican Majority* (1969); James L. Sundquist, *Dynamics of the Party System: Alignment and Realignment of Political Parties in the United States* (1973); and Paul Kleppner (ed.), *The Evolution of American Electoral Systems* (1981). On cycles of U.S. foreign policy, see Frank L. Klingberg, *Cyclical Trends in American Foreign Policy Moods* (1983); and Michael Roskin, "From Pearl Harbor to Vietnam: Shifting Generational Paradigms and Foreign Policy," *Political Science Quarterly,* 89, 3 (Fall 1974). On "long" (or "Kondratieff") cycles in economic history, see J. J. Van Duun, *The Long Wave in Economic Life* (1983); and Joshua S. Goldstein, *Long Cycles: Prosperity and War in the Modern Age* (1988). For a well-known theory of demographic cycles, see

Richard A. Easterlin, *Birth and Fortune: The Impact of Numbers on Personal Welfare* (2nd ed., 1987).

References

The Origin of the American Cycle
Jules Michelet, *Histoire de France* (1833–67), vol. VII. Jacob Burckhardt, *The Civilization of the Renaissance in Italy* (trans. in 1878; orig. *Die Kultur der Renaissance in Italien,* 1860). Martin Luther, in Erik H. Erikson, *Young Man Luther* (1958), 174. Since they are self-reported in U.S. Census surveys, "ancestry" figures are necessarily approximate; for 1900 and the 1920s, see David Hackett Fischer, *Albion's Seed* (1989), 870–73; for current figures, see Census figures reported in *Statistical Abstract of the United States* (annual), sec. 1; "English" is here assumed to include England, Wales, Scotland, Northern Ireland, and non-French Canada. For pre-1790 population figures by colony and race, see "Colonial and pre-Federal Statistics," *Historical Statistics of the United States, Colonial Times to 1970* (Bureau of the Census, 1975), ch. Z. For the estimated ancestry of population in 1720 and 1820, see sources and method outlined in *Generations,* 466–67; see also estimate for 1790 in John Mack Faragher, "Immigration," in Faragher (ed.), *The Encyclopedia of Colonial and Revolutionary America* (1990). On the usage of the English language, see Daniel J. Boorstin, *The Americans: The Colonial Experience* (1958), part 10, "The New Uniformity."

Archetypes in American History
José Ortega y Gassett, cited above in Chapter 3. François Mentré, in Julián Marías, *Generations: A Historical Method* (trans. in 1970; orig. *El metodo histórico de las generaciones,* 1967), 155ff.

Archetypes and Turnings
Abraham Lincoln, address to the Wisconsin State Agricultural Society (Milwaukee; Sep 30, 1859). David Donald, *An Excess of Democracy: The American Civil War and the Social Process* (1960), as excerpted in Kenneth M. Stampp (ed.), *The Causes of the Civil War* (1959), 98.

Rhythms in History
Harris, *op. cit.* Schlesinger Jr., *op. cit.,* ch. 2. For "young men born . . . ," see Ralph Waldo Emerson, *Life and Letters in New England* (1867). For "madmen . . . ," see Emerson (in "The Chardon Street Convention"), in Vernon L. Parrington, *The Romantic Revolution in America: 1800–1860* (1927; 1954 ed.), 337. Thomas Hobbes, *Behemoth, or an Epitome of the Civil Wars of England* (1679), as cited and discussed in Mark H. Curtis, "The Alienated Intellectuals of Early Stuart England," in Trevor Aston (ed.), *Crisis in Europe: Essays from 'Past and Present'* (1965). On cycles of campus unrest, see *Generations.* Michael Barkun, "Communal Societies as Cyclical Phenomena," *Communal Societies,* 4 (Fall, 1984)

Politics
Schlesinger, *op. cit.* Schlesinger Jr., *op. cit.* On Schlesinger Jr.'s forecast of the 1988 election, see Schlesinger Jr., "Wake Up, Liberals, Your Time Has Come," *WP* 5/1/88; and discussion in "Conventional Wisdom," *Newsweek* 11/21/88; and "Letters to the Editor," ibid. 12/19/88; see also more recent essays by Schlesinger Jr., in *WSJ* (2/8/89, 11/12/92, and 11/16/94). Burnham (1967), *op. cit.* Schlesinger Jr. (1986), *op. cit.* Paul Allen Beck, "A Socialization Theory of Partisan Realignment," in Richard G. Niemi and Associates, *The Politics of Future Citizens* (1974); see also Beck, "Young vs. Old in 1984: Generations and Life Stages in Presidential Nomination Politics," *PS* (Summer 1984). "The rate of turnout and political participation fell drastically between 1900 and 1920," according to Richard L. McCormick, "Political Parties," in Jack P. Greene (ed.), *Encyclopedia of American Political History* (1984).

Foreign Affairs
Frank L. Klingberg, "The Historical Alternation of Moods in American Foreign Policy," *World Politics,* IV, 2 (Jan 1952); later, Klingberg (1983), *op. cit.*

Economy
N. D. Kondratieff, "Die Langen Wellen der Konjunktur," *Archiv für Sozialwissenschaft und Sozialpolitik* (1926 trans. from 1925 Russian orig.); abridged English ed. first appeared in 1935, full English ed. in 1979. For quantifiable trends in poverty rates since the Civil War, see Eugene Smolensky and Michael M. Weinstein, "Poverty," in *EAEH.* For quantifiable trends in income and wealth distribution, see Lee Soltow, "Distribution of Income and Wealth," in *EAEH;* Alice Hansen Jones, *Wealth of a Nation To Be* (1980); and Jeffrey G. Williamson and Peter H. Lindert, *American Inequality: A Macroeconomic History* (1980).

Family and Society
Betty Friedan, *The Feminine Mystique* (1963). Mary Cable, *The Little Darlings* (1975), 105. On perceived changes in family life during the 1920s, see Mary Patrice Thaman, *Manners and Morals of the 1920s: A Survey of the Religious Press* (1977). On parallels between Garveyism in the 1920s and Black Muslims in the 1990s, see Orlando Patterson, "Going Separate Ways: The History of an Old Idea," *Time* 10/30/95; and Sean Wilentz, "Backward March," *New Republic* 11/6/95.

Population
For trends in total fertility rates since 1800, see Ansley J. Coale and Melvin Zelnick, *New Estimates of Fertility and Population in the United States* (1963) and recent Census figures. For earlier years and for trends in immigration, see *Generations,* appendix B.

Social Disorder
New York Gazette in 1749, in Carl Bridenbaugh, *Cities in Revolt: Urban Life in America, 1743–1776* (1955), 113. Available data on per-capita U.S. alcohol con-

sumption indicate that cyclical peaks were reached in 1980–1981, in 1906–1910, and in 1830–1840; see the *First Statistical Compendium on Alcohol and Health* (National Institute on Alcohol Abuse and Alcoholism; Feb 1981); *NIAAA Quick Facts* (CSR, Inc.; periodic); J. C. Burnham, "New Perspectives on the Prohibition 'Experiment' of the 1920s," *Journal of Social History* (Fall 1968); Jack S. Blocker Jr., *American Temperance Movements: Cycles of Reform* (1989); and statistical appendix to W. J. Rorabaugh, *The Alcoholic Republic: An American Tradition* (1979). For evidence that the late 1740s and 1750s may have been another peak era of alcohol consumption, see Rorabaugh, *op. cit.,* and Bridenbaugh, *op. cit.,* ch. 3. For similar trends in narcotics consumption, see H. Wayne Morgan, *Drugs in America: A Social History, 1800–1980* (1981); and David T. Courtwright, *Dark Paradise: Opiate Addiction in America before 1940* (1972). David Musto, in "Drug Use? America Can't Seem to Remember When," *WP* 8/27/90.

Culture
Edmund Morgan, "The American Revolution Considered as an Intellectual Movement" in Arthur M. Schlesinger Jr., and Morton White (eds.), *Paths of American Thought* (1963). Marilyn Ferguson, *The Aquarian Conspiracy* (1980). Cao Yu, in *Observer* (London) 4/13/80. Harris, *op. cit.*

Accidents and Anomalies
Bill Gates, *The Road Ahead* (1995), 105. Klingberg (1983), *op. cit.* For figures on the generational landslide of 1868, see *Generations,* appendix B.

OVERVIEW: SEVEN CYCLES OF GENERATIONS AND TURNINGS

BACKGROUND
A chapter-length biography (with bibliographical references) for every generation from the Puritans to the Millennials is available in *Generations.*

REFERENCES
Anthony Esler, *The Aspiring Mind of the Elizabethan Younger Generation* (1966), 165, 240, 68. Matthew A. Crenson, *The Federal Machine: Beginnings of Bureaucracy in Jacksonian America* (1975), 159. Emerson, "not a book . . ." (explicitly referring to New England between 1790 and 1820), in Russel Blaine Nye, *The Cultural Life of the New Nation, 1776–1830* (1960), 111. "Law of Competition," in Andrew Carnegie, *The Gospel of Wealth* (1900). Van Wyck Brooks, "The Younger Generation of 1870" in *New England: Indian Summer, 1865–1915* (1940), 438. "An end of ideology," in Daniel Bell, *The End of Ideology* (1960). "Morning in America," President Ronald Reagan's reelection campaign theme (summer and fall, 1984).

CHAPTER 5
REFERENCES
Nathaniel Hawthorne, "The Gray Champion," *Twice-Told Tales* (first series, 1837). For "a fiery gospel writ in burnished rows of steel" and "the fateful lightning of His terrible swift sword," see the third and first stanzas, respectively, of Julia Ward Howe, "The Battle Hymn of the Republic" (song lyrics, published 1862). Abraham Lincoln, Second Annual Message to Congress (Dec 1, 1862).

CHAPTERS 6, 7, AND 8
BACKGROUND

On the First Turning
See André Siegfried, *America at Mid-Century* (1955); Huston Smith (ed.), *The Search for America* (1959); William Manchester, *The Glory and the Dream: A Narrative History of America, 1932–1972* (1974); Roland Stromberg, *After Everything: Western Intellectual History Since 1945* (1975); Joseph Goulden, *The Best Years: 1945–1950* (1976); William O'Neill, *The American High: The Years of Confidence, 1945–1960* (1986); Elaine Tyler May, *Homeward Bound* (1988); Michael Barone, *Our Country: The Shaping of America from Roosevelt to Reagan* (1990); David Halberstam, *The Fifties* (1993); Alan Ehrenhalt, *The Lost City* (1995); Robert Samuelson, *The Good Life and Its Discontents* (1996); and James T. Patterson, *Grand Expectations: The United States, 1945–1974* (1996).

On the Second Turning
See Manchester, Stromberg, Barone, Samuelson, and Patterson *(op. cit.);* see also Theodore Roszak, *The Making of a Counterculture* (1969); Daniel Bell, *The Coming of Post-Industrial Society* (1973); Christopher Lasch, *The Culture of Narcissism in an Age of Diminishing Expectations* (1979); Marilyn Ferguson, *The Aquarian Conspiracy: Personal and Social Transformation in the 1980s* (1980); Marvin Harris, *America Now: The Anthropology of a Changing Culture* (1981); Daniel Yankelovich, *New Rules: Searching for Self-Fulfillment in a World Turned Upside Down* (1981); Richard Reeves, *American Journey: Traveling with Tocqueville in Search of Democracy in America* (1982); Stanley Karnow, *Vietnam: A History* (1983); Arnold Mitchell, *The Nine American Lifestyles* (1983); Robert N. Bellah, et al., *Habits of the Heart: Individualism and Commitment in American Life* (1985); and Todd Gitlin, *The Sixties: Years of Hope, Days of Rage* (1987); and Irwin Unger, *The Best of Intentions: The Triumphs and Failures of the Great Society Under Kennedy, Johnson, and Nixon* (1996).

On the Third Turning
See Samuelson, *op. cit.;* see also Louis Harris, *Inside America* (1987); Barbara Ehrenreich, *Fear of Falling* (1986); Benjamin Friedman, *Day of Reckoning* (1988); John Naisbitt, *Megatrands 2000* (1990); Alvin and Heidi Toffler, *Powershift* (1990); Kevin Phillips, *The Politics of Rich and Poor* (1990); Mary Ann Glendon, *Rights*

Talk (1991); E. J. Dionne Jr., *Why Americans Hate Politics* (1991); James Davison Hunter, *Culture Wars: The Struggle to Define America* (1991); Arthur M. Schlesinger Jr., *The Disuniting of America* (1992); Charles Sykes, *A Nation of Victims* (1992); Amitai Etzioni, *The Spirit of Community* (1993); Jonathan Rauch, *Demosclerosis* (1994); Stephen L. Carter, *The Culture of Disbelief* (1995); Bill Gates, *The Road Ahead* (1995); Jean Bethke Elshtain, *Democracy on Trial* (1995); and Phillip Longman, *The Return of Thrift* (1996).

On the Missionary through Millennial Generations
See *Generations* for extensive bibliographies. More recent noteworthy titles include, on the Missionaries, T. H. Watkins, *Righteous Pilgrim: The Life and Times of Harold L. Ickes, 1874–1952* (1990); Evelyn Brooks Higginbotham, *Righteous Discontent: The Women's Movement in the Black Baptist Church 1880–1920* (1993); David Fromkin, *In the Time of the Americans: The Generation that Changed America's Role in the World* (1995). On the Lost: David McCullough, *Truman* (1992); Marybeth Hamilton, *When I'm Bad, I'm Better: Mae West, Sex, and American Entertainment* (1995). On the G.I.s: Betty Friedan, *The Fountain of Age* (1993); and Richard Reeves, *President Kennedy: Profile of Power* (1994). On the Silent: Wini Breines, *Young, White, and Miserable: Growing up Female in the Fifties* (1992); William M. Tuttle Jr., *Daddy's Gone to War* (1993); Colin L. Powell, *My American Journey* (1995); and Gail Sheehy, *New Passages: Mapping Your Life Across Time* (1995). On the Boomers: Cheryl Russell, *The Master Trend* (1993); Katherine S. Newman, *Declining Fortunes* (1993); and Wade Clark Roof, *A Generation of Seekers* (1993). On the 13ers: Neil Howe and William Strauss, *13TH-GEN* (1993); Third Millennium, *Third Millennium Declaration* (1993); Children's Express, *Voices from the Future* (1993); Eric Liu (ed.), *Next: Young American Writers on the New Generation* (1994); Thomas French, *South of Heaven* (1994); Douglas Rushkoff (ed.), *The Generation X Reader* (1994); Rob Nelson and Bob Cowan, *Revolution X* (1994); David Lipsky and Alexander Abrams, *Late Bloomers* (1994); and Mike A. Males, *The Scapegoat Generation* (1996). On the Millennials: Sylvia Ann Hewlett, *When the Bough Breaks* (1991); Laurence J. Kotlikoff, *Generational Accounting* (1993); Linda and Richard Eyre, *Teaching Your Children Values* (1993); Nurith Zmora, *Orphanages Reconsidered* (1994); Jonathan Kozol, *Amazing Grace: The Lives of Children and the Conscience of a Nation* (1995); Mary Ann Glendon and David Blankenhorn (eds.), *Seedbeds of Virtue: Sources of Competence, Character, and Citizenship in American Society* (1995); Marian Wright Edelman, *Guide My Feet* (1995); Daniel Quayle and Dianne Medved, *The American Family: Discovering the Values That Make Us Strong* (1996); Hillary Clinton, *It Takes a Village And Other Lessons Children Teach Us* (1996); and Suzanne Logan, *The Kids Can Help* (1996).

CHAPTER 6
REFERENCES
Gunner Myrdal, "Is American Business Deluding Itself," *Atlantic Monthly* (Nov 1944). Quotations from *Fortune* are all from Jul, Aug, Dec of 1945, and Jan and Jun of 1946. *Saturday Evening Post,* in Alan Brinkley, "For America, It Truly Was a Great War," *NYT Magazine* 5/7/95. Sumner H. Slichter, "Jobs After the War," *At-*

lantic Monthly (Oct 1944). Leo Cherne, "The Future of the Middle Class," *Atlantic Monthly* (Jun 1944). For prediction in *Life,* see Landon Y. Jones, *Great Expectations* (1980), 18–19. John Kenneth Galbraith, *The Affluent Society* (1958). Robert Payne, in David Halberstam, *The Fifties* (1993), 49. President Dwight Eisenhower, final State of the Union message (Jan 1960). Paul Johnson, "Another 50 Years of Peace?" *WSJ* 5/9/95. Alan Valentine, *The Age of Conformity* (1954). Lewis Mumford, in Halberstam, *op. cit.,* 140. Michael Harrington, *The Other America* (1962).

First Turnings and Archetypes

Vachel Lindsay, *The Chinese Nightingale* (1917), end. Thomas Nashe, *Summer's Last Will and Testament* (1600). Wallace Stevens, *The Comedian as the Letter C* (1923), III, 4. Robert Browning, *Pippa Passes* (1841), pt. 1. Joel Barlow, *The Canal: A Poem on the Application of Physical Science to Political Economy* (1802). Vernon L. Parrington, *The Beginnings of Critical Realism in America: 1860–1920* (1930; 1958 ed.), 11. Increase Mather, *Pray for the Rising Generation* (1679). David Hackett Fischer, *Growing Old in America* (1977), 93, 88. John Adams, letters to Benjamin Rush (1809), in Zoltán Haraszti, *John Adams and the Prophets of Progress* (1952), 1. Benjamin Colman, in Perry Miller, *The New England Mind: From Colony to Province* (1953), 414. Thomas Jefferson, first inaugural address (Mar 4, 1801). For "docile and tutorable," see "Speeches of the Students of the College of William and Mary Delivered May 1, 1699," *William and Mary Quarterly* (Oct 1930). John Adams, in letter to *Columbian Centinel* (1793), in Samuel Flagg Bemis, *John Quincy Adams and the Foundations of American Foreign Policy* (1949), 36. For "a harmonious blending," see Sunday school spokesman Daniel Wise, in Joseph Kett, *Rites of Passage: Adolescence in America, 1790 to the Present* (1977), 120. David Leverenz, *The Language of Puritan Feeling: An Exploration in Literature, Psychology, and Social History* (1980), 3–4. Cotton Mather, *A Family Well-Ordered* (1699). Gary B. Nash, *The Urban Crucible: Social Change, Political Consciousness, and the Origins of the American Revolution* (1979), 133. Kett, *op. cit.,* 60. Mary Cable, *The Little Darlings* (1972), 105. Jane Addams, *Twenty Years at Hull House* (1910). Henry Canby, in Cable, *op. cit.,* 104.

Lost Entering Elderhood: Old Fogeys

Truman editorial, in William Manchester, *The Glory and the Dream* (1974), 367. Truman on Lewis, in William L. O'Neill, *The American High* (1986), 89. MacArthur, in Samuel Eliot Morison, *The Oxford History of the American People* (1965), 1045. Mott, in Sherwood Eddy, *Pathfinders of the World's Missionary Crusade* (1945), 310. Winston Churchill, *Mr. Crewe's Career* (1908), 53. Frederic Howe, *Confessions of a Reformer* (1925), 17. George Santayana, *Character and Opinion in the United States* (1920), 4–5. For "the rising generation," see Cornelia Comer, "A Letter to the Rising Generation," *Atlantic Monthly* (Feb 1911). For the first IQ tests, see Daniel J. Boorstin, *The Americans: The Democratic Experience* (1973), 220–23. President Franklin Roosevelt, in First Inaugural Address (Mar 4, 1933). Henry Miller, op-ed essay, *NYT* 9/7/74. Babe Ruth, in Warren I. Susman, *Culture as History: The Transformation of American Society in the Twentieth Century* (1984), 143–44. George Burns, in "After 100 Years . . . ," *WP* 3/10/96. F. Scott Fitzgerald, *This Side of Paradise* (1920). Edna St. Vincent Millay, *A Few Figs From Thistles* (1920). Malcolm Cowley, *Exile's Return* (1934, 1951 ed.), 306. For measures of self-esteem, see K. Warner Schaie and Iris Parham, "Stability of Adult Personality Traits: Fact or Fable?," *Journal of Personality and Social Psychology* (1976). Paul Tillich, in Tillich and Huston Smith, "Human Fulfillment," in Huston Smith (ed.), *The Search for America* (1959). Joseph Wood Krutch, *Human Nature and the Human Condition* (1959), 13. Thornton Wilder, *The Skin of Our Teeth* (1942). President Dwight Eisenhower, in letter to Henry Luce, in Fred Greenstein and Robert Wright, "Reagan . . . Another Ike?," *Public Opinion* (Dec–Jan 1981). William O'Neill, *op. cit.,* 287. For "mandatory retirement," see William Graebner, *A History of Retirement* (1980), chs. 9–10. Louis Kuplan, in ibid., 235. Ethel Andrus (in 1965), in "AARP's Catastrophe," *WSJ* 10/2/89. On 1961 White House Conference on Aging, see Graebner, *op. cit.,* 235. Bruce Barton, in Susman, *op. cit.,* 126. Paul Tillich, in O'Neill, *op. cit.,* 38.

G.I.s Entering Midlife: The Power Elite
Henry Malcolm, *Generation of Narcissus* (1971), 43. William Manchester, in "In America," *NYT* 3/11/96. Gene Shuford, in Calvin B. T. Lee, *The Campus Scene: 1900–1970* (1970), 36. Paula Fass, *The Damned and the Beautiful: American Youth in the 1920s* (1977). Stephen Ambrose, in Robert J. Samuelson, essay in *Newsweek* 1/17/94. For opinion data, see American Institute of Public Opinion, *Gallup Poll* (1972), poll of 5/28/45 on poison gas, of 10/19/45 on Japan, and of 11/19/54 on corporal punishment. Joseph Goulden, *The Best Years: 1945–1950* (1976), 427. Marynia Farnham and Ferdinand Lundberg, *The Lost Sex* (1946). *Look* magazine, in Jones, *op. cit.,* 24. Maxwell Taylor, *The Uncertain Trumpet* (1960). For G.I. voting record, see *Generations,* 267–68. Richard Rovere, *The Establishment* (1962).

Silent Entering Young Adulthood: Gray Flannel Suits
For surveys, see "The Class of '49," *Fortune* (Jun 1949). Frank Conroy, "My Generation," *Esquire* (Oct 1968). Philip Roth, in Steven Mintz and Susan Kellogg, *Domestic Revolutions* (1988), 181. For Silent fertility, see *Generations,* 284. On educational advance, see ibid., 252, 267, 284. Pauline Kael on Dean, in Halberstam, *op. cit.,* 484.

Boomers Entering Childhood: Dennis the Menace
Benjamin Spock, *The Common Sense Book of Baby and Child Care* (1946), ch. 1, "The Parents' Part." Eda Leshan, *The Wonderful Crisis of Middle Age* (1973). Kenneth Keniston, *Young Radicals* (1968), 51. On mothers, breastfeeding, and pediatrics, see *Generations,* 305. For TV-watching, see Manchester (1974), 586. For positive outlook, see Jones, *op. cit.* Kerr, in Jones, *op. cit.,* 98.

Toward the Second Turning
Stephen Spender, *The Struggle of the Modern* (1963). Donald Davie, *Brides of Reason* (1955), "Remembering the Thirties." Robert Frost, speech at Kennedy inaugural (Jan 20, 1961), in David Halberstam, *The Best and the Brightest* (1969), 38.

CHAPTER 7
REFERENCES

Theodore White, "The Assassination of the President," *World Book Encyclopedia Yearbook* (1965). Allen Drury, "Focus on the Economy," ibid. (1966). Sylvia Porter, "Focus on the Economy," ibid. (1965). Robert Theobald, *The Challenge of Abundance* (1961). Roy Harrod, "The Possibility of Economic Satiety," in Committee for Economic Development, *Problems of United States Economic Development* (1958), vol. 1, 207. John Kenneth Galbraith, *The New Industrial State* (1967). Alistair Cooke, "Focus on the Arts," *World Book Encyclopedia Yearbook* (1965). Myron Magnet, *The Dream and the Nightmare: The Sixties' Legacy to the Underclass* (1993). James Reston, "Focus on the Nation," *World Book Encyclopedia Yearbook* (1967–70). Charles Reich, *The Greening of America* (1970). Ayn Rand, "Apollo 11," in Leonard Peikoff (ed.), *Voice of Reason* (1988). James Reston, *op. cit.* Sargent Shriver, in Malcolm Gladwell, "The Failure of Our Best Intentions," *WP* 12/3/95. John Updike, in Landon Y. Jones, *Great Expectations* (1980), 293. Christopher Lasch, *The Culture of Narcissism: American Life in an Age of Diminishing Expectations* (1979). Daniel Yankelovich, *New Rules: Searching for Self-Fulfillment in a World Turned Upside Down* (1981). Julie Phillips, *The Seattle Weekly* (1992).

Second Turnings and Archetypes

William Shakespeare, *Sonnets* (1609), 18.3. Ralph Waldo Emerson, *The Conduct of Life,* "Fate" (1860). Joseph Wood Krutch, *The Twelve Seasons* (1949), "August." "Reformation must be universal . . ." (speech by Thomas Case, 1641), in Michael Walzer, *The Revolution of the Saints* (1968), 10–11. Benjamin Colman, in Perry Miller, *The New England Mind: From Colony to Province* (1953), 400. For Cotton Mather, see David E. Stannard, *The Puritan Way of Death* (1977), 150; and John Demos, "Old Age in Early New England" in Demos and Sarane Spence Boocock (eds.), *Turning Points: Historical and Sociological Essays on the Family* (1978). Thomas Jefferson, in Russel Blaine Nye, *The Cultural Life of the New Nation, 1776–1830* (1960), 31; and in Merrill D. Peterson, *The Great Triumvirate* (1987), 128. Albert Gallatin (at age 88), in Page Smith, *The Nation Comes of Age* (1981), 227. Jefferson, in Peter Charles Hoffer, *Revolution and Regeneration: Life Cycle and the Historical Vision of the Generation of 1776* (1983), 58. Benjamin Doolittle, *A Short Narrative* (1750). Nathaniel Appleton, *Faithful Ministers* (1743). Edward Wigglesworth, in Miller, *op. cit.,* 454. On the "post-heroic" theme, see Michael Paul Rogin, *Fathers and Children* (1975); and Michael Kammen, *A Season of Youth: The American Revolution and the Historical Imagination* (1978). William Wirt, in Leonard D. White, *The Jeffersonians* (1951), 346. Henry James, *What Maisie Knew* (1907–09), Preface. John Winthrop, in Edmund Morgan, *The Puritan Dilemma: the Story of John Winthrop* (1958), 29. Gilbert Tennent, *The Danger of an Unconverted Ministry* (1740). Benjamin Franklin, in Gary B. Nash, *The Urban Crucible: Social Change, Political Consciousness, and the Origins of the American Revolution* (1979), 220. William Lloyd Garrison, "The Liberator's Principles" (Jan 1, 1831). Margaret Fuller, in Smith (1981), *op. cit.,* 727. George Herron, in Page Smith, *The Rise of Industrial America: A People's History of the Post-Reconstruc-*

tion Era (1984), 483. Richard Mather, in Miller, *op. cit.,* 28. Eleazer Mather, in Emory Elliott, *Power and the Pulpit in Puritan New England* (1975), 18. For "sets them screaming," see Charles Chauncy, *Seasonable Thoughts on the State of Religion in New England* (1743). For "self-dependence," see Irene Quenzler Brown, "Death, Friendship, and Female Identity During New England's Second Great Awakening," *Journal of Family History,* 12 (1987). Foreign visitor was David Macrae, in Smith (1981), *op. cit.,* 914. Thomas Wolfe, *You Can't Go Home Again* (1934).

G.I.s Entering Elderhood: Senior Citizens
"America's Mood Today," *Look* 6/29/65. Eric Hoffer, in Richard Fox and T. Jackson Lears (eds.), *The Culture of Consumption* (1983). B. F. Skinner, *Walden Two* (1948). James MacGregor Burns, George Wald, and John Gardner, all in Ben Wattenberg, *The Real America: A Surprising Examination of the State of the Union* (1974), 15, 18, 22. Milton Mayer, in "Children's Crusade: A Search for Light," *LT* 11/16/69. For senior organizations and periodicals, senior benefits versus wages, and tests of anxiety and happiness, see *Generations,* 268–69. Ken Dychtwald and Joe Flower, *Age Wave: The Challenges and Opportunities of an Aging America* (1989), 134–35. Erik Erikson, *The Life Cycle Completed* (1982). Betty Friedan, *The Fountain of Age* (1993). Robert N. Butler, *Why Survive? Being Old in America* (1975). For "Is anyone still listening," see "In America," *NYT* 3/11/96. For G.I. gifts to Boomers, see "Aging Boomers Cut the Cord But Can't Let Go of the Wallet," *WSJ* 7/8/96. Eda Leshan, *The Wonderful Crisis of Middle Age* (1973), 279. Joan Erikson, in "Erikson, in His Own Old Age, Expands His View of Life," *NYT* 6/14/88. LeShan, *op. cit.,* 21.

Silent Entering Midlife: Vicars of Vacillation
On JFK assassination, see White, *op. cit.* Wade Greene, "Fiftysomething-and in Charge," *NYT* 1/2/90. Rose N. Franzblau, *The Middle Generation* (1971), x. Benita Eisler, *Private Lives: Men and Women of the Fifties* (1986), 308. On no-fault divorce laws, see *Generations,* 284. John Folger and Charles Nam, *Education of the American Population* (Census monograph, 1960). Barbara Gordon, *Jennifer Fever: Older Men and Younger Women* (1988). William Styron, in "My Generation," *Esquire* (Oct 1968). Alvin Toffler, *Future Shock* (1970), 430. Judith Viorst, *It's Hard to Be Hip Over Thirty, and Other Tragedies of Married Life* (1968). Russell Baker, "Observer," *NYT* 5/1/69. Ralph Nader, *Unsafe at Any Speed* (1965). For rise of public-interest law centers, see "Public Interest Law Groups: Prospering Amid Adversity," *WP* 11/17/88. Toffler, *op. cit.,* 230, 283. Lester Thurow, *The Zero-Sum Society* (1980). Schneider, "JFK's Children: The Class of '74," *Atlantic* (Mar 1989).

Boomers Entering Young Adulthood: Mystical Militants
For surveys on violence, see Seymour Martin Lipset and Everett Carll Ladd Jr., "The Political Future of Activist Generations" in Philip G. Altbach and Robert S. Laufer (eds.), *The New Pilgrims: Youth Protest in Transition* (1972). Daniel Moynihan, "Nirvana Now," *American Scholar* (Fall 1967). Annie Gottlieb, *Do You Believe in Magic? The Second Coming of the Sixties Generation* (1987). Michael Harrington, "Mystical Militants," in Alexander Klein (ed.), *Natural Enemies?* (1969). Ken-

neth Keniston, *Young Radicals* (1968), 80. Marilyn Ferguson, *The Aquarian Conspiracy: Personal and Social Transformation in the 1980s* (1980), 87. Keniston, *op. cit.,* 81. On young Wallace voters, see Lipset and Ladd, *op. cit.* Keniston, *op. cit.,* 55. Henry Malcolm, *Generation of Narcissus* (1971), 56. Lewis Feuer, *The Conflict of Generations* (1969), 470. Irving Kristol, "What's Bugging the Students," *Atlantic Monthly* (Nov 1965). On Boomers and the Vietnam War, see Lawrence M. Baskir and William Strauss, *Chance and Circumstance: The Draft, the War and the Vietnam Generation* (1978). For Boomer attitudes toward Vietnam War, see Daniel Yankelovich, et al., *The Sixties Generation: A Profile* (1986). Wanda Urbanska: *The Singular Generation: Young Americans in the 1980s* (1986). Bill Graham, in Jones, *op. cit.,* 135.

13ers Entering Childhood: Rosemary's Baby
On unwanted children, see Jones, *op. cit.,* 231. On G-rated films, see Cobbett Steinberg, *Real Facts: The Movie Book of Records* (1981), 41. Leslie Fiedler, in Jones, *op. cit.,* 241. Jones, ibid., 242. For "good life" survey, see Marvin Harris, *America Now: The Anthropology of a Changing Culture* (1981), 114. On abortion rates, see *Generations,* 324. Boston Women's Health Book Collective, *Ourselves and Our Children: A Book by and for Parents* (1978). Thomas Gordon, *Parental Effectiveness Training* (1970). Marie Winn, *Children Without Childhood* (1983). For parental time deficit, see studies by Joan Robinson, in Sylvia Ann Hewlett, *When the Bough Breaks* (1991), 73. For parental attitudes toward bad marriages, see Samuel Preston, "Children and the Elderly: Divergent Paths for America's Dependents," *Demography* (Nov 1984). Kyle Pruett, *The Nurturing Father: Journey Toward the Complete Man* (1987). For 13er children by family type, see *Generations,* 325. Bill Cosby, *Fatherhood* (1986), 93. Al Feldstein, in Winn, *op. cit.,* 64. Judy Blume, *Letters to Judy: What Your Kids Wish They Could Tell You* (1986), 273. John Holt, *Escape From Childhood* (1974). A. S. Neill, *Summerhill: A Radical Approach to Childrearing* (1960), 25, 29. For homework and grade inflation, see, "Grade Inflation, A Problem and a Proposal," *Education Week* 3/8/95; and Alexander Astin, et al., UCLA freshman surveys cited above in Chapter 3. For child poverty, see poverty rates by age in Bureau of the Census, *Poverty in the United States,* Current Population Reports, Series P-60 (annual). For rates of child suicide, homicide, and abuse, see *Generations,* 326.

Toward the Third Turning
Roland Stromberg, *After Everything* (1975), ch. 3.

CHAPTER 8
REFERENCES
See "Trust in Government, 1963–93," *WP* 8/23/93. For minorities and niche groups, see "A Distorted Image of Minorities," *WP* 10/8/95. For personal trust, see "Americans Losing Trust in Each Other," *WP* 1/28/96. For civility, "The American Uncivil Wars," *USNWR* 4/22/96. For ideological split, see David Broder, "Sharpening Party Lines," *WP* 1/22/95. Irving Kristol, "The Feminization of the Democrats," *WSJ* 9/9/95. For "Was there a time?" see "Newsweek Poll" in *Newsweek* 7/10/95. Charles

Murray, *Losing Ground* (1984). On legalized gambling, see "You Bet! It's a New National Pastime," *WP* 3/3/96. Times Mirror Center for The People and The Press, *Times Mirror Study of the American Electorate: The People, the Press, and Politics* (1988 and 1994). For survey on "moral and spiritual decline," see "Virtuecrats," *Newsweek* 6/13/94. For Roper polls showing pessimism of (esp. younger) Americans, see "Young Adults Now Are Most Pessimistic," *WSJ* 9/27/93. "The Whiney Nineties," *USA Weekend* (May 5–7, 1995). For popularity of decades, see Gallup poll for *CNN/USA Today* (May 1996).

Third Turnings and Archetypes
Richard Wilbur, *Advice to a Prophet* (1961), "Two Quatrains for First Frost." Edwin Way Teale, *North with the Spring* (1951), 3. Thomas Wolfe, *Of Time and the River* (1935), 39. Samuel Johnson, in Peter N. Carroll, *The Other Samuel Johnson: A Psychohistory of Early New England* (1978), 140. Nathaniel Appleton, in Clifford K. Shipton, *Sibley's Harvard Graduates* (1958), V, Class of 1712. Zachary Taylor, in Silas Bent McKinley and Silas Bent, *Old Rough and Ready: The Life and Times of Zachary Taylor* (1946), 286. Henry Clay, in Merrill D. Peterson, *The Great Triumvirate* (1987), 469. Woodrow Wilson, address to the Associated Press (Apr 20, 1915). Mark Sullivan, in Calvin B. T. Lee, *The Campus Scene: 1900–1970* (1970), 23. John Winthrop, in Richard S. Dunn, *Puritans and Yankees: The Winthrop Dynasty of New England, 1630–1717* (1962), 24. Michael Kammen, *Colonial New York: A History* (1975); see also, Richard L. Merritt, *Symbols of American Community, 1735–1775* (1966). Foreign visitors Captain Marryat, Frances Trollope, and Captain Basil Hall, all in Page Smith, *The Nation Comes of Age* (1981), 249, 914; and in Edward Pessen, *Jacksonian America: Society, Personality, and Politics* (1985), 27–8. Josiah Coale, in David Lovejoy, *Religious Enthusiasm in the New World* (1985), 116. Oscar Handlin, "The Significance of the Seventeenth Century" in Paul Goodman (ed.), *Essays in American Colonial History* (1967). William Pencak, *War, Politics, and Revolution in Provincial Massachusetts* (1981), 122. Strong, in Smith (1981), *op. cit.*, 753. Richard Hofstadter, *The American Political Tradition* (1948), 176. Stephen Carter, " 'These Wild Young People' By One of Them," *Atlantic Monthly* (Sep 1920). Randolph Bourne, "The Two Generations," *Atlantic Monthly* (May 1911). Increase Mather, *The Divine Right of Infant Baptism* (1690). On "preparation for salvation," see Robert G. Pope, *The Half-Way Covenant: Church Membership in Puritan New England* (1969). Jay Fliegelman, *Prodigals and Pilgrims: The American Revolution Against Patriarchal Authority, 1750–1800* (1982), 22. Kenneth S. Lynn, *A Divided People* (1977), 68. Leonard Cain, "Age Status and Generational Phenomena," *Gerontologist* (Sep 6, 1987).

Silent Entering Elderhood: High-Flex Neoseniors
David Broder, *Changing of the Guard* (1980); see also Broder, "Fit Fifties Generation," *WP* 8/15/89. Daniel Levinson, in "For Many, Turmoil of Aging Erupts in the '50s, Studies Find," *NYT* 2/7/89. On Silent performance in Congress, see *Generations,* 285. Michael J. Sandel, *Democracy's Discontent* (1996). Wade Greene, "Fiftysomething-and in Charge," *NYT* 1/2/90. Joseph Nye, "The Misleading Metaphor of Decline," *Atlantic Monthly* (Mar 1990). Union of International Associations, in "What's in Store for the 1990s?" *WP* 2/1/90. Pat Choate and J. K. Linger, *High-Flex Society* (1986). Tom Peters, *Liberation Management: Necessary Disor-*

ganization for the Nanosecond Nineties (1992). Ford Foundation, in "Philanthropically Correct," *Civilization* 11/12/95. For CEO pay, see "Winter of Discontent," *USNWR* 1/22/96. Russell Baker, "Surely He Is Spoofing," *WP* 8/20/96. Charles A. Reich, *Opposing the System* (1995). Calvin Trillin, *Remembering Denny* (1993). Paul Fussell *BAD Or, The Dumbing of America* (1991). Richard Cohen, "Critic at Large," *WP Magazine* 2/21/93. Gail Sheehy, *New Passages: Mapping Your Life Across Time* (1995). Lois Wyse, *Funny, You Don't Look Like a Grandmother* (1989). M. Hoffman and J. Burroughes, *My Grandma Has Black Hair* (1988). For children living with grandparents, see "Silent Saviors," *USNWR* 12/16/91. Frances Goldscheider, in "Cheaper by the Dozen," *Newsweek* 9/14/92. Peter Mayle, *A Year In Provence* (1990). John Updike, *Rabbit Run* (1960); *Rabbit Redux* (1971); *Rabbit Gets Rich* (1981); *Rabbit at Rest* (1990). For disappearing liberal donors, see "Vanishing Liberals," *WSJ* 8/7/95. For polls on support for the fine arts, see "Boomers Spell Gloom for the Arts," *WP* 5/15/96. Ellen Goodman, "Dance of Silence," *WP* 12/2/95.

Boomers Entering Midlife: The Cultural Elite

Rush H. Limbaugh III, *The Way Things Ought To Be* (1992). William Bennett, *The Book of Virtues* (1993). William Dunn, in "Demographers Track Down the Cause of Clinton's Behavior: He's a Boomer," *WSJ* 5/28/93. "Not baby killers," said James Johnson, Ohio militia leader, to the Senate Judiciary Committee, in "Militias Meet the Senate With Conspiracies to Share," in *WP* 6/16/95. "Critical mass," in "In Search of the Sacred," *Newsweek* 11/28/94. Evan Thomas, "Hooray for Hypocrisy," *Newsweek* 1/29/96. Robert Putnam, "Bowling Alone: America's Declining Social Capital," *Journal of Democracy* (Jan 1995). On the Boomer landslide in 1994, see Neil Howe and William Strauss, "Tired of Boomer leaders? Hang On," *USA Today* 11/13/95. For ranking members of Congress by spending proposals, see "Vote Tally" and "Bill Tally," semi-annual pubs. of the Congressional Budget Tracking System, National Taxapayers Union Foundation. For votes by age for Pat Robertson and Jesse Jackson (1988), see *Generations,* 306; for Paul Tsongas (1992), see "Recap of the Primaries," *WP* 7/12/92; for Pat Buchanan (1996), see exit polls in *WP* for Iowa (2/13/96), Arizona (2/28/96), South Carolina (3/3/96), and Maryland (3/6/96). Times Mirror Center, *op. cit.* For party identification, see Gallup Polls cited in *The American Enterprise* 1/2/96. For being "touched" by the supernatural, see "For Younger Baby Boomers, Deeper Faith," *Atlanta Constitution* 3/3/90. For God and churchgoing, see survey figures in Wade Clark Roof, *A Generation of Seekers* (1993); see also Roper poll on churchgoing, in *WSJ* 12/2/94. For angels, see "Angels: Hark! America's Latest Search for Spiritual Meaning Has a Halo Effect," *Newsweek* 12/27/93. For "shamanic journeys," see "Alien Invasion!" *Newsweek* 7/8/96. Clarissa Pinkola Estés, *Women Who Run With the Wolves* (1992). For political gender gap, see *The American Enterprise, op. cit.* On Boomer versus G.I. dads, see "Building a Better Dad," *Newsweek* 6/7/96. Stephen L. Carter, *The Culture of Disbelief* (1993). Shelby Steele, *The Content of Our Character* (1990). For Boomer blacks on religion and school prayer, see "Church Meets State," *USNWR* 4/24/95. Mickey Kaus, *The End of Equality* (1992). Martha Bayles, *Hole in Our Soul* (1994). For Boomers on neatness, see survey by the Soap and Detergent Association, in "Shampoo Planet," *USNWR* 4/22/96. For real worker income by generation, see Bureau of the Census, *Money Income of Households, Families, and Persons in the*

United States, Current Population Reports, Series P-60 (annual and historical). For self-esteem, see Ralph Whitehead, *Glory Days: The Baby Boom Generation and the American Dream* (Center for National Policy, 1986).

13ers Entering Young Adulthood: Top Guns

U.S. Department of Education, *A Nation at Risk: The Imperative for Educational Reform* (National Commission on Excellence in Education, 1983). Allan Bloom, *The Closing of the American Mind* (1987). Diane Ravitch and Chester Finn Jr., *What Do 17-Year-Olds Know?: A Report on the First National Assessment of History and Literature* (1987). David Leavitt, in Donald Kanter and Philip Mirvis, *The Cynical Americans* (1989). Doug Coupland, in John Marchese, "The Short Shelf Life of Generation X," *NYT* 6/17/95. For 13er entrepreneurs, see Roper Poll, in James Glassman, "When the Xers Come Marching In," *WP* 1/23/96. For comparisons of real median income, Census, *op. cit.* For median earnings by age, see Bureau of Labor Statistics, *Employment and Earnings* (monthly). For poverty rates, see Bureau of the Census, *Poverty in the United States,* Current Population Reports, Series P-60 (annual and historical). Jerald Bachman, "Premature Affluence: Do High School Students Earn Too Much?" *Economic Outlook USA* (Summer 1983); see also Bachman, more recently, in "All Work May Spell Trouble for Teens" *WSJ* 11/18/94. For black males in prison, see "1 in 3 Young Black Men in Justice System," *WP* 10/5/95. On teen and young-adult attraction to gambling, see "Sports Betting Rings Moving Into Schools," *WP* 4/12/95. On black-white marriages, see Richard Morin, "Unconventional Wisdom," *WP* 9/10/95. On political views of youth, see Alexander Astin, et al., *The American Freshman: Twenty-Five Year Trends, 1966–1990* (UCLA; 1991), plus more recent annual reports; see also Neil Howe and William Strauss, *13TH-GEN* (1993), ch. 19. James Glassman, *op. cit.;* see also, "Who Supports Ross Perot," *The American Enterprise* (Jan–Feb, 1996). On 13er trust in government, see poll by Louis Harris, in Jon Meachum, "The Truth About Twentysomethings," *Washington Monthly* (Jan–Feb 1995). For total taxation in Virginia, see William Strauss and Neil Howe, "Virginia Is for Seniors," *WP* 12/4/94. Third Millennium survey, in "Money for Nothing," *Details* (Mar 1995). On reading newspapers, see Times Mirror Center for the People and the Press, *The Age of Indifference* (1990). For "global village" survey, see The Wirthlin Group, *The Wirthlin Report* (Apr 1992). On professionalization, see Steven A. Sass, "The U.S. Professional Sector: 1950 to 1988," *New England Economic Review* (Jan–Feb 1990). On income inequality by age, see Bureau of the Census, *Workers With Low Earnings: 1964 to 1990,* Current Population Reports, P60-178, 1–8. Saren Sakurai, "Countercommerce," *Hyper Age Magazine* (Summer 1993). Mario Cuomo, nomination speech for Bill Clinton (New York, NY; Jul 15, 1992). "High-Tech Nomads Write New Program For Future of Work," *WSJ* 8/19/96.

Millennials Entering Childhood: Friends of Barney

Ellen Goodman, "Out of School and Into Trouble," *WP* 7/13/96. For tripling of popularity of staying home with family, see summary of surveys in "Balancing Act, Scale Tips Toward Family," *USA Today* (1995), *op. cit.* For survey on "giving up work indefinitely," see "Can Your Career Hurt Your Kids?" *Fortune* 5/20/91. For two out of three parents, see *USA Today* (1995), *op. cit.* For *Not With My Child You*

Don't, see "How to Win a Kingdom," *NYT* 9/16/95. James Garbarino, *Raising Children in a Socially Toxic Environment* (1995). Michael J. Sandel, "Easy Virtue," *New Republic* 9/2/96. For child savings, see Jane Bryant Quinn's essay in *WP* 5/31/92. For parental support for school uniforms, see "Sales of Uniforms are Looking Sharp," *WSJ* 8/22/95; and "School Uniforms Growing in Favor in California," *NYT* 9/3/94; see also "School Uniforms," *WP* 1/9/91. Hillary Clinton, *It Takes a Village* (1996). For home schooling, see "Fed Up with Schools, More Parents Turn to Teaching at Home," *WSJ* 5/10/94. Bennett, *op. cit.* William Damon, in "The Moral Child," *USNWR* 6/3/96.

CHAPTER 9
REFERENCES

Senator Daniel K. Inouye, speech to a joint meeting of Congress, excerpted in *WP* 10/12/95. Joseph Dawson, in *WP* 5/20/94. Sidney Hook, *The Hero in History* (1943). David Gelernter, *1939: The Lost World of the World's Fair* (1995), 27. William Cullen Bryant, "The Death of the Flowers," 1825. Victor Hugo, *Les Misérables* (1862; trans. by Charles E. Wilbour), "Fantine," 5.10. Algernon Charles Swinburne, *Atalanta in Calydon* (1865), chorus, stanza 1.

From Unraveling to Crisis

For "wonderful nonsense" and other phrases, see Mary Patrice Thaman, *Manners and Morals of the 1920s* (1977); Ernest Hemingway, *A Moveable Feast* (1964; posthumous memoirs). F. Scott Fitzgerald, in Andrew Trumbull, *Scott Fitzgerald* (1962), 183. Frederick Lewis Allen, *Only Yesterday: An Informal History of the 1920s* (1931), chs 13–14. *The New Yorker,* in ibid., 290. President Franklin Roosevelt, "fear," in First Inaugural Address (Mar 4, 1933); "nationwide," in speech (New York, NY; Apr 25, 1936). John Greenleaf Whittier, "Lines Inscribed to Friends Under Arrest for Treason Against the Slave Power" (1856); Hinton Rowan Helper, *The Impending Crisis of the South* (1857). William Seward, speech (Rochester, NY; Oct 25, 1858), in Kenneth M. Stampp (ed.), *The Causes of the Civil War* (1959), 105. Abraham Lincoln, speech at the Republican State Convention (Springfield, IL; Jun 16, 1858). Wendell Phillips, in C. Vann Woodward, *The Burden of Southern History* (1960), 52. Walt Whitman, *Years of the Modern* (1860, first pub. 1865). Edmund Ruffin, *Anticipations of the Future: To Serve as Lessons for the Present Time* (1860). Whitman, *The Eighteenth Presidency!* (1856). Lincoln, in George B. Forgie, *Patricide in the House Divided: A Psychological Interpretation of Lincoln and His Age* (1979), 287. James Otis, in Melvin Yazawa, *From Colonies to Commonwealth: Familial Ideology and the Beginnings of the American Republic* (1985), 90. Abigail Adams, in ibid., 90–91. Stephen Saunders Webb, *1676: The End of American Independence* (1985), xv–xvi. Estimates of the casualties at the Battle of Towton are discussed in Alison Weir, *The Wars of the Roses* (1995), 284.

Fourth Turnings and Archetypes

Perry Miller, *The New England Mind: The Seventeenth Century* (1939), 37–8. Sam Adams, in Pauline Maier, *The Old Revolutionaries* (1980). For "true religion and good morals," see Cushing Strout, *The New Heavens and New Earth: Political Re-*

ligion in America (1973), 67–8. Thaddeus Stevens, in Alphonse Miller, *Thaddeus Stevens* (1939), 182. Albert Barnes, *The Peaceful Death of the Righteous* (1858). Henry Adams, in Ken Burns (director), *The Civil War* (documentary film, 1990). For "like a Christian or a gentleman," see David C. Whitney, *The Colonial Spirit of '76* (1974), 296. Daniel J. Boorstin, *The Americans: The Democratic Experience* (1973), Part One. Lucius Annaeus Seneca (c. 4 B.C.–A.D. 65), *De providentia,* 5, 9. Cotton Mather, in Perry Miller, *The New England Mind: From Colony to Province* (1953), 159. T. H. Breen, *Puritans and Adventurers* (1980), "Transfer of Culture." For "all gaming" ballad of 1779, see Catherine Albanese, *Sons of the Fathers* (1976), 56. David Humphreys, *The Glory of America* (1783). Cotton Mather, *The Young Man's Preservative* (1701). For tithing men, see Edmund Morgan, *The Puritan Family* (1944), "Puritan Tribalism." Henry Clay, in Merrill D. Peterson, *The Great Triumvirate* (1987), 8–9. Foreigner was French visitor Georges Fisch, in George Winston Smith and Charles Judah, *Life in the North During the Civil War* (1966), 309–11. Joseph Kett, *Rites of Passage: Adolescence in America, 1790 to the Present* (1977), 116.

CHAPTER 10
REFERENCES

Benjamin Rush, in letters to his friends, in Melvin Yazawa, "Creating a Republican Citizenry," in Jack P. Greene (ed.), *The American Revolution* (1987).

Boomers Entering Elderhood: Gray Champions

For "Evangelization of the World," see Sherwood Eddy, *Pathfinders of the World's Missionary Crusade* (1945), 43. Louis Brandeis, *Burnet v. Colorado Oil and Gas* (1932). G. Stanley Hall, in Nathan G. Hale Jr., *Freud and the Americans: The Beginnings of Psychoanalysis in the United States, 1876–1917* (1971), 372. Vachel Lindsay, "Bryan, Bryan, Bryan, Bryan," *Collected Works* (1925). Arthur Schlesinger Jr., *The Crisis of the Old Order, 1919–1933* (1957), 19. Lyndon Johnson, in William Manchester, *The Glory and the Dream: A Narrative History of America, 1932–1972* (1974), 355. Bernard Berenson, *Aesthetics and History* (1948). Craig S. Karpel, *The Retirement Myth: What You Must Know to Prosper in the Coming Meltdown* (1995), ch. 16, "Owl Mountain." Ken Dychtwald and Joe Flower, *Age Wave: The Challenges and Opportunities of an Aging America* (1989). Cheryl Russell, *The Master Trend* (1993). Zalman Schachter-Shalomi and Ronald S. Miller, *From Age-ing to Sage-ing: A Profound New Vision of Growing Older* (1995). Harry Moody, in Schachter-Shalomi and Miller, *op. cit.,* 26. Gail Sheehy, *New Passages: Mapping Your Life Across Time* (1995). David Gutmann, *Reclaimed Powers: Toward a New Psychology of Men and Women in Later Life* (1987). Jean Bolen, *Goddesses in Everywoman* (1984). Deepak Chopra, *Quantum Healing: Exploring the Frontiers of Mind/Body Medicine* (1989). Ralph Waldo Emerson, *Journals* (1845). David Barker, *The K-Wave: Profiting from Cyclical Booms and Busts in the Global Economy* (1995), 250. For current share of retired-worker benefits awarded at age 62, see *Annual Statistical Supplement, 1995,* to the *Social Security Bulletin,* Social Security Administration. Eugene Bianchi, *Aging as a Spiritual Journey* (1982). Joan Halifax, in Schachter-Shalomi and Miller, *op. cit.,* 59. For "figure of an ancient man" and "fiery gospel," see references above in Chapter 5.

For "New Deal Isaiahs," see H. L. Mencken, "The New Deal Mentality" (1936). For "rendezvous with destiny," see President Franklin Roosevelt, in speech accepting renomination (Jun 27, 1936). Peter Collier and David Horowitz, *Destructive Generation: Second Thoughts About the Sixties* (1989), 335. James Redfield, in "The Prophecy Fulfilled," *Newsweek* 6/24/96. Cornel West, in Leon Wieseltier, "All and Nothing at All: The Unreal World of Cornel West," *New Republic* 3/6/95. Marcus Tullius Cicero (106–43 B.C.), *De senectute.* Winston S. Churchill, speech before the House of Commons (Apr 17, 1945).

13ers Entering Midlife: Doom Players
F. Scott Fitzgerald (1931), in Frederick J. Hoffman, "Some Perspectives on the 1920s," in Sidney Fine and Gerald S. Brown (eds.), *The American Past* (1970). Ernest Hemingway, *Death in the Afternoon* (1932). Niebuhr, *Moral Man in Immoral Society* (1932). Linklater, "Slackers," *Boston Phoenix* 10/11/91. Dorcas R. Hardy and C. Colburn Hardy, *Social Insecurity* (1991), 41.

Millennials Entering Young Adulthood: Power Rangers
For "I promise," see Manchester, *op. cit.,* 89. Malcolm Cowley, *Exile's Return* (1934, 1951 ed.), 294. Malcolm Cowley and Robert Cowley (eds.), *Fitzgerald and the Jazz Age* (1966), 48–9. For suicide rate, literacy, and college entry, see *Generations,* 252–53. Gene Shuford, in Calvin B. T. Lee, *The Campus Scene: 1900–1970* (1970), 36. President Franklin Roosevelt, speech (University of Pennsylvania, Philadelphia, PA; Sep 20, 1940). For G.I. generation's voting behavior, see *Generations,* 267–68. Roosevelt, radio address to the Young Democratic Clubs of America (1935), in E. Taylor Parks and Lois F. Parks (eds.), *Memorable Quotations of Franklin D. Roosevelt* (1965), 41. George Catlett Marshall, in Ronald Reagan, speech to Republican National Convention (Sep 15, 1988). Sinclair Lewis, *It Can't Happen Here* (1935).

New Silent Entering Childhood: Sweet Innocents
Benita Eisler, *Private Lives: Men and Women of the Fifties* (1986), 29. *Literary Digest,* in Paula Fass, *The Damned and the Beautiful: American Youth in the 1920s* (1977), 37. Daniel Rodgers, in Joseph Hawes and Ray Hiner, *Growing Up in America: Children in Historical Perspective* (1985), 130. For "total situation" parenting, see ibid., 504. Frank Conroy, "My Generation," *Esquire* (Oct 1968). William Raspberry, "Victims, Villains, Vision," *WP* 3/22/96.

Toward the First Turning
Hal Borland, *Sundial of the Seasons* (1964), "A Promise—April 29." Blaise Pascal, *Pensées* (1670), 355. For the "four old men," see J. C. Furnas, *The Americans: A Social History of the United States, 1587–1914* (1969), 550–51.

CHAPTER 11
References

How America Should Prepare
For America's demographic "Indian Summer," see Richard Jackson, "What to Expect as America Begins to Gray" *WSJ* 7/18/91.

Generational Scripts
The figures for the surviving shares of today's living generations in 2026 were derived from historical births and immigration (by age and year) and future projections as reported in Bureau of the Census, *Population Projections of the United States, by Age, Sex, Race, and Hispanic Origin: 1993 to 2050,* Current Population Reports, P25–1104 (Nov 1993). Sir Thomas Malory, *Morte Darthur* (1485), bk. XXI, ch. 7. Ella Wheeler Wilcox, *Collected Poems* (1917), "The World's Need." John Dewey, in Harvey Wish, *Society and Thought in Modern America* (1952), 519. David McClelland, *Power: The Inner Experience* (1975), 357. For Benjamin Franklin on the seal, see John F. Berens, *Providence and Patriotism in Early America, 1640–1815* (1978), 107. Ernest Hemingway, *Farewell to Arms* (1929), 261. Herbert Hoover, in Bob Herbert, "Turning Childrens' Rights Into Reality," *NYT* 5/27/96. For "The rising world," see Charles Royster, *A Revolutionary People at War* (1979), 8.

CHAPTER 12
References

On Navajos, see Nancy J. Parezo, *Navaho Sandpainting* (1983). Arnold Toynbee, *A Study of History* (twelve volumes, published from 1934 to 1961). Oswald Spengler, *Der Untergang des Abendlandes* (1918–22; trans. as *The Decline of the West,* 1926–28). Francis Fukuyama, *The End of History and the Last Man* (1992), 311. Friedrich Nietzsche, *Thus Spoke Zarathustra* (trans. in 1954 by Walter Kaufmann; orig. *Also Sprach Zarathustra,* 1892); see II, 20, "On Redemption," and III, 13, "The Convalescent"; see also Daniel Chapelle, *Nietzsche and Psychoanalysis* (1993), ch. 4, "Time and Its 'It Was'." Publius Cornelius Tacitus (c. A.D. 56–c. A.D. 120), *Annals* (trans. by D. R. Dudley, 1966), III, 55.

Index of Names

Dustin, Hannah, *71*, 129
Dychtwald, Ken, 183, 184, 280
Dyer, Mary, *71*
Dylan, Bob, 64, 187

E

Eastwood, Clint, 186
Eberly, Don, 228
Edison, Thomas Alva, *70*
Edsall, Thomas Byrne, 204
Edward IV, king of England, 124, 125
Edward V, king of England, 124
Edward VI, king of England, 126
Edwards, Jonathan, 48, *70*, *71*, 93, 96, 130, 131, 210
Einstein, Albert, 59, 154
Eisenhower, Dwight D.
  as an exemplar, *61*
  as general, 97, 155, 308
  peers of, 68
  presidency of, 3, *59*
  as president, 3, 17, 96, 147, 161, 164
  on religion, 156
Eisler, Benita, 186, 296
Elders, Joycelin, 214, 307
Eliade, Mircea, 9
Eliot, T. S., 32, 68
Elizabeth I, queen of England, 44, 45, 60, *71*, 126, 127, 128, 151, 264
Elizabeth of York, *71*
Ellis, Bret Easton, 236
Ellsberg, Daniel, 187
Emerson, Ralph Waldo, 35, 54, 107, 132, 133, 176, 282
Epicurus, 32
Erasmus, Desiderius, 34, 270
Erikson, Erik, 183, 190
Erikson, Joan, 184
Ervin, Samuel, 6
Esler, Anthony, 64, 127
Estés, Clarissa Pinkola, 228

Evers, Medgar, 185
Extreme, 235

F

Fallows, James, 286
Fass, Paula, 158
Feldstein, Al, 197
Ferdinand, king of Spain, 92
Ferguson, Marilyn, 114, 190
Ferrari, Giuseppe, 63, 65, 88, *90*
Ferrar, L. L., Jr., 37, 51
Ferraro, Geraldine, 212
Feuer, Lewis, 191
Fiedler, Leslie, 195
Fillion, Kate, 235
Finn, Chester, 233
Finney, Charles Grandison, 48, 132
Fischer, David Hackett, 151
Fitzgerald, F. Scott, *61*, 64, 135, 155, 259, 287
Flanagan, Father, 158
Fliegelman, Jay, 211
Flood, Curt, 188
Fogel, Robert, 47
Foley, Tom, 215
Fonda, Henry, 160
Forbes, Steve, 230
Ford, Gerald, 160
Foster, Jodie, *71*, 80, 137, 196
Franco, Francisco, 120
Frank, Anne, 135
Frank, Barney, 186
Franklin, Benjamin, 5, 131, 140, 179, 298, 326
  as an exemplar, 80, 96
Franzblau, Rose, 186
Freberg, Stan, 165
Freud, Sigmund, 73, 133
Friedan, Betty, 111, 159, 183
Frodo, 76
Frost, Robert, 169
Fukuyama, Francis, 12, 331
Fuller, Margaret, 179

Fulton, Robert, 131
Fussell, Paul, 217

G

Galbraith, John Kenneth, 147, 172
Galileo Galilei, 34, 127
Gallatin, Albert, 177
Gallup, George, 159
Gama, Vasco da, 92
Gandalf, 76
Gardiner, Stephen, 125
Gardner, John W., 181
Garfunkel, Art, 187
Garland, Judy, 135
Garrison, William Lloyd, *70*, 96,
    133, 140, 179
Garroway, Dave, 160
Garvey, Marcus, 112
Gates, Bill, 80, 117, 137, 231
Gehrig, Lou, 309
Gelernter, David, 254
George III, king of Great Britain,
    131
Gephardt, Dick, 212
Gergen, David, 213
Gillette, Douglas, 73
Gingrich, Newt, 51, 64, *70*, *71*,
    137, 224, 226, 229, 286
Ginsberg, Allen, 165
Gitlin, Todd, 194
Giuliani, Rudolph, 247
Gleason, Jackie, 160
Goldman, Emma, *71*
Goldscheider, Frances, 220
Goldstein, Joshua, 51
Goldwater, Barry, 157, 171
Goodman, Ellen, 196, 222, 244
Gorbachev, Mikhail, 135
Gordon, Barbara, 186
Gordy, Berry, Jr., 187
Gore, Albert, Jr., 64, 225, 226,
    231, 286
Gore, Tipper, 246
Gottlieb, Annie, 190

Goulden, Joseph, 159
Gourmont, Rémy de, 35
Graham, Bill, 194
Gramm, Phil, 212, 215
Grandmother Willow, 281
Grant, Ulysses, 67, *71*, 80, 96, 97,
    133, 269
  peers of, 122
  as president, 56
Greene, Wade, 186, 214
Greenfield, Meg, 214
Green Mountain Boys, 131
Gresham, Sir Thomas, 127
Grocyn, William, 125
Gruening, Ernest, 181
Guthrie, Woody, 158
Gutmann, David, 281

H

Hackney, Sheldon, 203, 214
Halberstam, David, 161, 164
Halifax, Joan, 285
Hall, G. Stanley, 279
Hamilton, Alexander, 141
Hammett, Dashiell, 156
Hammurabi, 77
Handel, George Frideric, 129
Handlin, Oscar, 211
Hansel and Gretel, 77
Hardy, Dorcas, 290
Hardy, Thomas, 56
Harkin, Tom, 212
Harrington, Michael, 148, 190
Harrison, William Henry, 270
Harris, Peter, 106, 115
Harrod, Roy, 172
Hart, Gary, 82, 212, 215, 222,
    307
Harvard, John, 129
Hawkins, Sir John, 127, 269
Hawthorne, Nathaniel, 139–41
Hayakawa, S. I., 192
Hefner, Hugh, 165
Hegel, G. W. F., 12, 43

Steinbeck, John, 68
Steinem, Gloria, 17, *61*, 186
Stevenson, Adlai, 156
Stevens, Thaddeus, 268, 298
Stevens, Wallace, 150
Stewart, Jimmy, *61*, 158, 160, 184
Stimson, Henry, 59
Stockman, David, 193
Stoughton, William, 96, 97, 129
Stravinsky, Igor, 79
Streisand, Barbra, 222
Stromberg, Roland, 200
Strong, George Templeton, 211
Styron, William, 187
Sullivan, Ed, 17, 164, 171
Sullivan, Mark, 209
Sunday, William Ashley "Billy,"
    134
Superman, 75
Swinburne, Algernon Charles, 255

T

Tacitus, Cornelius, 333
Taft, William Howard, 134
Taney, Roger, 324
Tarantino, Quentin, 137
Tarquin (Tarquinius Superbus),
    last king of Rome, 27
Taylor, Maxwell, 160
Taylor, Zachary, 209
Teale, Edwin Way, 208
Tecumseh, 131
Telemachus, 86
Temple, Shirley, *61*, 296
Tennent, Gilbert, 179
Thatcher, Margaret, 120
Theobald, Robert, 172
Theseus, 76
Thomas, Clarence, 228
Thomas, Evan, 224
Thompson, Hunter, 215
Thompson, William Irwin, 73
Thompson, William R., 38, 51
Thomson, Virgil, 155

Thoth, 76
Thucydides, 87
Thurow, Lester, 189
Tillich, Paul, 155, 157
Tipton, Steve, 199
Tobin, James, 164
Toffler, Alvin, 12, 187, 188
Tōjō, Hideki, 118, 120, 260
Tolkien, J. R. R., *76*
Toynbee, Arnold, 15, 32, 35, 89,
    90, 330
  on the cycle of war and peace,
    14, 36–37, 38, 41
Trillin, Calvin, 217
Truman, Harry S, *71*, 97, 135,
    153–54, 157, 161
  as president, 3, 17, 59, 96
Tsongas, Paul, 188, 212, 220, 226
Tudor, Henry. *See* Henry VII
Tung Chung-shu, 31
Turgenev, Ivan, 88
Turner, Nat, 48, *70*, 132, 133, 140
Twain, Mark, 133, 211
Tweed, William Marcy "Boss,"
    133, 269
Tyndale, William, 48, 92, 126, 127

U

Ueberroth, Peter, 205
Uncle Remus, 78
Updike, John, 165, 174, 186, 221
Urbanska, Wanda, 193

V

Varro, Marcus Tarentius, 25
Vedder, Eddie, 235
Vere, John de, 125
Vere, Sir Francis, 127
Vesey, Denmark, 48, 132
Vespucci, Amerigo, 92
Vico, Giambattista, 32